EUROPEAN SOCIETY
OF INTERNATIONAL LAW SERIES

The European Convention on Human Rights and General International Law

The ESIL Book Series publishes high quality volumes primarily on the themes of ESIL Annual Conferences and ESIL joint events. The volumes include chapters that are based on selected papers presented at ESIL events, revised to fit the focus of the volume, and complemented by additional chapters that address topics that were not fully explored at the events, but that are essential for a full coverage of the theme.

The European Convention on Human Rights and General International Law

Edited by

ANNE VAN AAKEN

and

IULIA MOTOC

OXFORD
UNIVERSITY PRESS

OXFORD
UNIVERSITY PRESS

Great Clarendon Street, Oxford, OX2 6DP,
United Kingdom

Oxford University Press is a department of the University of Oxford.
It furthers the University's objective of excellence in research, scholarship,
and education by publishing worldwide. Oxford is a registered trade mark of
Oxford University Press in the UK and in certain other countries

First Edition published in 2018

Impression: 1

Published in the United States of America by Oxford University Press
198 Madison Avenue, New York, NY 10016, United States of America

British Library Cataloguing in Publication Data
Data available

Library of Congress Control Number: 2018942411

ISBN 978–0–19–883000–9

Printed and bound by
CPI Group (UK) Ltd, Croydon, CR0 4YY

Preface

It is with pleasure that I welcome the appearance of this excellent work, which will make an important contribution to the scholarly literature on the mutual influence and relationship between the European Convention on Human Rights and general international law. The question, or more correctly the many questions, about the Convention and general international law are of inexhaustible interest for those engaged in either, or both, of these disciplines.

The calibre of this volume attests to the very high level of the contributions and discussions that took place during the conference held at the Court in June 2015. It was an extremely fruitful collaboration between our institution and the scholars of the European Society of International Law, whose membership extends well into the judicial ranks of the Court. Opening the proceedings, the then-President of the Court, Dean Spielmann, told the participants that the seminar had all the makings of a landmark event. I would agree. The seminar not only set a precedent for cooperation, but also a standard of intellectual quality that has inspired subsequent joint ventures with the ESIL at Strasbourg. It was natural for me, during my presidency of the Court, to support and encourage these meritorious initiatives. I take this opportunity to record my appreciation for the great efforts in this connection of my colleague, Judge Iulia Motoc, who has been both instrumental and indispensable in developing this productive intellectual partnership.

As the editors recall in their introduction, a deliberately broad approach was taken, encompassing various aspects and dimensions of a subject matter both wide and fundamental. Well-balanced panels of speakers, including judges and academics (not a watertight distinction in international courts), brought their differing perspectives to bear on substantive questions—the notion of 'jurisdiction' under the Convention, State responsibility, State immunity—and on questions of the Court's methodology in interpreting the Convention, with its distinctive reliance on other normative sources. Their debates play out in these pages. To say that these debates are not new is not at all to downplay the interest that they will undoubtedly hold for international lawyers and international human-rights lawyers. The intersection and interactions between these two dynamic disciplines merit the continuing attention of legal commentators. The debate is anything but repetitious, and the discussion is far from closed. The Court's jurisprudential output is considerable and continuous. Since the date of the Strasbourg seminar, some highly significant judgments have been delivered by the Court's Grand Chamber. Happily the authors have been able to take account of some of these recent rulings, for example the *Al-Dulimi* judgment[1] commented on by Vice-President Alexander Sicilianos in his article on the responsibilities of states under the Convention when

[1] *Al-Dulimi and Montana Management Inc v Switzerland* [GC] App no 5809/08 (ECtHR, 2016).

giving effect to economic sanctions decided by the UN Security Council. Further jurisprudential clarifications, innovations, and refinements are no doubt in store, sustaining the debate among legal scholars.

The appearance of this book is timely in that it comes at a moment when the Contracting States have opened a discussion among experts, in the forum of the Council of Europe's Steering Committee for Human Rights, about the place of the Convention mechanism in the European and international legal order[2]. The insights and nuances, the justifications, and the criticisms aired at the seminar will be a valuable source of reference in that ongoing process.

Addressing the seminar in its closing session, Judge Antonio Cançado Trindade alluded to the place and importance of judicial dialogue as a means for courts—national and international—to guard against fragmentation within the international legal system. That message, previously delivered by Dame Rosalyn Higgins in a lecture at Strasbourg in 2009, is well understood in the precincts of the European Court. This is an institution deeply committed to dialogue, be it dialogue within the Convention system or, in the present context, a wider dialogue with international courts, fellow protagonists in the wider international legal system. Shortly after the ESIL seminar, a delegation of the International Court of Justice paid a visit to the European Court of Human Rights for discussions with their counterparts at Strasbourg. Complementing the well-known phenomenon of the 'dialogue of judgments' among international courts, this dialogue among international judges deserves to become a regular practice.

Guido Raimondi
President of the European Court of Human Rights
Strasbourg

[2] As foreseen in Chapter V of the report of the Steering Committee for Human Rights, 'The Longer-term Future of the System of the European Convention on Human Rights', 2015.

Contents

Table of Cases

TABLE OF NATIONAL CASES

TABLE OF EUROPEAN CASES

TABLE OF CASES OF THE INTER AMERICAN COURT OF HUMAN RIGHTS

TABLE OF CASES OF THE WORLD TRADE ORGANISATION (WTO)

TABLE OF CASES OF THE INTERNATIONAL COURT OF JUSTICE (ICJ)

TABLE OF CASES OF THE HAGUE DISTRICT COURT

TABLE OF CASES OF THE HRC

TABLE OF CASES OF THE INTERNATIONAL TRIBUNAL FOR THE LAW OF THE SEA (ITLOS)

TABLE OF CASES OF THE INTERNATIONAL CRIMINAL COURT (ICC)

TABLE OF CASES OF THE INTERNATIONAL CRIMINAL TRIBUNAL FOR THE FORMER YUGOSLAVIA

TABLE OF CASES RELATING TO ARBITRATION

TABLE OF CASES OF THE UNITED NATIONS

Table of Legislation

TABLE OF INTERNATIONAL INSTRUMENTS

Table of Treaties and Conventions

TABLE OF EUROPEAN INSTRUMENTS

Table of Treaties and Conventions

Table of European Regulations

Table of European Directives

TABLE OF UNITED NATIONS RESOLUTIONS

Table of UN General Assembly Resolutions

Table of UN Security Council Resolutions

TABLE OF NATIONAL LEGISLATION

Korea

Turkey

United Kingdom

United States of America

TABLE OF INTERNATIONAL COURT OF JUSTICE INSTRUMENTS

TABLE OF COURT RULES

INTERNATIONAL LABOUR ORGANISATION (ILO) INSTRUMENTS

NORTH ATLANTIC TREATY ORGANISATION (NATO) INSTRUMENTS

List of Contributors

Anne van Aaken, Alexander von Humboldt Professor, Director of the Institute for Law and Economics, Professor for Law and Economics, Legal Theory, Public International Law and European Law, University of Hamburg, Germany; Former Vice-President of the European Society of International Law

Hasan Bakırcı, Deputy Registrar, Second Section, Registry of the European Court of Human Rights

Samantha Besson, Professor of Public International Law and European Law, University of Fribourg (Switzerland)

Antônio Augusto Cançado Trindade, Judge of the International Court of Justice; Former President of the Inter-American Court of Human Rights; Emeritus Professor of International Law of the University of Brasilia; Former President of the Latin American Society of International Law; Member of the Curatorium of the Hague Academy of International Law, and of the Institut de Droit International

James Crawford, Judge of the International Court of Justice; Former Whewell Professor of International Law at the University of Cambridge and Fellow in Law at Jesus College, Cambridge and Director of the Lauterpacht Centre for International Law (Cambridge)

Işıl Karakaş, Judge of the European Court of Human Rights; Former Vice-President of the European Court of Human Rights

Amelia Keene, Associate at Three Crowns LLP; Formerly Associate Legal Officer at the International Court of Justice

Marko Milanovic, Associate Professor, University of Nottingham School of Law; Vice-President, European Society of International Law

Iulia Motoc, Judge of the European Court of Human Rights; Professor of International Law University of Bucharest; Former Judge at the Constitutional Court of Romania

Angelika Nußberger, Vice-President of the European Court of Human Rights, Director of the Institute of Eastern European Law and Professor of Constitutional Law, International Law and Comparative Law at the University of Cologne

Riccardo Pavoni, Professor of International and European Law, University of Siena

Paulo Pinto de Albuquerque, Judge of the European Court of Human Rights; Ordinary Professor at the Faculty of Law of the Catholic University Lisboa

Anja Seibert-Fohr, Hengstberger Professor and Director of the Institute for Constitutional Law and Legal Philosophy, University of Heidelberg; Vice-Chair of the United Nations Human Rights Committee

Linos-Alexandre Sicilianos, Vice-President of the European Court of Human Rights; Associate Member of the Institute of International Law

Geir Ulfstein, Professor of Law, Department of Public and International Law, University of Oslo

Johann Justus Vasel, Dr. iur. LLM (NYU) Post-Doctoral Researcher at the Law School University of Hamburg, Germany

Ganna Yudkivska, PhD, Judge and Section President of the European Court of Human Rights; Associate Professor of European and International Law at the Academy of Advocacy of Ukraine

Ineta Ziemele, PhD (Cantab), President of the Constitutional Court of the Republic of Latvia; Professor at the Riga Graduate School of Law; Former Judge and Section President at the European Court of Human Rights

Dr. Philippa Webb (LLM and JSD Yale),Reader (Associate Professor) in Public International Law at The Dickson Poon School of Law, King's College London, formerly Special Assistant and Legal Officer to Judge Rosalyn Higgins at the ICJ (2006-2009) and Associate Legal Adviser to Prosecutor Luis Moreno-Ocampo at the ICC.

Introduction

The European Convention on Human Rights and General International Law

Anne van Aaken, Iulia Motoc, and Johann Justus Vasel

1. Introduction

The title of this book—The European Convention on Human Rights and General International Law—is almost vacuous but this is intentional. There are many ways of looking at the relationship between international human rights law (IHRL) and general international law.[1] One may look at the influence of IHRL on general international law, and vice versa, by tracking judgments and their effect on other international courts.[2] One may also discuss the relationship under the heading of fragmentation, taking a broader, systemic, and institutional view.[3] This discussion of fragmentation and/or convergence has been the subject of academic and judicial debate for a while now.[4] Both pessimistic (the 'fragmentation' approach) and optimistic (the 'reconciliation' approach)[5] voices are heard on this issue

[1] General international law is not very often defined, but often referred to. We understand it as in Menno T. Kamminga, 'Final Report on the Impact of International Human Rights Law on General International Law' in Menno T. Kamminga and Martin Scheinin (eds), *The Impact of Human Rights Law on General International Law* (OUP 2009) 2 as the opposite of *lex specialis*, which governs particular topics of international law. Examples are the Vienna Convention on the Law of Treaties or the law of State responsibility as codified in the Articles on State Responsibility for Internationally Wrongful Acts (ARSIWA), (2001) II(2) ILC Yearbook.

[2] This has been the approach of the International Law Association, see Kamminga and Scheinin (eds) (n 1). Other systematic examinations of the impact of IHLR on general international law have been provided by Theodor Meron, *The Humanization of International Law* (Martinus Nijhoff Publishers 2006); Bruno Simma, 'International Human Rights Law and General International Law: A Comparative Perspective in *Collected Courses of the Academy of European Law* (Kluwer 1993) Vol IV Book 2.

[3] ILC, 'Fragmentation of International Law: Difficulties arising from the Diversification and Expansion of International Law, Report of the Study Group of the International Law Commission, finalized by Martti Koskenniemi' (13 April 2006) A/CN.4/L.682.

[4] See, recently, Mads Adenas and Eirik Bjorge (eds), *A Farewell to Fragmentation: Reassertion and Convergence in International Law* (CUP 2015).

[5] For these expressions, see Kamminga (n 1) 1. An example of the latter, optimistic approach, is Alain Pellet, 'Should we (still) worry about fragmentation?' in Geir Ulfstein and Andreas Follesdal (eds), *The Judicialization of International Law—A Mixed Blessing?* (OUP 2018).

and the discussion is becoming ever more refined. Given that the judicial dialogue between international courts as well as with national courts is increasing, the optimistic perspective seems to be gaining the upper hand. A distinction has been made between substantive, methodological, and institutional fragmentation.[6] We will deal only with the first two, although institutional fragmentation is of course at the heart of the matter, especially from a social-science perspective.

There is no doubt that the European Court of Human Rights (ECtHR) does not consider the European Convention on Human Rights (ECHR) in isolation from general international law, but when, why, and where does it take different paths? What are the means that it uses to reconcile human rights protection with general international law? Under what circumstances does the ECtHR deviate from general international law? Under what circumstances is the jurisprudence of the ECtHR taken up in general international law, especially by the International Court of Justice (ICJ)?

The ECtHR is one of the main players in the interpretation of IHRL where issues of general international law arise. While developing its own jurisprudence for the protection of human rights in the European context, it remains embedded in the developments of general international law; the ECHR is not interpreted in 'clinical isolation' from general international law and does not always follow general international law closely but the Court develops its own doctrines. Its decisions however are important for national courts as well as other international courts and tribunals, and therefore guides general international law. The direction of influence thus goes both ways.

This book is intended to be a contribution to the ongoing debate on fragmentation and convergence, taking as a special case the ECtHR and its interaction with general international law and looking at their mutual influence. It explores the interaction, including the problems arising in the context of human rights, between the ECHR and general international law. Some of the chapters suggest reconciling methods and convergence while others stress the danger of fragmentation. The focus is on specific topics which we deem to be of merit, namely: sources, interpretation, jurisdiction, State responsibility, and immunity. In all these areas, the relationship between the ECHR and general international law has either been one-sided (only from general international law to the ECHR), or confused and meandering, or general international law has been adapted to the European human rights context. All the chapters discuss either new aspects or new case law in the respective areas under consideration and thus contribute to the ongoing discussion of the overall topic of the book. They reflect the dialogue between judges of the ECtHR, judges of the ICJ, and academics at a conference co-organized by the ECtHR and the European Society of International Law on 5 June 2015.

In this introduction, we will first recall the distinct character of human rights law and the discussion on fragmentation in this regard. Here, we allude to the two-way street of fragmentation and integration, drawing on a typology by Philippa

[6] Mads Adenas and Eirik Bjorge, 'Introduction: from fragmentation to convergence in international law' in Adenas and Bjorge (eds) (n 4) 4 et seq.

Webb (part 2). Building on that, we go through the different areas treated in this book as discussed by the respective authors to answer the questions when and why IHLR differs from or coincides with general international law (part 3). The last part concludes the discussion (4).

2. Fragmentation and Conciliation: A Two-Way Street

The distinct character of the ECHR (compared with general international law) has long been acknowledged. Thus, the relationship between the ECHR and general international law is rather intricate. Formally, the Convention came into being as a traditional or common international covenant, shaped by the established rules and principles of general international law. However, its very nature as a human rights instrument born out of the atrocities of the Second World War prefigured, from the outset, a somewhat idiosyncratic character and thus a special relationship with general international law. Over time, the formerly predominantly State-centred and reciprocal nature of international law has been influenced and changed by the special and non-reciprocal character of human rights obligations.[7] *Jus cogens* and *inter omnes* obligations, both drawing on human rights, have mainly been shaped by the ICJ[8] and the International Law Commission (ILC)[9] but are used by human rights courts.

Human rights courts, including the ECtHR, have stressed the special character of human rights treaties. The Convention's distinct and inimitable character is already reflected in the Court's ruling in *Ireland v The United Kingdom* of 1978: 'Unlike international treaties of the classic kind, the Convention comprises more than mere reciprocal engagements between contracting States. It creates, over and above a network of mutual, bilateral undertakings, objective obligations which, in the words of the Preamble, benefit from a "collective enforcement".'[10] According to this passage, the ECHR has to be distinguished from general international law ('Unlike international treaties of the classic kind') and can be qualified as something 'beyond' classic treaties of international law ('more than mere reciprocal engagements') exhibiting a superordinate status ('over and above'). Moreover, one can infer from this excerpt that—contrary to traditional public international law—it is not the signatory States but the system itself that generates the protection mechanism ('It creates') and creates 'objective obligations'.

There is no doubt that the ECHR is a law-making treaty and thus is different from classic bilateral and reciprocal treaties. It constitutes an '*ordre public européen*'[11] and is—as was held in *Loizidou*—a 'constitutional instrument of European public order'.[12] This also means that the obligations of States create a special mode of

[7] Sandesh Sivakumaran, 'Impact on the Structure of International Obligations' in Kamminga and Scheinin (eds) (n 1).

[8] In *Barcelona Traction, Light and Power Company, Limited (New Application: 1962), Belgium v Spain* [1970] ICJ Rep 3, para 33.

[9] Article 48 ARSIWA.

[10] *Ireland v The United Kingdom* App no 5310/71 (ECtHR, 18 January 1978), para 239.

[11] Peter Häberle, 'Gemeineuropäisches Verfassungsrecht' (1991) EuGRZ 264.

[12] *Loizidou v Turkey* (Preliminary Objections) App no 15318/89 (ECtHR, 23 March 1995), para 75.

enforcement—namely, they must be understood as obligations *erga omnes*—in contrast to the traditional bilateral obligations of international law. It also suggests that, whereas classic treaties must be interpreted according to the will of the States Parties, the ECtHR understands the Convention as a living instrument and accordingly uses a dynamic, teleological interpretation. This allows the Court to gradually objectivize the Convention. Positive obligations, surpassing the negative rights dimension, have a constitutional dimension since they demand positive action by the State. There is a broad consensus that there has been an 'anthropocentric turn' in international law,[13] and other human rights courts, not only the ECtHR, have certainly played an important role in this development.

Over the last six decades, the Convention has developed significantly. It has built its own unique identity, simultaneously challenging conventional institutional setups of international courts.[14] Two factors have had a tremendous impact in shaping and changing the identity of the Convention and thus its relationship with general international law. First, the end of the Cold War period and the subsequent accession of new members of the Council of Europe (CoE), and second the significant reform process in accordance with Protocol No. 11 in 1998 establishing a permanent Court and a compulsory individual complaint mechanism.

The tremendous development of the Convention has had significant and substantial consequences and changed the very character of the instrument. Due to this, it has been described as 'emancipated' from general international law, unfolding in a 'mezzanine' level between national and international law.[15] Others have argued that the ECHR may be seen as a factor contributing to the 'fragmentation' of international law. At the same time, however, it has also been seen as an important element of the 'constitutionalization' of international law and thus as having a conciliatory impact.

This is in line with more recent studies, which contend that the fragmentation of international law is far exceeded by its convergence, as international bodies find ways to take account of each other and of the interaction of emerging fields,[16] including human rights law.[17] Maybe Alain Pellet is right in asking 'Should we (still) worry about fragmentation?' and even more so in answering that 'there is nothing to worry about'.[18] All in all, the relationship between the ECHR and general international law seems somewhat shimmering and fluctuating. Over time the ECHR challenges it, over time it improves it, and over time it strengthens and reaffirms it.

[13] Markus Kotzur, 'Die anthropozentrische Wende—menschenrechtlicher Individualschutz im Völkerrecht' in Michael Sachs and others (eds), *Der grundrechtsgeprägte Verfassungsstaat. Festschrift für Klaus Stern zum 80. Geburtstag* (Duncker & Humblot 2012); Meron (n 2); Christian Tomuschat, 'International Law: Ensuring the Survival of Mankind on the Eve of a New Century, General Course on Public International Law' in Collected Courses of the Hague Academy of International Law (Brill 1999) Vol 281,13.

[14] Ed Bates, *The Evolution of the European Convention on Human Rights: From Its Inception to the Creation of a Permanent Court of Human Rights* (OUP 2010).

[15] Johann Justus Vasel, *Regionaler Menschenrechtsschutz als Emanzipationsprozess* (Duncker & Humblot 2017).

[16] Adenas and Bjorge (eds) (n 4).

[17] Dean Spielmann, 'Fragmentation or partnership? The reception of ICJ case-law by the European Court of Human Rights' in Adenas and Bjorge (eds) (n 4).

[18] Pellet (n 5).

Thus, the process of development, or 'emancipation' from general international law, is not linear, nor has it emerged in all relevant fields in the same manner. And of course, views differ on how far the ECtHR should go in reaffirming human rights protection when challenging general international law or ICJ judgments.

More generally, the phenomenal increase in number of international courts and quasi-judicial bodies over the last decades has had a tremendous impact on international law. International law is no longer created and interpreted by States, but predominantly by the decisions of judicial bodies in the international realm. This finding begs the question whether the coherence of international law is threatened by international tribunals[19] or whether an emerging judicial dialogue is contributing to conciliation. As Dame Higgins said, 'the plethora of judicial and quasi-judicial bodies operating in the field of human rights does pose the risk of divergent jurisprudence'.[20] But she also underlined, stressing the importance of judicial dialogue, the frequent references in the Strasbourg case law to the case law of the ICJ, which itself often looks to the Convention jurisprudence. Even if one does not share the rather 'optimistic' perspective of Alain Pellet, remaining scepticism regarding fragmentation may be attenuated or even eliminated by Philippa Webb's observation that fragmentation is often accompanied by integration. They are two sides of the same coin.

Philippa Webb has identified and examined several factors influencing fragmentation and convergence.[21] Although her study focuses on international courts, her findings—*mutatis mutandis*—may hold true with regard to the ECtHR being the very epitome of a regional court and her criteria provide a good framework for looking at the chapters in this book. First, the identity of the court matters. Since the permanent nature of a court, like that of the ECtHR, is associated with authority and stability, this factor increases its tendency towards convergence, and is likely to promote integration.[22] While the function of a court in itself may not define its tendency towards fragmentation or integration, it is nevertheless relevant since fragmentation may occur more often when a court trespasses beyond the boundaries and limitations defined by its function.[23] The ECtHR has been criticized on that account and some of the chapters in this book caution the Court against going any further.[24] Institutional context matters in this regard: The Court is the CoE's

[19] Jonathan I Charney, 'Is International Law Threatened by Multiple International Tribunals?' (1998) 271 *Recueil des Cours* 101, 117.

[20] Rosalyn Higgins, 'The International Court of Justice and the European Court of Human Rights: Partners for the Protection of Human Rights, European Court of Human Rights' in *Dialogue between Judges, Fifty Years of the European Court of Human Rights viewed by its Fellow International Courts* (Council of Europe 2009) 82.

[21] Philippa Webb, 'Factors influencing fragmentation and convergence in international courts' Adenas and Bjorge (eds) (n 4). She also deals with procedural issues which we will not address in this context.

[22] ibid 147.

[23] See, for an overview, Philippa Webb, International Judicial Integration and Fragmentation (OUP 2016) <https://global.oup.com/academic/product/international-judicial-integration-and-fragmentation-9780198743729?cc=de&lang=en&

[24] See especially the chapters by Anja Seibert-Fohr and Geir Ulfstein in this volume on the interpretational approaches.

principal judicial organ and it has a compulsory complaint mechanism which may have led to a decreased appreciation of the views of States on human rights. But it is also embedded in the CoE and this is obvious when it refers to the 'European consensus', that is, drawing on other norms of the CoE.[25] Nevertheless, the ECtHR must rely on the cooperation of the member States, which may narrow down the framework within which it acts. Secondly, the substance of the law matters. The Court adjudicates on the basis of a treaty and is thus bound by it as well as by the Vienna Convention on the Law of Treaties (VCLT). Whenever it bases itself on custom, there is much more dispute about the decisions (for example, in immunity cases[26]). Just as customary international law provides courts with greater scope for creativity, the relative sparseness of judicial practice in an area of law also provides space for judicial innovation.[27] Conflicting approaches between courts and a change of doctrine or facts both increase the tendency towards fragmentation, at least in the short term, as Webb says. The issue of extraterritoriality and responsibility are examples of that.[28] But they may also lead to convergence if different courts take each other's position into account as far as possible.

3. Typologies—Confirmation of and Emancipation from General International Law

The following section discusses the exemplary areas of mutual influence set out in the book, namely, sources, interpretation, jurisdiction, State responsibility, and immunity. These chapters explore whether there has been confirmation of, or emancipation from, general international law in those areas.

3.1 Sources

Traditionally, sources are viewed as a means of integration of international law since they are common to all international treaties; they thus form the common basis for IHRL and general international law. But of course, the use of sources differs between courts. Also, the way in which custom and other sources are identified varies and the ECtHR meanders between tradition and deviation from general international law in this regard. This problem is connected to its interpretational approach, dealt with in the next section but, in the view of the editors, it merits special attention.

Judge Ineta Ziemele focuses on custom and European consensus. Customary international law is said to have been influenced by IHRL, not only substantively (that is undisputed) but also in the way custom is identified—at least by human rights courts. Hitherto, it has been widely assumed that the 'human rights method' of ascertaining customary international law emphasizes *opinio juris* over State

[25] See the chapter by Angelika Nußberger.
[26] See the chapter by Riccardo Pavoni and Philippa Webb.
[27] See the chapters by Samantha Besson and Ganna Judkivska.
[28] See the chapters by Marko Milanovic, Isıl Karakas/Hasan Bakirci, and Ganna Judkivska.

practice, more so than was established by the ICJ in the *Nicaragua* case.[29] It has been argued that the more important the common interests of States or humanity are, the greater the weight that may be attached to *opinio juris* as opposed to State practice.[30] Judge Ziemele considers the role of European consensus in the jurisprudence of the Court. Is it a way of ascertaining (regional) custom or does European consensus denote a normative concept of its own? Although methodological clarity is still missing in the case law, she discusses how the Court uses and identifies European consensus. The question arises whether the Court's approach is compatible with the way the existence of a rule of customary law is established in international law. The Court uses three ways of finding a European consensus: First, it reads into the provisions of the Convention the content of other applicable rules of international law via Article 3(3)(c) of theVCLT;[31] second, the Court sees that through consistent practice the States have amended the Convention provision via Article 31(3)(b) of the VCLT; third, European consensus may be found where there is enough legal material showing that most States have taken a consistent position on a specific issue over a certain period. Thus, the Court takes consistent tendencies in State practice into account as relevant either for the purposes of establishing a regional custom or a general principle, or as development in interpretation of the Convention. Furthermore, the Court may establish a European consensus if that is compatible with the object and purpose of the Convention and considering the special character of the Convention as a human rights treaty. This use of the concept of European consensus in the case law of the ECtHR may be considered as European-consensus regional customary law. However, Judge Ziemele shows that, while it is a legitimate point of departure, it does not fully explain the notion. As the notion has developed historically, it is fair to say that it was meant to have an autonomous meaning, especially given the difficulties surrounding the concept of customary law and in particular *opinio juris*. Over time, the notion of European consensus has permitted the Court to operate with the very same rule of treaty interpretation in a more dynamic and less dogmatic manner. The Court thus expands on the notion of custom as understood in general international law.

Judge Angelika Nußberger shows in her article how the Court does (or does not) integrate other international norms by referring to soft law. She tackles the question as to how far it matters for the Court if a rule of international law is to be considered as hard law or soft law when referring to it in its jurisprudence, a problem closely linked to the legitimacy of the Court. Soft law is defined as all principles, rules, and standards governing international relations, which are not considered to stem from one of the sources of international law enumerated in Article 38(1) of the Statute

[29] *Military and Paramilitary Activities in and Against Nicaragua (Nicaragua v United States)* [1984] ICJ Rep 392.

[30] Jan Wouters and Cedric Ryngaert, 'Impact on the Process of the Formation of Customary International Law' in Kamminga and Scheinin (eds) (n 1). For a more general account on that issue, see Anthea Elizabeth Roberts, 'Traditional and Modern Approaches to Customary International Law' (2001) 95 American Journal of International Law 757.

[31] Vienna Convention on the Law of Treaties (adopted 23 May 1969, entered into force 27 January 1980) 1155 UNTS 331.

of the ICJ or unratified treaties, communications from treaty bodies (soft jurisprudence) etc. Common to all these regulations is the lack of formalized consent by States, which are nevertheless expected to take them into account. Since soft law has become an important governing mechanism in international relations,[32] it is even more important to analyse how the ECtHR deals with this kind of 'relative normativity'.[33] The Court treats hard law, which may create conflicting legal obligations, differently from soft law. The role of the ECtHR may be seen as an especially important one, as it can and does act as a catalyst upgrading (and downgrading) soft law. Quotations from soft law can enhance knowledge about otherwise unknown rules; references can give them weight, and reliance on them can change their nature. If soft law is ignored, considered to be irrelevant, or contradicted, a major drawback for the work of the respective originator of the soft law, eg a treaty body, is to be expected. It also matters in which context soft law is taken up in the ECtHR's judgments. Basically, three scenarios can be distinguished according to Judge Nußberger.

First, soft law can be found in the ECtHR judgments under the heading 'Relevant international law', in which the Court gives a comprehensive overview of relevant norms adopted within the CoE or other international organizations, as well as of relevant judgments and decisions. Here, the Court does not distinguish between hard law and soft law, but sets out the relevant norms. Second, international legal material can be included in the part of the judgment under the heading 'The Law' without being a decisive part of the reasoning. Third, soft law can gain a prominent place in the Court's reasoning and become part of the *ratio decidendi*. This usually happens in the context of an evolutive interpretation of the Convention, when the Court needs to prove the existence of new approaches in the international legal environment to justify a change in its case law and therefore relies on what is called European consensus, being based on international and comparative law. It thus uses soft law in evolutive interpretations and in filling gaps within the Convention but without necessarily justifying its position. Conflicts between the ECHR and soft law are solved by accepting their parallelism and coexistence, and not necessarily interpreting soft law in a harmonious way. The Court reserves its right to give an answer to a concrete case which is incompatible with the general approach in international soft jurisprudence. Case law confirms that potential disharmony between the ECHR's case law and soft law or soft jurisprudence is not per se considered as a threat to the consistency of international human rights protection and does not, at least not under all circumstances, require a justification of the Court's diverging approach. This differs from its approach to hard law or hard jurisprudence, where the Court often tries to solve conflicts by deferring to the judgments of other courts (particularly those of the ICJ). The Court accepts an obligation to interpret the Convention as far as possible in harmony with other international treaties. Thus, since soft law or soft jurisprudence may lead to 'controversial results', it is not to be

[32] Joost Pauwelyn, Ramses Wessel, and Jan Wouters (eds), *Informal International Lawmaking* (OUP 2012).

[33] Prosper Weil, 'Towards Relative Normativity in International Law?' (1983) 77 American Journal of International Law 413.

feared that they might result in 'irreconcilable legal obligations' as with hard law or hard jurisprudence. The Court has thus differentiated in its approach to dealing with other international law, be it general or not. Its own judgments can be considered hard jurisprudence though, at least in Europe, and other courts may deal with them on that basis.

3.2 Interpretation

The ECtHR relies, as do other international courts and tribunals, on the VCLT, and thus a common body of interpretational methods exists. The ILC has cautiously criticized the approach of the VCLT, which does not differentiate between different types of treaties, especially bilateral and reciprocal treaties and multilateral and law-making treaties.[34] The ILC study, 'Treaties over time',[35] illustrates the point that, as a common point of reference, all international courts—including those interpreting international human rights instruments—consider Article 31 of the VCLT as the basis for treaty interpretation the study makes no special reference to human rights treaties, although it acknowledges the different emphasis of international courts and tribunals.[36] Human rights treaties or treaties protecting common interests thus may require special rules of interpretation or at least a different emphasis regarding the methods codified in Articles 31 and 32 of the VCLT. Indeed, the Court uses the methods in a distinct way, since the Convention has a 'special character as a treaty for the collective enforcement of human rights'.[37] The object and purpose, as mandated in Article 31(1) of the VCLT, is heavily used to give effect to the ECHR. The principle of dynamic interpretation can be said to be reflected in Article 31(3)(b) of the VCLT. Nevertheless, the IL found that it '[could not] be said that there ha[d] been a significant impact from international human rights law on general international law in this field'[38] of interpretation. The Court itself has given different decisions, from which one may draw the conclusion that it sometimes situates itself strictly within the framework of the VCLT and sometimes goes beyond it or at least understands it loosely.

Anja Seibert-Fohr analyses the effect of subsequent practice on the ECHR from a general international law perspective, based on the VCLT. On what basis can the meaning of a treaty legitimately be advanced? What role do Contracting States play in this endeavour? Can they advance or even modify the treaty after its conclusion by way of State practice? She specifies the preconditions under which subsequent State practice can legitimately be considered in human rights treaty interpretation and tackles the broader question of whether human rights jurisprudence follows

[34] International Law Commission, Fragmentation of International Law: Difficulties arising from the Diversification and Expansion of International Law (n 3) 250–51. See also Kamminga (n 1) 9.

[35] Relevant for the purpose of the issue at hand: See on the latest work ILC, 'Report of the International Law Commission on the Work of its 67th Session' (4 May–7 August 2015) UN Doc A/CN.4/L.854, 84.

[36] See ILC, Report of the International Law Commission on the Work of its 65th Session (6 May–9 August 2013) UN Doc A/68/10), Draft Commentary Conclusion no 1, para 16.

[37] *Soering v The United Kingdom* App no 14038/88 (ECtHR, 7 July 1989), para 87.

[38] Kamminga (n 1) 10.

its own rules of interpretation or can be accommodated within the realm of general international law. Any evolutive interpretation of the meaning of a term must, according to the ILC, result from the ordinary process of treaty interpretation.[39] It requires a presumed intention of the States Parties.[40] She describes international law as a matrix which draws the outer limits for treaty interpretation, and at the same time allows for sufficient flexibility to accommodate the specific nature of human rights law within this perimeter, and develops a framework in which it can be reconciled. At the heart of the matter is a phenomenon which might become ever more important in the times we live in: State practice can contribute to advancing human rights (the context in which the Court usually uses State practice) in accordance with the object and purpose of the ECHR, but it can also lead to a lower level of protection if State practice retreats. What is the solution to this? On the one hand, the obligations under the Convention are undertaken by States and their consent provides the source of these obligations. As the authors of the Convention, they remain competent to modify it, arguably even by means of practice. On the other hand, the specific nature of the Convention as a human rights instrument solicits a cautious approach. Seibert-Fohr develops a general theoretical framework, which rationalizes the normative value of subsequent practice in accordance with its respective function: State practice in teleological interpretation, in textual interpretation, in contextual interpretation, and State practice as a subsidiary means of interpretation. Lastly, State practice can potentially be a means of modifying the Convention.

But it remains unclear in practice and theory how many States Parties need to engage in this practice, how agreement can be established, and whether State practice needs to be uniform. Seibert-Fohr thus places the requirements for subsequent practice on a normative scale. If State practice is only referred to in a supplementary manner to confirm a meaning which is based on textual, contextual, and teleological interpretation, State practice does not need to be uniform because the treaty itself backs it up. If it is considered in the context of a textual or teleological interpretation, State practice needs to be sufficiently broad, and not at odds with the text, context, and purpose of the Convention, to warrant evolutive interpretation. Beyond this, when an interpretation cannot be based on the text or purpose of a treaty, and thus is not grounded in the fundamental consensus of the treaty itself, it is necessary to establish that practice is sufficiently consistent to presume that the relevant Contracting States agree. Seibert-Fohr then answers the broader question of whether human rights jurisprudence follows its own rules of interpretation or can be accommodated within the realm of general international law in the affirmative: that is, if evolutive interpretation is not framed as a separate means of interpretation but recognizes progress as the result of a textual, teleological, and contextual analysis. If State practice is regressive, or if it jeopardizes the object and purpose of the Convention as an instrument for the protection of the individual, it lacks the

[39] ibid para 8.

[40] See also Eirik Bjorge, 'The Vienna Rules, Evolutionary Interpretation, and the Intentions of the Parties' in Andrea Bianchi, Daniel Peat, and Matthew Windsor (eds), *Interpretation in International Law* (OUP 2015) 189, 203–4.

necessary legitimacy and effect on treaty interpretation. Subsequent practice is then devoid of normative value.

Geir Ulfstein looks at the law and legitimacy of evolutive interpretation in the light of other international instruments. He argues, first, that the significance of the VCLT has been subject to qualifications in some of the Court's judgments. In *Demir and Baykara v Turkey*[41], the Court talked about applying a method of interpretation that was guaranteed to be 'practical and effective', a method not present in the VCLT. In other cases the Court's reasoning can be accommodated within the bounds of the VCLT. Furthermore, the ECtHR has gone beyond the bounds of Article 31(3)(b) and (c) and primarily relies on Article 31(1) when it takes account of other international instruments than the ECHR. In Ulfstein's view, the Court is also 'collapsing' an evolutive interpretation based on European consensus in domestic law and on practice in the form of international instruments. Ulfstein mainly deplores the lack of clarity in the Court's reasoning. The Court thus risks allegations of going beyond its legal mandate and becoming an activist court. There is also a danger that States may be unwilling to implement judgments which are seen as legally unpersuasive.

Both Seibert-Fohr and Ulfstein tend to caution the ECtHR not to go beyond the limits of the VCLT and thus stay within the realm of general international law. Neither, however, would object to favouring certain methods of interpretation in order to take account of the special character of a human rights treaty. But they both make it clear that this is a fine line and that more clarity in the application of the interpretational methods in the Court's jurisprudence would be desirable.

3.3 Jurisdiction

The jurisdiction and applicability of the ECHR have been a contentious issue for some time now. The Court is said to go beyond general international law, but opinion differs as to whether it should. Furthermore, there is debate as to whether jurisdiction is, or should be, conflated with attribution and responsibility, thus overlaps in the chapters of this book are unavoidable. In the *Nicaragua* case, the ICJ held that 'to give rise to legal responsibility of the United States, it would in principle have to be proven that that State had *effective control* of the military and paramilitary operations in the course of which the alleged violation was committed'.[42] This *'effective control'* test was reaffirmed in the *Bosnian Genocide* case[43] by refusing to apply the broader *'overall control'* test[44] of the International Criminal Court for the Former Yugoslavia in the *Tadic* decision.[45] The ECtHR went beyond

[41] *Demir and Baykara v Turkey* [GC] App no 34503/97 (ECtHR, 12 November 2008) para 66.

[42] ibid §115. In the same vein, Article 8 of the Articles on State Responsibility, see James Crawford, *The International Law Commission's Articles on State Responsibility: Introduction, Text and Commentaries* (CUP 2002).

[43] *Application of the Convention on the Prevention and Punishment of the Crime of Genocide (Bosnia and Herzegovina v Serbia and Montenegro)* (Merits) [2007] ICJ Rep 43, paras 402–7.

[44] See Antonio Cassese, 'The Nicaragua and Tadic Tests revisited in light of the ICJ Judgment on Genocide in Bosnia' (2007) 18(4) EJIL 650.

[45] *Tadic Case* (Judgment) ICTY-94-1-A (15 July 1999).

that when establishing jurisdiction under Article 1 of the Convention, arguably because Article 1 of the ECHR is a threshold question of jurisdiction, not a question of attribution or responsibility, thus setting a lower threshold for a finding of jurisdiction.

In his contribution, Marko Milanovic focuses on the extraterritorial applicability of the Convention and analyses trends in the jurisprudence of the Strasbourg Court with regard to State jurisdiction (Article 1 of the ECHR) and State responsibility. His chapter aims to clarify the notion of jurisdiction, and State responsibility is thus put first. Although the extensive case law seems rather diverse and 'plagued with inconsistencies and uncertainties',[46] Milanovic identifies a clear tendency. The chapter examines the overarching trends in the jurisprudence of the ECtHR on questions of State jurisdiction, in the sense of Article 1 of the ECHR, and State responsibility, after its seminal judgment in the *Al-Skeini* case. The Court allows for two models: the spatial model (jurisdiction as effective overall control by a State over an area or territory)[47] and the personal model (jurisdiction as an exercise of authority or control by State agents over an individual). While the chapter does not claim to cover the subject comprehensively, it first discusses the threshold question of the extraterritorial applicability of human rights treaties, and analyses the relationship between the notions of jurisdiction and responsibility, specifically looking at the *Jaloud v The Netherlands*[48] case. The verdict is clear: the Court itself has over the decades been 'the greatest culprit in conflating jurisdiction and State responsibility'. The chapter then examines the issue of the relationship between human rights and international humanitarian law and the Court's judgment in *Hassan v The United Kingdom*.[49] The main argument put forward in this chapter is that the Court is growing increasingly comfortable with applying the Convention extraterritorially and in armed conflict, and with directly invoking rules of international humanitarian law (IHL). While some human rights bodies, especially in the inter-American system,[50] have a long history of applying IHL, this is a recent development in the European system where the Court has so far generally avoided relying on IHL. But this seems to be changing now. However, several important caveats and uncertainties remain in the Court's jurisprudence, which will inevitably be an issue in important cases currently pending before it, eg the many inter-state and individual applications dealing with the conflict in the Ukraine. By showing that the Court is becoming more and more comfortable with an extraterritorial application of the Convention in general, and in armed conflicts in particular, Milanovic's analysis seems to point towards an increasing dissociation of the ECHR from general international law. However, the Court's repeated

[46] See the chapter in this volume by Marko Milanovic.

[47] *Al-Skeini and Others v The United Kingdom* [GC] App no 55721/07 (ECtHR, 7 July 2011) paras 138–39.

[48] *Jaloud v The Netherlands* [GC] App no 47708/08 (ECtHR, 20 November 2014).

[49] *Hassan v The United Kingdom* [GC] App no 29750/09 (ECtHR, 16 September 2014).

[50] See F Hampson, 'The Relationship between International Humanitarian Law and Human Rights Law from the Perspective of a Human Rights Treaty Body' (2008) 90 IRRC 549.

reliance on IHL appears to be integrative, rather than challenging, with regard to general international law.

Judge Işıl Karakas and Hasan Bakırcı also address the issue of extraterritorial jurisdiction. Their chapter analyses the evolution of the Strasbourg case law on the concept of jurisdiction within the meaning of Article 1 of the Convention and attempts to provide a comprehensive answer to the question of extraterritorial jurisdiction by neatly grouping different cases *ratione loci* and *ratione personae*. It also ascertains whether there is any truth in the criticism directed towards the Court's case law and, more importantly, whether there is any room for its further development. It is on the basis of the historical and contemporary practice of State authorities' endeavours to find ways to deny individuals their basic human rights, and to escape accountability and responsibility for human rights violations occurring outside their home territories in the course of their extraterritorial activities, that the interpretation of Article 1 of the ECHR by the Court must be understood. In their view, there is no direct conflict between the above-mentioned cases of attribution as decided by the ICJ, since the issue of jurisdiction under Article 1 of the ECHR is a threshold requirement in the Convention; the question of State responsibility or attribution would only arise once the Court was satisfied that the matters complained of were within the jurisdiction of the respondent State. But the question is whether Article 1 of the ECHR is also subject to the 'living instrument' doctrine or whether that doctrine is inapplicable. In their view, it is, thereby allowing for a more extensive interpretation of jurisdiction.

Both chapters argue that the jurisprudence of the Court is in line with that of other human rights bodies, if not necessarily with the ICJ. Referring to the object and purpose of the Convention, they deem it justified to favour an extensive reading of jurisdiction, despite the criticism by certain member States which argue that the concept of 'effective control' as applied by the Court to establish the extraterritorial jurisdiction is not in harmony with the principles of international law.

Clearly, the issue remains topical: not only regarding extraterritorial humanitarian action of the member States, but also cases on extraterritorial electronic surveillance and other cyber activities, in which the application of the Court's test based on physical control will not be straightforward—although, in Milanovic's view, those cases should end up being decided extensively as well.

Judge Ganna Judkivska takes an unconventional perspective on territorial jurisdiction and analyses the positive obligations of an occupied State and the evolving issues under Article 1 of the ECHR. The task of the international law of occupation, as it has developed since the nineteenth century as part of the law of war, is to regulate the conduct of occupying forces. Indeed, it is all about what an occupying power should and should not do. Very little has been said about the obligations of an occupied State, or a 'victim' State—the State that has lost part of its territory following a belligerent occupation. The chapter elaborates on this issue, which has not been sufficiently developed in either the doctrine or the practice of international tribunals including the ECtHR. Specifically, the chapter aims to outline the nature—and defines the scope—of the human rights obligations of an occupied State, in conjunction with the potential concurrent duties and responsibilities of an occupying State. It discusses the posture of international law with respect to the duties of an injured State and argues that the

Court's approach in the case of *Ilaşcu and Others*[51] represented a new development in international law, according to which human rights obligations are primarily triggered by effective territorial control. The requirements to achieve respect for human rights and freedoms in a territory outside a State's control are rather controversial and call for a more nuanced methodology.

Clearly though, the Court is at the forefront of developing doctrines which might be relevant for other international courts as well. This chapter also has a lot to say on responsibility, which is the next area we will turn to.

3.4 Responsibility

Samantha Besson argues in favour of concurrent responsibilities under the ECHR, namely the concurrence of human rights jurisdictions, duties, and responsibilities. This is a problem not only of primary obligations but also of State responsibility. After dwelling for a long time on the notion, conditions, and related duties, the debate about jurisdiction—territorial or extraterritorial—in the ECHR has now moved on to the issue of its normative implications for States' duties and responsibilities in circumstances where many States exercise concurrent jurisdiction. In response to this new challenge, this chapter discusses how one should articulate the concurrent effective control, and hence jurisdictions, of different States; how one should specify and allocate their concurrent duties stemming from this concurrence of jurisdiction; and, lastly, how one should attribute and then allocate their concurrent responsibilities when concurrent duties have been violated. This chapter thus helps to unravel distinct issues whose relationship with the elusive notion of State 'control' has remained unclear in the jurisprudence of the Court. More generally, it shows how much the ECtHR's practice has promoted, and could promote even further, the development of the still largely underexplored regime of concurrent or 'shared' responsibility in general international law. Since the concept of 'shared' responsibility in international law, including Article 47 of the Articles on the Responsibility of States for Internationally Wrongful Acts (ARSIWA) is highly unclear, the Court has the potential to be a trendsetter in this respect.[52]

Judge James Crawford and Amelia Keene ask whether there is an integrated approach to be found between the UN Security Council, ARSIWA, and the ECtHR. They start with Malcolm Evans' claim that the human rights character of the ECHR 'makes the international principles of State responsibility *irrelevant* to its operation, so it is not clear why they should be referred to at all'. The ARSIWA, in contrast, operate on the completely contrary assumption that they fully apply in the human rights context as the relevant secondary rules on State

[51] *Ilaşcu and Others v Moldova and Russia* [GC] App no 48787/99 (ECtHR, 8 July 2004).

[52] André Nollkaemper and Dov Jacobs, 'Shared Responsibility in International Law: A Conceptual Framework' (2013) 34 Michigan Journal of International Law 359; and generally the 'shares' project at the University of Amsterdam: <http://acil.uva.nl/research/research-projects/content/shared-responsibility-in-international-law-shares.html> accessed 27 July 2018.

responsibility. The jurisprudence of the ECtHR sits somewhere between these two positions. In some cases the State responsibility rules have not been applied. The Court has developed a novel 'acquiescence or connivance' rule to hold a third State responsible for the acts of another State on its territory (*El-Masri*[53]) that has no place in Article 16 of the ARSIWA. It has also refused to apply the Articles on the Responsibility of International Organisations (ARIO) in finding that an 'ultimate authority' test was to be preferred to the 'effective control' rule set out in what is now Article 7 of the ARIO (*Behrami*[54]). Moreover, the Court has broadly interpreted Article 3 of the ECHR so as to engage States' direct responsibility for the acts of private actors without reference to the attribution rules under the ARSIWA (*Costello-Roberts*[55]). But recently, the Court has more fully applied the rules on State responsibility and has pulled back from some of its earlier departures (*Kotov*[56]*;Al Nashiri*[57]). It is also making its own contribution to the rules on the responsibility of States for the acts of international organizations, influencing the drafting of the ARIO (*Bosphorus*[58]).

So, in a way, the relationship between the ECtHR and general international law in the sphere of State responsibility is not on settled ground, but one may cautiously call it a two-way street.

Judge Iulia Motoc and Johann Justus Vasel analyse the recent jurisprudence of the ECtHR reaching the conclusion that the Court's approach is evolving towards judicial integration, this evolution being sustained by arguments concerning the way in which the Court analyses and rationalizes the differences between human rights and general international law. The question of fragmentation and integration has haunted the doctrine of jurisdiction and responsibility. After analysing the notion of *lex specialis* with regard to the question of responsibility and jurisdiction as (implicitly) proposed by the ECtHR in the *Catan*[59] judgment, the contribution considers the question of the attribution of conduct introduced for the first time in the *Jaloud*[60] judgment. The chapter draws a parallel between the notion of effective control used in the ICJ's *Nicaragua* case and the *Chiragov*[61] case. It argues that the Court's ruling in *Chiragov* is closer to the criterion of effective control imposed by the ICJ. The analysis shows that, in both the recent decisions of *Jaloud* and *Chiragov*, the Court is moving towards judicial integration in the sense of a reasoned difference between the responsibility of human rights and general

[53] *El-Masri v The Former Yugoslav Republic of Macedonia* [GC] App no 39630/09 (ECtHR, 13 December 2012).

[54] *Behrami and Behrami v France* and *Saramati v France, Germany and Norway* [GC] App nos 71412/01 and 78166/01 (ECtHR, 2 May 2007).

[55] *Costello-Roberts v The United Kingdom* App no 13134/87 (ECtHR, 25 March 1993).

[56] *Kotov v Russia* [GC] App no 54522/00 (ECtHR, 3 April 2012).

[57] *Al Nashiri v Poland* App no 28761/11 (ECtHR, 24 July 2014).

[58] *Bosphorus Hava Yolları Turizm ve Ticaret Anonim Şirketi v Ireland* [GC] App no 45036/98 (ECtHR, 30 June 2005).

[59] *Catan and Others v The Republic of Moldova and Russia* [GC] App nos 43370/04, 8252/05, and 18454/06 (ECtHR, 19 October 2012).

[60] *Jaloud* (n 48).

[61] *Chiragov and Others v Armenia* [GC] App no 13216/05 (ECtHR, 16 June 2015).

international law. Although, in future, judgments of the ECtHR will have to offer even more consistent legal reasoning to maintain this trend, it is evident that the ECHR is not a self-contained regime.

Judge Linos-Alexandre Sicilianos tackles the relationship between the ECHR and the question of the responsibility of States acting in execution of a Security Council resolution, which has repeatedly arisen in the Court's case law. The central question raised involves the relationship between the UN system and that of the ECHR, and consequently the Court's role in this vast geopolitical framework, while at the same time its function in guaranteeing the fundamental values of the European public order. An examination of the cases may sometimes give the impression that the Court oscillates between a somewhat reserved, or even self-effacing, attitude and a significantly more assertive approach, at times showing reverence towards the Security Council and at other times a form of defiance. Judge Sicilianos attempts to conceptualize this issue as a whole. He thus makes a distinction between Security Council resolutions that involve, or could potentially involve, the use of armed force on the one hand and those which impose economic or targeted sanctions on the other. First, the two types of resolutions have a different legal basis: economic sanctions are imposed on the basis of Article 41 of the UN Charter, whereas military operations are based mainly on Article 42 or—at least in the case of authorized operations—on Chapter VII of the Charter as a whole. The two types of resolutions also, and above all, differ as to the means and procedure for their implementation: the latter involves the deployment of military troops abroad, while the former requires the establishment of a legal and regulatory framework to enforce the economic sanctions within the territory of the forum State—corresponding to the respondent State before the Court. Military operations involve the problem of extraterritoriality, and the principle established in the Court's case law in this sphere is that, while being essentially territorial in its application, the ECHR may be applicable outside the territory of the State concerned in a range of specific situations, including—and particularly—when that State's armed forces are operating abroad. This position is corroborated by the case law of the ICJ and the practice of the Human Rights Committee and other international human rights protection bodies. Thus, where the implementation of resolutions involving the use of force is concerned, the Court's recent case law has shown a shift towards systematic acceptance of the extraterritorial scope of the ECHR. The—not always very clear—distinction between the concepts of jurisdiction and attribution cannot call into question the fundamental principle that every internationally wrongful act of a state entails its international responsibility, irrespective of the place where the act was perpetrated. As to whether the conduct in issue should be attributed to the States Parties or to the UN, the Court now makes a clear distinction between operations authorized by the Security Council and UN peacekeeping operations. The former are placed under national command and control authorities, and consequently the question of the UN's responsibility does not even arise. In the case of UN operations, however, it remains important to undertake a more detailed examination of the question of shared responsibility between the UN and the States contributing troops.

The question of the responsibility of the Contracting Parties to the ECHR in the implementation of resolutions imposing economic sanctions is addressed differently according to whether the respondent State is or is not a member of the EU. The criterion of 'equivalent protection' (as in the 2005 *Bosphorus* judgment[62]) is only applicable in the former scenario. And in any event, it needs to be applied cautiously on a case-by-case basis, bearing in mind that the prospect of EU accession to the ECHR has receded following the European Court of Justice's opinion 2/13 and that, as a result, the protection of human rights is still not complete in Europe. As regards the enforcement of economic sanctions by non-EU member States, the Court tends to interpret Security Council resolutions in a manner consistent with the obligations deriving from the ECHR. Without ruling out the applicability of Article 103 of the Charter in the circumstances of each individual case, such an approach seeks to avoid a conflict of obligations, and thus tension between the UN and ECHR systems. The Court favours an integrated and harmonized interpretation and application of (potentially conflicting) obligations of States under the two systems. In other words, the Court's approach is oriented towards systemic complementarity rather than towards normative conflict. Judge Sicilianos notes that the Court is in the process of refining its conceptual tools for determining the responsibility of the States Parties to the ECHR acting in execution of a Security Council resolution.

Judge Paulo Pinto de Albuquerque and Anne van Aaken address the issue of the nature of damages awarded in international law. 'Punitive damages' have long been the subject of controversy in national as well as in international law. This is no different for the ECtHR. Until now, the Court has considered it inappropriate, in accordance with the Court's Practice Directives of March 2007 and January 2016, to accept claims for damages with labels such as 'punitive', 'aggravated', or 'exemplary'. One would thus expect that punitive damages would not be awarded by the Court. But is this really the case? This chapter finds that the Court has been at the forefront of an international trend, using just satisfaction to prevent further violations of human rights and punish governments that have engaged in wrongdoing. The acknowledgment of punitive damages under the Convention is essential in at least three cases: (i) gross violations of human rights protected by the Convention or the additional Protocols, especially when there are multiple violations at the same time, repeated violations over a significant period of time, or a single continuing violation over a significant period of time; (ii) prolonged, deliberate non-compliance with a judgment of the Court delivered with regard to the recalcitrant Contracting Party; and (iii) the severe curtailment, or threat thereof, of the applicant's human rights with the purpose of avoiding, impairing, or restricting his or her access to the Court as well as the Court's access to the applicant.

They thus argue first that the aforementioned Practice Directive is no longer up to date in that the Court uses punitive damages implicitly and second that there are well-established social-science reasons why punitive damages should be used.

[62] *Bosphorus* (n 58).

The idea of punitive damages is strongly connected to the effectiveness of law. Wherever enforcement might be weak, punitive damages can set the correct incentives for following the law. Punitive damages may serve, inter alia, to implement the *inter omnes* obligations of States as well as the human rights of the people of the CoE. The Court is thus at the forefront of a development in international law. Whether other courts will follow remains to be seen.

3.5 Immunity

Immunity has been a complicated issue in international law, given its reliance on national law and, to a lesser extent, on treaty or custom.

Philippa Webb's chapter calls immunity—correctly in our view—a moving target. The last fifty years have seen significant changes in the law of State immunity. The ECtHR has, over the past fifteen years in particular, played an influential role in the law applicable to this 'moving target'. This chapter examines three approaches of the ECtHR: (i) the ECtHR looking to the ICJ; (ii) the ECtHR looking to national practice; and (iii) the ECtHR looking to the ILC and the provisional application of treaties. Although the ECtHR strives to place itself within general international law, it necessarily approaches questions of immunity through the lens of Article 6 of the ECHR and taking into account whether immunity constitutes a legitimate and proportionate restriction on the right of access to a court. This has, at times, taken the Court down a different path from other judicial bodies and Webb identifies the emergence of a 'European approach' to the role of immunity in employment disputes. Whether other courts will follow the ECtHR's approach remains an open question.

Riccardo Pavoni critically reviews the jurisprudence of the Court on State immunity, calling into question the customary nature of the 2004 UN Convention on Jurisdictional Immunities of States and Their Property (UNCSI) as used by the Court. The modern jurisprudence of the ECtHR involving questions of foreign State immunity is usually informed by the premise that such questions are governed by customary international law, 'the codification of which is enshrined' in the UNCSI, a multilateral treaty which is not yet in force. This chapter takes the view that the alleged customary nature of the UNCSI largely constitutes a myth. A primary illustration is offered by Article 11 on the employment exception to State immunity, which is at the heart of most of the ECtHR's decisions relating to the UNCSI. The multiple reasons why the UNCSI, and that provision in particular, cannot be regarded as a reflection of customary law are outlined. The chapter considers that, in its UNCSI decisions, the ECtHR may have favoured a consequentialist posture, according to which the ultimate end of safeguarding human rights impaired by measures taken by ECHR Parties pursuant to controversial immunity rules would justify every legal means, however questionable, espoused for that purpose. However, it is not to be taken for granted that the ECtHR's calculus has been accurate in this area, ie that the Court has carefully considered the pros and cons of its UNCSI jurisprudence. A dilemma remains as to whether the end justifies the means. Thus, both authors conclude that, at least in employment issues, the Court takes its own path, even if trying to conceal it by the use of putative custom.

Judge Antônio Cançado Trindade, in his concluding chapter, clearly states that in a *jus naturale* mode of thinking, to which he adheres, the notion of justice has always occupied a central position, guiding the law as a whole. For him, justice is found, in sum, at the beginning of all law, being moreover its ultimate end. Accordingly, the interpretation of human rights treaties must be guided less by the objective of securing the uniformity of international law in general, in any context and circumstances, than by the concern and purpose to respond effectively to the needs and the imperatives of the international protection of human rights. One specific example is the law of immunity, where uniformity of international law has been considered important by the ECtHR. For Judge Cançado Trindade, *jus cogens* stands above the prerogative or privilege of State immunity, with all the consequences that flow from that, thus avoiding denials of justice and impunity, even if that would mean giving up the coherence of international law. The evolution of international human rights law should not be hindered by an attachment to the classic postulates of the law of treaties irrespective of the context in which they apply.

4. Conclusion: The ECHR and General International Law—Osmosis and Concentric Circles

The question of fragmentation and convergence with in international law is a dynamic one: it may change over time. The ECHR and general international law can be described as being in an osmotic relationship: osmosis takes place in both directions, well documented by the mutual citation of cases of the ECtHR (eg in immunities) and the ICJ.[63] The ECtHR has not only followed general law,[64] the ICJ also cites the decisions of the ECtHR.[65] Simultaneously, it is possible to describe concentric circles from the point of view of human rights law. Whereas the inner circle constitutes perfect alignment between human rights law and general international law, the further one gets to the outer circles, the further the alignment may stray. Let's start with the inner circle. Clearly, all international law, while being codified in treaties, rests on the VCLT, or, as Judge Cançado Trindade says in his concluding remarks, there is a common ground of treaty hermeneutics. Furthermore, this inner circle is made up of the general principles of international law. But already in the next circle, even if relying on the first inner circle, there are special ways adopted in the methods of interpretation by the Court due to the 'special character' of the ECHR and other human rights treaties (Seibert-Fohr and Ulfstein).[66] This is well illustrated by Judge

[63] Spielmann (n 17).

[64] Adamantia Rachovitsa, 'Fragmentation of International Law Revisited: Insights, Good Practices, and Lessons to be Learned from the Case Law of the European Court of Human Rights' (2015) 28 Leiden Journal of International Law 863.

[65] See, for example, *Jurisdictional Immunities of the State (Germany v Italy: Greece intervening)* (Judgment) [2012] ICJ Rep 143, citing *Al-Adsani v The United Kingdom* [GC] App no 35763/97 (ECtHR, 21 November 2001).

[66] See *Mamatkulov and Askarov v Turkey* [GC] App nos 46827/99 and 46951/99 (ECtHR, 4 February 2005), para 111: 'the Convention must be interpreted in the light of the rules set out in the Vienna Convention of 23 May 1969 on the Law of Treaties', but the Court must do so 'taking into

Nußberger when analysing the soft law the Court uses—including CoE norms and the European consensus. The next circle diverges even more from general international law. In the field of responsibility (Sicilianos, Motoc and Vasel, Crawford and Keene) and damages (Pinto de Alberquerque and van Aaken), the Court can be seen to be going further than general international law while still trying to integrate it as far as possible. Then, in a further circle, there are areas where the Court breaks new ground, having the potential to shape general international law. In those cases, where jurisprudence is not 'thick' and the law is still in flux, the Court may be able to establish itself as a trendsetter, namely in the question of shared responsibility (Besson) and in cases of occupation (Judkivska). The same happens with immunities due to Article 6 of the ECHR, at least in employment issues, even if the Court tries to place itself within general international law (Webb and Pavoni). The views of the different authors on fragmentation and conciliation, as practised by the Court, differ though, with the ECtHR judges being more tempted to view the attitude of the Court as conciliatory.

As Judge Cançado Trindade stresses in his conclusion, the best way of dealing with fragmentation is dialogue: dialogue between international and constitutional courts, ie between judges of a multilayered system. This can be on a formal basis or on a more personal and informal level. Even if this dialogue is still young, 'it contains the seeds for greater linkages among international courts that may in turn enhance convergence'.[67] The attempt at systemic harmonization was stressed by the Grand Chamber—as far as possible, the Court will try to harmonize with international law.[68]

Having said that, and noting that convergence and coherence of international law are in principle desirable, we would like to stress that fragmentation has its own merits, duly accounting for the special and objective character of human rights treaties, as also stressed by Judge Cançado Trindade. This responsibility of human rights courts, including the ECtHR, might be challenged by States in times of crisis. The Court would, in our view, be making a mistake if it gave in to those challenges and if it gave up its determination to protect the rights of all people of the CoE. A call for convergence cannot impede what Judge Cançado Trindade has put succinctly:

> The ILHR has ... enriched and legitimized Public International Law, in developing its aptitude to govern relations not only at inter-State, but also at intra-State levels. And we are all fortunate to witness and to contribute to the ongoing historical process of humanization of international law, the new *jus gentium* of our times.

It is also the responsibility of the Court to prevent reversal—as far as it can.

account the *special nature* of the Convention as an instrument of human rights protection (see *Golder* v. *United Kingdom*, judgment of 21 February 1975, Series A no 18, p. 14, § 29)'.

[67] Webb (n 21) 167.

[68] Separate opinion of Judge Motoc, *Jaloud* (n 48) paras 2 et seq and separate opinion of Judge Sicilianos, *Al-Dulimi and Montana Management Inc v Switzerland* App no 5809/08 paras 9 et seq (ECtHR, 26 November 2013) (referred to the Grand Chamber 14 April 2014).

PART I

SOURCES

1

European Consensus and International Law

Ineta Ziemele

1. Introduction—Setting the Stage

The concept of 'European consensus' is the creation of the European Court of Human Rights (ECtHR).[1] One of the first cases in which it was resorted to in substance concerned judicial corporal punishment of juveniles. The Court in *Tyrer v The United Kingdom* found that such punishment is contrary to Article 3 of the European Convention on Human Rights (ECHR). It observed that:

> The Court must also recall that the Convention is a living instrument which, as the Commission rightly stressed, must be interpreted in the light of present-day conditions. In the case now before it the Court cannot but be influenced by the developments and commonly accepted standards in the penal policy of the member States of the Council of Europe in this field.[2]

The Court accepts that it will be influenced by 'the developments and commonly accepted standards' in the member States of the Council of Europe. In other words, the Court takes note of changing attitudes in Europe and, in this case, it in effect determines that, by 1978, judicial corporal punishment of juveniles as such is contrary to Article 3. Judge Sir Gerald Fitzmaurice disagreed with this conclusion because he considered that the Court in fact legislated on the matter. Interestingly, Fitzmaurice did not disagree with the principle that the Convention is a living instrument. The above cited *Tyrer* passage shows that the principle of the Convention as a living instrument and the interpretation of the Convention in light of developments in member States are part of the same phenomenon. However, the Court neither elaborates on the methodology for taking note of the changing attitudes nor provides for any further definitions.

In scholarly writings, this approach of the Court has been called a consensual interpretation deriving from the Preamble and it has been argued that such reference

[1] Early reflections on the topic can be found in the presentation delivered at the CADHI conference 'The Judge and International Custom' in Paris on 21 September 2012. See *The Judge and International Custom/Le Juge et la Coutume International* (Council of Europe 2012).

[2] See *Tyrer v The United Kingdom* App no 5856/72 (ECtHR, 25 April 1978), para 31.

to domestic law legitimizes the Court's interpretation of the Convention[3] over time. The scholarly debate discusses evolutive interpretation since 'it is closely linked to consensual interpretation carried out on the basis of domestic or international law, which allows the Court to determine whether the European legal common ground has evolved'.[4] Another view suggests that the principles of evolutive and dynamic interpretation of the Convention explain the so-called 'rights' principle which is the basis of the Convention, ie a constitutional principle.[5] In other words, the whole purpose of the Convention and its application is to ensure that the rights remain effective over time.

It is evident that the notion of European consensus, as it is referred to in the case law of the Court, places us in the very middle of the Court's work in interpreting the Convention. There is an agreement among scholars that European consensus, as an element of the evolutive interpretation of the Convention, is important for the further development of the Convention system. At the same time, it is also pointed out that the lack of 'further details as to its origins, advantages, and disadvantages' is the basis for criticism, especially the argument that the Court engages in judicial activism.[6] This position indicates the problem attributed to evolutive interpretation of treaties, ie the risk of overshadowing State consent thus giving rise to legitimacy issues.

The notions of the Convention as a living instrument and European consensus are linked to fundamental issues with regards to the evolving nature of law, and international law in particular, and relate to the issues of change and time, and adjudication in time.[7] However, this possible reflection will not be the focus of this chapter. The scope of this chapter will be to focus on any possible analogy that the notion of European consensus brings up with reference to the sources of international law as well as the general rule of interpretation of a treaty.[8] In international law, State consent remains the paradigm mechanism for the creation of rules in the form of treaties, custom, or general principles of law. However, expressions of and influences upon State consent evolve. Certainly, the ECtHR is such a procedural avenue through which new State consent may emerge or can be promoted. Since the Court has been criticized for its evolutive interpretation of the Convention and the assessment of European consensus, it is important to see whether the Court's methods may have indeed overshadowed State consent on the scope and content of the European Convention. Therefore, it is proposed to examine within the limits of

[3] See Magdalena Forowicz, *The Reception of International Law in the European Court of Human Rights* (OUP 2010) 9 (with references).

[4] ibid 11.

[5] See Steven Greer, *The European Convention on Human Rights. Achievements, Problems and Prospects* (CUP 2006) 203, 213.

[6] Forowicz (n 3) 12.

[7] See concurring opinion of Judge Ziemele in *O'Keeffe v Ireland* App no 35810/09 (ECtHR, 28 January 2014); See Ineta Ziemele, *Separate Opinions at the European Court of Human Rights* (Riga: RGSL, 2017) 62.

[8] European consensus has attracted important attention within the discourse on the Convention specifically. See, eg Konstantsin Dzehtsiarou, 'European Consensus and the Evolutive Interpretation of the European Convention on Human Rights' (2011) 12 German Law Journal 1730. However, there is not much reflection on consensus from the perspective of general international law.

this chapter whether in fact international law provides a better explanation of the notion of European consensus.

In 2008, in the seminar at the opening of its judicial year, the ECtHR prepared its own background paper on consensus, which was the theme of the seminar. In that paper, two conceptual propositions were the subject of reflection. First, that consensus can be seen as 'an element in the development of customary law', and second, that 'consensus in the context of the European Convention on Human Rights is generally understood as being the basis for the evolution of Convention standards through the case-law of the European Court of Human Rights ... Consensus legitimises progress and facilitates its reception into domestic law'.[9] The paper did not explain whether, within the first proposition, European consensus might be seen as an element of State practice which is at the core of the development of customary law. It did not link consensus to the element of subsequent practice in the law of treaties. Nor did it explain the second option, which primarily emphasizes the role of the Court in the evolution of the human rights standards, and thus does not help to address the above-mentioned criticism directed at the Court for its alleged judicial activism.

This chapter, through analysis of a number of leading judgments, looks at the Court's resort to State practice in interpreting the Convention and seeks to explain European consensus through the tools available in international law, notably the general rule of interpretation of a treaty.

It is generally known that the Court has always declared that it interprets the Convention in accordance with the rule of interpretation of treaties as enshrined in the Vienna Convention on the Law of Treaties (VCLT). In order to determine the meaning of the terms and phrases used in the Convention, the Court is guided mainly by Articles 31 to 33 of the VCLT.[10] At the same time, the Court interprets the Convention rights in light of present-day conditions; which approach goes back to the *Tyrer* case. Often within a case at hand, the Court has had to admit that there is either a growing acceptance of the social phenomenon among European States or in international instruments. There are several questions that arise. What are the sources for establishing the views and practices of the States? How many States are sufficient for the purpose of European consensus? What is the legal value of such consensus vis-à-vis the Convention as an international treaty? Is European consensus in fact akin to regional custom or does it reflect new State consent more broadly, which the Court cannot ignore?

These questions will be answered by examining certain leading judgments of the Court. I will first examine the *Demir and Baykara v Turkey* case followed by *Hassan v The United Kingdom*, which exemplify the Court's approach to types and sources of state practice. I will then look at the cases *Cudak v Lithuania* and *A B and C v Ireland*,

[9] See *Dialogue Between Judges: The Role of Consensus in the System of the European Convention on Human Rights* (European Court of Human Rights 2008) 17–18.

[10] See, for example, *Golder v The United Kingdom* App no 4451/70 (ECtHR, 21 February 1975), para 29; *Johnston and Others v Ireland* App no 9697/82 (ECtHR, 18 December 1986), paras 51 et seq.; and *Witold Litwa v Poland* App no 26629/95 (ECtHR, 4 April 2000), paras 57–59.

and will address more specifically the Court's approach to customary international law and its relationship to European consensus.

2. The Convention, Relevant Rules of International Law, and Subsequent Practice

The general rule of interpretation as set forth in Article 31 of the VCLT defines the context for the purposes of the interpretation of a treaty and notes that any subsequent agreement or practice, or other relevant rules of international law, shall be taken into account. Since European consensus is part of evolutive interpretation of the Convention, reference to the VCLT provides an indication that the notion of European consensus could be seen as any of the elements mentioned in Article 31(3) of the VCLT which take note of relevant developments subsequent to the adoption of a treaty.

It can be recalled that the Court's jurisdiction proper is limited to the Convention and the Protocols.[11] The Court's case law shows that it often resorts to Article 31(3)(c) of the VCLT. It does so when confronted with other rules of international law which allegedly may limit its interpretation of the Convention or, on the contrary, invite the Court to expand the scope of the rights. In the case *Demir and Baykara v Turkey*, the Court takes the opportunity to explain in detail its understanding of the two notions in Article 31(3)(c) of the VCLT, ie 'other rules' and 'applicable between the parties'. The reason for this approach was that, in accordance with the facts of the case, the Court had to establish whether the right to collective bargaining that had evolved within the International Labour Organization standards, and was provided for by the European Social Charter, could have also instructed the scope of Article 11 of the Convention. Thus, the Court had to determine whether there were sufficient grounds to include the right to collective bargaining of at least some groups of civil servants within the scope of the right to assembly. In other words, this was the case in which seemingly other rules of international law based on State consent suggested that the Court should include, within the scope of Article 11, a right that originally may not have been there. In the *Demir and Baykara* case, the Court sums up its approach. The Court explains that 'it must also take into account any relevant rules and principles of international law applicable in relations between the Contracting Parties'.[12]

The Court continues to spell out what could be seen as its pronouncement of an open and integrationist approach to international law. The Court thus says:

> Being made up of a set of rules and principles that are accepted by the vast majority of States, the common international or domestic law standards of European States reflect a reality

[11] In accordance with Article 32 of the Convention:

1. The jurisdiction of the Court shall extend to all matters concerning the interpretation and application of the Convention and the Protocols thereto which are referred to it as provided in Articles 33, 34, 46 and 47.
2. In the event of dispute as to whether the Court has jurisdiction, the Court shall decide.

[12] See *Demir and Baykara v Turkey* [GC] (ECtHR, 12 November 2008), para 67.

that the Court cannot disregard when it is called upon to clarify the scope of a Convention provision that more conventional means of interpretation have not enabled it to establish with a sufficient degree of certainty. The Court observes in this connection that in searching for common ground among the norms of international law it has never distinguished between sources of law according to whether or not they have been signed or ratified by the respondent State.[13]

Admittedly, the *Demir and Baykara* case is very rich in important methodological pronouncements which might not always follow a logical order but certainly require, when subject to examination, a fairly comprehensive citation. From the above passage, one of the important statements refers to the Court's explanation of what makes up current reality which the Court cannot ignore. That reality is made up of common international and domestic standards. The Court further concludes by explaining that:

[I]n defining the meaning of terms and notions in the text of the Convention, [the Court] can and must take into account elements of international law other than the Convention, the interpretation of such elements by competent organs, and the practice of European States reflecting their common values. The consensus emerging from specialised international instruments and from the practice of Contracting States may constitute a relevant consideration for the Court when it interprets the provisions of the Convention in specific cases.[14]

This view of the Court can be seen to reflect both subsequent State practice and other applicable rules of international law as elements for the interpretation of a treaty. It also adds a broader statement to what could be considered classical language:

It will be sufficient for the Court that the relevant international instruments denote a continuous evolution in the norms and principles applied in international law or in the domestic law of the majority of member States of the Council of Europe and show, in a precise area, that there is common ground in modern societies.[15]

The clarification of the Court's method is accompanied by a reminder as to the special character of the Convention as a human rights instrument and the principle of the Convention as a living instrument to be interpreted in the light of present-day conditions and taking 'account of evolving norms of national and international law in its interpretation of Convention provisions'.[16] In other words, in *Demir and Baykara*, the Court answers the questions that the above cited passage in *Tyrer* had opened concerning the impact of developments in domestic and international law on the interpretation of the Convention. First, the Court considers that common standards in domestic laws or other international pronouncements may in fact form other rules of international law in the sense of Article 31(3)(c) of the VCLT and, secondly, that this is the relevant context for the interpretation of the terms of the Convention. The Court does not require that State practice should have formed a treaty, a custom, or a principle for it to be taken into account. The Court adopts a more flexible reading of the notion 'relevant rules of international law' when it does

[13] ibid paras 76, 78. [14] ibid para 86. [15] ibid para 85. [16] ibid para 68.

not require a specific form and normative character of a rule. It is also clear that international instruments, which would normally be considered as soft law, will be relevant for the Court in its search for common ground among European States. The Court also decides to clarify that it is not necessary that the relevant developments are reflected in the practices of all States; it is rather the majority of States that the Court will look at. It transpires that the Court examines domestic legislation and case law, and various sources of international law, which reflect the views of European States.

Thus, the Court delimits the living nature of the Convention within the framework of the general rule of interpretation of a treaty. However, the Court does not take a dogmatic approach to the wording of Article 31 or to the sequence in which the article lists the methods of interpretation. As evidenced by the language of *Demir and Baykara*, the Court may not be too concerned as to whether the State has ratified the treaty or whether the common domestic practices emerge specifically in the application of the European Convention, as the wording of Article 31(3) would indicate. The Court is interested in seeing the common developments and trends relevant to the scope of the European Convention without necessarily identifying the binding character of these developments and practices. In other words, while Article 31 of the VCLT offers a frame of reference for the Court as such, the Court follows the methods of interpretation with certain flexibility. This may give rise to the argument that, when the VCLT was drafted, the original intention of its drafters was not to provide those applying international treaties with such flexibility.[17]

The Court prefers to approach the developments in State practice at a domestic level or on an international scene through Article 31(3)(c), ie in identifying whether these practices and developments suggest that a new relevant rule may have emerged affecting its interpretation of the Convention. In *Hassan v The United Kingdom*, the Court rather exceptionally decided to consider subsequent State practice in the application of the Convention and also to follow Article 31(3)(b) of the VCLT. This was the case about the deprivation of liberty of a young man by British armed forces during active hostilities in Iraq. Article 5 of the ECHR, among its permitted exceptions from the right to liberty, does not contain internment of civilians during armed hostilities. The Court is faced with a three-fold question. First, it has to address the question of the relationship between the ECHR and international humanitarian law (IHL). Secondly, it has to decide whether the Convention States when exercising their powers under IHL have to make a derogation from the ECHR in accordance with Article 15 of the Convention. Finally, the Court has to assess whether there is any subsequent State practice which provides any relevant indications as to the first two issues.[18]

[17] However, for a more dynamic reading of Article 31, see Mark Villiger, *Commentary on the 1969 Vienna Convention on the Law of Treaties* (Martinus Nijhoff Publishers 2009) 432–33.

[18] See further Cedric De Koker, 'Hassan v United Kingdom. The Interaction of Human Rights Law and International Humanitarian Law with regard to the Deprivation of Liberty in Armed Conflicts' (2015) 31(81) Utrecht Journal of International and European Law 90.

The Court, therefore, has the opportunity to provide its view concerning the impact of subsequent State practice on the very clear text of the Convention. For the purposes of this chapter, it is this aspect that will be elaborated, leaving the other equally complex and interesting questions outside the scope of the analysis. The Court says:

> in respect of the criterion set out in Article 31 § 3(b) of the Vienna Convention, the Court has previously stated that a consistent practice on the part of the High Contracting Parties, subsequent to their ratification of the Convention, could be taken as establishing their agreement not only as regards interpretation but even to modify the text of the Convention.[19]

In other words, the Court accepts that subsequent practice of the Convention States is relevant for the interpretation of the Convention; this observation may lead us back to the assessment of other relevant rules of international law. It may also be the basis for the question of whether new agreement has emerged as to the modification of the particular treaty. The latter is part of the context for the interpretation of a treaty, but it does raise the question of whether the Court means an agreement as to the interpretation of the existing text or rather a new agreed rule going beyond the treaty. Certainly, the language of the above passage is unclear and may appear to go beyond the limits of the general rule of interpretation. The Court ought to have been more nuanced as to the latter option, even if the judgment is not based on the argument that the Convention would have been amended through some subsequent State practice.[20]

This case raises questions concerning the available methods for the identification of subsequent State practice. It can be seen from the *Hassan* judgment that the Court offers the information it has gathered from scholarly research, and the practice of the Human Rights Committee, and its own practice.[21] This research shows that no subsequent practice could be identified whereby the States, when required to apply Geneva Conventions III and IV, would have derogated from their international human rights obligations, ie that they would have displaced their application during armed hostilities. The Court decides to give space to the application of IHL within the frame of Article 5, and without asking for derogations from the Convention. The Court argues:

> By reason of the co-existence of the safeguards provided by international humanitarian law and by the Convention in time of armed conflict, the grounds of permitted deprivation of liberty set out in sub-paragraphs (a) to (f) of that provision should be accommodated, as far as possible, with the taking of prisoners of war and the detention of civilians who pose a risk to security under the Third and Fourth Geneva Conventions.[22]

[19] See *Hassan v The United Kingdom* [GC] App no 29750/09 (ECtHR 16 September 2014), para 101 (with references to *Soering v The United Kingdom* App no 14038/88 (ECtHR, 7 July 1989) and *Al-Saadoon and Mufdhi v The United Kingdom* App no 61498/08 (ECtHR, 2 March 2010)).

[20] For the same call for careful consideration of subsequent practice and its true meaning, see ILC, 'Second Report of Special Rapporteur Georg Nolte, 65th Sess.' (2014) para 19.

[21] ibid paras 41–42. [22] ibid para 104.

While it is obvious that the Court does not consider that the Convention as such would have been amended by subsequent practice, and this judgment therefore is not helpful for further reflections in this regard, it is clear that the Court interprets Article 5 to include, within the margin of discretion of the States, the internment of civilians during armed hostilities. In so doing, the Court relies on the absence of State practice as concerns derogations from human rights treaties in such a scenario. One of the results of this judgment is a closer integration of the two branches of international law and a clearer approach of the Court towards international law as a coherent legal system. This case also shows that the possibility of inquiring as to whether all 47 States Parties to the Convention could have agreed with this interpretation, and what the consequences might be in the future, are limited not least because the Court has yet to reflect on the procedure for obtaining comprehensive State practice, nor does it have enough resources to do so itself. The Court really needs to reflect on ways and means for its inquiry into State practice in the future.

It is to be noted that the International Law Commission's (ILC) Special Rapporteur Georg Nolte, while generally accepting the Court's approach, nevertheless points out that:

> the European Court of Human Rights mostly limits itself to broad and sometimes rough comparative assessments of the domestic legislation or international positions adopted by States. In this context, it must be borne in mind that the rights which are articulated in human rights treaties are usually not designed to be authoritatively interpreted and applied by State organs, but they must rather correctly translate (within the given margin of appreciation) the treaty obligations into the law, the executive practice and international arrangements of their respective State. For this purpose, sufficiently strong commonalities in the national legislations of a significant number of member States can already be relevant for the determination of the scope of a human right or the necessity of its restriction. In addition, the character of certain rights sometimes speaks in favour of taking less specific practice into account.[23]

The Court's engagement with Article 31(3)(b) in the *Hassan* case has solicited some critical views in scholarly comments, primarily for the reason of the absence of citations of the work of the ILC Special Rapporteur on treaties and subsequent practice.[24] First of all, it has to be noticed that the parties to the proceedings did not submit such information, nor did they examine the legal issues in accordance with this element of the general rule of interpretation. The choice to interpret the Convention by looking at subsequent practice of the States was that of the Court and, in view of the legal issues involved, in particular the unhelpful reference to *lex specialis* in the facts of the case, that choice was an important clarification of the Court's methodology.

Over the last decade, the Court has provided sufficient detail as to how it views other sources of international law and their relation with the Convention. It clearly does not apply the Convention in a vacuum. It interprets the Convention by taking

[23] ibid para 40.

[24] See Lawrence Hill-Cawthorne, 'The Grand Chamber Judgment in Hassan v UK' (2014) EJIL: *Talk!* <http://www.ejiltalk.org/the-grand-chamber-judgment-in-hassan-v-uk/> accessed 1 October 2017.

cognizance of other relevant rules of international law that either give rise to new obligations for member States relevant for the Convention's purposes, or instruct the scope of the Convention rights as such. For the Court, State practice takes several different forms which are all relevant for the interpretation of the Convention in accordance with modern-day conditions. The devil, as always, is in the detail, ie how comprehensive a study of domestic and international practices of States should the Court carry out, and by what means should it do so given that parties to human rights proceedings would normally stay within the narrative of the specific facts of the alleged human rights violation? Even if Special Rapporteur Georg Nolte has, in a way, justified the approach of the Court in view of the nature of protected rights, it would be advisable for the Court to guide the parties to the proceedings with its own questions in requesting the relevant information on State practice.

Some specific methodological statements cited earlier continue to pose several questions for an international lawyer. For example, the following statement that 'when searching for common ground among the norms the Court' neither distinguishes 'between sources of law'[25] nor pays particular attention as to whether a State has ratified them. Basically, what the Court says is that, even if a State has not ratified a particular treaty, it does not mean that international law does not provide for a relevant obligation and that obligation could not be found in another source of international law. It could be another treaty that the State has ratified. It could be an obligation deriving from a customary norm, which may be the same or very similar to that provided for in a treaty. This reading of the above cited language from *Demir and Baykara* would still fall within the element of interpretation of a treaty provided for in Article 31(3)(c) of the VCLT. But it may also be understood to go beyond existing rules and to provide the Court with more flexibility in identifying common ground with regard to the developments in State practice, an approach which has also been noted by the ILC Special Rapporteur Georg Nolte.

In the cases examined in this section of the chapter, the Court provides an answer to the question of what, in its view, is sufficient State practice to pronounce on the new scope of the right. It says that a consistent tendency that emerges from domestic law or international instruments might be enough to make positive pronouncements in Convention terms. In principle, the Court attempts to assess the practice of all State parties to the Convention. However, in some cases this has been a difficult issue.[26] It is also true, as pointed out by the ILC Special Rapporteur, that the nature of the right may speak in favour of a less stringent approach as to the extent of the State practice assessed.

To sum up, the Court clearly pays attention to any common trends that may be reflected in domestic legislation, domestic case law, international case law, other international treaties, and statements of the governments. It also seeks information in scholarly writings, but to a lesser extent. This information will, most of the time, be considered relevant for detecting European consensus. But it is those times when

[25] *Demir* (n 12) para 78.

[26] See *X and Others v Austria* [GC] App no 19010/07 (ECtHR, 19 February 2013). See dissenting opinion of Judges Casadevall, Ziemele, Jočiene, Šikuta, De Gaetano, and Sicilianos.

the Court does not refer to European consensus and remains purely within the context of Article 31(3)(c) or (b) of the VCLT that are instructive for the purposes of this chapter. The *Hassan* case indeed did not refer to European consensus, thus suggesting a distinction between notions of subsequent State practice in the application of the Convention or other rules of international law and European consensus. In other words, both cases examined here show that the Court can provide effective protection of Convention rights by taking into account the relevant developments in European States through a simple resort to Article 31(3)(b) and (c) as tools. The question remains: What then is the scope of European consensus?

3. Two Main Scenarios Relevant for Discussion on European Consensus and Custom

With a view to attempting to narrow down the meaning of European consensus, I propose to look at, in my opinion, two paradigmatic cases, ie *Cudak v Lithuania* and *A, B and C v Ireland*. In these cases, the Court engages with the notions of State practice, European consensus, and customary law and draws conclusions as to the scope of the Convention.

3.1 Affirming the rule of customary law

The first scenario could be viewed as classical. It happens when the Court has a case which is directly linked to a subject matter regulated by general rules of international law, for example all cases that deal with State immunity. In the case of *Cudak v Lithuania*,[27] the Court is faced with the question of whether it can be said that, in view of the developments in State practice, a rule of limited State immunity in certain situations has emerged. Was it applicable in relation to Lithuania and thus required that the Lithuanian courts, as a matter of Article 6 of the Convention, pronounce upon the complaint of the dismissed receptionist at the Polish embassy in Vilnius?

The Court examines the developments with regard to the drafting of the 2004 Convention on Jurisdictional Immunities of States and their Property (hereafter, the 2004 Convention) and the rule with regard to employment contracts in particular. It notes that:

> the application of absolute State immunity has, for many years, clearly been eroded. In 1979 the International Law Commission was given the task of codifying and gradually developing international law in the area of jurisdictional immunities of States and their property ... The report appended to the 1991 Draft Articles stated that the rules formulated in Article 11 appeared to be consistent with the emerging trend in the legislative and treaty practice of a growing number of States (ILC Yearbook, 1991, Vol. II, Part 2, p. 44, § 14).[28]

[27] See *Cudak v Lithuania* [GC] App no 15869/02 (ECtHR, 23 March 2010).
[28] ibid paras 64–66.

The Court draws the conclusion that this must also hold true for the 2004 Convention. The Court traces the trend in the area of employment contracts and State immunity primarily by looking at the work done by the ILC and the adopted text of the 2004 Convention. One could argue that this is a rather general assessment, which does not provide for sufficient detail as concerns the contested aspect as to whether or not the applicant in the *Cudak* case exercised government authority.[29] On the other hand, based on various sources of information, including domestic doctrine and case law, the Court does spend time examining the nature of the applicant's duties at the Polish embassy. It notes that even the Supreme Court of Lithuania had been unable to obtain any information from the embassy allowing it to establish the scope of the applicant's duties.[30] The Court also notes that the background of the dispute related to allegations by the applicant of sexual harassment. The Court goes through the exceptions to the non-immunity rule as spelled out in the 2004 Convention and does not find anything in the case file in front of it to suggest that any such exceptions applied.

Another issue that the Court has to deal with concerns the fact that Lithuania has not ratified the 2004 Convention and it is therefore unclear whether, and in what manner, the emerging trend engages Lithuania. The Court decides to be guided by the theory of a treaty provision as a reflection of an established or a new custom enunciated by the International Court of Justice (ICJ) in the *North Sea Continental Shelf* cases.[31]

The Court does not gather more evidence to confirm that the growing trend has become a rule of customary law. It uses another technique, ie it examines whether States, and Lithuania in particular, had objected to the drafting or adoption of Article 11 of the 2004 Convention. The Court finds that 'there were no particular objections by States to the wording of Article 11 of the International Law Commission's Draft Articles, at least not by the respondent State. As to the 2004 Convention, Lithuania has admittedly not ratified it but did not vote against its adoption either'.[32] This language indicates that the Court has been inspired by the persistent objector doctrine and has applied it in the process of its assessment of whether an applicable rule of customary law exists. The Court concludes:

> Consequently, it is possible to affirm that Article 11 of the International Law Commission's 1991 Draft Articles, on which the 2004 Convention was based, applies to the respondent State under customary international law. The Court must take this into consideration in examining whether the right of access to a court, within the meaning of Article 6 § 1, was respected.[33]

The ILC Draft Conclusions on customary law prepared by Special Rapporteur Michael Wood accept that 'inaction may also serve as evidence of acceptance as law'.[34]

[29] See Roger O'Keefe and Christian J Tams (eds), *The United Nations Convention on Jurisdictional Immunities of States and their Property. A Commentary* (OUP 2013) 198–200.

[30] See *Cudak v Lithuania* (n 27) paras 69–71.

[31] ibid para 66.

[32] ibid paras 64–66.

[33] ibid para 67.

[34] Draft Conclusion 11. See ILC, 'Second Report of Special Rapporteur Michael Wood, 66th Sess.' (2015), Annex.

The question must be asked whether the Court's approach is compatible with the manner in which, in international law, the existence of a rule of customary law is identified. It could be recalled that the ICJ said in the *Nicaragua* case that: '[I]n the field of customary international law, the shared view of the Parties as to the content of what they regard as the rule is not enough. The Court must satisfy itself that the existence of the rule in the *opinio juris* of States is confirmed by practice.'[35] In other words, is it correct to pass judgment based on a consistent tendency reflected in domestic laws and practice or in the views of the States concerned found in different international instruments, rather than their belief of what the rule might be? It is true that in the 2004 Convention one can find support for the Court's approach in opening up Article 6 of the ECHR to labour disputes at the diplomatic representations. But it still remains unclear whether there is State practice which would evidence relevant *opinio juris* concerning exemption of employment contracts from the rule of State immunity. There are also indications in State practice that the developments towards limited State immunity remain controversial. European States are not among those keenly ratifying the 2004 Convention. In other words, did the Court read too much into this progressive development of international law by the ILC? In the *Cudak* case did the Court assess the available material with regard to State practice as it ought to when dealing with customary law?

James Crawford has attempted to disentangle the mysterious *opinio juris* and has come up with the following explanation: 'Customary rules arise from a dialogue between international actors over time. And that dialogue must include, at the very least, proto-legal and legal steps.'[36] ILC Special Rapporteur Michael Wood has proposed the following ways to find evidence of custom:

> The forms of evidence include, but are not limited to, statements by States which indicate what are or are not rules of customary international law, diplomatic correspondence, the jurisprudence of national courts, the opinions of Government legal advisers, official publications in fields of international law, treaty practice and action in connection with resolutions of organs of international organizations and of international conferences.[37]

In other words, *opinio juris* is not about the ability to read the minds of international actors. It is first and foremost the question of taking note of attitudes of States in different fora over a certain period of time. The Court's approach in looking at the attitude of Lithuania towards the normative process leading to the adoption of the 2004 Convention corresponds to the idea that States are part of the process and accept it unless they clearly object. At the same time, it has to be recognized that the Court's approach in *Cudak* and similar cases is the support that the drafters of the 2004 Convention needed and, in the field of employment contracts,

[35] *Case Concerning Military and Paramilitary Activities in and against Nicaragua* [1986] ICJ Rep, para 185. See ILC, 'Second Report of Special Rapporteur Michael Wood, 66th Sess.' (2015), Annex.

[36] See James Crawford, *Chance, Order, Change: The Course of International Law* (Hague Academy of International Law 2014) 82.

[37] Draft Conclusion 11. See Second Report of Special Rapporteur Michael Wood, 66th Sess., ILC 2015, Annex.

the Court may have indeed taken up somewhat the function as a 'driving force in international law'.[38]

In *Cudak*, the European Court tries to see whether the scope of Article 6, as concerns access to court, is in any way further elaborated by possible obligations of the State concerned under other rules of international law, including customary norms. In this process, it is clear that the Court has to know whether there is a rule of customary law and for that purpose whether, as the Court points out in the *Cudak* judgment, it is guided by relevant principles determined by the ICJ in the *North Sea Continental Shelf* case. This is, however, a delicate exercise. On the one hand, the Court does not have jurisdiction to establish the existence of a rule of customary law in the field of State immunity as such. On the other hand, the Court should pronounce on the question of whether access to court would be violated if the State immunity rule was upheld. The Court cannot refuse to address the question of access to court under Article 6 just because it may not have the competence to establish the rules of state immunity. It is in view of these considerations that, in the *Cudak v Lithuania* case, the Court chooses 'to affirm' the existence of a rule of customary law, having reviewed the ILC debate and the debate in the sixth committee of the General Assembly, rather than to establish such a rule. In the absence of relevant decisions from the ICJ, these were the authoritative international law sources that the Court could rely on.

Cudak is one of the clearest cases in which the Court has to examine the States' interaction within international processes relevant for the Court's position as to the existence of a rule of customary law. It is to be hoped that the methodology of the *Cudak* judgment is reflected in its future case law and further elaborated. It appears that the Court's position in *Demir and Baykara* and *Cudak* in relation to relevant State practice, especially that of the respondent States, is rather in line with the approach in international law towards finding the relevant rules, including evidence for custom.

In view of the *Cudak* and *Hassan* judgments, it has to be said that the Court changes or expands upon the scope of rights provided for in the Convention originally in a number of ways: First, when the Court reads into the Convention provision the content of other applicable rules of international law *qua* Article 31(3)(c) VCLT and, secondly, when the Court sees that, through consistent subsequent practice, the States have expanded upon the interpretation of the scope of the Convention provision *qua* Article 31(3)(b) VCLT. It seems that the Court's consistent perspective that the Convention is part of a wider legal system, and that it has to be interpreted in accordance with the general rule of interpretation of a treaty and in harmony with other branches and rules of international law, has by and large allowed it to interpret the Convention progressively. Questions nevertheless will continue to arise in relation to the sufficiency and exact relevance of the evidence of State practice. That issue, however, is not new to the discipline of international law, which strives for

[38] Luzius Wildhaber, 'The European Convention on Human Rights and International Law' (2007) 56 International and Comparative Law Quarterly 221.

answers exactly on these issues. In this context, the importance of the reasoning in the Court's judgment cannot be overstated.

3.2 European consensus entangled

The above discussed judgments indicate that, at least in situations in which other rules of international law are relevant for the purposes of the interpretation of the Convention, the establishment of State practice does not necessarily lead to, or require discussion about, European consensus. However, it needs to be recalled that, in *Demir and Baykara*, the Court, having shown in detail its approach to State practice, links it to the notion of consensus stating that: 'The *consensus* emerging from specialised international instruments and from the practice of Contracting States may constitute a relevant consideration for the Court when it interprets the provisions of the Convention in specific cases.'[39]

The Court does not disentangle the notions of subsequent State practice and consensus, and that is problematic. The Court should try to address this issue in the future even if what it really means by consensus is the same thing as State practice and *opinion juris* or subsequent State practice. At this point, it is relevant to look at another case law scenario which evokes European consensus in a slightly different context.

The *A, B and C v Ireland*[40] case can be referred to as a rather instructive case for our purposes. The case concerns the legislation regarding abortion in Ireland raising problems under Article 8 as concerns the right to privacy of women. The Court recalls that, in such matters, States enjoy a wide margin of appreciation, and indeed rights guaranteed by Article 8 have been formulated in a rather open-ended manner. However, in this case, the Court goes on to examine whether this wide margin of appreciation is narrowed by the existence of a relevant European consensus.

In the judgment, the Court explains how it understands European consensus. Importantly, it refers back to the *Tyrer* case. The Court says:

> The existence of a consensus has long played a role in the development and evolution of Convention protections beginning with Tyrer v. the United Kingdom [and] ... the Convention being considered a 'living instrument' to be interpreted in the light of present-day conditions. Consensus has therefore been invoked to justify a dynamic interpretation of the Convention.[41]

This passage confirms that the Court considers that it has created concepts of European consensus and the living instrument for the interpretation of the Convention, thus giving space for evolutive and dynamic adjudication. The Court does not engage with Article 31 of the VCLT. European consensus appears to have an autonomous meaning in the context of *Tyrer* and *A, B and C*, and other similar cases.

[39] *Demir and Baykara* (n 12), para 85 (emphasis added).

[40] See *A, B and C v Ireland* App no 25579/05 (ECtHR, 16 December 2010).

[41] ibid 234. Other references in the judgment are to the following cases: *Marckx v Belgium* App no 6833/74 (ECtHR, 13 June 1979), para 41; *Dudgeon v The United Kingdom* App no 7525/76 (ECtHR, 22 October 1981), para 60; *Soering v The United Kingdom* App no 14038/88 (ECtHR, 7 July 1989), para 102; *L and V v Austria* App nos 39392/98 and 39829/98 (ECtHR, 9 January 2003), para 50.

The *A, B and C* case represents an interesting choice by the Court in this regard. It reads as follows:

In the present case, and contrary to the Government's submission, the Court considers that there is indeed a consensus amongst a substantial majority of the Contracting States of the Council of Europe towards allowing abortion on broader grounds than accorded under Irish law. Given this consensus amongst a substantial majority of the Contracting States, it is not necessary to look further to international trends and views which the first two applicants and certain of the third parties argued also land in favour of a broader access to abortion.[42]

Here the Court establishes that allowing abortion on broader grounds is part of European consensus. This is evidenced for the Court by domestic laws and practices of a great majority of States. Although the Court suggests that it may look further into evidence available in international law, it decides that having European consensus is sufficient in this case. In other words, this is a case in which the Court does not resort to such practice that may evidence other rules of international law. It stays purely within the domestic European context. Is this approach in any way linked to the elements of Article 31 of the VCLT?

It is relevant to recall that the ILC Special Rapporteur Georg Nolte considered the nature of evolutive interpretation of treaties and compared it with the elements of subsequent agreements and subsequent practice. He recalled the ICJ judgment in the *Dispute regarding Navigational and Related Rights (Costa Rica v Nicaragua)* case as providing the ICJ's position in this regard. He concluded that:

The *Costa Rica v. Nicaragua* judgment demonstrates that subsequent agreements and subsequent practice of the parties can have both a supportive and a restrictive effect on the possibility of an evolutive interpretation. The supportive effect consists in confirming that an evolved understanding of a treaty can be based on subsequent practice as an authentic means of interpretation. The restrictive effect of subsequent practice emerges when it is contrasted with an evolutive interpretation which is based on other grounds, in particular on the object and purpose of the treaty.[43]

This is also a relevant observation for the ECtHR because, if followed, it explains the essence and the limits of its evolutive interpretation. In other words, European consensus might in fact only mean that the Court has established subsequent practice which instructs the interpretation of the Convention.

However, in the *A, B and C* case, the Court acknowledges that, even if there is European consensus and even if it instructs the scope of Article 8, it does not automatically follow that non-compliance with such consensus leads to a violation of the Convention. This approach may raise the question in relation to a normative character of European consensus or, once again, the question as to what it is. The key passage states:

It follows that, even if it appears from the national laws referred to that most Contracting Parties may in their legislation have resolved those conflicting rights and interests in favour of greater legal access to abortion, *this consensus cannot be a decisive factor* in the Court's

[42] *A, B and C* (n 40) para 235. [43] A/CNN.4/660 para 60.

examination of whether the impugned prohibition on abortion in Ireland for health and well-being reasons struck a fair balance between the conflicting rights and interests, notwithstanding an evolutive interpretation of the Convention.[44]

This passage requires further examination. The Court recalls that European consensus lies with the greater legal access to abortion and that, based on evolutive interpretation of the Convention, the Court determines that Article 8 provides for such a scope of the right to privacy. The scope of the Convention in accordance with the present-day conditions is clear. The judgment shows that the establishment of European consensus does not require every member State to have followed a particular practice. In other words, if the consent of all States is not required then what should be the position of the Court in relation to arguably those very few States which follow a different practice? This becomes a question of the application of the Convention and the Court acknowledges that, at least for those human rights with an open-ended character, evolution of the scope of the right through subsequent practice does not automatically impose specific Convention obligations on the State with different practice. In the case *A, B and C*, it appears a relevant factor that the restrictive Irish approach stems from several popular referenda and, therefore, the Court is confronted with a rather clear will of the people.[45] This raises a very interesting question both in international and domestic law. It relates to the legitimacy of the Court's approach in the context of the broader issue of confrontation between the strong democratic legitimacy of the particular domestic position and the new Article 8 reading. There is no question that the Irish approach stemming from the view of the people has the democratic legitimacy par excellence. But when compared to the overall aims of the European Convention, which strives to advance the protection of human rights in Europe, one cannot say that the decision of the Court lacks a democratic character. Therefore, no evident or automatic solution in favour of the domestic law or the ECHR is available.

In such a situation, it is important that the right at stake is of such a character that States, in implementing their obligations, may enjoy a wide margin of appreciation. It would indeed be a rather different confrontation where absolute rights were concerned, since there are grounds to believe that a popular will to restore, for example, the death penalty in Europe would not be acceptable. In this context, why did the Court in this case decide that the consensus is not a decisive factor? What does this tell us about consensus?

In view of the above, there are several possible readings of the judgment. First, it is possible to view the case as one of new subsequent practice in the application of the right to privacy in the member States, except for a few, whereby States have agreed on a new interpretation of the Convention. Secondly, it is possible to consider the case as one that takes note of a new regional custom with regard to greater access to abortion for reasons of self-determination and privacy of women. As noted, the Court

[44] *A, B and C* (n 40) para 237 (emphasis added).

[45] See more generally on the problem of sources and democracy, Samantha Besson, 'Theorizing the Sources of International Law' in Samantha Besson and John Tasioulas (eds) *The Philosophy of International Law* (OUP 2010) 163 et seq.

did not refer to Article 31(3)(b) or (c) of the VCLT, which leaves space for the third possible reading of the judgment, ie the autonomous notion of European consensus.

I suggest the following reflection. The subsequent practice approach explains the new content of the right, but it does not help to explain the outcome of the case, ie why Ireland was allowed to maintain its own different practice. The Court's own notion of European consensus along the lines proposed during the opening of the Court's judicial year of 2008, keeping in mind the object and purpose of the Convention, is a possibility but, in view of the outcome in the case, it may lead to the criticism of inconsistency, incoherence, and casuistic case law. However, if it is accepted that, in this case we have indeed evidenced the emergence of a regional customary norm, which the Court ought to take into consideration based on Article 31(3)(c) and its own case law, the customary law perspective also allows for the acceptance of the persistent objector to the emergence of the rule. This too, the Court has to consider in its application of the Convention. I submit that, in the *A, B and C* case, the persistent objector perspective offers a sounder basis for the Court's conclusion that Ireland has acted within its margin of appreciation. Ireland can be afforded a broad margin of appreciation in balancing individual rights and the morals of society, first, because the Convention has already foreseen the balancing in the area of privacy and, secondly, precisely because it has persistently objected to the evident formation of this State practice. One should accept that the reader of this judgment would have been helped by a more conceptual explanation on the part of the Court as concerns the relationship between the treaty provision and the European consensus, and in particular the difference between the scope of the right *qua* consensus and the balance struck *qua* objection to the consensus.

To sum it up, resort to the concept of European consensus in the case law of the ECtHR may legitimately make an international lawyer think about both subsequent State practice and regional customary law. The examination above shows that the Court should be clearer on its use of these international law concepts. It also shows that the Court has attempted to read an autonomous scope into the notion of European consensus probably, and at least partly, because some elements of Article 31 of the VCLT may have appeared too rigid for the effective protection of human rights. The examination has shown, however, that the general rule of interpretation of a treaty does not prevent the use of evolutive interpretation.

4. Concluding Remarks

The notion of European consensus, similar to the notion of European public order, has been important for the purposes of the constitutionalist vision of European integration. Indeed, the special character of the Convention, often invoked by the Court when following evolutive interpretation, has also inspired the constitutionalist discourse with regards to the Convention.[46] However, the Court itself has not

[46] See eg Jan Klabbers, Anne Peters, and Geir Ulfstein, *The Constitutonalization of International Law* (OUP 2009) 345 (alerting to the risks of oversell of this approach).

developed any particular link between European consensus and a possible vision of the Convention as a constitutional instrument. So far, the notion of European consensus has been employed along with the other methods for interpreting the Convention largely within the confines of the general rule of interpretation of a treaty, although, as noted in this chapter, more clarity would be welcome. It may well be that the Court will one day consider it necessary to provide further explanations on the notion of European consensus and its link to the special character of the Convention or its relevance for European public order beyond the confines of international law. For the time being, however, it would be helpful if the Court clarified further how it comes to establish common ground among the State parties to the Convention as well as different legal consequences that may arise once the common ground is found.[47] It is especially important that the Court is very clear about the methodological basis for those situations when it takes the position of a driving force in international law.[48] In other words, the determination of European consensus has to lie on very sound grounds so as to be legitimate and clear, and to carry the necessary authority. In that regard, clearer resort to the relevant international law concepts would only help.

[47] For some further reflections, see Ineta Ziemele, 'Other Rules of International Law and the European Court of Human Rights: A Question of A Simple Collateral Benefit?' in D Spielmann et al (eds), *La Convention Européenne des Droits de l'Homme, un Instrument Vivant/The European Convention on Human Rights, a Living Instrument* (Bruylant 2011) 741–58.

[48] See Wildhaber, 'The European Convention' (n 38).

2

Hard Law or Soft Law—Does it Matter?

Distinction Between Different Sources of International Law in the Jurisprudence of the ECtHR

*Angelika Nußberger**

1. Introduction

Many discussions about how international law stemming from different sources is used in the jurisprudence of the European Court of Human Rights (ECtHR) focus on a famous quotation in the judgment *Demir and Baykara v Turkey*: 'The Court observes . . . that in searching for common ground among the norms of international law it has never distinguished between sources of law according to whether or not they have been signed or ratified by the respondent State.'[1] There are, however, also other statements of the Court to be found which seem to suggest a different approach to the distinction to be made between hard law and soft law. In the judgment *Mamatkulov v Turkey*, the Court emphasizes that, 'unlike the Court and the Committee of Ministers, the Commission had no power to issue a binding decision that a Contracting State had violated the Convention. The Commission's task

* The views expressed in this chapter are personal only.

[1] *Demir and Baykara v Turkey* App no 34503/97 (ECtHR, 12 November 2008); see Laurence Burgorgue-Larsen, '"Nothing is Perfect" Libres propos sur la méthodologie interprétative de la Cour européenne' in *L'homme et le droit. En hommage au Professeur Jean-Francois Flauss* (Pedone 2014); Sébastien Van Drooghenbroeck 'Les frontiers du droit et le temps juridique: La Cour européenne des droits de l'homme repousse les limites. Cour Européenne des droits de l'homme (Grande Chambre), Demir et Baykara c. Turquie, 12 novembre 2008' (2009) Rev trim dr h 811; Patrick Wachsmann, 'Réflexions sur l'interprétation "globalisante" de la Convention européenne des droits de l'homme' in *La conscience des droits. Mélanges en l'honneur de JP Costa* (Dalloz 2011); Julian Arato, 'Constitutional Transformation in the ECtHR: Strasbourg's Expansive Recourse to External Rules of International Law' (2012) 37 Brook J Intl Law 350; Francoise Tulkens, Sébastien van Drooghenbroeck, and Frédéric Krenc, 'Le soft law et la Cour européenne des droits de l'homme: questions de légitimité et de méthode' (2012) 89 Rev trim dr h 433; Cesare Pitea, 'Interpretation and Application of the European Convention on Human Rights in the Broader Context of International Law: Myth or Reality' in Yves Haeck and Eva Brems (eds), *Human Rights and Civil Liberties in the 21st Century* (Springer 2014) 1; Klaus Lörcher, 'The New Social Dimension in the Jurisprudence of the European Court of Human Rights (ECtHR): The Demir and Baykara Judgment, its Methodology and Follow-up' in F Dorssemont, K Lörcher, and I Schömann (eds), *The European Convention on Human Rights and the Employment Relation* (Hart Publishing 2014).

with regard to the merits was of a preliminary nature and its opinion on whether or not there had been a violation of the Convention was not binding'.[2] Thus, on the one hand, the message seems to be that it does not matter if an international rule stems from a treaty binding on the Contracting States on the basis of the Vienna Convention on the Law of Treaties (VCLT) while, on the other hand, the Court differentiates between a non-binding finding of the (former) European Commission on Human Rights and a binding judgment of the Court. This raises the basic question of how far it matters for the Court if a rule of international law is to be considered as hard law or soft law when referring to it in its jurisprudence, a question closely linked to the legitimacy of the Court's way of adjudicating conflicts. In as far as State consent is considered to be a basic element in international law, it would be a provocative approach to do away with it. The main argument of this chapter is, however, that even if the dichotomy between hard law and soft law gives way to what is called 'normative relativity'[3] and the Court seems to dilute the differences between rules coming from different sources in developing its evolutive jurisprudence, it nevertheless takes hard law more seriously than soft law. State consent matters and still makes a difference.

The present chapter starts with a discussion on the differences between hard law and soft law focusing not only on soft lawmaking and hard lawmaking, but also on what may be called 'soft jurisprudence' and 'hard jurisprudence' (2). Against this background the differentiated approach of the ECtHR is discussed (3). In this context, the following aspects are highlighted: First, it makes a difference in which part of the judgment references to soft law are made and which functions are accordingly attributed to them (3.1). Second, it is analysed in which way soft law is used for interpreting vague legal terms and filling gaps (3.2). Third, it is discussed in how far soft law contributes to the evolutive interpretation of the Convention (3.3). As it is understood to be revelatory to compare the Court's reactions to clashes between the Convention and soft law on the one hand and between the Convention and hard law on the other hand, this aspect is taken up in the last part of this chapter (3.4). This allows for general conclusions on the relevance of the different forms of international law for the Court's jurisprudence (4).

2. Difference Between Hard Law and Soft Law

While the variety of soft law is by definition unlimited, two different subcategories can be discerned: the more traditional form of 'soft lawmaking' on the one hand and 'soft jurisprudence' on the other hand, a phenomenon that has come to the fore only quite recently but has visibly developed over the last years. Both forms of soft law have to be compared to hard law, although there is no black-and-white contrast

[2] *Mamatkulov and Askarov v Turkey* App nos 46827/99 and 46951/99 (ECtHR, 4 February 2005), para 119.

[3] Prosper Weil, 'Towards Relative Normativity in International Law?' (1983) 77 American Journal of International Law 413.

but rather manifold transitions both from hard law to soft law and from soft law to hard law.

2.1 Soft lawmaking vs hard lawmaking

Soft law can be basically said to comprise all 'principles, rules, and standards governing international relations which are not considered to stem from one of the sources of international law enumerated in Article 38(1) International Court of Justice (ICJ) Statute'.[4] Thus it can be defined *ex negativo* as all norms of international origin that are neither treaties, nor customary law, nor general rules of international law. Nature and origin of the norms, as well as legitimacy of those involved in the lawmaking process, can vary considerably. The range stretches from non-binding resolutions or recommendations made by State representatives in a formal setting to informal rules agreed upon by lobby groups such as the International Association of Judges or the World Medical Association; the norms can be not only soft, but very soft indeed.[5] Treaties can also be considered as part of soft law before being signed and ratified.[6]

What is common to all these regulations is the lack of formalized consent by States who are nevertheless expected to take them into account. This raises the question of legitimacy of this form of lawmaking, as it might be seen as a circumvention of national parliaments who are often not even informed but, in any case, not involved in the adoption of soft law rules. Lack of transparency and inclusiveness is difficult to reconcile with basic principles of democracy.[7] Nevertheless, it has become clear that it would be an illusion to equate non-bindingness with negligibility.[8]

At the same time formal consent in creating hard law should not be overestimated either. The consent to be bound by a treaty covers the text of the treaty and is necessarily linked to a certain historical context which is, however, only of secondary importance in interpreting the treaty.[9] If a court is endowed with the competence

[4] Daniel Thürer, 'Soft law' (2015) MPEPIL 5; this can be considered as the 'classical' or 'conservative' approach, see also Graf Vitzthum, 'Begriff, Geschichte und Rechtsquellen des Völkerrechts' in Graf Vitzhum (ed) *Völkerrecht* (5th edn, De Gruyter 2010) paras 14, 68, 152; see H Hillgenberg, 'A Fresh Look at Soft Law' (1999) 10 EJIL 499; M Bothe, 'Legal and Non-Legal Norms—A meaningful Distinction in International Relations' (1980) 11 Netherlands YIL 65; in contrast to these 'positivist' approaches in international law studies, see also the overview on 'rational institutionalist' and 'constructivist' approaches in studies on international relations in G Shaffer and MA Pollack, 'Hard Law and Soft Law' in JL Dunhoff and MA Pollack (eds), *Interdisciplinary Perspectives on International Law and International Relations The State of the Art* (CUP 2013) 196, 197 et seq.

[5] See on the choices between soft law and hard law in the international arena Shaffer and Pollack (n 4) 202 et seq; AT Guzman and T Meyer, 'International Soft Law' (2010) 2 Journal of Legal Analysis 171.

[6] Thürer (n 4) 4.

[7] Armin v Bogdandy and Ingo Venzke interpret this as a problem of technocratic global governance, see Armin v Bogdandy, Ingo Venzke *In wessen Namen* (Suhrcamp Taschenbuch 2014) 280.

[8] See the empirical study by Daniel E Ho, 'Compliance and International Soft Law: Why Do Countries Implement the Basle Accord?' (2002) 5 Journal of International Economic Law 647.

[9] Article 32 VCLT referring to 'supplementary means of interpretation'.

of authentic interpretation—as in the case of the European Convention on Human Rights (ECHR)[10]—it is not always foreseeable what concrete obligations might be deduced from the general clauses of a treaty. This is especially true in as far as human rights treaties are concerned. Giving a 'living consent' to a 'living instrument'[11] means opening a door without knowing exactly what is behind it.

In as far as customary international law is concerned, the notion of consent (*opinio juris*) is also blurred to a certain extent. In the context of the present chapter it might be sufficient to allude to the fact that customary international law is formed by the 'majority of States', not by 'all States'; in practice this may include only a few States seen to be of major importance.[12] The idea of the non-applicability of customary international law to the 'persistent objector' remains doubtful.[13] There is no clear understanding of how *jus cogens*—from which no derogation is possible—comes into being.[14] Thus, consent matters, but the lack of consent is not an absolute barrier for the creation and application of rules of customary international law.

In differentiating between hard law and soft law, it is also important to be aware of potential transitions.[15] Treaties which are to be considered as soft law before their entry into force are gradually being transformed into hard law, the first step being signature, the second ratification.[16] Non-binding recommendations and resolutions may be transformed into hard law as well.[17] The adoption of such instruments can be relevant for assessing the existence of *opinio juris* and thus become a decisive element for the creation of customary international law.[18] In the EU law context, soft law has an increasingly important role to play as part of new governance methods.[19] Interestingly, soft law need not always be complementary to hard law, but can also

[10] cf Article 32 of the Convention: 'The jurisdiction of the Court shall extend to all matters concerning the interpretation and application of the Convention and the Protocols thereto.'

[11] Angelika Nußberger, 'The Concept of "Jurisdiction" in the Jurisprudence of the European Court of Human Rights' (2012) 65 Current Legal Problems 241.

[12] cf Malcolm N Shaw, *International Law* (7th edn, CUP 2014) with reference to de Visscher (*Theory and Reality in International Law* (Princeton University Press 1957) 149) who speaks of 'heavier footprints' of the 'more influential states'.

[13] T Stein, 'The Approach of the Different Drummer: The Principle of the Persistent Objector in International Law' (1985) 26 Harvard International Journal 457; J Charey, 'The Persistent Objector Rule and the Development of Customary International Law' (1985) 56 BYIL 1.

[14] See Weil (n 3); see also the ILC Report which takes up the question of the requirements for the identification of a norm of *jus cogens*, ILC, 'Second report on *jus cogens* by Dire Tladi, Special Rapporteur' (16 March 2017) UN Doc A/CN.4/706.

[15] See D Shelton, 'Soft Law' in *Handbook of International Law* (Routledge Press 2008) 68.

[16] See the respective obligations attached to signature and ratification under the VCLT (Articles 14, 18).

[17] This procedure has often been followed in the codification of human rights of special groups, cf eg United Nations General Assembly Resolution 2263 (XXII) of 7 November 1967 on the Elimination of Discrimination against Women, which was followed on 18 December 1979 by the adoption of the Convention on the Elimination of Discrimination against Women (CEDAW).

[18] Francoise Tulkens and Sébastien van Drooghenbroeck, 'Le soft law des droits de l'homme est-il vraiment si soft? Les développements de la pratique interprétative récente de la Cour européenne des droits de l'homme' in *Liber Amicorum Michel Mahieu* (Larcier 2008) 505, 508 et seq.

[19] See DM Trubek, P Cottrell, and M Nance, '"Soft Law," "Hard Law," and European Integration: Toward a Theory of Hybridity' (2005) 2/05 Jean Monnet Working Paper <http://jeanmonnetprogram.org/archive/papers/05/050201.html> accessed 14 May 2018.

be used as promoting concepts contrary to those laid down in hard law and help in bridging antagonistic positions.[20]

Relative normativity, even if often approached with reluctance and critique,[21] is thus reality.[22]

2.2 Soft jurisprudence vs hard jurisprudence

A comparatively new phenomenon is what might be called soft jurisprudence in comparison to hard jurisprudence. While the latter comprises binding judgments of international courts, the former refers to all sorts of 'conclusions', 'views', 'communications', and 'recommendations' of international expert bodies endowed with the task of observing the implementation of a treaty, but not given the competence to adopt binding judgments. Although the non-binding nature of such treaty bodies' conclusions are, as a rule, explicitly or implicitly fixed in the relevant international instruments,[23] those conclusions are nevertheless often addressed as 'jurisprudence'.[24] This applies to reports on States' compliance with treaty obligations, as well as for concrete observations on individual complaints or abstract comments on the interpretation of specific treaty provisions. Even if this terminology might be unfortunate and misleading, it is true that, here again, hard law and soft law are not just black and white.

Judgments of international courts are, as a rule, binding only *inter partes*. As an example Article 46 ECHR might be cited: 'The High Contracting Parties undertake to abide by the final judgment of the court in any case to which they are parties.' A similar provision is to be found in Article 68 of the American Convention on Human Rights.[25] The same is also true for the ICJ, as confirmed in Article 59 of the Statute: 'The decision of the Court has no binding force except between the parties and in respect of that particular case.' Nevertheless, these courts' judgments can be said to have effects that go far beyond the narrow scope of the parties'

[20] See Shaffer and Pollock (n 4) 209 et seq with reference, for example, to the Codex alimentarius of the WTO.

[21] See GJH Van Hoof, *Re-thinking the Sources of International Law* (Deventer 1983) 187, 190; Jan Klabbers, 'The Undesirability of Soft Law' (1998) 67 Nordic Journal of International Law 381.

[22] Matthias Goldmann, 'Inside Relative Normativity: From Sources to Standard Instruments for the Exercise of International Public Authority' in Armin v Bogdandy et al (eds), *The Exercise of Public Authority by International Institutions* (Springer 2010) 661, 668; Angelika Nußberger, *Sozialstandards im Völkerrecht. Eine Studie zu Entwicklung und Bedeutung der Normsetzung der Vereinten Nationen, der Internationalen Arbeitsorganisation und des Europarats zu Fragen des Sozialschutzes* (Nomos 2005) 452 et seq.

[23] See, for example, the Regulation for the Human Rights Committee: Article 5 para 4 Optional Protocol: 'The Committee shall forward its views to the State Party concerned and to the individual'; Regulation on the European Committee on Social Rights: 'Turin Protocol', Council of Europe Treaty Series No 142: to 'assess from a legal standpoint the compliance of national law and practice with the obligations arising from the Charter', a regulation which has, however, not entered into force as several member States have refused to ratify it.

[24] Compare, for example, the official homepage of the Human Rights Committee summarizing the individual statements under the title 'Jurisprudence'.

[25] 'The States Parties to the Convention undertake to comply with the judgment of the Court in any case to which they are parties.'

conflict involved. The ICJ referred to the *erga omnes* effect decades ago in the famous *Barcelona Traction* case.[26] The *erga omnes* effect of the judgments of the ECtHR is also widely acknowledged in legal literature, even if member States might stress that they only feel obliged to abide by the judgments concerning them directly. In any case, an indirect *erga omnes* effect or the principle of *res iudicata*[27] is encouraged by the Steering Committee of the Council of Europe.[28] As the Court has to be consistent in its jurisprudence, it is foreseeable that a violation found in respect of one Member State will be confirmed in a similar case against another State as well.[29] The indirect *erga omnes* effect of judgments 'officially' binding only *inter partes* can also be seen as a specific form of soft jurisprudence.

Similar developments are to be expected when Protocol No. 16 to the ECHR enters into force. Article 16 of the Protocol explicitly provides that the advisory opinions the Court will give to national supreme courts are not binding. As they are adopted by the Grand Chamber, they will nevertheless form part of the Court's jurisprudence and, in practice, have similar effects to those of Grand Chamber judgments.

An interesting phenomenon is furthermore the integration of supreme courts' judgments worldwide into judicial argumentation. Even if that is technically only a source of inspiration, it might have considerable weight for finding a solution, especially in cases on new societal questions. Convincingly argued judgments used on a comparative basis may thus constitute another soft, but decisive, factor in adjudicating cases.[30] This is especially true for the judgments of international human rights courts which influence even courts outside the respective treaty system. One famous example is the Japanese Supreme Court's judgment in 2013[31] on discrimination of children born out of wedlock, in which it changed its jurisprudence with a reference to the ECtHR's judgment *Mazurek v France*.[32]

[26] *Barcelona Traction, Light and Power Company, Limited (Belgium v Spain)* [1970] ICJ Rep 3–51, para 33 <http://www.icj-cij.org/files/case-related/50/050-19700205-JUD-01-00-EN.pdf> accessed 15 May 2018: 'In particular, an essential distinction should be drawn between the obligations of a State towards the international community as a whole, and those arising vis-à-vis another State in the field of diplomatic protection. By their very nature the former are the concern of all States. In view of the importance of the rights involved, all States can be held to have a legal interest in their protection; they are obligations *erga omnes*.'

[27] See A Bodnar, 'Res Interpretata: Legal effect of the European Court of Human Rights' Judgments for other States than those which were party to the proceedings' in Y Haeck and E Brems (eds), *Human Rights and Civil Liberties in the 21st Century* (Springer 2014).

[28] CDDH report on the longer-term future of the system of the European Court of Human Rights, CDDH (2015) R84, Addendum I, para 37.

[29] See, as an interesting example of an analysis of a foreseeable Convention violation, the judgment of the German Supreme Administrative Court which analyses the Court's jurisprudence on the interdiction of a complete ban on the right to strike for civil servants developed in cases against Turkey and its potential transfer on similar cases in Germany (BVerwG 2 C 1.13, 27 February 2014).

[30] See Christopher McCrudden, 'Using Comparative Reasoning in Human Rights Adjudication: The Court of Justice of the European Union and the European Court of Human Rights Compared' (2013) 15 Cambridge Yearbook of European Legal Studies 383 considers such material for the ECtHR in some cases even as 'basis for its decision'.

[31] The decision of the SCJ (GB), 4 September 2013, 67(6) *Minshu* 1320 <http://www.courts.go.jp/hanrei/pdf/20130904154932.pdf> accessed 15 May 2018 (in Japanese).

[32] Akiko Ejima, 'Emerging Transjudicial Dialogue on Human Rights in Japan: Does it Contribute in Making a Hybrid of National and International Human Rights Norms?' (2014) 14 Meiji Law School Review 139.

The fact that international treaty bodies, unlike international courts, are not allowed to adopt binding judgments does not automatically mean that they are also denied the right to authentic treaty interpretation. Practice shows that international treaty bodies assume this competence and adopt abstract comments,[33] in exceptional cases even if authentic interpretation is explicitly forbidden. An interesting example in this context is the ILO Committee of Experts, which was, at the moment of its foundation in the late 1920s, explicitly denied the right to interpret the ILO Conventions as this right was reserved for the Permanent Court of International Justice (PCIJ),[34] to whom controversial cases were, however, almost never referred. The Committee argues that 'in so far as [its] views are not contradicted by the International Court of Justice, they should be considered as valid and generally recognized'.[35]

As it is rare that Contracting States explicitly contradict the findings in abstract 'general comments' on the interpretation of specific treaty clauses,[36] they might be seen to be accepted on the basis of acquiescence. On the other hand, it might be questionable if a formal protest is necessary against officially non-binding conclusions. Practice shows that governments are not only failing to take seriously the far-reaching requirements and wishful thinking contained in the growing number of comments elaborated by a growing number of treaty bodies, but are actively ignoring them.[37]

In any case, soft jurisprudence is, similar to soft law in general, characterized by flexibility and relative normativity. There are many forms of soft law between non-law and hard law; their impact on decision-making processes depends on many factors and remains basically unpredictable.

Last but not least, it has to be mentioned that even the binding nature of final judgments of an international court can be undermined and put to a test. Thus, constitutional courts have insisted on having the competence—despite the clear rule in Article 27 VCLT—to take final decisions if there is a contradiction between

[33] See Deutsches Institut für Menschenrechte (ed), *Die 'General Comments' zu den VN-Menschenrechtsverträgen. Deutsche Übersetzung und Kurzeinführungen* (Nomos 2005).

[34] See Article 37 ILO Constitution.

[35] See on the dispute concerning the Committee's competences the foreword to 'Collective Bargaining in the Public Service: A Way Forward', a report of the ILO Committee of Experts to the 102nd session of the International Labour Conference, 2013.

[36] A famous exception is provided by the reactions of the United States and France to the Human Rights Committee's General Comment 24(52), 'General Comment on issues relating to reservations made upon ratification or accession to the Covenant or the Optional Protocols thereto, or in relation to declarations under Article 41 of the Covenant' (1994) UN Doc CCPR/C/21/Rev 1/Add 6.

[37] One example might be the General Comment of the Committee on Economic, Social, and Cultural Rights No 14 on the 'Right to the Highest Attainable Standard of Health' 11 August 2000 E/C.12/2000/4 <http://www.refworld.org/pdfid/4538838d0.pdf> accessed 15 May 2018, which holds a maximalist position on health care to be provided even to illegal migrants: 'In particular, States are under the obligation to respect the right to health by, inter alia, refraining from denying or limiting equal access for all persons, including prisoners or detainees, minorities, asylum-seekers and illegal immigrants, to preventive, curative and palliative health services' (point 34). It does not seem that this demand has had any impact on government policy in this field. Neither has it ever been quoted by the ECtHR although it had to adjudicate a lot of questions concerning the level of health care to be guaranteed to vulnerable groups.

a binding judgment of an international court and basic constitutional principles. While the German Constitutional Court's theoretical explanations in the famous *Görgülü* judgment[38] have been without any follow-up,[39] a more radical approach of the Russian Constitutional Court[40] has led to the adoption of a new law which grants the Constitutional Court the right of the last word on the compatibility of the ECtHR's judgments with the Russian constitution.[41] Thus it has to be admitted that there is no guarantee against attempts to soften hard law.

3. Approach of the ECtHR

International courts in general may play different roles with a view to the growth of international soft law. The role of the ECtHR may be seen as an especially important one as it can act and acts as a catalyst grading up (and down) soft law. Quotations can enhance the knowledge about otherwise unknown rules of soft law, references can give them weight, reliance on them can change their nature. Are they ignored, considered to be irrelevant, or contradicted, a major drawback for the work of the respective treaty body is to be expected.

3.1 Contextuality of soft law references

It matters in which context soft law is taken up in the ECtHR's judgments. Basically, three scenarios can be differentiated.[42]

First, soft law can be found in the ECtHR judgments under the heading 'Relevant international law' in which the Court gives a comprehensive overview of relevant norms adopted within the Council of Europe (CoE) or other international organizations as well as of relevant judgments and decisions. This basically serves the same purpose as the documentation of the national law applied in a specific case. The idea is to explain the basis for the legal analysis. It may be compared to the bibliography in a research work as it shows what material has been used. It is controversial which legal acts have to be included and which ones can be left out. According to one school of thought, the material quoted should be restricted to what will be directly used and quoted in the legal analysis. Others argue that even material consulted

[38] BVerfGE 111, 307.

[39] Angelika Nußberger, 'Enhancing National Mechanisms for Effective Implementation of the European Convention on Human Rights. Report on Germany' (2015) Working paper at the St Petersburg conference 'Enhancing national mechanisms for effective implementation of the European Convention on Human Rights' <https://rm.coe.int/16806fe1a5> accessed 15 May 2018.

[40] Judgment of the Russian Constitutional Court 14 July 2015 , 21-П/2015.

[41] Федеральный конституционный закон от 14.12.2015 № 7-ФКЗ "О внесении изменений в Ф едеральный конституционный закон "О Конституционном Суде Российской Федерации" <http://publication.pravo.gov.ru/Document/View/0001201512150010?index=0&rangeSize=1> accessed 15 May 2018 (in Russian); see 'Putin Enables Russia to Overturn European Court of Human Rights Decisions' *The Moscow Times* (Moscow, 15 December 2015).

[42] Luis López Guerra, 'Soft law y sus efectos en el ámbito des derecho europeo de los derechos humanos' (2012) 11 Teoria y Derecho 151, 154.

but not relied upon should be included. In any case, the Court does not distinguish between hard law and soft law in this respect. This is mainly due to the structural distinction between CoE documents and others, but might be seen as granting soft law the same status as hard law. It is interesting to note that soft law material quoted in a judgment of the ECtHR might be taken up in the implementation procedure of the judgments and be interpreted as an authoritative source of law although the Court has not qualified it as such.[43]

Second, international legal material can be included in the part of the judgment under the heading 'The law' without being a decisive part of the argumentation. The Court can, while making a general statement about the legal problem it is confronted with, refer to rules of soft law which are in line with its own approach.[44] It thus fortifies its position and shows that it is compatible with other international expert bodies' approaches to the same problem.

Third, soft law can gain a prominent place in the Court's argumentation and become part of *ratio dicendi*.[45] This is especially true in the context of evolutive interpretation of the Convention when the Court needs to prove the existence of new approaches in the international legal environment in order to justify a change in its case law and therefore relies on what is called 'European consensus'.[46] But, as the provisions of the ECHR are vague and open, soft law can also serve the purpose of providing general guidelines for interpretation and filling in gaps in the text of the Convention. The Court is, in this context however, free to decide which rules of soft law it wants to accept as guidelines and which ones it rather puts aside as not to the point, be they outdated or too far-reaching. Due to the 'soft' character of these norms, the Court does not necessarily have to justify its position.[47]

These two approaches, the use of soft law in evolutive interpretation and in filling gaps in the Convention, which are a 'phenomenon in constant expansion',[48] have to be explored more in detail.

[43] An example would be the case *Etxebarria Caballero v Spain* App no 74016/12 (ECtHR, 7 October 2014) para 48 where the Court referred to recommendations of the Committee for the Prevention of Torture and Inhuman and Degrading Punishment (CPT) and the Human Rights Commissioner ('The Court insists on the importance of adopting the measures recommended by the CPT ... ; the Court supports the recommendations by the CPT taken up by the Human Rights Commissioner'). The Spanish government contested the Committee of Ministers' view that the execution of the Court's judgment included implementing these measures as they were only an obiter dictum; cf Document of the Committee of Ministers DHDD(2015)923, 11 September 2015.

[44] López Guerra (n 42) 155 refers in this context to the judgment *Salduz v Turkey*, in which the Court explains the vulnerable position of the accused during the investigation stage for the preparation of the criminal proceedings and then refers to the recommendations of the European Committee for the Prevention of Torture and Inhuman or Degrading Treatment or Punishment, in order to confirm 'that the right of a detainee to have access to legal advice is a fundamental safeguard against ill-treatment' (*Salduz v Turkey* App no 36391/02 (ECtHR, 27 November 2008), para 54).

[45] López Guerra (n 42) 157.

[46] See the chapter by Ineta Ziemele in this volume.

[47] See Magdalena Forowicz, *The Reception of International Law in the European Court of Human Rights* (OUP 2010) 377 who calls the Court's approach 'functional' as it is meant 'to reinforce the ECHR system and the protection of human rights at the European level'.

[48] Tulkens and Drooghenbroeck (n 18) 513.

3.2 The role of soft law in filling in gaps in the text of the Convention

Human rights treaties are characterized by vague notions such as 'inhuman treatment' or 'best interest of the child'. Even if those notions are widely used, it is unclear what 'inhuman' or 'best interests' mean. The same is true for permitting restrictions to human rights only when they are 'necessary' in a 'democratic society'.

The interpretation of such vague terms depends primarily on the context. In many specific fields the CoE and other international organizations have elaborated standards in the form of soft law.[49] One prominent example is the standardization of prison conditions.[50] While the Court has to take into account the specific circumstances and to weigh and balance them in each case, standards facilitate its task. Thus, in its assessment of the inhuman character of prison conditions, it regularly takes note of various resolutions and recommendations of the Committee of Ministers, such as the European Prison Rules,[51] as well as of the reports of the Committee for the Prevention of Torture and Inhuman and Degrading Punishment (CPT).[52] Its recommendation of ensuring that the living space per prisoner should attain a certain minimum in all establishments is regularly taken up by the Court in its judgments and forms the basis for the assessment of living space in prison.[53] Even if the legal (non-binding) nature of the CPT's reports is not changed by the Court's long-standing jurisprudence, factually the standards have acquired an authoritative normative value, notwithstanding that the adoption of binding European prison rules had been envisaged but then abandoned by the CoE.[54]

In as far as the Court develops a consistent case law in taking such standards as a basis for its legal assessment, it is bound to give a justification if it considers taking a different approach. This is a basic requirement of rule of law and legal certainty in the Court's jurisprudence. On the contrary, as long as there is no generalized approach, the non-binding character of such norms would leave a leeway to the Court to take such standards up and to follow them or to interpret the vague notions in the Convention in a different way.

Soft law is thus an auxiliary means at the disposal of the Court which is basically free to use it or not to use it. It has, however, to be consistent in its approach.

In individual cases, the Court can, where appropriate, also take into account concrete reports, eg reports of the CPT on the situation in specific prisons or even

[49] See Jörg Polakiewicz, 'Alternatives to Treaty-Making and Law-Making by Treaty and Expert Bodies in the Council of Europe' in Rüdiger Wolfrum and Volker Röben (eds), *Developments of International Law in Treaty Making* (Springer 2005).

[50] See for many more examples Tulkens and Drooghenbroeck (n 18) 512 et seq.

[51] Approved by Recommendation no R(87)3 of the Committee of Ministers to the Member States.

[52] Compare the latest update Strasbourg, 15 December 2015 CPT/INF(2015)44 <http://hudoc.cpt.coe.int/eng#{"fulltext":["CPT/INF(2015)44"],"sort":["CPTDocumentDate Descending,CPTDocumentID Ascending,CPTSectionNumber Ascending"],"CPTSectionID":["p-standards-inf-2015-44-en-1"]}> accessed 15 May 2018.

[53] See, for example, *Davydov and Others v Ukraine* App nos 17674/02 and 39081/02 (ECtHR, 1 July 2010) paras 101–8.

[54] Tulkens and Drooghenbroek (n 18) 520, 521.

concrete events. The Court does not, however, necessarily come to the same assessment as the CPT.[55]

3.3 The role of soft law in the evolutive interpretation of the Convention

The role of soft law in the evolutive interpretation of the Convention has often been described;[56] it suffices in the context of the present chapter to summarize the most important findings. The methodological approach has first been developed in the famous case *Marckx v Belgium*. The basic assumption was that notions used in the Convention had held a special meaning in the 1950s when the Convention was drafted, but that this meaning had not remained unchanged. When interpreting the Convention, the Court would have to explore those changes. As it could not resort to sociological research or statistical data, it was bound to rely on normative material. The Court was ready to accept all indications for changes contained in relevant norms such as non-ratified international treaties, comparative law, and soft law. The legal nature was not considered to be decisive. While this was explicitly outlined only in *Demir and Baykara* with reference to Article 31 (3)(c) VCLT, it was already clear in *Marckx* because of the soft law character of the norms referred to.[57] What matters for the Court is to prove changes in society on the basis of changes in normative approaches, be they vague. The Court, therefore, highlights the dynamics of change and explains that the 'living' nature of the Convention 'must be interpreted in the light of present-day conditions', taking account of 'evolving norms of national and international law in its interpretation of Convention provisions'.[58]

This reading of the Convention as a 'living instrument' is widely accepted even if it raises issues under the headings of 'legal security' and 'limits of State consent';[59] the method in determining changes in society on the basis of international and comparative law is further refined on the basis of what is called 'European consensus'.[60]

[55] See the controversy about prison conditions in Malta which the CPT had considered to be 'far below any acceptable standard', whereas the majority of the Chamber denied a violation of Article 3 (*Story and Others v Malta* App nos 56854/13, 57005/13, and 57043/13 (ECtHR, 29 October 2015), dissenting opinion by Josep Casadevall).

[56] See the literature quoted in n 1.

[57] In *Marckx v Belgium* App no 6833/74 (ECtHR, 13 June 1979), the Court relied on the European Convention of 15 October 1975 on the Legal Status of Children born out of Wedlock ratified by four member States and the Brussels Convention of 12 September 1962 on the Establishment of Maternal Affiliation of Natural Children also ratified by four member States, although none had been ratified by the defendant State Belgium. The Court mentions the small number of signatures and ratifications and then explains: 'However, this state of affairs cannot be relied on in opposition to the evolution noted above. Both the relevant Conventions are in force and there is no reason to attribute the currently small number of Contracting States to a refusal to admit equality between "illegitimate" and ["]legitimate" children on the point under consideration. In fact, the existence of these two treaties denotes that there is a clear measure of common ground in this area amongst modern societies' (para 41).

[58] See also 'classics' such as *Soering v The United Kingdom* App no 14038/88 (ECtHR, 7 July 1989), para 102; *Vo v France* App no 53924/00 (ECtHR, 8 July 2004), para 82 and *Mamatkulov and Askarov v Turkey* App nos 46827/99 and 46951/99 (ECtHR, 4 February 2005), para 121.

[59] See for an interesting discussion on both problems Tulkens and Drooghenbroeck (n 18) 520 et seq.; Wachsmann (n 1).

[60] Luzius Wildhaber, Arnaldur Hjartarson and Stephen Donelly, 'No consensus on consensus' (2013) 33 HRLJ 248.

While this approach is uncontested, it is worth highlighting the Court's prudent language. Thus in the famous judgment *Demir and Baykara*, where the Court explains the theoretical basis of its innovative interpretation method, it uses the interesting expression 'searching for common ground among the norms of international law'.[61] The metaphor of the 'common ground' is to be understood as indication of a certain tendency, a general development. It is not the specific obligation fixed in a legal act which counts, but the 'spirit' of the norm. Another metaphor is also revelatory in this context: the metaphor of the 'international law background'.[62]

It is furthermore worth mentioning that the Court uses the soft expression 'may' and not 'must' when explaining its method of interpretation: 'The consensus emerging from specialised international instruments and from the practice of Contracting States *may* constitute a relevant consideration for the Court when it interprets the provisions of the Convention in specific cases.'[63] In this context it also uses the metaphor of an 'interpretation in the light of . . . ' which is deliberately imprecise and leaves room for different conclusions.

3.4 Clashes

This prepares the ground for better understanding how clashes are solved between, on the one hand, soft law and the ECHR and, on the other hand, between hard law and the ECHR.[64] The Court's argumentation in the different constellations is revelatory for its well-nuanced approach to binding and non-binding sources of international law.

3.4.1 Clashes between the ECHR and soft law

The prudent language used in *Demir and Baykara v Turkey* allows the Court in the follow-up case *National Union of Rail, Maritime and Transport Workers v The United Kingdom*[65] to remain consistent in its approach to the interpretation of the Convention in the light of international soft law without feeling itself bound by soft jurisprudence. It is worth having a closer look at the argumentation.

Both cases concern questions of international labour law, the first one the more general question of public servants' right to strike, the second one the more specific question of a ban on taking secondary industrial action against an employer who is not party to a labour dispute. While the first case was decided with reference to

61 *Demir* (n 1) 78.
62 *Demir* (n 1) para 76.
63 *Demir* (n 1) para 85, emphasis added.
64 See Gregory C Shaffer and Mark A Pollack, 'Hard vs. Soft Law: Alternatives, Complements, and Antagonists in International Governance' (2010) 94 Minnesota Law Review 706, who also focus on the antagonistic relationship between hard law and soft law from a sociological point of view analysing distributive conflicts.
65 *National Union of Rail, Maritime and Transport Workers v The United Kingdom* App no 31045/10 (ECtHR, 8 April 2014).

soft law norms of international labour law, in the second case the Court refused to follow a long-standing and consistent soft jurisprudence of the relevant international treaty bodies.

The starting point in the second case for the Court is that not the core of freedom of association is affected, but only 'a secondary or accessory aspect'.[66] Even if international (soft) law is accepted as one of the factors determining the margin of appreciation, it is clear that the Court sees this as a possibility, not as an obligation. With reference to *Demir and Baykara* it explains: 'The degree of common ground between the member States of the Council of Europe in relation to the issue arising in the case *may* also be relevant, as *may* any international consensus reflected in the apposite international instruments (Demir and Baykara, para 85).'[67] The Court acknowledges that the restrictive British position is 'out of line with a discernible international trend calling for a less restrictive approach'.[68] It also accepts that it clashes with the position of the international treaty bodies' view, ie the long-standing 'jurisprudence' of the ILO Expert Committee and the Social Rights Committee of the CoE. Nevertheless, the Court does not feel bound by this soft jurisprudence because of the 'distinct character of the Court's review compared with that of the supervisory procedures of the ILO and the European Social Charter'.[69] In the end, it comes to the conclusion 'that the negative assessments made by the relevant monitoring bodies of the ILO and European Social Charter are not of such persuasive weight'.[70]

The clash between different normative approaches is thus solved by accepting their parallelism and coexistence. The Court reserves its right to give an answer to a concrete case which is incompatible with a general approach in international soft jurisprudence. While it carefully avoids discrediting the findings of the other treaty bodies,[71] it obviously does not fear to upset or undermine the whole system. Therefore its aim is not to find a harmonious interpretation at any price.

The Court's argumentation in *National Union of Rail, Maritime and Transport Workers v The United Kingdom* is an example for a straightforward and direct discussion of a clash between international soft law and the ECHR. It is based on the parties' argumentation, as both the government and the applicant heavily relied on the findings of the international treaty bodies.

[66] *National Union of Rail* (n 65) para 87.
[67] ibid para 86.
[68] ibid para 98.
[69] ibid.
[70] ibid. The judgment has been criticized in legal literature cf, for example, Klaus Lörcher, 'Kein Recht auf Sekundärstreik in Großbritannien—Roll-back des EGMR?' Newsletter zum Europäischen Arbeitsrecht 2/2014 <http://www.hugo-sinzheimer-institut.de/hsi-newsletter/europaeisches-arbeitsrecht/2014/newsletter-022014.html#c5724> accessed 15 May 2018.
[71] See its appraisal of the role of the relevant treaty bodies as a reply to the government's argument they lacked judicial or quasi-judicial status. The Court defends the European Committee on Social Rights' (ECSR) 'interpretative value' which is 'certainly accepted by the Court'. It adds that it 'has repeatedly had regard to the ECSR's interpretation of the Charter and its assessment of State compliance with its various provisions' (*National Union of Rail* (n 65) para 94). The same is true according to the Court for the ILO expert committee 'as a point of reference and guidance for the interpretation of certain provisions of the Convention' (*National Union of Rail* (n 65) para 97).

But there are other cases where the Court has not explicitly distinguished its approach from other findings in international soft jurisprudence.[72] A well-known example is the case *Koufaki et Adedy v Greece*[73] which concerns austerity measures, such as the reduction of remuneration, benefits, bonuses, and retirement pensions of public servants, deemed necessary to overcome the economic crisis. The cuts were part of a broader programme drawn up by the Greek authorities after consultation with the European Commission, the European Central Bank, and the International Monetary Fund to buttress the fiscal adjustment effort and restoration of competitiveness. The Court accepted that there was an exceptional crisis, which was unprecedented in the recent history of Greece, and called for an immediate reduction in public spending. In this context, it accorded a large margin of appreciation to Greece to choose the best measures and argued that there was no excessive burden for the applicants. The complaints under the right to property (Article 1 of Protocol No. 1) were dismissed as 'manifestly ill-founded'.

The European Committee of Social Rights (ECSR) had to pronounce itself on the same reform laws adopted in 2010 and analysed them on the basis of various articles contained in the European Social Charter (ESC), among others Article 12 para 3 ESC, the right to social security.[74] It found several violations 'due to the cumulative effect of the restrictive measures and the procedures adopted to put them into place'.[75] Although the Committee's decisions[76] preceded the Court's decision by one year and the Committee had referred to the Court's relevant case law in the area of cuts in social rights, the Court did not deem it necessary to either quote the Committee's findings, or the common ground in the approaches of other international treaty bodies criticizing the austerity measures. This can, once again, be explained by the 'distinct character' of the Court's review compared with that of the other supervisory procedures. The Court's perspective is a different one, as it is confronted with the assessment of the austerity measures in only one concrete case and has to answer the question of whether there is an 'excessive individual burden'. But it is also clear that the underlying philosophy is different. The ECSR takes as a starting point its conclusion that 'the economic crisis should not have as a consequence the reduction of the protection of the rights recognised by the Charter. Hence, governments are bound to take all

[72] See the critique on this point Klaus Lörcher, 'EGMR prüft drastische Sparmaßnahmen' Newsletter zum Europäischen Arbeitsrecht 2/2013, <http://www.hugo-sinzheimer-institut.de/hsi-newsletter/europaeisches-arbeitsrecht/2013/newsletter-022013.html> accessed 15 May 2018.

[73] *Koufaki et Adedy v Greece* App nos 57665/12 and 57657/12 (ECtHR, 7 May 2013).

[74] The wording of the relevant provision is very open: 'With a view to ensuring the effective exercise of the right to social security, the Contracting Parties undertake: ... to endeavour to raise progressively the system of social security to a higher level.'

[75] *Pensioners' Union of the Agricultural Bank of Greece (ATE) v Greece* Complaint no 80/2012 (ECSR, 7 December 2012) para 78; see also similar decisions on Complaints nos 76/2012, 77/2012, 78/2012, 79/2012.

[76] The relevant decisions are the ones cited in n 75 as well as the following: Complaint no 66/2011 (ECSR, 23 May 2012).

necessary steps to ensure that the rights of the Charter are effectively guaranteed at a period of time when beneficiaries most need the protection'.[77] The Court, on the contrary, generally accepts the necessity to reduce social benefits if necessary in a situation of crisis and focuses on potentially disproportionate results of the respective austerity measures. While the ECSR approaches the problem on the basis of the right to social security, the Court's legal point of reference is the protection of property.

Another discrepancy is evident between the finding of the ECSR allowing the right to organize as guaranteed in Article 5 ESC to be totally suppressed in as far as the army is concerned,[78] whereas the ECtHR decided in *Matelly v France*[79] and *Adefdromil v France*[80] that an 'absolute interdiction' of all rights connected to freedom of association is disproportionate. This difference in interpretation is all the more remarkable as the wording of the relevant articles is very similar.[81] In this case, the Court quotes the relevant conclusions of the ECSR and refers to its statement in *Demir and Baykara* that 'the common international or domestic law standards of European States reflect a reality that the Court cannot disregard when it is called upon to clarify the scope of a Convention provision that more conventional means of interpretation have not enabled it to establish with a sufficient degree of certainty'.[82] With a view to its own long-standing jurisprudence on the applicability of Article 11 to armed forces, it denies, however, that the meaning of Article 11 ECHR is unclear in this respect. An obvious contradiction to the ECSR's approach is not seen as a reason for a detailed analysis and clarification of the respective positions. It is also interesting to note that the Court does not rely on Article 53 ECHR in order to solve conflicts between more or less far-reaching approaches to international human rights protection.

All these examples confirm that potential disharmony between the ECtHR's case law and soft law or soft jurisprudence is not per se considered as a threat to the consistency of international human rights protection and does not, at least not under all circumstances, require a justification of the Court's deviant approach.

[77] *General Federation of employees of the national electric power corporation (GENOP-DEI) and Confederation of Greek Civil Servants' Trade Unions (ADEDY) v Greece* Complaint no 66/2011 (ECSR, 23 May 2012) para 12.

[78] *Fédération européenne du Personnel des Services publics contre la France* Complaint no 2/1999 (ECSR, 4 December 2000) para 28: Comme le Comité l'a toujours affirmé, il résulte des termes de la dernière phrase de l'article 5 de la Charte sociale européenne de 1961 que les Etats sont autorisés à apporter « n'importe quelle limitation et même la suppression intégrale de la liberté syndicale des membres des forces armées » (Conclusions I, p 32).

[79] *Matelly v France* App no 10609/10 (ECtHR, 2 October 2014).

[80] *Adefdromil v France* App no 32191/09 (ECtHR, 2 October 2014).

[81] cf Article 5 ESC: 'The principle governing the application to the members of the armed forces of these guarantees and the extent to which they shall apply to persons in this category shall equally be determined by national laws or regulations.'; Article 11 para 2 ECHR: 'This article shall not prevent the imposition of lawful restrictions on the exercise of these rights by members of the armed forces, of the police or of the administration of the State.'

[82] *Demir* (n 1) para 76.

3.4.2 Clashes between the ECHR and hard law

Clashes between the ECHR and other norms of hard law or binding judgments of international courts are treated in a different manner. Instead of the word 'may', the Court uses the word 'must' and thus makes clear that it accepts an obligation to interpret the Convention so far as possible in harmony with other international treaties.

One good example for this approach is the judgment *Jones v The United Kingdom* where the Court explains that the judgment of the ICJ '*must* be considered by this Court as authoritative as regards the content of customary international law'.[83] This quotation is part of a dialogue between the ECtHR and the ICJ. In 2001, the ECtHR had decided that the denial of access to court on the basis of State immunity is compatible with Article 6 ECHR even in cases concerning compensation for torture.[84] This finding was taken up by the ICJ in the case *Jurisdictional Immunities of the State* (*Germany v Italy*, Greece intervening) of 3 February 2012[85] where State immunity was confirmed as part of customary law even in a case concerning compensation for war crimes.[86] The judgment in the case of *Al-Adsani,* as well as other relevant judgments of the European Court, were explicitly quoted.[87] In *Jones v The United Kingdom*, the ECtHR was confronted with the demand to revisit its approach in *Al-Adsani*. The Court found, however, that in *Al-Adsani*, it had been 'acting in accordance with its obligation to take account of the relevant rules and principles of international law and to interpret the Convention so far as possible in harmony with other rules of international law of which it forms part'.[88] The Court thus confirmed its interpretation of the right of access to court guaranteed in Article 6 ECHR in light of the rules of customary international law concerning State immunity. It is interesting to note that the Court accepted restricting the scope of the applicability of Article 6 so as to avoid contradictions with general international law.

A similarly restrictive approach to the interpretation of the Convention was also necessary in other areas of international law where rules of general international law clashed with the European Convention. That is especially true in the case of *Hassan v The United Kingdom*,[89] which concerned the interaction between humanitarian law and the Convention. In this case, the Human Rights Centre of the University of Essex, as third party intervener, held that the interpretation of the Convention in harmony with other rules of public international law 'was desirable and necessary, to avoid States being faced with irreconcilable legal obligations and controversial

[83] *Jones v United Kingdom* App nos 34356/06 and 40528/06 (ECtHR, 14 January 2014) para 197, emphasis added.

[84] *Al-Adsani v The United Kingdom* App no 35763/97 (ECtHR, 21 November 2001).

[85] *Jurisdictional Immunities of the State* (*Germany v Italy*) (Judgment) [2012] ICJ Rep 99 <http://www.icj-cij.org/files/case-related/143/143-20120203-JUD-01-00-EN.pdf> accessed 15 May 2018.

[86] Benjamin Nußberger and Victoria Otto, 'Jurisdictional Immunities of the State (Germany v Italy, Greece Intervening)' [2016] MPEPIL <http://opil.ouplaw.com/view/10.1093/law:epil/9780199231690/law-9780199231690-e2184?rskey=ModboK&result=1&prd=EPIL> accessed 15 May 2018.

[87] *Jurisdictional Immunities of the State* (n 85) para 90.

[88] *Jones* (n 83) para 195.

[89] *Hassan v The United Kingdom* App no 29750/09 (ECtHR, 16 September 2014).

results'.[90] This comment highlights the differences in the clashes between hard law and soft law with the obligations deduced from the Convention. Whereas different approaches in soft law and ECHR law may lead to 'controversial results', it is not to be feared that they might result in 'irreconcilable legal obligations'. This explains why the Court in those situations puts much more effort in finding compromise solutions. This is especially true for clashes between human rights law and humanitarian law as can be seen in the argumentation in *Hassan v The United Kingdom*. In finding no violation in this case, the Court is ready to accept 'to disapply [a Member State's] obligations under Article 5 or in some other way to interpret them in the light of powers of detention available to it under international humanitarian law'[91] for the sake of consistency in international law. The compromise formula is summarized in the following words: 'the Court considers that, even in situations of international armed conflict, the safeguards under the Convention continue to apply, albeit interpreted against the background of the provisions of international humanitarian law. By reason of the co-existence of the safeguards provided by international humanitarian law and by the Convention in time of armed conflict, the grounds of permitted deprivation of liberty set out in subparagraphs (a) to (f) of that provision should be accommodated, as far as possible, with the taking of prisoners of war and the detention of civilians who pose a risk to security under the Third and Fourth Geneva Conventions.'[92] This is a far-reaching step not accepted by all judges as can be seen from the dissenting opinions.[93]

It is clear that such an 'accommodation' of the interpretation of the Convention would never be deemed necessary in a conflict with soft law.

The argumentation of the Court in the case *Hassan v The United Kingdom* can—once again—be seen as a part of an ongoing dialogue between the Court and other courts as well as opinions held in legal literature on the problem of fragmentation in international law. The same is true in the case of *X v Latvia*,[94] where the Court reacts to critique voiced against its judgment *Neulinger and Shuruk v Switzerland*[95] and tried to align its case law to the basic principles of international treaties ratified much more widely than the Convention itself, in this case the Hague Convention on the Civil Aspects of International Child Abduction of 25 October 1980. The Court admits that the judgment in *Neulinger and Shuruk* 'may and has indeed been read as suggesting that the domestic courts were required to conduct an in-depth examination of the entire family situation and of a whole series of factors', ie in a way incompatible with the Hague Convention. Against this background, the Court 'considers it opportune to clarify' its jurisprudence and to explain how 'a harmonious interpretation of the European Convention and the Hague Convention' can be achieved.[96]

90 *Hassan* (n 89) para 91. 91 ibid para 99. 92 ibid para 104.

93 See the partly dissenting opinion of Judge Spano joined by Judges Nicolaou, Bianku, and Kalaydjieva.

94 *X v Latvia* [GC] App no 27853/09 (ECtHR, 26 November 2013).

95 *Neulinger Shuruk v Switzerland* [GC] App no 41615/07 (ECtHR, 6 July 2010).

96 *X v Latvia* (n 94) paras 104–06.

All these examples show that the Court is ready to rethink its interpretation of Convention provisions when confronted with the reproach that member States are confronted with 'irreconcilable obligations'.

4. Conclusion

To conclude, it can be argued that the Court takes both hard law and soft law seriously as 'international law background' when interpreting the provisions of the Convention. This is especially true when it is necessary to adapt them to changed conditions in European societies and to explore what is called the 'European consensus'. Nevertheless, the Court does not treat hard law and soft law in the same way. When clashes occur and the interpretation of the Convention has to be accommodated it takes hard law more seriously than soft law, especially when the scope of the protection provided by the Convention has to be restricted. This finding can be linked to the acceptability and legitimacy of the Court's jurisprudence. The Court is legitimized to interpret the Convention, but it is not only bound by the generally accepted rules of interpretation,[97] but also by the member States' consent which can be stretched to include rules not explicitly accepted, such as soft law, but cannot go beyond what is possible to fulfil. An interpretation of the Convention creating irreconcilable treaty obligations is generally not acceptable, unless the collision concerns clearly outdated treaty provisions or treaties where there is a consensus that they should be denounced.[98] An interpretation of the Convention going less far or further than rules of soft law might be criticized, but does not create unsolvable problems for member States. Thus, while there is no black-and-white scenario, and the difference between hard law and soft law might have been qualified to a large extent by the Court, it still matters in its jurisprudence.

[97] In the literature there are critical voices arguing that the Court 'seems to be ready to bend generally accepted rules of interpretation to a breaking point and beyond' Pitea (n 1) 11; see also G Letsas 'Strasbourg's Interpretive Ethic: Lessons for the International Lawyer' (2010) 21 EJIL 503 arguing that the Court favours a 'moral reading' of the Convention. Arato (n 1) 385 interprets the Court's approach as an 'informal constitutional change through interpretation'.

[98] An example would be ILO Convention No 89 on the prohibition of night work for women which was considered as discriminatory; see *Case No 158/91* [1993] ECR I-04287.

PART II

INTERPRETATION

3

The Effect of Subsequent Practice on the European Convention on Human Rights

Considerations from a General International Law Perspective

*Anja Seibert-Fohr**

1. Introduction

Almost 200 years ago—in 1816—Thomas Jefferson wrote: 'laws and institutions must go hand in hand with the progress of the human mind.'[1] According to him, requiring society to remain ever under the same rules would be tantamount to asking a man to wear the same coat which fitted him when a boy. Though the European Convention on Human Rights (ECHR)[2] only claims a 67-year-old history, the question to what extent the Convention is able—in Jefferson's terms—'to go hand in hand with progress of human mind' has been subject to debate for quite some time now.[3] On what basis can the meaning of a treaty legitimately be advanced? What role do Contracting States play in this endeavour? Can they advance or even modify the treaty after its conclusion by way of State practice?

To answer these questions, two competing considerations come to mind. On the one hand, the obligations under the Convention are undertaken by States. Their consent provides the source of these obligations. As the authors of the Convention, they remain competent to modify it, arguably even by means of practice. On the other hand, the specific nature of the Convention as a human rights instrument

* The author thanks Torben Schlüter, Thomas Thamm, and Anton Müller for their valuable research assistance and careful editing.

[1] Letter from Thomas Jefferson to Samuel Kercheval (12 July 1816).

[2] Convention for the Protection of Human Rights and Fundamental Freedoms (European Convention on Human Rights, as amended) (1953).

[3] See, for example, Rudolf Bernhardt, 'Rechtsfortbildung durch den Europäischen Gerichtshof für Menschenrechte' in S Breitenmoser, B Ehrenzeller, M Sassòli, W Stoffel, and B Wagner Pfeifer (eds), *Human Rights, Democracy and the Rule of Law: Liber amicorum Luzius Wildhaber* (Nomos 2007) 91–101; George Letsas, 'The ECHR as a living instrument: its meaning and legitimacy' in Andreas Føllesdal, Birgit Peters, and Geir Ulfstein (eds), *Constituting Europe—The European Court of Human Rights in a National, European and Global Context* (CUP 2013) 106; Daniel Moeckli and Nigel D White, 'Treaties as "Living Instruments"' in Dino Kritsiotis and Michael Bowman (eds), *Conceptual and Contextual Perspectives on the Modern Law of Treaties* (CUP 2018).

solicits a cautious approach.[4] Seen from this perspective, it is debatable whether, and to what extent, State practice can be a legitimate source of treaty interpretation.[5] Since it is the very object of human rights protection to restrain State conduct, States cannot overrule the guarantees set out in the Convention simply by way of practice.

The European Court of Human Rights (ECtHR) takes a pragmatic approach to this dilemma when it considers State practice. It acknowledges the relevance of State practice when it engages in 'dynamic interpretation' of substantive rights.[6] In this context, State practice is used to advance the protection of rights so that it does not compete but rather accords with the object of the Convention. However, this approach has not gone unchallenged. Some authors have criticized the Court's dynamic interpretation for the lack of methodological consistency and for not being subject to democratic accountability in the member States if it cannot be traced back to sufficient relevant State practice.[7] The issue becomes even more controversial in cases where reference to State practice leads to a lower level of protection. For example, in *Hassan v The United Kingdom*,[8] State practice became relevant when the Court had to determine whether States are relieved from a formal derogation in extraterritorial military missions.[9] The Court relied on State practice in order to hold that Contracting States who detain persons on the basis of the Third or Fourth Geneva Convention during an international armed conflict do not need to formally derogate from Article 5 for such detention.[10] However, this holding did not go unchallenged. In a partial dissent, Judges Spano, Bianku, Nicolaou, and Kalaydjeieva questioned whether State practice was sufficiently consolidated ('common to all Parties') to warrant this potentially modifying reading of the Convention.[11]

The discussion among the judges shows that this is an area of international law which continues to engage the Court. While State practice has traditionally played

[4] For a value-based approach to the interpretation of the ECHR, see George Letsas, 'Strasbourg's Interpretive Ethic: Lessons for the International Lawyer' (2010) 21 EJIL 509–41.

[5] For the limited role of state consent and the special value of 'non-uniform practice' and 'non-binding rules' as supplementary means of interpretation for the ECHR in accordance with Article 31 VCLT, see Moeckli and White (n 3).

[6] *Tyrer v The United Kingdom* App no 5856/72 (ECtHR, 25 April 1978), para 31. The Court refused to apply the living instrument approach in *Banković and Others v Belgium and Others* [GC] App no 52207/99 (ECtHR, 12 December 2001), paras 64–65. For a critique of this narrow application of the living instrument approach see Eirik Bjorge, 'What Is Living and What Is Dead in the European Convention on Human Rights? A Comment on Hassan v. United Kingdom' (2015) 15 QIL 23, 29.

[7] Daniel Moeckli and Nigel White argue that the legitimacy of the ECtHR's evolutive interpretation cannot draw from the availability of a democratic corrective, as in the case of constitutional interpretation by domestic constitutional courts, but only from the consent of as many States parties as possible. See Moeckli and White (n 3). Therefore, the authors demand at least a detailed explanation of the 'living instrument' approach backed up by evidence rather than mere reference to the *Tyrer* judgment.

[8] *Hassan v The United Kingdom* [GC] App no 29750/09 (ECtHR, 16 September 2014).

[9] For a critical assessment of the Court's approach in this case, see, eg Luigi Crema, 'Subsequent Practice in Hassan v. United Kingdom: When Things Seem to Go Wrong in the Life of a Living Instrument' (2015) 15 QIL 3, 10; Bjorge (n 6) 23, 25. See also Matthias Lippold, 'Between Humanization and Humanitarization? Detention in Armed Conflicts and the European Convention on Human Rights' [2016] ZaöRV 53.

[10] *Hassan* (n 8)

[11] Partly Dissenting Opinion of Judge Spano joined by Judges Nicolaou, Bianku, and Kalaydjieva, *Hassan* (n 8) para 13.

some role in the interpretation of the Convention, such as in the well-known *Tyrer* case,[12] the methodology applied by the Court to determine under what circumstance, and to what extent, State practice is able to affect the scope and meaning of the Convention remains uncertain. How much State practice is needed in order to sustain an evolving interpretation of the Convention? Is it only relevant if it is common and agreed by all Contracting States? Can State practice lead to a lowering of the Convention standards? Do the same standards apply irrespective of whether practice relates to substantive or procedural matters?

Most attention by literature has been devoted so far to the Court's dynamic interpretation of substantive rights whereas the role of State practice for formal issues has attracted less interest by academia.[13] The current chapter considers State practice more comprehensively and seeks to explain its normative relevance for different means of interpretation. At the same time, it concentrates exclusively on the relevance of State practice for the interpretation of the European Convention, rather than on the general issue of dynamic interpretation which also involves elements other than State practice.[14]

In an effort to clarify the area of treaty interpretation, which is informed by State practice, the chapter turns to the recent work of the International Law Commission (ILC) on 'Subsequent agreements and subsequent practice in relation to interpretation of treaties'. [15] Based on a comprehensive study of international jurisprudence and in an effort to delineate a general methodology, the Commission has adopted draft conclusions on the role of subsequent agreements and practice in treaty interpretation.[16] The study offers a frame under which the European human rights jurisprudence can be systematically analysed.

The chapter outlines the work of the ILC and compares it to the jurisprudence of the ECtHR. After setting out the VCLT's normative framework for the

[12] *Tyrer* (n 6) para 31. See also, eg *Marckx v Belgium* App no 6833/74 (ECtHR, 13 June 1979) para 41; *Christine Goodwin v The United Kingdom* [GC] App no 28957/95 (ECtHR, 11 July 2002) para 85; *Öcalan v Turkey* [GC] App no 46221/99 ECHR 2005-IV; *Demir and Baykara v Turkey* [GC] App no 34503/97 (ECtHR, 12 November 2008) paras 65–86. For further details see Geir Ulfstein, 'Evolutive Interpretation in the Light of Other International Instruments: Law and Legitimacy' in this volume.

[13] Eirik Bjorge, *The Evolutionary Interpretation of Treaties* (OUP 2014); David McGrogan, 'On the Interpretation of Human Rights Treaties and Subsequent Practice' (2014) 32 NQHR 347–78; George Letsas, 'The ECHR as a living instrument: its meaning and legitimacy' in Andreas Føllesdal, Birgit Peters, and Geir Ulfstein (eds), *Constituting Europe—The European Court of Human Rights in a National, European and Global Context* (CUP 2013) 106; Moeckli and White (n 3).

[14] See Bianchi who considers subsequent practice as one tool amongst others that may lead to changes in the law over time. Andrea Bianchi, 'Law, Time, and Change: The Self-Regulatory Function of Subsequent Practice' in Georg Nolte (ed), *Treaties and Subsequent Practice* (OUP 2013) 140. For the relevance of international instruments for dynamic interpretation see Ulfstein (n 12).

[15] Georg Nolte, 'Subsequent Treaty Practice: The Work of the International Law Commission' in A Reinisch, ME Footer, and C Binder (eds), *International Law and... Select Proceedings of the European Society of International Law* (Volume 5, Hart Publishing 2016) 219–25; Georg Nolte, 'Third report on subsequent agreements and subsequent practice in relation to the interpretation of treaties' UN Doc A/CN.4/683 A/CN.4/683; Georg Nolte, 'Fourth report on subsequent agreements and subsequent practice in relation to the interpretation of treaties' UN Doc A/CN.4/694 A/CN.4/694.

[16] See on the latest work ILC, 'Report of the International Law Commission on the Work of its 68th Session' (2 May–10 June and 4 July–12 August 2016) UN Doc A/71/10, 118–240.

interpretation of the European Convention, the second part distinguishes between the different means of interpretation and describes to what extent subsequent practice may become relevant respectively. In the third part, the question of whether the European Convention can be modified is considered.

Since the ultimate goal of this chapter is to specify the preconditions under which subsequent State practice can be legitimately considered in human rights treaty interpretation, the fourth part develops a general theoretical framework, which rationalizes the normative value of subsequent practice in accordance with its respective function and sets out the relevant standards for the consideration of State practice. It draws from the previous analysis and places the requirements for subsequent practice on a normative scale. The final part of the contribution turns to the broader question of whether human rights jurisprudence follows its own rules of interpretation or can be accommodated within the realms of general international law.[17] It describes international law as a matrix, which draws the outer limits for treaty interpretation and, at the same time, allows for sufficient flexibility to accommodate the specific nature of human rights law within this perimeter. From this perspective, subsequent practice can serve as a catalyst for the advancement of human rights without compromising the legitimate value of treaty interpretation.

2. State Practice and Treaty Interpretation

2.1 Normative framework for interpretation

In order to determine the normative value of State practice for the interpretation of the ECHR, we need to consider the relevant rules of general international law. The ILC study illustrates that, as a common point of reference, all international courts, including those interpreting international human rights instruments, consider Article 31 of the Vienna Convention on the Law of Treaties (VCLT) as the basis for treaty interpretation.[18] The ECtHR already recognized the relevance of the

[17] For the issue of constitutional interpretation, see Ineta Ziemele, 'European Consensus and International Law' chapter 1 in this volume.

[18] Vienna Convention on the Law of Treaties (adopted 23 May 1969, entered into force 27 January 1980) 1155 UNTS 331; **ICJ**: *Arbitral Award of July 1989 (Guinea-Bissau v Senegal)* (Judgment) [1991] ICJ Rep 53, para 48; *Land, Island and Maritime Frontier Dispute (El Salvador v Honduras, Nicaragua intervening)* (Judgment) [1992] ICJ Rep 351, paras 373, 376; *Application of the Interim Accord of 13 September 1995 (Macedonia v Greece)* [2011] ICJ Rep 644, para 91; **ECtHR**: *Golder v The United Kingdom* App no 4451/70 (ECtHR, 21 February 1975) para 30; *Mamatkulov and Askarov v Turkey* [GC] App nos 46827/99 and 46951/99 (ECtHR, 4 February 2005) paras 111, 123; *Hassan* (n 8) para 100; **HRC**: *Alberta Union v Canada* (1986) 2 Selected Decisions of the Human Rights Committee (HRC SD) 34, para 6.3; *Setelich v Uruguay* (1981) 1 HRC SD 101, para 6.3; **ITLOS**: *Responsibilities and Obligations of States Sponsoring Persons and Entities with Respect to Activities in the Area* (Advisory Opinion of 1 February 2011) 2011 ITLOS Reports 10, paras 57–58; **ICC**: *Prosecutor v Lubanga Dyilo* (Decision on the Final System of Disclosure and the Establishment of a Timetable) ICC-01/04-01/06-102 (15 May 2006) Annex I, para 1; *Situation in the Democratic Republic of the Congo* (Judgment on the Prosecutor's Application for Extraordinary Review of Pre-Trial Chamber I's 31 March 2006 Decision Denying Leave to Appeal) ICC-01/04-168 (13 July 2006), paras 6, 33; **WTO DSB**: WTO, *Japan: Alcoholic Beverages II—Report of the Appellate Body* (4 October 1996) WT/DS8/AB/R, WT/DS10/AB/R, WT/DS11/AB/R, section D; **ECJ**: Case C-386/08 *Brita GmbH v Hauptzollamt Hamburg-Hafen* [2010] ECR I-01289, paras 40–43.

VCLT in 1975 in *Golder v The United Kingdom* where it held with respect to treaty interpretation:

The Court [. . .] should be guided by Articles 31 to 33 of the Vienna Convention of 23 May 1969 on the Law of Treaties. That Convention has not yet entered into force and it specifies, at Article 4, that it will not be retroactive, but its Articles 31 to 33 enunciate in essence generally accepted principles of international law to which the Court has already referred on occasion.[19]

The UN Human Rights Committee (HRC) shares this approach.[20] In reviewing the International Covenant on Civil and Political Rights, it considers that 'as required by the Vienna Convention on the Law of Treaties, a treaty should be interpreted in good faith and in accordance with the ordinary meaning to be given to the terms of the treaty in their context and in the light of its object and purpose'.[21]

Despite this common ground for treaty interpretation, the ILC study reveals that there are considerable differences in the application of Articles 31 to 33 VCLT.[22] The comparison of the ECtHR with the WTO Appellate Body shows that, while both affirm Article 31 VCLT as a general rule, the former emphasizes the object and purpose in its interpretation whereas the latter has been described as more text oriented.[23] For example, the WTO Appellate Body engages in a detailed analysis of the ordinary meaning of treaty terms referring to dictionaries, such as the Concise Oxford English Dictionary and Black's Law Dictionary, in order to determine the meaning of a treaty provision.[24] The European Court of Human Right, on the other hand, gives considerable weight to the purpose, as evidenced, for example, in *Soering*

On the jurisprudence of international courts and tribunals regarding Article 31 VCLT see eg ILC, 'First Report on Subsequent Agreements and Subsequent Practice in Relation to Treaty Interpretation' (13 March 2013) UN Doc A/CN.4/660, paras 8ff; For evolutive interpretation, see also eg Pierre-Marie Dupuy, 'Evolutionary Interpretation of Treaties' in Enzo Cannizzaro (ed), *The Law of Treaties Beyond the Vienna Convention* (OUP 2011) 123; Osamu Inagaki, 'Evolutionary Interpretation of Treaties Re-examined: The Two-Stage Reasoning' (2015) 22 [2–3] Journal of International Cooperation Studies 127; Julien Arato, 'Subsequent Practice and Evolutive Interpretation: Techniques of Treaty Interpretation over Time and Their Diverse Consequences' (2010) 9 J Int'l L & Prac 443.

[19] *Golder* (n 18) para 29. See also Ulfstein (n 12); Sorel and Boré Eveno, Article 31(3) in Corten and Klein, *VCLT—A Commentary* (OUP 2011) 827–29; Sean D Murphy, 'The Relevance of Subsequent Agreement and Subsequent Practice for the Interpretation of Treaties' in Georg Nolte (ed), *Treaties and Subsequent Practice* (OUP 2013) 82, 87f; Alexander Orakhelashvili, *The Interpretation of Acts and Rules in Public International Law* (OUP 2008) 362.

[20] See Moeckli and White (n 3). Arguing that the Human Rights Committee favours teleological effectiveness over original intent: Başak Çali, 'Specialized Rules of Treaty Interpretation: Human Rights' in Duncan B Hollis (ed), *The Oxford Guide to Treaties* (OUP 2012) 539f.

[21] International Covenant on Civil and Political Rights (adopted 16 December 1966, entered into force 23 March 1976) 999 UNTS 171; *Judge v Canada* (2003) 8 HRC SD 85, para 10.4. See also Kerstin Mechlem, 'Treaty Bodies and the Interpretation of Human Rights' (2009) 42 Vanderbilt Journal of Transnational Law 905.

[22] This does not surprise given the differences between textualist, intentionalist, and telological approaches, which informed the debate in the drafting of Article 31 in Vienna. See Mark E Villiger, *Commentary on the 1969 Vienna Convention on the Law of Treaties* (Martinus Nijhoff 2009) 421–23.

[23] ILC, 'Report of the International Law Commission on the Work of its 63rd Session' (26 April–12 August 2011) UN Doc A/66/10, para 344.

[24] See eg, WTO, *Brazil: Export Financing Programme for Aircraft, Recourse by Canada to Article 21.5 of the DSU—Report of the Appellate Body* (21 July 2000) WT/DS46/AB/RW, para 45.

v The United Kingdom when the Court had to determine whether the extradition of Jens Soering to Virginia, where he faced the risk of exposure to the 'death row phenomenon', amounted to inhuman or degrading treatment in violation of Article 3 ECHR. The Court held that:

> [I]n interpreting the Convention regard must be had to its special character as a treaty for the collective enforcement of human rights and fundamental freedoms [...]. Thus, the object and purpose of the Convention as an instrument for the protection of individual human beings require that its provisions be interpreted and applied so as to make its safeguards practical and effective.[25]

The ILC does not give preference to either method of interpretation.[26] Instead, it is the combination of textual, teleological, contextual, and other modes of interpretation which makes it a single combined operation.[27] This operation places appropriate emphasis on the various means of interpretation outlined in Articles 31 and 32. The term 'appropriate' indicates that the application of these means of interpretation depends on each treaty and case.[28] Therefore, the weight of a particular means may vary from treaty to treaty.[29] Nevertheless, despite these variances the ILC after some debate, and in an effort to preserve the unity of international law, decided not to refer to the nature of a treaty.[30] Its approach is based on the understanding that Articles 31 and 32 VCLT provide for the general framework, which can be applied with some flexibility to various treaties. Different approaches to treaty interpretation can be accommodated within this framework.[31] This reading of the Vienna Convention also has implications for the European Court of Human Rights.[32] It gives the Court enough room to pursue its teleological approach provided that it does not lose sight of the equal value of textual and contextual analysis.

[25] *Soering v The United Kingdom* App no 14038/88 (ECtHR, 7 July 1989), para 87. For the particular nature of the European Convention, see also *Mamatkulov* (n 18) para 111.

[26] According to the ILC, there is no priority of one over other means of interpretation; ILC, 'Report of the International Law Commission on the Work of its 68th Session' (2 May–10 June and 4 July–12 August 2016) UN Doc A/71/10, Draft Commentary Conclusion no 2, para 13.

[27] ILC, 'Report of the International Law Commission on the Work of its 68th Session' (2 May–10 June and 4 July–12 August 2016) UN Doc A/71/10, Draft Commentary Conclusion no 2, para 5. See also *Golder* (n 18) para 30: unity, combined operation, same footing of the various elements of interpretation; *Banković* (n 6) para 56; *Loizidou v Turkey* (Preliminary Objections) App no 15318/89 (ECtHR, 23 March 1995), para 89.

[28] Çali argues that the European Convention requires a flexible application of Article 31 VCLT and solicits an interpretation guided by the principle of effectivity. Çali (n 20) 525–48.

[29] ILC, 'Report of the ILC on the Work of its 68th Session'(2 May–10 June and 4 July–12 August 2016) UN Doc A/71/10, Draft Commentary Conclusion no 2, para 15; ILC, 'First Report on Subsequent Agreements and Subsequent Practice' (n 18) Draft Conclusion no 1(2).

[30] ILC, 'Report of the International Law Commission on the Work of its 68th Session' (2 May–10 June and 4 July–12 August 2016) UN Doc A/71/10, Draft Commentary Conclusion no 1, para 16. For the discussion, see ILC, 'Report of the ILC on the Work of its 65th Session' Draft Commentary Conclusion no 1, para 16.

[31] See Çali (n 20) 525.

[32] For the jurisprudence of the ECtHR see, eg Mark E Villiger, 'Articles 31 and 32 of the Vienna Convention on the Law of Treaties in the Case-Law of the European Court of Human Rights' in Jürgen Bröhmer and others (eds), *Internationale Gemeinschaft und Menschenrechte—Festschrift für Georg Ress zum 70. Geburtstag* (Carl Heymanns 2005) 317.

2.2 Dynamics of treaty interpretation

As a common point of reference, Article 31 VCLT is relevant for the question of whether the meaning of a treaty can evolve over time under general international law.[33] The ILC does not take a position on the appropriateness of an evolutive approach to treaty interpretation in general.[34] The draft conclusions neither refer to terms such as 'dynamic interpretation' nor do they describe treaties as 'living instruments'. Instead, the Commission states a need for caution.[35] Any evolutive interpretation of the meaning of a term must, according to the ILC, result from the ordinary process of treaty interpretation.[36] It requires a presumed intention of the States Parties.[37] Whether a treaty was intended to be capable of evolving must be established through the various means of interpretation recognized in Articles 31 and 32.[38] Subsequent agreements and practice may be relevant for this analysis according to the draft conclusions.[39]

While this approach may serve as a theoretical ground for evolutive interpretation, in practice, the European Court of Human Rights has never engaged in a detailed examination of the intention of the Contracting States in order to establish a genuine agreement with respect to evolutive interpretation.[40] In *Tyrer v The United Kingdom,* the Court simply held that 'the Convention is a living instrument which [. . .] must be interpreted in the light of present-day conditions'.[41] This approach

[33] Taslim Olawale Elias, 'The Doctrine of Intertemporal Law' (1980) 45 AJIL 285; Ruth Higgins, 'Some Observations on the Inter-Temporal Rule in International Law' in Jerzy Makarczyk (ed), *Theory of International Law at the Threshold of the 21st Century* (Kluwer Law International 1996) 173, 174ff; Malgosia Fitzmaurice, 'Dynamic (Evolutive) Interpretation of Treaties, Part I' (2008) 21 Hague YB Int'l L 101; Giovanni Distefano, 'L' Interprétation Évolutive de la Norme Internationale' (2011) 115 [2] RGDIP 373, 384, 389ff; Dupuy (n 18), para 123, 125ff; Ulf Linderfalk, *On the Interpretation of Treaties: The Modern International Law as Expressed in the 1969 Vienna Convention on the Law of Treaties* (Springer 2007) 179–89; Richard Gardiner, *Treaty Interpretation* (OUP 2008) 252–56. See also, eg *Island of Palmas Case (Netherlands v USA)* (Award by Arbitrator Huber) (1928) 2 UNRIAA 829, 845; *Arbitration regarding the Iron Rhine ('Ijzeren Rijn') Railway (Belgium v Netherlands)* (Award) (2005) 17 UNRIAA 35, para 81; *Legal Consequences for States of the Continued Presence of South Africa in Namibia (South West Africa) notwithstanding Security Council Resolution 276 (1970)* (Advisory Opinion) [1971] ICJ Rep 16, para 53; ILC, 'Reports of the International Law Commission on the Second Part of its Seventeenth Session and its Eighteenth Session (3 January–19 July 1966)' (1966) [2] UNYBILC 220–21, para 11; ILC, 'Report of the Study Group on the Fragmentation of International Law, Finalized by Martti Koskenniemi' (13 April 2006) UN Doc A/CN.4/L.682, para 478; ILC, 'Reports of the International Law Commission on the Second Part of its Seventeenth Session and its Eighteenth Session' (3 January–19 July 1966) [2] UNYBILC 220–21, para 11.

[34] ILC, 'Report of the International Law Commission on the Work of its 68th Session' (2 May–10 June and 4 July–12 August 2016) UN Doc A/71/10 Draft Commentary Conclusion no 8, para 4.

[35] ibid para 10. [36] ibid para 8.

[37] See also Eirik Bjorge, 'The Vienna Rules, Evolutionary Interpretation, and the Intentions of the Parties' in Andrea Bianchi, Daniel Peat, and Matthew Windsor (eds), *Interpretation in International Law* (OUP 2015) 189, 203–4.

[38] ILC, 'Report of the ILC on the Work of its 68th Session' (2 May–10 June and 4 July–12 August 2016) UN Doc A/71/10 Draft Commentary Conclusion no 3, para 9.

[39] ibid, Draft Commentary Conclusion no 3. [40] Inagaki (n 18) 139.

[41] Its interpretation of the term 'degrading punishment' was therefore influenced by 'the developments and commonly accepted standards in the penal policy of the member States of the Council of Europe'. See *Tyrer* (n 6) para 31. See also Moeckli and White (n 3); ILC, 'Report of the ILC on the Work of its 68th Session' (2 May–10 June and 4 July–12 August 2016) UN Doc A/71/10 Draft Commentary Conclusion no 8, para 14.

resembles the one applied by the UN Human Rights Committee, which also applies evolutive interpretation.[42] In *Judge v Canada,* the Committee recognized 'that the protection of human rights evolves' and considered that 'the Covenant should be interpreted as a living instrument and the rights protected under it should be applied in context and in the light of present–day conditions'.[43] It recognized that a 'review of the scope of application of the rights protected in the Covenant' may be required 'if there have been notable factual and legal developments and changes in international opinion in respect of the issue raised'.[44]

Both treaty bodies presume that human rights treaties are *intended* to be capable of evolving. A prominent example of evolutive interpretation is the recognition of the right to conscientious objection, which the Committee and the European Court of Human Rights initially denied and later recognized as the result of an evolutionary development.[45] In *Yoon and Choi v Republic of Korea,* the Human Rights Committee held that the understanding of Article 18 of the Covenant, which guarantees the right to freedom of thought, conscience, and religion, 'evolves as that of any other guarantee of the Covenant over time in view of its text and purpose'. In this case, *Yeo-bum Yoon* and more than a hundred other authors, all citizens of the Republic of Korea, had been convicted for refusing to perform military service because of their beliefs as Jehovah's Witnesses. The Constitutional Court of Korea had held that the freedom of conscience, as guaranteed in Article 19 of the Korean Constitution, did not grant individuals a right to refuse military service. Hence, more than 700 conscientious objectors had been imprisoned for one and a half years. The authors brought their case to the Human Rights Committee claiming a violation of the right to freedom of conscience and religion under Article 18 International Covenant on Civil and Political Rights (ICCPR). The Committee reversed its earlier jurisprudence holding that Article 8 ICCPR does not preclude a right of conscientious objection. Taking into account the evolving understanding of Article 18 ICCPR, it recognized that the provision provides protection against being forced to act against genuinely-held religious belief.

The ECtHR followed this approach in *Bayatyan v Armenia.*[46] The author of this case had also refused to perform military service because of his beliefs as a Jehovah's Witness. His offer to do alternative civil service was rejected by state authorities on the basis that there was no law providing for such service and Mr Bayatyan was convicted for draft evasion and sentenced to imprisonment. When the case was brought to Strasbourg, the Court, in contrast to the earlier jurisprudence of the European Commission of Human Rights, recognized a right to conscientious objection to military service as falling under Article 9 ECHR, which guarantees the freedom of

[42] *Kindler v Canada* (2003) 5 HRC SD 113, para 14.2; *Judge v Canada* (n 21) para 10.3; *Barrett and Sutcliffe v Jamaica* (1992) 4 HRC SD 71, para 8.4; *Simms v Jamaica* (1995) 5 HRC SD 18, para 6.5; *Kim Jong-Cheol v Republic of Korea* (2005) UN Doc CCPR/C/84/D/968/2001, para 8.3 (Committee member Wedgwood attached a dissenting opinion, criticizing the perspective of the majority as selective (at p 10)).

[43] *Judge v Canada* (n 21) paras 10.3, 10.7.

[44] ibid para 10.3.

[45] *Yoon and Choi v Republic of Korea* (2007) 9 HRC SD 218, para 8.2.

[46] *Bayatyan v Armenia* [GC] App no 23459/03 (ECtHR, 7 July 2011) para 105.

thought, conscience, and religion. It explained its deviation from the earlier jurisprudence of the Commission inter alia with domestic legal changes of the Council of Europe (CoE) member States. The Court did so out of the fear that 'a failure by the Court to maintain a dynamic and evolutive approach would risk rendering it a bar to reform or improvement'.[47] It is noteworthy that neither the European Court of Human Rights nor the Human Rights Committee explained this evolutive interpretation on the basis of an agreement between the States Parties to reinterpret the Convention or the Covenant but only on the basis of changing *domestic* perceptions.

Whereas this progress has not been linked directly to an explicit international state consent, evolutive interpretation can nevertheless be rationalized on the basis of Article 31 VCLT.[48] It can be explained based on the object and purpose (2.2.1), the text (2.2.2), and context (2.2.3) of the Convention. These rationales overlap to a certain extent as evidenced by the following overview.

2.2.1 State practice in teleological interpretation

Progress follows in particular from the Convention's object and purpose as a living instrument.[49] The European Court in the conscientious objection case of *Bayatyan v Armenia* implicitly recognized this when it found that it had to have regard to the changing conditions in Contracting States in order to determine the scope of Article 9 ECHR and respond to any emerging consensus as to the standards to be achieved because the Convention created a system for the protection of Human Rights.[50] In other words, the intention of the Contracting States to envisage the Convention as capable of evolving can be derived from its nature as a human rights instrument, which requires its ability to adapt to changing circumstances in order to keep human rights protection effective.[51] Arguably, by creating a supervisory organ like the European Court of Human Rights, member States accepted this evolving judicial interpretation.[52] Accordingly, it is in the determination of the evolving meaning of a provision (not with respect to the intention of the Contracting States to render

[47] ibid para 98 with reference to *Vilho Eskelinen and Others v Finland* [GC] App no 63235/00 ECHR 2007-II.

[48] Bjorge argues that evolutionary interpretation is evolution intended by the parties, Eirik Bjorge, *The Evolutionary Interpretation of Treaties* (OUP 2014). According to Matscher, subsequent acceptance by States justifies evolutive interpretation under Article 31(3)(b) VCLT: Franz Matscher, 'Wie sich die 1950 in der EMRK festgeschriebenen Menschenrechte weiterentwickelt haben' in S Breitenmoser, B Ehrenzeller, M Sassòli, W Stoffel, and B Wagner Pfeifer (eds), *Human Rights, Democracy and the Rule of Law: Liber amicorum Luzius Wildhaber* (Nomos 2007) 440–41. See also Irina Buga, 'A Critical Look at the Law of Treaties: Giving Recognition to Informal Means of Treaty Adaption' in C Ryngaert, EJ Molenaar, and SMH Nouwen (eds), *What's Wrong with International Law? Liber Amicorum A.H.A. Soons* (Brill Nijhoff 2015) 232, 240–42. Other authors have argued that evolutive interpretation can be explained on the basis of 'ordinary meaning' and 'object and purpose' (Article 31(1) VCLT) as well as 'relevant rules of international law' (Article 31(3)(c) VCLT); Moeckli and White (n 3).

[49] See eg *Christine Goodwin* (n 12) para 74. The Grand Chamber held in *Demir and Baykara v Turkey* that in the consideration of the object and purpose of the Convention provisions it also takes into account common domestic law standards of European States. See *Demir* (n 12) para 76. See also Inagaki (n 18) 138–39. See also Ulfstein (n 12).

[50] *Bayatyan* (n 46) para 102. [51] See also Moeckli and White (n 3). [52] ibid.

the treaty dynamic) that the Court considers subsequent practice. The Court has explained this approach with the nature of the Convention as 'a living instrument which [...] must be interpreted in the light of present-day conditions' and that 'the Court cannot but be influenced by the developments and commonly accepted standards in the penal policy of the member States of the Council of Europe in this field'.[53] Hence, when State practice, such as national legislation, becomes relevant for the determination of the current interpretation of the Convention it informs the *modality* of adjustment rather than its terms and conditions. The consent to the widening scope of the respective provisions derives already from the original consent to the Convention as a human rights instrument. In the case of *Bayatyan v Armenia*, it was the adoption of a provision on the freedom of thought, conscience, and religion, followed by the increasing acceptance of conscientious objection in CoE States, which laid the basis for the relevant State consent.

2.2.2 State practice in textual interpretation

Apart from the Convention's object and purpose, the Court can also rely on its text to justify an evolving interpretation. The adoption of generic terms,[54] such as 'inhuman or degrading' in the text of Convention suggests that the Contracting States intended them to be receptive to evolving interpretation and to accommodate changes in the understanding of these terms.[55] As a result, State practice becomes relevant when the Court determines how a term needs to be interpreted nowadays. For example, in *Tyrer v The United Kingdom*, the Court had to evaluate whether corporal punishment is degrading. Anthony M Tyrer had been convicted at the age of 15 by a local juvenile court on the Isle of Man of an assault, which he had committed together with three others, against an older pupil at his school. In accordance with the relevant legislation, he had been sentenced to three strokes of the birch. The ECtHR found that this corporal punishment constitutes degrading punishment in violation of Article 3 ECHR. In its evaluation, the Court considered the changing perception of what is degrading as manifested 'by the developments and commonly accepted standards in the penal policy of the member States of the Council of Europe in this field'[56] and therefore found judicial corporal punishment in violation of Article 3.[57] A similar approach was taken in *Herrmann v Germany*

[53] See *Tyrer* (n 6) para 31.

[54] See also the rationale applied by the ICJ with respect to 'generic' terms as warranting an evolutive interpretation in *Dispute regarding Navigational and Related Rights (Costa Rica v Nicaragua)* (Judgment) [2009] ICJ Rep 213, paras 64–71 concerning the term 'commerce'. See also *Legal Consequences for States of the Continued Presence of South Africa in Namibia* (n 33) para 53.

[55] For this approach in other fields of international law see *Gabčíkovo-Nagymaros Project (Hungary v Slovakia)* (Judgment) [1997] ICJ Rep 7, para 104 'formulation [...] designed to accommodate change'; *Navigational and Related Rights* (n 54) para 66. See also Dupuy (n 18) para 129–31.

[56] *Tyrer* (n 6) para 31. See also *Marckx* (n 12) para 41; *Mazurek v France* App no 34406/97 (ECtHR, 1 February 2000) para 52 with reference to changed 'factual and temporal circumstances'.

[57] Arguably this is a matter of evolutive application rather than evolutive interpretation. See Marko Milanovic, 'The ICJ and Evolutionary Treaty Interpretation' (2009) EJIL: *Talk!* <http://www.ejiltalk.org/the-icj-and-evolutionary-treaty-interpretation> accessed 4 August 2017. See also the Court in

where the evolving convergence of the domestic standards with regard to mandatory hunting had an impact on the Court's interpretation of Article 1 of Protocol No. 1.[58] In these cases, the Court could rely on the general wording of the treaty, the meaning of which was informed by subsequent State practice.

The jurisprudence of the Court thus demonstrates that State practice becomes relevant for the textual and teleological interpretation of the Convention. Against this backdrop, the question of whether treaty interpretation by the European Court of Human Rights can be reconciled with general international law can be answered in the affirmative—provided that evolutive interpretation is not framed as a separate means of interpretation, but as the result of a textual and teleological interpretation in accordance with Article 31(1) VCLT.

2.2.3 State practice in contextual interpretation

State practice may also become relevant under Article 31(3) VCLT, which provides that any subsequent practice in the application of a treaty shall be taken into account in treaty interpretation, together with its context, provided that this practice establishes the agreement of the parties regarding interpretation.[59] This requires a two-prong test: First, there needs to be practice under a treaty, second, an agreement with respect to interpretation must be established. However, the VCLT does not specify how much practice is needed to establish an agreement.[60] It is therefore unclear how many States Parties need to engage in this practice, how agreement can be established, and whether State practice needs to be uniform.

The ILC study, which is based on a detailed analysis of international jurisprudence by its Special Rapporteur Georg Nolte, reveals that exigencies vary.[61] For example, the WTO Appellate Body rigidly asks for a 'concordant, common and consistent' practice in order to satisfy article 31(3)(b) of the VCLT.[62] It does so in

Marckx (n 12) para 41 where the Court stressed that the Convention must be interpreted in the light of present-day conditions.

[58] *Herrmann v Germany* [GC] App no 9300/07 (ECtHR, 26 June 2012) para 78 with reference to *Chapman v The United Kingdom*[GC] App no 27238/95 (ECtHR, 18 January 2001) para 70; *Bayatyan* (n 46) para 98. See also *Marckx* (n 12) para 41. In *VO v France* [GC] App no 53924/00 (ECtHR, 8 July 2004) para 84, however, the Court found no consensus on the nature and status of the embryo which could lead to an evolutive interpretation.

[59] See David McGrogan (n 13) 347–78; Oliver Dörr, 'Article 31' in O Dörr and K Schmalenbach (eds), *Vienna Convention on the Law of Treaties: A Commentary* (Springer 2012) 552–68; Jean-Marc Sorel and Valerie Bore-Eveno, 'Article 31' in O Corten and P Klein (eds), *Vienna Convention on the Law of Treaties: A Commentary* (OUP 2011) 825–29.

[60] For this issue, see Gardiner (n 33) 239.

[61] Georg Nolte, 'Jurisprudence of the International Court of Justice and Arbitral Tribunals of Ad Hoc Jurisdiction Relating to Subsequent Agreements and Subsequent Practice—Introductory Report for the ILC Study Group on Treaties over Time' reprinted in Georg Nolte (ed), *Treaties and Subsequent Practice* (OUP 2013) 169, 190ff; ILC, 'First Report on Subsequent Agreements and Subsequent Practice' (n 18) para 92ff; ILC, 'Second Report on Subsequent Agreements and Subsequent Practice' (26 March 2014) UN Doc A/CN.4/671, para 42ff; Georg Nolte, 'Jurisprudence Under Special Regimes Relating to Subsequent Agreements and Subsequent Practice—Second Report for the ILC Study Group on Treaties over Time' reprinted in George Nolte (ed), *Treaties and Subsequent Practice* (OUP 2013) 210, 247, 255ff, 266f, 278ff, 284f, 295, 305.

[62] *Japan: Alcoholic Beverages II* (n 18) section E.

order to establish a pattern, which implies the agreement of the parties regarding the interpretation. Arguably, this rigid approach corresponds to the nature of trade agreements. They provide for reciprocal rights and obligations of States Parties so that any changes require state consent.[63] However, the wording of Article 31 does not suggest that agreement can be established only by way of a common practice.[64] Accordingly, the ILC clarifies in its draft conclusions that the number of parties actively engaging in subsequent practice may vary if there is a common understanding regarding the interpretation of the treaty which the parties are aware of and accept.[65] Silence can constitute acceptance when the circumstances call for a reaction.[66] There is no mention of concordant, common, and consistent practice—as stipulated by the Appellate Body in *Japan: Alcoholic Beverages II*—in any of the ILC draft conclusions.

The European Court of Human Rights which typically refers to Article 31(3)(b) VCLT when it determines its relationship to member States or deals with questions of general international law, requires State practice to be *consistent*.[67] The Court has declined to adjust its interpretation of the Convention if State practice is insufficiently consolidated. An emerging consensus alone is not enough. An example is the judgment in *SH and Others v Austria* where the court was asked to determine whether the prohibition to use donated sperm or ova for *in vitro* fertilization constitutes a discrimination in regard of the right to respect for private and family life. Though the Grand Chamber acknowledged 'a clear trend in the legislation of the Contracting States towards allowing gamete donation for the purpose of in vitro fertilisation, which reflects an emerging European consensus', this emerging consensus was not based on 'settled and long-standing principles established in the law of the member States but rather reflects a stage of development within a particularly dynamic field of law and does not decisively narrow the margin of appreciation of the State [under article 8 of the Convention]'.[68] Mere trends are thus insufficient to serve as a basis for contextual interpretation.

Nevertheless, the Court does not require that the practice is common to all Contracting States. For example, in *Loizidou v Turkey* the Court relied on the fact that 'almost all' of the parties to the Convention had accepted the competence of the Court to examine complaints without restrictions *ratione loci*.[69] The applicant, a Cypriot national, complained that Turkish forces had prevented her, since the occupation in 1974, from returning to Kyrenia, a city in northern Cyprus where she

[63] For the difference between contractual and law-making treaties see Moeckli and White (n 3).

[64] For the practice of the ICJ see ILC, 'Report of the International Law Commission on the Work of its 68th Session' (2 May–10 June and 4 July–12 August 2016) UN Doc A/71/10, Draft Commentary Conclusion no 9, para 9 with reference to *Kasikili/Sedudu Island (Botswana v Namibia)* (Judgment) [1999] ICJ Rep 1045.

[65] ILC, 'Report of the International Law Commission on the Work of its 68th Session' (2 May–10 June and 4 July–12 August 2016) UN Doc A/71/10, Draft Commentary Conclusion no 10.

[66] ibid.

[67] *Cruz Varas and Others v Sweden* App no 15576/89 (ECtHR, 20 March 1991) para 100; *Loizidou* (n 27) para 73; *Banković* (n 6) para 56. See also ILC, 'First Report on Subsequent Agreements and Subsequent Practice' (n 18) para 37. See *Al-Saadoon and Mufdhi v The United Kingdom* App no 61498/08 (ECtHR, 2 March 2010) para 120; *Hassan* (n 8) para 101 on the term 'consistent'.

[68] *SH and Others v Austria* [GC] App no 57813/00(ECtHR, 3 November 2011) para 96.

[69] *Loizidou* (n 27) para 79.

owned property.[70] The Turkish government filed preliminary objections challenging the Court's jurisdiction. The government relied on two earlier declarations placing territorial limitations upon the Court's jurisdiction and argued that it had not accepted the Court's competence to examine acts outside its metropolitan territory.[71] At the time, Articles 25 and 46 ECHR required recognition of the Commission's and the Court's jurisdiction by the Respondent State. However, the Court found 'practically universal agreement' amongst the Contracting Parties that Articles 25 and 46 ECHR did not permit any territorial or substantive restrictions.[72] This 'uniform and consistent State practice' led the Court to rebut the respondent government's argument that the drafters had envisaged a different interpretation.[73] In other cases, the exigencies for State practice have been even less demanding and the Court in practice only required a number of Contracting States to be directly engaged in it.[74]

Since practice as an objective element is only one aspect of Article 31(3)(b) VCLT, it is necessary to show also the agreement of those States Parties who do not participate in the practice (voluntary element).[75] The ILC asks for a common understanding regarding the interpretation of the treaty, which *the parties are aware of and accept.*[76] According to the ILC, State Parties must have taken a position regarding the interpretation of the treaty.[77]

The ECtHR, however, does not engage in a lengthy analysis to establish the agreement of all Contracting States.[78] Neither does it examine to what extent State practice is in the application of the Convention.[79] When it relies on Article 31(3), it usually only refers to State practice without identifying a corresponding agreement between the parties.[80] Such agreement is usually presumed from practice.[81] For example in *Soering v The United Kingdom,* the Court explained that subsequent practice in national penal policy could be taken as establishing State party agreement with respect to the death penalty.[82] In other

[70] ibid para 11. [71] ibid para 55. [72] ibid para 80. [73] ibid para 82.

[74] *Hassan* (n 8) para 101. [75] Gardiner (n 33) 236.

[76] ILC, 'Report of the ILC on the Work of its 68th Session' (2 May–10 June and 4 July–12 August 2016) UN Doc A/71/10, Draft Commentary Conclusion no 10, para 1. According to the ILC, States parties must have taken a position regarding the interpretation of the treaty. ibid Draft Commentary Conclusion no 6, para 1.

[77] ibid Draft Commentary Conclusion no 6, para 1.

[78] See, eg *Soering* (n 25) para 103. See also ILC, 'Report of the ILC on the Work of its 68th Session' (2 May–10 June and 4 July–12 August 2016) UN Doc A/71/10, Draft Commentary Conclusion no 6, para 14. In *Cruz Varas v Sweden* the Court found that the practice of complying with the Court's interim measures was a matter of good-faith cooperation and not based on a 'belief that these indications gave rise to a binding obligation', *Cruz Varas* (n 67) para 100. See also Luigi Crema (n 9) 3, 10.

[79] ILC, 'First Report on Subsequent Agreements and Subsequent Practice' (n 18), para 97.

[80] ibid.

[81] An exception is *Cruz Varas v Sweden* in which the Court explained that the practice of complying with interim measures could not be explained as being based on a 'belief that these indications gave rise to a binding obligation' but rather on a matter of good-faith cooperation with the Commission. *Cruz Varas* (n 67) para 100. Later in *Mamatkulov and Askarov v Turkey*, the Court referred instead to general principles of international law, the object and purpose of the Convention ('living instrument'), and contextual arguments in order to find interim measures to be binding. See *Mamatkulov* (n 18) paras 110–27.

[82] *Soering* (n 25) para 103.

words, if there is sufficient State practice, agreement is presumed even though the practice may not be specifically related to the Convention as an international legal instrument. Another example is the judgment in *Öcalan v Turkey* where the Court referred to the almost complete abolition of the death penalty in Europe without, however, considering whether this change in domestic penal policy was in fact motivated by the Convention.[83]

Though this analysis may appear to be at odds with the exigencies of Article 31(3)(b) VCLT, there are valid reasons for this approach. In a system of multilevel human rights protection, which is first and foremost directed at domestic implementation, it would be artificial to distinguish between domestic legislation on the one hand and the implementation of the Convention on the other hand or to maintain that a measure of protection is purely domestic and not in application of the Convention. There is a valid expectation that CoE Members States are mindful of their obligations under the Convention when they legislate. Their domestic practice, therefore, can be presumed bona fide to reflect how they understand their multilevel human rights commitments.[84] Measures undertaken to protect human rights in domestic law are presumably also in application of the Convention unless there are indications to the contrary. In other words, agreement can generally be derived from practice in such cases.[85] This results from the Convention's particular character as a human rights instrument.

The ILC accepts this practice by pointing out that a position regarding the interpretation of a treaty may be inferred from the character of a treaty.[86] However, in order to presume the necessary agreement by the Contracting States, it is necessary to show that State practice is sufficiently consistent and common in these instances. The above analysis of the European Court's jurisprudence shows that it requires more than an emerging consensus. Practice needs to be shared by a plurality of the States Parties; it must be consistent in content and consolidated over time. If this is the case, State Parties' agreement can be presumed.

2.2.4 State practice as subsidiary means of interpretation

If State practice lacks the necessary agreement by all States or is insufficiently consistent and thus does not meet the threshold of Article 31(3)(b) VCLT, it can still be relevant as a subsidiary means of interpretation. As such, subsequent practice can contribute to the clarification of the meaning of a treaty if it remains within the limits of treaty interpretation.[87] This is why the European Court of Human Rights

[83] *Öcalan* (n 12) para 163 with reference to para 195 of the Chamber judgment.

[84] See also ILC, 'Report of the ILC on the Work of its 68th Session' (2 May–10 June and 4 July–12 August 2016) UN Doc A/71/10 Draft Commentary Conclusion no 6, para 14.

[85] The case is different if practice relates to procedural issues, such as derogation, and leads to a lower level of protection. See Crema (n 9) 3, 10.

[86] See ibid.

[87] ILC, 'First Report on Subsequent Agreements and Subsequent Practice' (n 18) para 107. See also ILC, 'Report of the International Law Commission on the Work of its 68th Session' (2 May–10 June and 4 July–12 August 2016) UN Doc A/71/10, Draft Commentary Conclusion no 2, para 4 and no 7, para 2.

frequently refers to subsequent practice in order to confirm an interpretation.[88] One example is the reference by the Grand Chamber to the 'vast majority' of European States recognizing in principle the right of public servants to bargain collectively in *Demir and Baykara v Turkey*.[89] The applicants were the president and a member of a Turkish trade union formed by civil servants.[90] This trade union entered into a collective agreement with a municipal council regulating all working conditions in 1993.[91] After the council failed to fulfil certain obligations, particularly financial ones, the trade union initiated civil proceedings.[92] Though the District Court acknowledged a lack of express statutory provisions in Turkish law recognizing a right for trade unions formed by civil servants to enter into collective agreements, it held that this right could be derived from international agreements, in particular the International Labour Organization (ILO) conventions, which were directly applicable in domestic law according to the Turkish constitution.[93] The Court of Cassation, however, overruled the lower court holding that the trade union had never gained legal personality because Turkish legislation did not permit civil servants to form trade unions.[94]

The European Court of Human Rights found a violation of the Convention. It recognized a right of civil servants to organize and form trade unions[95] and found support of its position 'in the practice of European States'.[96] At the same time, the Court maintained that the remaining exceptions in State practice from public officials' right to bargain collectively in certain areas or categories of civil servants could be justified by particular circumstances.[97] It explained its final holding also by reference to international instruments.[98] This is in line with its usual jurisprudence, in which the Court often relies on subsequent State practice, not alone but also on international agreements, in order to confirm a progressive reading of the Convention.

3. State Practice and Treaty Modification

When we consider the question to what extent State practice may have an impact on international treaties, interpretation in light of subsequent practice is only one aspect.[99] An additional and even more controversial issue is the question of whether treaties may be modified by way of State practice.[100] It was controversially discussed

88 See eg *Loizidou* (n 27) para 79.
89 *Demir* (n 12) para 52.
90 ibid para 14.
91 ibid para 16.
92 ibid para 17.
93 ibid para 21.
94 ibid para 29.
95 ibid para 97.
96 ibid para 98.
97 ibid para 52.
98 ibid paras 101ff. For this issue see Ulfstein (n 12).
99 See also Murphy (n 19) 82, 83ff.
100 According to Mark Villiger, State Parties as the masters of a treaty are entitled to amend, extend, or delete a text by means of State practice pursuant to Article 31(3)(b) VCLT. See Villiger (n 22) 429. But see Marcelo G Kohen, 'Keeping Subsequent Agreements and Practice in Their Right Limits' in Nolte (ed), *Treaties and Subsequent Practice* (n 19) 34, 36, 44. On this issue see also, eg Irina Buga, 'Subsequent Practice and Treaty Modification' in Dino Kritsiotis and Michael J Bowman (eds), *Conceptual and Contextual Perspectives on the Modern Law of Treaties* (CUP 2015) 13, and Irina Buga (n 48) 242–46. For the jurisprudence of the ICJ see ILC, 'Second Report on Subsequent Agreements and Subsequent Practice' (n 61), para 125 ff. *Nota bene*, modification is not always easy to distinguish

already at the Vienna Conference where the originally proposed draft Article 38 on the modification of treaties by subsequent practice was later withdrawn from the Convention.[101] The provision provided that a treaty 'may be modified by subsequent practice in the application of the treaty establishing the agreement of the parties to modify its provisions'.[102] In favour of the proposed article, the ILC cited an arbitration between France and the United States regarding a bilateral air transport services agreement.[103] The tribunal had recognized that the parties' subsequent practice was not merely a means of interpretation but a possible source of modification.[104] This holding was taken as indicating that the required agreement to any modification could in fact be established by subsequent practice.[105] Delegates at the Vienna conference argued that sovereign States were, in principle, free to act as they wished and that agreement to modification did not need to be declared formally.[106] Other delegates, however, found it inappropriate to deal with the complex relationship of customary and treaty law in a convention on the law of treaties.[107] Since subsequent practice could be considered as a means of interpretation, the proposed draft Article 38 was deemed unnecessary.[108] The main argument against the proposed rule was that any practice incompatible with a treaty generally constituted a violation rather than a new rule.[109] Practice itself seemed to be insufficient to legalize a new situation. Rather, the conclusion of a new agreement was required in order to comply with the principle of *pacta sunt servanda*.[110] In addition, several constitutional issues were raised because in some States the principle of formal parallelism required that treaty modifications followed the same procedure as the original text.[111] Modification by practice would give rise to unconstitutional modifications without parliamentary approval.[112] Low-level officials might even interpret treaties erroneously.[113] Delegates also argued that the draft Article would deprive specific provisions for revision, contained in many treaties, of their meaning.[114] Finally, modification by subsequent practice raised issues of legal certainty and security.[115]

Given this controversy, it does not surprise that the ILC's approach remains cautious even today. There is not a single sentence in its draft conclusions, which would

from interpretation. For the distinction see Gerhard Hafner, 'Subsequent Agreements and Practice: Between Interpretation, Informal Modification, and Formal Amendment' in Nolte (ed), *Treaties and Subsequent Practice* (n 19) 105, 114.

[101] See ILC, 'Report of the International Law Commission on the Work of its 18th Session' (4 May–19 July 1966) UN Doc A/CN.4/191, 236; UN Conference on the Law of Treaties 'Summary Records of the Plenary Meetings and of the Meetings of the Committee of the Whole' (Vienna 26 March–24 May 1968) (1969) UN Doc A/CONF.39/11, 207, 215. For the drafting history see Orakhelashvili (n 19) 356.

[102] (1966) II ILC Yearbook, 182.

[103] ILC, 'Report of the International Law Commission on the Work of its 18th Session' (4 May–19 July 1966) UN Doc A/CN.4/191, 236.

[104] ibid. [105] ibid.

[106] UN Conference on the Law of Treaties 'Summary Records of the Plenary Meetings and of the Meetings of the Committee of the Whole' (Vienna 26 March–24 May 1968) (1969) UN Doc A/CONF.39/11, 211.

[107] ibid 207, 209f. [108] ibid 207f., 213. [109] ibid 208.

[110] ibid 208, 210, 212f. [111] ibid 208. [112] ibid 209. [113] ibid 211.

[114] ibid 208f. [115] ibid 208.

allow States to modify a treaty by way of State practice. Instead, draft conclusion no 7(3) stipulates that the possibility of modifying a treaty by subsequent State practice has not been generally recognized and that the parties to a treaty, by a practice in the application of the treaty, presumably intend to interpret the treaty, not to amend or to modify it. According to the Special Rapporteur, international jurisprudence suggests, however, that—absent indications in the treaty to the contrary—agreed subsequent practice of the parties 'may lead' to limited treaty modification. Nevertheless, courts should try to consider State practice as an effort to interpret a treaty rather than to modify it.[116] Whether there is additional room for modification depends on the treaty and the provisions concerned.[117]

The European Court of Human Rights has not entirely ruled out the possibility of modification.[118] This issue became relevant when the Court considered the admissibility of the death penalty under the European Convention. In *Soering v The United Kingdom*, it indicated in a dictum that subsequent practice in national penal law could have the effect of abrogating the exception for the death penalty under Article 2:

> Subsequent practice in national penal policy, in the form of a generalised abolition of capital punishment, could be taken as establishing the agreement of the Contracting States to abrogate the exception provided for under Article 2 § 1 [. . .] and hence to remove a textual limit on the scope for evolutive interpretation of Article 3 [. . .] However, Protocol No. 6 [. . .], as a subsequent written agreement, shows that the intention of the Contracting Parties as recently as 1983 was to adopt the normal method of amendment of the text in order to introduce a new obligation to abolish capital punishment in time of peace and, what is more, to do so by an optional instrument allowing each State to choose the moment when to undertake such an engagement. In these conditions, notwithstanding the special character of the Convention [. . .], Article 3 [. . .] cannot be interpreted as generally prohibiting the death penalty.[119]

Though the Court ultimately followed a cautious approach because of the Protocols amending the Convention, it indicated that, in other cases, textual limits could be overcome by means of subsequent State practice. This approach was later confirmed in *Al-Saadoon and Mufdhi v The United Kingdom* despite the fact that the text usually provides a limit for evolutive interpretation.[120]

It was again confirmed in *Hassan v The United Kingdom* with respect to a procedural issue when the Grand Chamber held in respect of Article 31(3)(b) that consistent subsequent State practice 'could be taken as establishing agreement not only

[116] ILC, 'Second Report on Subsequent Agreements and Subsequent Practice' (n 61) para 142.

[117] See also ILC, 'Report of the ILC on the Work of its 68th Session' (2 May–10 June and 4 July–12 August 2016) UN Doc A/71/10, Draft Commentary Conclusion no 7, para 35.

[118] In *Cruz Varas* (n 67) para 100, the Court indicated however: 'Subsequent practice could be taken as establishing the agreement of Contracting States regarding the interpretation of a Convention provision (see, mutatis mutandis, the above-mentioned *Soering* judgment, [. . .] and Article 31 § 3 (b) of the Vienna Convention of 23 May 1969 on the Law of Treaties) but not to create new rights and obligations which were not included in the Convention at the outset.' See also *Johnston and Others v Ireland* App no 9697/82 (ECtHR, 18 December 1986) para 53. See also Bernhardt (n 3) 91–101.

[119] *Soering* (n 25) para 103.

[120] *Al-Saadoon* (n 67) para 120.

to interpret but even to modify the text of the Convention'.[121] The case was brought to the Court on behalf of an Iraqi national who had been arrested by British troops in Iraq and taken to a camp that was jointly operated by British and US troops. The respondent State requested the Court to disapply its obligations under Article 5 or to interpret them in the light of powers of detention available to it under international humanitarian law. The applicant disagreed, arguing that there had been no derogation in this case and that there could be no implied displacement of Convention rights.

The Court did not consider it harmful that the United Kingdom had not made a derogation. It noted that the practice of the High Contracting Parties was not to derogate from their obligations under Article 5 in order to detain persons on the basis of the Third and Fourth Geneva Conventions during international armed conflicts. No State had ever made a derogation in order to detain persons based on the Geneva Conventions during an international armed conflict abroad.[122] Consequently, the lack of a formal derogation did not prevent the Court from interpreting Article 5 of the Convention in line with international humanitarian law.

While I do not take issue with the outcome in this case (for somewhat different substantive reasons), the question remains whether this holding can be based on Article 31(3)(b).[123] Is it enough to consider practice by States or is it necessary to evaluate also whether other Contracting States agree? Arguably, for the modification of a treaty, agreement amongst all Contracting States cannot simply be presumed from the practice of some States. Accordingly, the partly dissenting judges criticized the holding and questioned whether the State practice was sufficient to fulfil the criteria of concordant, common, and consistent in order to modify the text of the Convention.[124]

I agree and would argue that, while it is not necessary to find concordant, common, and consistent practice in the context of textual, teleological, or contextual interpretation, the threshold for modification is higher if it leaves the realm of textual limits. Exigencies are particularly high in those cases in which State practice limits the substantive reach of the Convention.[125] If neither the text nor the purpose of the Convention provides a basis for a particular reading, it becomes even more essential to back it up by way of agreement. In other words, for the modification of a treaty, it is insufficient to consider subsequent practice alone; it is also necessary to establish a corresponding *opinio juris*, comparable to customary international law. Accordingly, Judges Caflisch, Türmen, and Kovler in their Joint Partly Dissenting Opinion in *Mamatkulov and Askarov v Turkey* maintained:

[121] *Hassan* (n 8) para 101. [122] ibid.

[123] See also Eirik Bjorge who finds it unclear whether the requisite practice was actually obtained. Bjorge (n 6) 23, 25. Lippold argues that it is not self-evident that the lack of derogations implied an interpretative statement. Lippold (n 9) 53, 83. According to Crema the crucial issue was whether the lack of a declaration was in the application of the treaty. Crema (n 9) 3, 9–10.

[124] Partly Dissenting Opinion of Judges Spano, Nicolaou, Bianku, and Kalaydjieva, *Hassan* (n 8), para 13. For a critique of the 'concordant, common and consistent' approach see Luigi Crema (n 9) 3, 12–13; Matthias Lippold (n 9) 53, 82–83.

[125] See Partly Dissenting Opinion of Judges Spano, Nicolaou, Bianku, and Kalaydjieva, *Hassan* (n 8), para 13.

while the Court is entitled to interpret the provisions of the Convention it may not—by way of interpretation [...]—write new rules into the Convention, not even if there is a fairly widespread practice in the desired sense, as long as that practice is not uniform accompanied by a corresponding *opinio juris*.[126]

4. Scaling Subsequent Practice

The analysis of the European Court of Human Rights' jurisprudence shows that subsequent practice is relevant for different aspects of treaty interpretation: as supplementary means of interpretation, as means of textual and teleological interpretation, and as a matter of context; potentially, even as a means to modify the Convention. In its interaction with different means of interpretation, State practice contributes to the clarification of the meaning of a treaty.[127] For this matter, it needs to be considered in view of the object and purpose of a human rights treaty. State practice is one element for the interpretation of the treaty but not an exclusive or necessarily decisive one.[128]

The general rules of treaty interpretation, which have been codified in Articles 31 and 32 VCLT, provide the starting point for the consideration of State practice with respect to human rights treaties. While Article 31(3)(b) VCLT explicitly refers to subsequent practice, it is not the only relevant provision for the consideration of State practice in human rights treaty interpretation. If it comes to the interpretation of substantive rights, the Court can usually rely on the wording and purpose of the European Convention in accordance with Article 31(1) VCLT. Since the Convention is intended to provide for effective human rights protection, a certain dynamic is already built into it. The Court can refer to subsequent practice in the context of its living instrument jurisprudence in order to sustain its interpretation of the evolving meaning of its terms and the changing perceptions of its scope. Thus, in the context of textual and teleological interpretation, State practice can support a particular interpretation when an evolving practice renders the protection of a particular right more effective or when it demonstrates an evolving meaning. In these cases, evolutive interpretation is the result of a textual and teleological interpretation of the Convention, while state practice informs the way in which the meaning of a right is adjusted to present-day conditions.

The normative value of State practice varies according to its respective role for treaty interpretation. For this matter, we need to distinguish between modification, ordinary, and supplementary means of interpretation. If State practice is resorted to only as a supplementary means it represents just one element to sustain a particular interpretation and thus is less significant than in those cases in which State practice is resorted to for purpose of treaty modification. This has an impact on

[126] Joint Party Dissenting Opinion by Judges Caflisch, Türmen, and Kovler, *Mamatkulov* (n 18) para 146.

[127] ILC, 'Report of the ILC on the Work of its 68th Session' (2 May–10 June and 4 July–12 August 2016) UN Doc A/71/10, Draft Conclusion no 7, para 1.

[128] See, eg *Christine Goodwin* (n 12) para 85.

the prerequisites for the density of State practice. The higher the normative value attributed to State practice, the higher are the exigencies. Its requirements can be scaled according to the following increments: If State practice is only referred to in a supplementary manner (Article 32 VCLT) in order to confirm a meaning, which is based on textual, contextual, and teleological interpretation, State practice is only complemental and does not need to be uniform because the treaty itself backs it up. If it is considered in the context of a textual or teleological interpretation (Article 31(1) VCLT), State practice needs to be sufficiently broad[129] and not at odds with the text, context, and purpose of the Convention in order to warrant evolutive interpretation.[130] This standard is relevant for the interpretation of substantive rights.

Beyond this, when an interpretation cannot be based on the text or purpose of a treaty and thus is not grounded in the fundamental consensus of the treaty itself, it is necessary to establish that practice is sufficiently consistent, consolidated over time, and shared by a plurality of Contracting States to presume the respective agreement by the Contracting States (Article 31(3)(b) VCLT).[131] This standard is relevant in particular for the interpretation of procedural rules, such as the Court's jurisdiction.

Finally, if it comes to modification, it is insufficient to presume such agreement. In cases where a reading cannot be backed up by the text, context, and purpose of the Convention, close attention is warranted not only with regard to the consistency of State practice but also with regard to the agreement of the Contracting States in order to legitimize modification. Without the relevant *opinio juris*, it is difficult to reconcile such modification with general international law. According to the conventional understanding of international law, there is a need for consent in order to bind States. With respect to treaty obligations, the primary source of consent lies in the ratification of, or the accession to, a treaty. It establishes the fundamental consensus from which interpretation derives its normative force. If a treaty is insufficiently clear, subsequent practice may convey supplementary consent if it confirms an interpretation which is nevertheless guided by the text, purpose, and context of a treaty. As such, subsequent practice translates consent. It can provide additional legitimacy to treaty interpretation and ensure acceptance thereof, if it does not diverge from the object and purpose of the treaty. With respect to treaty modification, State practice cannot rely on the fundamental consensus of the treaty as a basis of consent. It thus needs to be based on *opinio juris* like customary international law.

[129] For example in *Bayatyan v Armenia*, the Court based its holding inter alia on the fact that there was 'nearly a consensus' among CoE member States. See *Bayatyan* (n 46) para 103. See also the analysis of international jurisprudence by Arato which demonstrates that the evidentiary standards in this area are lower than for subsequent practice under Article 31(3)(b). See Arato (n 18) 476.

[130] In the 'single combined operation' of treaty interpretation, these different means of interpretation need to be considered in combination.

[131] See Article 31(3)(b) VCLT. The ILC notes in its draft conclusions that the number of parties actively engaging in subsequent practice may vary (ILC, 'Report of the ILC on the Work of its 68th Session' (2 May–10 June and 4 July–12 August 2016) UN Doc A/71/10, Draft Commentary Conclusion no 10, para 2) provided that there is a common understanding regarding the interpretation of the treaty which the parties are aware of and accept. (Draft Commentary Conclusion no 10, para 1). Silence can constitute acceptance when the circumstances call for a reaction (ibid, para 2). There is no mention of concordant, common, and consistent in the conclusions.

Based on this understanding, the two competing considerations outlined in the introduction of this chapter, the consent-based character and the State-restraining nature of the European Convention, can be reconciled. Though on first sight it appears counterintuitive to allow State practice to change or develop the meaning of a treaty that seeks to restrain State practice, such practice can claim normative value if it enhances the meaning of the Convention in the interest of increased human rights protection. If State practice is guided by a genuine commitment to the protection of human rights, both aspects, the consent-based and and the protective nature of the Convention, are mutually reinforcing. However, if this is not the case, subsequent practice is devoid of normative value. When such practice is regressive or jeopardizes the object and purpose of the Convention as an instrument for the protection of the individual, it lacks the necessary legitimacy and effect on treaty interpretation.[132]

5. Conclusion: Subsequent Practice as Catalyst

The consideration of subsequent practice in the application and interpretation of the ECHR can be accommodated within the framework of the law of treaties. It can be rationalized under the rules recognized in Articles 31 and 32 VCLT. They provide the matrix for the consideration of subsequent practice in treaty interpretation with the necessary flexibility to accommodate the particular nature of the European Convention as a human rights instrument. The object and purpose, as well as the text, demonstrate that a certain dynamic is built into the Convention as a human rights instrument, which is intended to be capable of evolving so that the protection of the individual becomes effective. Accordingly, some variances in the application of the rules of treaty interpretation can be explained by the nature of the Convention. For example, it is not necessary to demonstrate a common agreement of the Contracting States regarding the interpretation of the Convention if domestic changes commonly lead to a higher standard of protection.[133]

Whereas the European Court's dynamic interpretation has been criticized for the lack of methodological consistency, it is possible to reconcile human rights jurisprudence with the rules of interpretation set out in the VCLT. As a template, Articles 31 and 32 VCLT outline the perimeters for the interpretation of the ECHR.[134] They remind the European Court of Human Rights not to forget the equal value of textual and contextual analysis when it engages in teleological interpretation and not to frame evolutive interpretation as a separate means of interpretation but to recognize progress as the result of a textual, teleological, and contextual analysis.

The normative scale of subsequent practice, which I have outlined above, provides a theoretical frame, which can guide the Court when it refers to State practice and help to enhance its methodological consistency. It explains under what

[132] See also Nolte, 'Jurisprudence Under Special Regimes Relating to Subsequent Practice' (n 61) 254.

[133] See 2.2.3.

[134] According to Villiger, interpretation of the Convention must abide by Article 31 VCLT, see Villiger (n 32) 330.

circumstances, and to what extent, State practice is able to affect the scope and meaning of the Covenant. The exigencies vary depending on the nature of the rule and the normative value of State practice. The higher the normativity, the higher are the exigencies. The Court should be particularly cautious if it comes to treaty modification.

Once State practice meets the required standard it can sustain the legitimacy of treaty interpretation. By considering State practice in the course of its textual, teleological, and contextual interpretation, it can be a valuable source of legitimacy for the evolving scope of treaty obligations if the rules of interpretation are duly respected.[135] As such, subsequent practice can serve as a catalyst for the advancement of human rights.[136]

There is sufficient leeway for evolution within the theoretical framework outlined above. In Jefferson's terms: public international law does not require a man (or woman!) to still wear the same coat, which fitted when a child. However, clothes can serve a valuable purpose for keeping a check on weight gain. A tight fit may indicate that it is time to keep an eye on extra calories; otherwise, a garment becomes useless. It is thus the task of international jurisprudence to keep this in mind, in an effort to preserve the legitimacy and integrity of human rights treaties. However, treaties should not become straitjackets, which do not give room to breathe. A careful consideration of subsequent practice as outlined above can serve a valuable function in this undertaking.

[135] See section 4 of this chapter.

[136] Bianchi considers subsequent practice as 'a self-regulatory device where meaning is adjusted to a range of expectations and demands of the epistemic communities that control subject-specific regimes'. Bianchi (n 14) para 140.

4

Evolutive Interpretation in the Light of Other International Instruments

Law and Legitimacy

*Geir Ulfstein**

1. Introduction

Treaties can change over time through evolutive (or 'evolutionary') interpretation. Such interpretation may be based on the general rule of interpretation in the Vienna Convention on the Law of Treaties (VCLT) Article 31(1), which provides that a treaty shall be interpreted 'in accordance with the ordinary meaning to be given to the terms of the treaty in their context and in the light of its object and purpose'. Evolutive interpretation is warranted if the treaty contains terms or other indications of an *evolutive intention* of the States Parties at the time of the treaty's adoption.[1]

However, the interpretation of a treaty can also change as a result of *subsequent practice* showing 'the agreement of the parties regarding its interpretation' (VCLT Article 31(3)(b)). The reliance on subsequent practice reflects the control of the States Parties over developments in their mutual obligations. Alternatively, treaties may change as a result of *systemic interpretation*, in which other legal instruments are taken into account (Article 31(3)(c)). Such interpretation seeks to extract the intention of the parties from other international legal interaction. It also serves the comprehensiveness of international law as a legal system.

Interpretation on the basis of Article 31(1) and (3)(b) and (c) may overlap to the extent that evolutive intention is supported by subsequent practice and/or other legal instruments. But interpretation based on Article 31(3)(b) or Article 31(3)(c) need not coincide with interpretation based on the original intention of the parties. They may or may not be indicative of an evolutive interpretation, they may suggest a more or less evolutive interpretation, or they may point in different directions.

* This paper was supported by the Research Council of Norway through its Centres of Excellence Funding Scheme, project number 223274 PluriCourts—The Legitimacy of the International Judiciary.

[1] Eirik Bjorge, *The Evolutionary Interpretation of Treaties* (OUP 2014) 5.

In this chapter I discuss how the European Court of Human Rights (ECtHR) uses international instruments in its evolutive interpretation of the European Convention on Human Rights (ECHR) (section 2). I argue that the ECtHR, in its use of such instruments, goes beyond the bounds of Article 31(3)(b) (subsequent practice) and (c) (systemic interpretation) and uses them as guidance in giving effect to the original intention of the parties based on Article 31(1) (evolutive intention). However, this is not made clear in the Court's reasoning. Moreover, it prefers extensive discretion in how it should use such instruments in its evolutive interpretation. This makes the Court vulnerable to allegations of extrajudicial approaches and activism, which can threaten its legitimacy. Therefore, I propose certain guidelines for the interpretational use of international instruments (section 3). Finally, I end with some conclusions (section 4).

2. The Practice of the Court

The *Tyrer* case (1978) introduced the doctrine of the European Convention as a 'living instrument'.[2] But in this case, the Court relied on developments in member States' domestic policy in its evolutive interpretation, not on other international instruments. Reliance on domestic, rather than international, legal instruments has become a prominent part of the Court's evolutive interpretation based on 'European consensus'.[3]

However, in the *Marckx* case one year later, the Court used, in addition to developments in domestic law of the member States, two conventions, ie the Brussels Convention on the Establishment of Maternal Affiliation of Natural Children and the European Convention on the Legal Status of Children Born out of Wedlock. Despite the limited number of States Parties to the conventions, the Court stated that 'there is a clear measure of common ground in this area amongst modern societies'.[4]

In the *Goodwin* case (2002), the Court attached:

> less importance to the lack of evidence of a common European approach to the resolution of the legal and practical problems posed, than to the clear and uncontested evidence of a continuing international trend in favour not only of increased social acceptance of transsexuals but of legal recognition of the new sexual identity of post-operative transsexuals.[5]

The Court did not specify which international material was of importance, or why. But the case is interesting in its reliance on what the Court described as an international trend rather than on a European consensus.

The Court has also addressed the significance of international instruments and practice in other cases. For example, on the abolition of the death penalty in the *Soering* case [Plenary] (1989),[6] on reservations regarding the territorial application

[2] *Tyrer v The United Kingdom* App no 5856/72 (ECtHR, 25 April 1978) para 31.

[3] Kanstantsin Dzehtsiarou, *European Consensus and the Legitimacy of the European Court of Human Rights* (CUP 2015).

[4] *Marckx v Belgium* App no 6833/74 (ECtHR, 13 June 1979) para 41.

[5] *Christine Goodwin v The United Kingdom* [GC] App no 28957/95 (ECtHR, 11 July 2002) para 85 (emphasis added).

[6] *Soering v The United Kingdom* App no 14038/88 (ECtHR, 7 July 1989).

of the ECHR in the *Loizidou* case (1995),[7] and on the legal status of interim measures in the *Mamatkulov and Askarov* [Grand Chamber] case (2005).[8] However, in the case of *Demir and Baykara*[9] (2008), the Court devoted a full section to 'The practice of interpreting Convention provisions in the light of other international texts and instruments'.[10] I will therefore discuss this case and subsequent case law in more detail.

The applicants claimed in *Demir and Baykara* that Article 11 ECHR was violated because Turkey had denied them the right to form trade unions, to engage in collective bargaining, and to enter into collective agreements. The Court started by saying in its subsection entitled '(a) Basis' that it is 'guided mainly by the rules of interpretation provided for in Articles 31 to 33 of the Vienna Convention on the Law of Treaties'.[11] This is followed by the standard formulation that '[s]ince the Convention is first and foremost a system for the protection of human rights, the Court must interpret and apply it in a manner which renders its rights practical and effective, not theoretical and illusory'. It is worth noting that the Court felt a need to qualify the application of the VCLT Articles 31 to 33 both by using the term 'mainly' and by adding that the ECHR should be interpreted in a way that renders it 'practical and effective'.

The Court said that it 'has never considered the provisions of the Convention [the ECHR] as the sole framework of reference for the interpretation of the rights and freedoms enshrined therein'.[12] When it comes to the use of other instruments, the Court did not mention VCLT Article 31(3)(b). It referred to its case law, but stated rather undecidedly: 'see *also* Article 31 § 3 (c) of the Vienna Convention'.[13] Finally, the Court explained that in determining the 'living' nature of the Convention, it has 'taken account of evolving norms of national *and* international law'.[14] It is interesting to note that no distinction is made between national and international norms, and that the combined set of norms seems to be a separate basis for an evolutive interpretation, which reaches beyond the use of subsequent practice according to VCLT Article 31(3)(b) and systemic interpretation based on VCLT Article 31(3)(c).

In the next subsection of the judgment, '(b) Diversity of international texts and instruments used for the interpretation of the Convention', the Court divided its discussion into two parts: (i) General international law, and (ii) Council of Europe (CoE) instruments. In the first part, the Court referred to the relevance of global conventions, specialized international treaties, general principles of law, and peremptory norms. As regards CoE instruments, the Court said that it also has taken into account non-binding CoE instruments from the Committee of Ministers and the Parliamentary Assembly, as well as from other CoE organs, even if they are not representing States Parties (such as specialized organs like the Venice Commission and treaty bodies like the European Committee for the Prevention of Torture and

[7] *Loizidou v Turkey* (Preliminary Objections) App no 15318/89 (ECtHR, 23 March 1995).

[8] *Mamatkulov and Askarov v Turkey* [GC] App nos 46827/99 and 46951/99 (ECtHR, 4 February 2005).

[9] *Demir and Baykara v Turkey* [GC] App no 34503/97 (ECtHR, 12 November 2008).

[10] ibid paras 65–86.

[11] ibid para 65.

[12] ibid para 67.

[13] ibid (emphasis added).

[14] ibid para 68 (emphasis added).

Inhuman and Degrading Treatment or Punishment (CPT)). In subsection (iii) 'Consideration by the Court', it emphasized that it has never distinguished between sources of law ratified or not by the respondent state, and that it has also relied on non-binding instruments.

In the final section '4. Conclusions' the Court stated:

> 85. The Court, in defining the meaning of terms and notions in the text of the Convention, can and must take into account *elements of international law* other than the Convention, the *interpretation of such elements by competent organs*, and *the practice of European States reflecting their common values*. The *consensus emerging* from *specialised international instruments* and from the *practice of Contracting States* may constitute a relevant consideration for the Court when it interprets the provisions of the Convention in specific cases.
>
> 86. In this context, it is *not necessary for the respondent State to have ratified* the entire collection of instruments that are applicable in respect of the precise subject matter of the case concerned. It will be sufficient for the Court that *the relevant international instruments* denote a *continuous evolution* in the norms and principles applied in *international law* or in the *domestic law of the majority of member States* of the Council of Europe and show, in a precise area, that there is *common ground in modern societies* [. . .].[15]

The emphasized terms indicate that the Court does not distinguish between the significance of international instruments and the domestic law of member States. What is important for the Court is that the practice shows that there is common ground in modern societies—this is not explicitly limited to member States. The Court also emphasizes interpretations applied by 'competent organs', but without distinguishing between different kinds of organs, such as between international courts and supervisory organs. Finally, the respondent State does not need to have ratified the relevant international legal instrument.

This leaves the Court with a rather open-ended list of what it can take into consideration, without any reasoning for why these elements are of significance, or a prioritization between the relevant elements, or an indication of how these elements should be used.

I will examine to what extent the Court in its later case law has acknowledged the relevance of the VCLT for the interpretation of the ECHR (section 2.1), as well as the significance of, respectively, the member States' subsequent practice (section 2.2), and a systemic interpretation (section 2.3) in the Court's evolutive interpretation.

2.1 The Vienna Convention on the Law of Treaties

The Court has constantly confirmed the relevance of the Vienna Convention for the interpretation of the ECHR. But, as in *Demir and Baykara*, the significance of the

[15] ibid (emphasis added).

VCLT has been subject to qualifications. For example, in *Rantsev* (2010), the Court stated that the ECHR must be interpreted *in the light of* the VCLT.[16]

Hassan [Grand Chamber] (2014) has more robust wording, saying that 'the *starting point* for the Court's examination must be its constant practice of interpreting the Convention in the light of the rules set out in the Vienna Convention on the Law of Treaties'.[17] Even stronger expressions are used in *Cyprus v Turkey* [Grand Chamber] (2014):

> The Court reiterates that the provisions of the Convention cannot be interpreted and applied in a vacuum. *Despite its specific character* as a human rights instrument, the Convention is an international treaty to be interpreted *in accordance with* the relevant norms and principles of public international law, and, *in particular*, in the light of the Vienna Convention on the Law of Treaties of 23 May 1969 (the 'Vienna Convention').[18]

The *Al-Dulimi* case [Grand Chamber] (2016) uses a wording identical to that of *Cyprus v Turkey*.[19]

This seems to settle that there is no contradiction between the ECHR as a human rights instrument and its interpretation on the basis of accepted canons of interpretation in general international law in which the Vienna Convention has a particular role. Consequently, the concerns expressed in earlier case law, including in *Demir and Baykara*, about applying a method of interpretation to ensure that the ECHR is 'practical and effective' can be accommodated within the bounds of the Vienna Convention, which is generally seen as expressing customary international law.[20] But the next question is how the Court uses VCLT Article 31(3)(b) and (c) in its evolutive interpretation.

2.2 The Vienna Convention Article 31(3)(b)

The Vienna Convention Article 31(3)(b) on subsequent practice is only relevant to the extent that other international instruments can be seen as 'application of the treaty which establishes the *agreement* of the parties regarding its interpretation' (emphasis added). But such agreement need not take the form of a subsequent treaty and does not necessarily need to be binding.[21] Nor does it need participation of all parties as long as their agreement on the interpretation is sufficiently clear.[22]

The ECtHR generally recognizes the significance of Article 31(3)(b)—although it was not even mentioned in *Demir and Baykara*. In *Hassan*, the Court said that

[16] *Rantsev v Cyprus and Russia* App no 25965/04 (ECtHR, 7 January 2010) para 273.

[17] *Hassan v The United Kingdom* [GC] App no 29750/09 (ECtHR 16 September 2014) para 100 (emphasis added).

[18] *Cyprus v Turkey* [GC] App no 25781/94 (ECtHR, 12 May 2014) para 23 (emphasis added).

[19] *Al-Dulimi and Montana Management Inc v Switzerland* [GC] App no 5809/08 (ECtHR, 21 June 2016) para 134.

[20] See Başak Çali, 'Specialized Rules of Treaty Interpretation: Human Rights' in Duncan B. Hollis (ed), *The Oxford Guide to Treaties* (OUP 2012) 537; Bjorge (n 1) 6.

[21] ILC, Georg Nolte, Special Rapporteur, 'Second report on subsequent agreements and subsequent practice in relation to treaty interpretation' (26 March 2014) UN Doc A/CN.4/671, para 56.

[22] ibid para 60.

'in respect of the criterion set out in Article 31 § 3 (b) of the Vienna Convention […], the Court has previously stated that a consistent practice on the part of the High Contracting Parties, subsequent to their ratification of the Convention, could be taken as establishing their agreement not only as regards interpretation but even to modify the text of the Convention'.[23] This case illustrates that subsequent practice can establish the agreement between the parties on an evolutive interpretation. It also demonstrates the gradual connection between evolutive interpretation and amendment through practice.

In this case, the Court referred to the practice of the States Parties not to derogate from Article 5 on detention in order to detain persons on the basis of the Third and Fourth Geneva Conventions during international armed conflicts.[24] However, the Court did not find this practice determinative. It rather relied on a systemic interpretation on the basis of international humanitarian law in its restrictive interpretation of the ECHR (see section 2.3).

The *Al-Saadoon and Mufdhi* case (2010) is made interesting by the fact that the Court held that subsequent practice had modified the ECHR. The Court concluded that the internal legislation by the States Parties and their acceptance on Protocols Nos. 6 and 13 on the abolition of the death penalty meant that the wording of Article 2 of the ECHR on allowing this penalty did not any longer prevent the death penalty from being regarded as inhuman or degrading treatment under Article 3.[25] Hence, the ECHR was considered modified on the basis of a combination of domestic law and international instruments in the form of Protocols Nos. 6 and 13.

However, this use of the subsequent practice is exceptional. The Court regularly uses both domestic law and international instruments as a basis for evolutive interpretation far beyond the requirements of Article 31(3)(b).[26] Rather than determining whether there is *agreement* among the States Parties on an interpretation based on Article 31(3)(b), the Court has, based on *both* domestic law and international instruments, assessed whether there exists a European consensus on the appropriate human rights standard.[27] Consensus has been defined as consisting of a practice by a *majority* of the member States.[28] Such consensus is used to give effect to the evolutive intention of the States Parties based on Article 31(1).

2.3 The Vienna Convention Article 31(3)(c)

Article 31(3)(c) on systemic interpretation through taking into account '[a]ny relevant rules of international law applicable in the relations between the parties' raises

[23] *Hassan* (n 17) para 101. [24] ibid.

[25] *Al-Saadoon and Mufdhi v The United Kingdom* App no 61498/08 (ECtHR, 2 March 2010) para 120. Article 2(1) reads: 'Everyone's right to life shall be protected by law. *No one shall be deprived of his life* intentionally *save in the execution of a sentence of a court* following his conviction of a crime for which this penalty is provided by law' (emphasis added).

[26] ILC, Georg Nolte, Special Rapporteur, 'First report on subsequent agreements and subsequent practice in relation to treaty interpretation' (19 March 2013) UN Doc A/CN.4/660, para 37 (footnotes omitted, emphasis added).

[27] Dzehtsiarou (n 3) 38. [28] ibid 9.

both issues about what should be considered 'relevant rules of international law' and which rules are 'applicable in the relations between the parties'. As regards the first question, the rules can be found in treaties and customary international law, and possibly in general principles of law as reflected in Article 38 of the Statute of the International Court of Justice. It is more debatable to what extent non-binding instruments are also included.[29]

Difficult questions may arise if the membership of the other instruments does not cover all parties to the treaty being interpreted. A panel of the World Trade Organization's dispute settlement system required that the parties to the treaty under interpretation also needed to be bound by the other international instrument.[30] But several alternative interpretations are possible, including interpreting Article 31(3)(c) as meaning that all parties to the relevant treaty must at least implicitly have accepted the external rule to be applied in the interpretation.[31]

The ECtHR has generally expressed its commitment to interpreting the ECHR consistently with other international instruments. In *Demir and Baykara*, the Court only made a passing reference to Article 31(3)(c). But in the *Tănase* case [Grand Chamber] (2010), the Court said that it '*must* take into account relevant international instruments and reports, and *in particular* those of other Council of Europe organs'.[32] In the *Neulinger and Shuruk* case [Grand Chamber] (2010), the Court noted that 'there is currently a *broad consensus*—including in international law—in support of the idea that in all decisions concerning children, their best interests must be paramount'.[33] The Court stated in the *National Union* case (2014) that account should be taken of Article 31(3)(c) and that this applies '*in particular* [to] the rules concerning the international protection of human rights'.[34] It also referred to 'any international *consensus* reflected in the apposite instruments'.[35]

The *Hassan* case is remarkable as it provides a rare example of the Court feeling compelled towards a restrictive interpretation of the ECHR on the basis of other international instruments. The Court emphasized that it 'has made it clear on many occasions that the Convention *must* be interpreted in harmony with other rules of international law' and furthermore that '[t]he Court *must endeavour* to interpret and apply the Convention in a manner which is consistent with the framework under international law delineated by the International Court of Justice'.[36] In this case, the Court tried—as best as possible—to accommodate the ECHR Article 5 and the Third and Fourth Geneva Conventions on detention, but without allowing more restrictions on the ECHR than necessary. This case also shows the ECtHR's respect

[29] Richard K Gardiner, *Treaty Interpretation* (OUP 2008) 307.

[30] *European Communities—Measures Affecting the Approval and Marketing of Biotech Products*, Reports of the Panel, 29 September 2006, WT/DS291/R, WT/DS292/R, WT/DS293/R at 333, para 7.68 (footnotes omitted).

[31] Gardiner (n 29) 275.

[32] *Tănase v Moldova* [GC] App no 7/08 (ECtHR, 27 April 2010) para 176 (emphasis added).

[33] *Neulinger and Shuruk v Switzerland* [GC] App no 41615/07 (ECtHR, 6 July 2010) para 135 (emphasis added).

[34] *National Union of Rail, Maritime and Transport Workers v The United Kingdom* App no 31045/10 (ECtHR, 8 April 2014), para 76 (emphasis added).

[35] ibid para 86 (emphasis added).

[36] *Hassan* (n 17) para 102 (emphasis added).

for the practice of the International Court of Justice. Four partly dissenting judges held, however, that the Court should have given priority to the ECHR in this conflict with international humanitarian law.[37]

Hassan shows that other international instruments can have decisive importance in the interpretation of the ECHR. However, it is worth noting that this case concerns restrictive interpretation of the Convention, not an evolutive interpretation.

There are several cases concerning evolutive interpretation in which the Court does *not* discuss the content and limits of Article 31(3)(c). In *Rantsev*, the Court referred both to practice by the International Criminal Tribunal for the former Yugoslavia (ICTY) and to the Protocol to Prevent, Suppress and Punish Trafficking in Persons, especially Women and Children (the Palermo Protocol) and the European Convention on Action against Trafficking in Human Beings (the Anti-Trafficking Convention) in its interpretation of slavery, servitude, or forced and compulsory labour under Article 4.[38] But it did not explain the importance of these instruments and the judicial practice for the interpretation of the ECHR. Instead, it seems that the Court preferred to keep the influence of such instruments extremely vague and to allow itself absolute discretion. Such discretion is explicitly confirmed by the *Tănase* (2010) and the *Kiyutin* (2011) cases. In both cases, the Court said: 'It is for the Court to decide which international instruments and reports it considers relevant and how much weight to attribute to them.'[39]

The freedom of the Court has been recently confirmed in the *A-MV v Finland* case (2017).[40] Under the heading 'Recapitulation of general principles', the Court establishes its understanding of the relevance of other international legal instruments and recapitulates the formulation in *Tănase* and *Kiyutin*:

> Furthermore, the Court reiterates its consistent practice according to which the Court *takes into account relevant international instruments and reports* in order to interpret the guarantees of the Convention and to establish whether there is a *common standard* in the field concerned. *It is for the Court to decide which international instruments and reports it considers relevant and how much weight to attribute to them* (see *Tănase v. Moldova* [GC], no. 7/08, § 176, ECHR 2010; and *Demir and Baykara v. Turkey* [GC], no. 34503/97, §§ 85-86, ECHR 2008). In the present case, the Court *considers relevant* the United Nations Convention on the Rights of Persons with disabilities (see paragraphs 39–41 above), having also regard to the interpretation given by the UN Committee (see paragraphs 42–45 above), as well as the related recommendations, resolutions and strategy statements adopted by the Council of Europe bodies (see paragraphs 46–48 above).[41]

The Court sets out that the United Nations Convention on the Rights of Persons with Disabilities and interpretations by the UN Committee are relevant, but includes also non-binding 'recommendations, resolutions and strategy statements' by CoE bodies. It does not provide any reasons for why these instruments and interpretations are selected, nor is any distinction made between binding and

[37] ibid para 19. [38] *Rantsev* (n 16) paras 278–80.
[39] *Tănase* (n 32) para 176; *Kiyutin v Russia* App no 2700/10 (ECtHR, 10 March 2011) para 67.
[40] *A-MV v Finland* App no 53251/13 (ECtHR, 23 March 2017).
[41] ibid para 74 (emphasis added).

non-binding instruments, and nothing is said about the weight accorded to the different instruments.

It can be concluded that the Court recognizes the need for systemic interpretation based on VCLT Article 31(3)(c). *Hassan* is the exception in the sense that the Court felt compelled to a restrictive interpretation based on other international instruments. But generally the Court has emphasized its discretion in selecting the relevant instruments and in according weight to such instruments. It seems clear that the Court feels that it is not inhibited by the bounds of Article 31(3)(c) in its evolutive interpretation. The Court will go beyond Article 31(3)(c) if it deems it desirable, based on the evolutive intention of the member States under Article 31(1).

3. Evaluation of the Court's Practice

The ECtHR has recognized, albeit somewhat hesitantly in its earlier case law, that the ECHR's character as a human rights treaty does not prevent the application of general principles of treaty interpretation as reflected in the VCLT. This means that it acknowledges the relevance of Article 31(1) (evolutive intention), as well as Article 31(3)(b) (subsequent practice) and (c) (systemic interpretation), for its evolutive interpretation.

But the Court rarely discusses whether the requirements set out in Article 31(3)(b) and (c) are fulfilled in the relevant cases. Exceptions are *Al-Saadoon and Mufddhi* in which the Court relied on Protocols Nos. 6 and 13 on abolition of the death penalty (31(3)(b)), and *Hassan* in which the Court relied on the Third and Fourth Geneva Conventions (31(3)(c)). Nor does it generally clarify when it uses international instruments as guidance for the evolutive intention of State Parties based on Article 31(1), as opposed to use of, respectively, Article 31(b) and (c). But what is clear is that the Court goes beyond the bounds of Article 31(3)(b) and (c) in its evolutive interpretation. This means that, in practice, Article 31(1) is by far the most important basis for the Court's use of international instruments in its evolutive interpretation.

Applying international instruments in the interpretation of the ECHR without the constraints of Article 31(3)(b) and (c) leaves considerable freedom to the Court. Indeed, it has, as demonstrated in the *Tănase, Kiyutin,* and *A-MV* cases, insisted on its freedom to decide which instruments to use and the weight they should be accorded. But such freedom means that the Court can be accused of being an activist court which bases its decisions on extralegal factors.[42] This may undermine its legitimacy in a situation in which the Court is criticized by some States for going too far in its expansive interpretation. Ultimately, it may result in unwillingness by States to comply with the Court's judgments. This raises the question of why and how international instruments should guide the Court in giving effect to the evolutive intention of the parties based on Article 31(1).

[42] See Ragnar Nordeide, *The Interaction between the European Convention on Human Rights (ECHR) and Other International Law: What Role for a Purposive Conception of the ECHR?* (Faculty of Law, University of Oslo, 2015) 285 [available at the University Library, Oslo].

One reason for relying on international instruments is that such practice represents objective factors, rather than the Court's subjective assessment or its own 'moral reading' of the Convention.[43] This promotes foreseeability as an aspect of the rule of law. It does not mean that the relevance of international instruments is objective in the sense that their use is without interpretational challenges. But their use is comparatively more objective than leaving complete discretion to the Court itself.

Another reason for giving effect to international instruments in evolutive interpretation is that member States are the 'masters of the treaty'. They have adopted the ECHR, they can make formal amendments, and they can formally abolish it. It is consonant with the consensual character of the ECHR that the practice of States in the form of international instruments is accorded interpretational weight in giving effect to the evolutive intention of the member States.

But while Article 31(3)(b) and (c) contains restrictions on which practice and rules can be taken into account, the question arises about what should control evolutive intention based on Article 31(1).

First, the Court should in each case make clear what follows from Article 31(3)(b) and (c), and what is an interpretation based on the original evolutive intention under Article 31(1). This would, to a greater extent, ensure that the restrictions contained in Article 31(3)(b) and (c) are respected. It would also challenge the Court to explain how it uses Article 31(1) in its evolutive interpretation.

The Court collapses evolutive interpretation based on European consensus in domestic law and that found in the form of international legal instruments. But while developments in national legislation indicate the attitudes of member States on rights protection as an aspect of domestic law, it does not necessarily establish a basis for assessing their views on their international obligations. Therefore, developments in domestic law and practice in the form of international instruments should be distinguished. Furthermore, to the extent international instruments express the view of ECHR State Parties on relevant international obligations, they should be accorded greater value than developments in the domestic law of member States.

When it comes to the weight accorded to different kinds of international instruments, a distinction should be made between binding and non-binding instruments. Both binding and non-binding instruments may give guidance in the evolutive interpretation of the ECHR. This is also reflected in *Demir and Baykara*. But, generally, binding instruments should be accorded more weight as expressions of a firmer commitment by member States.

A distinction between regional and global instruments is also set out in *Demir and Baykara*. Treaties, decisions, and recommendations adopted by the representative organs of the CoE, ie the Parliamentary Assembly and the Committee of Ministers, should carry special weight as expressions of the views of ECHR State Parties. Other

[43] See on a moral reading of the ECHR: George Letsas, 'The ECHR as a Living Instrument: Its Meaning and Legitimacy' in Andreas Føllesdal, Birgit Peters, and Geir Ulfstein (eds), *Constituting Europe: the European Court of Human Rights in a National, European and Global Context* (CUP 2013) 106–42. See also Malgosia Fitzmaurice, 'Dynamic (Evolutive) Interpretation of Treaties Part II' in *Hague Yearbook of International Law* (Brill 2009) 16.

international instruments can also give guidance. But the Court should give special emphasis to the support by European member States for such instruments.

More weight should be given to international instruments commanding widespread support among ECHR parties. But the Court should avoid using the term 'consensus' in this respect. This term gives connotations to practice as an informal agreement between the States Parties as required by Article 31(3)(b). Nor should it be required that the instruments are accepted by a majority of the States. The weight should correspond to the number of European ratifications or other means of support. Moreover, the fact that the instruments have been ratified by the respondent State should not be given much weight as a manifestation of the general evolutive interpretation of States Parties.

However, there may be situations in which the ECtHR should *not* respect the practice by European States as expressed in international legal instruments. Such instruments can indicate a static while more precise interpretation, or even retrogressive interpretation, eg in weighing the need for counterterrorism measures as opposed to the protection of human rights. The Court has the responsibility to uphold certain minimum requirements of human rights protection based on the Convention, even when this goes against the policy of one or more of the parties. This must be ensured by the Court whether or not some, or even a considerable number, of States accept international instruments threatening the ECHR human rights standards.

4. Conclusions

The Court has acknowledged that the ECHR should be interpreted on the basis of the principles set out in the VCLT. But the ECtHR should be clearer about the legal basis for the application of international instruments in its evolutive interpretation: is it based on the original evolutive intention of States Parties under Article 31(1) or, respectively, Article 31(3)(b) (subsequent practice) or (c) (systemic interpretation)?

This uncertainty leaves too much discretion to the ECtHR. The Court risks allegations of going beyond its legal mandate and being an activist court. There is also a danger that States may be unwilling to implement judgments which are seen as legally unpersuasive. I have instead argued that the Court should make its use of international legal instruments as part of Article 31(3)(b) and (c) clear, but also how it uses such instruments in its evolutive interpretation based on Article 31(1). The use of these instruments in giving effect to the evolutive intention based on Article 31(1) means not only that the Court would be guided by some objective factors, rather than its subjective preferences, it also means that States—as masters of the ECHR—influence the interpretation of the European Convention.

The Court has applied developments in European domestic law as a basis for its evolutive interpretation. European support of international instruments may be an even better indication of the commitment of the member States to developments in international obligations. There is, however, a need to specify why such material is used, which material is of interest, and how much weight different instruments should be accorded.

International instruments should generally be accorded more weight than developments in the domestic law of member States. Such instruments adopted by the European States should be given special weight. It should not be required that these instruments are legally binding or that they have been ratified by the respondent State. But binding instruments should generally be given more weight as an expression of deeper commitment by the States. However, the Court may, in upholding certain minimum human rights standards, choose not to apply the solutions found in international instruments—whether or not they are supported by European States.

PART III

JURISDICTION

5

Jurisdiction and Responsibility

Trends in the Jurisprudence of the Strasbourg Court

Marko Milanovic

1. Introduction

This chapter will examine the overarching trends in the jurisprudence of the European Court of Human Rights (ECtHR) on questions of state jurisdiction in the sense of Article 1 of the European Convention on Human Rights (ECHR)[1] and state responsibility, after its seminal judgment in the *Al-Skeini* case.[2] While the chapter makes no claim to comprehensiveness of coverage, it will first discuss the threshold question of the extraterritorial applicability of human rights treaties, and analyse the relationship between the notions of jurisdiction and responsibility. It will then look at the issue of the relationship between human rights and international humanitarian law and the European Court's judgment in *Hassan v The United Kingdom*.[3] This chapter's main thesis is that the Court is growing increasingly comfortable with applying the Convention extraterritorially and in armed conflict, as well as in directly invoking rules of international humanitarian law. However, a number of important caveats and uncertainties remain in the Court's jurisprudence, a number of which will inevitably be at issue in important cases currently pending or soon to be pending before it.

2. Article 1 Jurisdiction: Two Basic Models of Extraterritorial Application

The European Court and other human rights bodies have produced an extensive body of case law on the extraterritorial application of human rights treaties.[4]

[1] Providing that the 'High Contracting Parties shall secure to everyone within their jurisdiction the rights and freedoms defined [in the] Convention'.

[2] *Al-Skeini and others v The United Kingdom* [GC] App no 55721/07 (ECtHR, 7 July 2011). See also M Milanovic, '*Al-Skeini* and *Al-Jedda* in Strasbourg' (2012) 23 EJIL 121.

[3] *Hassan v The United Kingdom* [GC] App no 29750/09 (ECtHR, 16 September 2014).

[4] See generally F Coomans and M Kamminga (eds), *Extraterritorial Application of Human Rights Treaties* (Intersentia 2004); M Gibney and S Skogly, *Universal Human Rights and Extraterritorial*

The European Court's case law in particular has been the most rich and varied, but also one plagued with inconsistencies and uncertainties. In *Al-Skeini*, the Court took to heart much of the criticism levied against some of its earlier cases, most of all *Banković*,[5] in which the Court controversially held that the ECHR would not apply to situations of aerial bombing outside the borders of the State using force, and tried to set its conceptual approach on a sounder footing. It thus reaffirmed and clarified the two basic models of state jurisdiction: the spatial model (jurisdiction as effective overall control by a State over an area or territory)[6] and the personal model (jurisdiction as an exercise of authority or control by State agents over an individual).[7]

In particular, the Court in *Al-Skeini* departed from the *Banković* position that the application of the Convention is an all or nothing proposition, holding that 'whenever the State, through its agents, exercises control and authority over an individual, and thus jurisdiction, the State is under an obligation under Article 1 to secure to that individual the rights and freedoms under Section I of the Convention that are relevant to the situation of that individual. In this sense, therefore, the Convention rights can be "divided and tailored"'.[8] With respect to both models, the Court emphasized their *factual* nature, as encapsulated in the notion of control. It resolved the case by holding that all six applicants in that case—who were killed in varying circumstances by British troops in Iraq—were within the UK's jurisdiction by virtue of the personal model.[9] However, the Court also introduced a significant level of uncertainty into its analysis of the personal model—uncertainty that it needed to prevent that model from collapsing, since it is essentially not limitable by reference to any non-arbitrary principle. It emphasized the 'exceptional' nature of the British mission in Iraq, and pointed to nebulously defined 'public powers' that the UK was exercising there. At least at first glance, the implication of this analysis was that the mere fact that an individual is killed by a State acting extraterritorially would not, without more, constitute jurisdiction under the personal model.[10]

The Court thus managed to partially overrule *Banković* while maintaining its final result and some of its misguided conceptual foundations, such as the insistence

Obligations (University of Pennsylvania Press 2010); M Gondek, *The Reach of Human Rights in a Globalising World: Extraterritorial Application of Human Rights Treaties* (Intersentia 2009); M Milanovic, *Extraterritorial Application of Human Rights Treaties: Law, Principles, and Policy* (OUP 2011); K da Costa, *The Extraterritorial Application of Selected Human Rights Treaties* (Nijhoff 2012); G Grisel, *Application extraterritoriale du droit international des droits de l'homme* (Helbing Lichtenhahn 2010). Among dozens of scholarly articles, see esp J Cerone, 'Jurisdiction and Power: The Intersection of Human Rights Law and the Law of Non-International Armed Conflict in an Extraterritorial Context' (2007) 40 Israel Law Review 72; R Wilde, 'Triggering State Obligations Extraterritorially: The Spatial Test in Certain Human Rights Treaties' (2007) 40 Israel Law Review 503; A-M Baldovin, 'Impact de la Jurisprudence Récente de la Cour Européenne des droits de l'Homme sur la Planification et l'Exécution des Opérations Militaires à Venir: Application Extraterritoriale de la Convention, Imputabilité des Faits des Troupes et Fragmentation du Droit International' (2011) 50 Revue de Droit Militaire et de Droit de la Guerre 369.

[5] *Banković and Others v Belgium and Others* (Dec) [GC] App no 52207/99 (ECtHR, 12 December 2001).

[6] *Al-Skeini* (n 2) paras 138–39. [7] ibid paras 133–37.

[8] ibid para 137. [9] ibid para 149.

[10] See more Milanovic (n 2).

that the concept of State jurisdiction in Article 1 of the Convention stems from the grounds of prescriptive jurisdiction in general international law, when in fact the two are categorically different in kind.[11] While a significant improvement upon *Banković*, *Al-Skeini* left many doors open—perhaps too many. Thus, for example, after the judgment, the UK government argued that it was confined to the specific facts of Iraq, and that the Convention largely does not apply to UK activities in Afghanistan.[12]

3. A More Factual and Expansive Approach to Extraterritoriality

In the years after *Al-Skeini*, the European Court has demonstrated a trend towards a clearer, more factual, and, most importantly, more *expansive* approach towards the question of the Convention's extraterritorial application and the interpretation of the jurisdiction clause in Article 1. It has done so with regard to both the spatial and the personal tests outlined above. For example, when it comes to the spatial model, in *Chiragov and Others v Armenia*, the Court found by fourteen votes to three that Armenia exercised effective control over the area of Nagorno-Karabakh.[13] In doing so, the Court took a very relaxed approach to the question of non-exhaustion of effective domestic remedies, a key admissibility requirement that the Court generally applies quite strictly, and, even more importantly, to its evaluation of the *evidence* on the basis of which it established Armenia's control.[14] In other words, it really did not take much to persuade the Court that Armenia controlled Nagorno-Karabakh, and this has significant implications for pending or future cases raising similar issues. For example, currently pending before the Court is an interstate case between Georgia and Russia,[15] where a key question for the application of the spatial model will be whether Russia controls the separatist entities of Abkhazia and South Ossetia in Georgia, while also pending are several interstate cases between Ukraine and Russia, where again a key question will be whether Russia controls Crimea and the Donbas region.[16] The Court's flexibility in applying the spatial model is also

[11] See also R Wilde, 'The Extraterritorial Application of International Human Rights Law on Civil and Political Rights' in S Sheeran and N Rodley (eds), *Routledge Handbook of International Human Rights Law* (Routledge, 2013) 635, at 640.

[12] See Communication from the United Kingdom concerning the case of *Al-Skeini* against United Kingdom to the Committee of Ministers, DH—DD(2012)438, 2 May 2012, at <https://wcd.coe.int/com.instranet.InstraServlet?command=com.instranet.CmdBlobGet&InstranetImage=2082643&SecMode=1&DocId=1885434&Usage=2> accessed 1 June 2017.('The UK considers that the Al Skeini judgment is set in the factual circumstances of UK's past operations in Iraq and that it has no implications for its current operations elsewhere, including in Afghanistan.')

[13] *Chiragov and Others v Armenia* [GC] App no 13216/05 (ECtHR, 16 June 2015).

[14] *Chiragov* (n 13) paras 172–87. See also the dissenting opinion of Judge Pinto de Albuquerque.

[15] *Georgia v Russia (No. 2)* App no 13255/07.

[16] See 'European Court of Human Rights communicates to Russia new inter-State case concerning events in Crimea and Eastern Ukraine' Press Release of the European Court, 1 October 2015 (available on HUDOC), explaining that there are three pending interstate applications between Ukraine and Russia and more than 1,400 individual applications related to Crimea or the conflict in Eastern Ukraine.

shown by the *Catan* case, dealing with Russia's continued control of a separatist region in Moldova.[17]

More interesting and more difficult is the Court's treatment of the personal model, but there too the expansive trend is clear. For example, in *Hassan v The United Kingdom*, the Court ruled categorically that physical custody will ipso facto constitute Article 1 jurisdiction within the personal model of jurisdiction as authority and control over an individual.[18] The Court did not seem to put any limits on this principle (and rightly so), not even the vague idea of 'public powers' that it invented in *Banković* and imported into the personal model of jurisdiction in *Al-Skeini*.[19]

The bottom line of this approach is that, whenever the military forces of a European State capture any individual, the Convention will apply by virtue of the personal conception of Article 1 jurisdiction as authority and control over individuals, no matter where that individual is located. The Convention will apply on this basis not only to detention operations in Afghanistan, but also to situations such as the French intervention in Mali, the capture of Ukrainian soldiers by Russian forces in Crimea etc. This is also fully consistent with the English High Court's *Serdar Mohammed* judgment, which rejected the UK government's attempts to confine *Al-Skeini* to the facts of Iraq.[20] Such is also the recently reaffirmed position of the Human Rights Committee with regard to the extraterritorial applicability of the International Covenant on Civil and Political Rights.[21]

Another important recent case in which the European Court applied the personal model of jurisdiction was *Jaloud v The Netherlands*,[22] holding that individuals who passed through and were shot at a Dutch-manned checkpoint in Iraq were within the authority and control, and thus jurisdiction, of the Netherlands. The Court was unanimous on this point.[23] However, the Court was sharply divided (ten votes to seven) on just how strictly to assess the State's compliance with the positive obligation to investigate under Article 2.

After *Al-Skeini*, the European Court did not have the opportunity to pronounce itself on the Article 1 jurisdiction question in purely kinetic operations without

[17] See *Catan and Others v Moldova and Russia* [GC] App nos 43370/04, 8252/05, and 18454/06 (ECtHR,19 October 2012) and its predecessor case *Ilaşcu and others v Moldova and Russia* [GC] App no 48787/99 (ECtHR, 8 July 2004) paras 382–94 (speaking of a 'decisive influence' of Russia over a separatist part of Moldova as sufficing for jurisdiction).

[18] *Hassan* (n 3).

[19] cf the Court's finding in *Hassan* para 75 that the events took place *before* the UK assumed responsibility for the maintenance of security in South East Iraq, which was the basis for the 'public powers' in *Al-Skeini*. Similarly, the Court (again, rightly) focused on factual control, disregarding some of the formal arrangements under a memorandum of understanding between the UK and the US (para 78), and found that 'Tarek Hassan fell within the jurisdiction of the United Kingdom from the moment of his capture by United Kingdom troops, at Umm Qasr on 23 April 2003, until his release from the bus that took him from Camp Bucca to the drop-off point, most probably Umm Qasr on 2 May 2003' (para 80).

[20] *Serdar Mohammed v Ministry of Defence* [2014] EWHC 1369 (QB) paras 147–48.

[21] See General Comment No 35 on the right of liberty and security of person, CCPR/C/GC/35, 16 December 2014, para 63.

[22] *Jaloud v The Netherlands* [GC] App no 47708/08, (ECtHR, 20 November 2014).

[23] ibid para 152.

territorial control, which were excluded from the ambit of the Convention under *Banković*. As I have explained, however, once State jurisdiction is defined as the exercise of authority or control over an individual, there is no reasonable, non-arbitrary way to limit this personal model.[24] If detention qualifies as jurisdiction under the personal model, and if passing through a checkpoint is also authority or control over an individual, then why should not killing that individual, or even reading their email, also qualify as jurisdiction?

In an important recent judgment in the *Al-Saadoon* case, the High Court of England and Wales, per Mr Justice Leggatt, applied *Al-Skeini* even to kinetic operations without territorial control, in effect collapsing the personal threshold despite *Al-Skeini*'s caveats and ambiguities:

> The essential principle that I derive is that whenever and wherever a state which is a contracting party to the Convention purports to exercise legal authority or uses physical force, it must do so in a way that does not violate Convention rights. That is still a far-reaching principle of jurisdiction. It creates real and difficult problems as to how human rights law under the Convention can be accommodated to the realities of international peacekeeping operations and situations of armed conflict. There are strong reasons of policy for seeking to interpret the territorial scope of the Convention in a way which limits the extent to which it impinges on military operations in the field, particularly where actual fighting is involved. There is also reason to be concerned that, once the Convention is held to apply to the use of force in overseas military operations, then the inevitable consequence of any major foreign intervention such as the British involvement in Iraq will be a flood of claims. That this concern is not fanciful is shown by the very large number of claims which have in fact been brought in the English courts since the decisions in the *Al-Skeini* and *Al-Jedda* cases were issued by the European Court.
>
> I do not think, however, that it would be an effective solution, even if it were legitimate, to seek to stem this tide by drawing a line between cases where force is used to detain and cases where force is used to kill. By far the majority of both the public law and private law claims arising out of the British involvement in Iraq have been brought by individuals who were detained by British forces and who allege that their detention was unlawful and that they were ill-treated while in British custody. There are comparatively few claims alleging unlawful killing. In any event, in the light of the decision in Al-Skeini, most if not all of the claims involving the killing of individuals who had not been detained will fall within the jurisdiction of the UK on the basis that the deaths occurred during security operations which involved the exercise of public powers. That applies in relation to all the relevant cases which have been chosen as test cases for the purpose of this issue. Drawing a line in the manner contended for by the Secretary of State would therefore be largely futile as well as illogical. When the lesser use of force involved in apprehending someone has been held to bring that person within the article 1 jurisdiction of a contracting state, it makes no sense to hold that the greater use of force involved in killing someone does not have that effect.[25]

This reasoning is in my view entirely correct. It remains to be seen, however, whether the UK appellate courts and ultimately the European Court will follow Mr Justice

[24] See Milanovic (n 4) 207–8.

[25] *Al-Saadoon and Others v Secretary of State for Defence* [2015] EWHC 715 (Admin) 17 March 2015, paras 106–7.

Leggatt in collapsing the personal model so soon after *Al-Skeini*.[26] In the long run, as I said above, the collapse of the threshold seems inevitable.

To conclude this section on jurisdiction:

1. Recent cases provide clear confirmation of the trend in the European Court's jurisprudence towards a more expansive approach to the Convention's extraterritorial application. This is in line with the case law of other human rights bodies.[27] The trend is evident not only from the outcome of the relevant cases, but also from the Court's unanimity or near-unanimity in reaching those outcomes, and in its flexible approach to evidence. The Court currently has before it a number of cases (some of them interstate) in which this trend will probably be reaffirmed. Further cases on Iraq and Afghanistan are also likely. A further challenge that the Court will have to face with are cases on extraterritorial electronic surveillance and other cyber activities, in which the application of the Court's tests based on physical control will not be straightforward—although, in my view, those cases should end up decided expansively as well.[28]
2. The Convention's applicability to detention operations is clear, and begins from the moment of capture. Its applicability to kinetic operations is less clear when the state does not control the territory in which the operation takes place, but the likely trend, in the long-term, is for these operations to be covered as well.
3. This simply means that focusing too much attention on the threshold question of extraterritorial applicability is ultimately a losing, counter-productive strategy, which detracts from the far more important and more difficult questions on the merits, as indeed happened in *Jaloud*. There is only so much time, space, and energy that can be devoted to any given case, and the more effort is invested in jurisdictional issues, the less remains for the merits.
4. The position under the European Convention inevitably has ripple effects even for States which are not parties thereto, if they engage (as they frequently do) in multinational operations which include States which are parties to the Convention. Thus, for example, although the United States, Canada, and Australia are not bound in any way by the ECHR, they routinely cooperate

[26] See *Serdar Mohammed v Secretary of State for Defence* [2015] EWCA Civ 843, 30 July 2015, para 95 (where the Court of Appeal seems to be approvingly citing Mr Justice Leggatt's reasoning in *Al-Saadoon*).

[27] See, eg the Human Rights Committee's General Comment No 35 (n 21); the Committee's (unreasoned but quite expansive) position that the ICCPR applies to extraterritorial use of armed force with drones and extraterritorial surveillance in its Concluding Observations on the Fourth Report of the United States of America, CCPR/C/USA/CO/4, 23 April 2014, paras 9 and 22; The Inter-American Court and Commission of Human Rights have historically also had a generous approach to the extraterritorial application of the American Declaration and Convention—see, eg C Cerna, 'Extraterritorial Application of the Human Rights Instruments of the Inter-American System' in Coomans and Kamminga (n 4) 141.

[28] See more M Milanovic, 'Human Rights Treaties and Foreign Surveillance: Privacy in the Digital Age' (2015) 56 Harvard International Law Journal 81.

with States like the United Kingdom, Belgium, and France which are bound by the Convention, and they must necessarily take into account the legal limits their partners are subjected to.

4. The Relationship Between Article 1 Jurisdiction and State Responsibility

A further point of uncertainty in the Court's case law—that unfortunately shows no signs of abating—is the frequent conceptual confusion between Article 1 jurisdiction, as the prerequisite for the Convention's application, and attribution of conduct as a matter of state responsibility. Recently, the relationship between the two concepts was particularly vexing for the judges in the *Jaloud* case. In particular, in their separate opinion, Judges Spielmann and Raimondi found the Court's use of the attribution concept and its references to the case law of the ICJ and the International Law Commission's (ILC) Articles on State Responsibility[29] to have been exceptionally objectionable, indeed 'ambiguous, subsidiary and incomprehensible'. For the two judges, attribution was a 'non-issue' in the case, which the Court should have avoided:

> There was therefore no need to examine the non-issue of 'attribution', which is completely separate from the question of 'jurisdiction'. More fundamentally, the Court should in any event be careful not to conflate the notions of jurisdiction under Article 1 with the concept of State responsibility under general international law. Efforts to seek to elucidate the former by reference to the latter are conceptually unsound and likely to cause further confusion in an already difficult area of law.[30]

The two judges are right that the two concepts are distinct. But that does not mean that there is no relationship between them, or that attribution was truly a non-issue in *Jaloud*, even if the Court could have been clearer in explaining what it was doing.[31]

In fact, it is the Court itself that has over the decades been the greatest culprit in conflating jurisdiction and state responsibility. As I explain in detail elsewhere,[32] the Court has serially confused jurisdiction and responsibility in cases such as *Loizidou*[33] and *Ilaşcu*, often by using hopelessly imprecise terminology, eg by talking about the 'responsibility' of State Parties 'under Article 1'—as if that Article set standards of responsibility—or by saying that a respondent State's responsibility 'was engaged' (whatever that may mean exactly). It has thus been exceedingly difficult for outside observers to understand what the Court was actually

[29] Report of the International Law Commission on the work of its 53rd session 'Official Records of the General Assembly' (56th session) UN Doc A/56/10 chp.IV.E.2 Supplement no 10, hereinafter ILC ASR.

[30] *Jaloud* (n 22) Concurring Opinion of Judges Spielmann and Raimondi, para 7.

[31] See also *Jaloud* (n 22) Concurring Opinion of Judge Motoc.

[32] See Milanovic (n 4) 41–53.

[33] *Loizidou v Turkey* (Preliminary Objections) App no 15318/89 (ECtHR, 23 March 1995).

doing in such cases, eg whether the respondent States in cases such as *Loizidou* and *Ilaşcu* were found directly responsible for the conduct of non-State actors whose conduct was attributable to them, or rather for their own failing to prevent such conduct by third parties.

When the counsel for Russia in the *Catan* case pointed out the ambiguities in the Court's approach and its possible inconsistency with attribution tests devised by the ICJ and endorsed by the ILC, the Court responded with a commendable, if somewhat disingenuous, paragraph which it now reaffirmed in *Jaloud*: 'The Court reiterates that the test for establishing the existence of "jurisdiction" under Article 1 of the Convention has never been equated with the test for establishing a State's responsibility for an internationally wrongful act under general international law.'[34] The Court has, in fact, frequently 'equated' the two, or at least it has never explained how the two are distinct.

How exactly then are these concepts different? Because they are intellectual operations which involve different questions. *Attribution of conduct* is a question of whether the acts or omissions of a living, breathing human being (or group of human beings) should *in law* be regarded as the conduct of a state, a constructed, abstract entity, which (just like a corporation in domestic law) can in reality only act through human beings.[35] *State jurisdiction*, whether under Article 1 ECHR or under the comparable clauses of other human rights treaties, is a concept which poses two different questions—does a state exercise effective control of an area or territory in which the victim of the alleged human rights violation is located (spatial model), or does the state through its agents exercise authority and control over the individual victim of the alleged human rights violation (personal model).[36]

Attribution and jurisdiction may at times use similar terminology (eg effective control), which facilitates confusion between the two. But the questions posed are nonetheless different, even if the terminology is similar—control *over whom or what?*—is it an actor, or a territory, or a victim. If we look at the matter through the ILC's conceptual framework, attribution is an issue under Article 2(a) of the ILC Articles (is the conduct that of the relevant State?), while jurisdiction is an issue under Article 2(b) (did the conduct breach an obligation of the state, ie did that obligation even apply to that particular conduct?).

To give an example, when Osama bin Laden was killed by US Navy Seals in Pakistan, the attribution issue was perfectly clear: the conduct in question is attributable to the United States, because the deed was done by organs of the United States. But the jurisdiction issue is a separate one, and is not as clear—did, through killing him, US agents exercise authority/power/control (and thus jurisdiction) over

[34] *Jaloud* (n 22) para 154.

[35] See ILC commentary to Article 2 ASR (n 29) 71, para 5: 'For particular conduct to be characterized as an internationally wrongful act, it must first be attributable to the State. The State is a real organized entity, a legal person with full authority to act under international law. But to recognize this is not to deny the elementary fact that the State cannot act of itself. An "act of the State" must involve some action or omission by a human being or group.'

[36] See also Wilde (n 11).

Osama bin Laden as an individual, so that he had rights under the International Covenant on Civil and Political Rights vis-à-vis the United States? Or, to give a different example, when the UK's Government Communications Headquarters (GCHQ) intercepts my email while I am in Switzerland, the attribution issue is again clear—the conduct in question is undoubtedly that of the United Kingdom. But there is a separate jurisdiction issue[37]—whether by reading my email the UK exercised jurisdiction over me, so that I would have privacy rights under the ECHR vis-à-vis the UK.

The two judges are thus correct when they say that the two questions are conceptually separate. But they are *not* correct when they say that attribution was a 'non-issue' in *Jaloud.* In fact, attribution is an issue in *every single case, Jaloud* included. For a State to be responsible for any violation of the Convention, the conduct of some human being has to be *attributed* to that State. Again, there is no way that a State can act except through individuals, or groups of individuals, and the conduct of these individuals must be assigned in law to the State (whether we call this process attribution, imputation, something else, or do not give it a name at all). What is true is that in the vast majority of Strasbourg cases (say 99 per cent) the attribution issue is not explicitly *raised* by the parties or by the Court, since on the facts of the case the answers to the attribution inquiry are *obvious*: the conduct which violates human rights is that of the State's *de jure* organs, per Article 4, ILC ASR. In other words, when Italy is found responsible because Italian courts unduly delay a trial, or Bulgaria is found responsible because the Bulgarian police kill an unarmed fugitive, nobody really bothers with an attribution inquiry or invokes the ILC Articles. But the attribution inquiry is nonetheless still done *sub silentio*, since without it there can be no State responsibility for an internationally wrongful act.[38]

Attribution was in fact a very important issue in *Jaloud.* But to understand how this was so, we must also understand which conduct exactly is being attributed, and what the relationship between jurisdiction and attribution can look like. First, recall that we have defined jurisdiction as either effective control of an area *by a State,* or as authority, power, or control over individuals *by a State.* Both the spatial and personal types of jurisdiction can only be exercised *by a State* through its own organs or agents, ie *persons whose acts are attributable to it.* For example, in *Loizidou*, Turkey could not have exercised effective control over Northern Cyprus if there were no Turkish soldiers and other agents in that part of the island. Similarly, the UK cannot exercise personal jurisdiction except through its own agents, who exert authority or control over the victim of human rights violation, as in *Al-Skeini.*

[37] See more Milanovic (n 28).

[38] Note, in that regard, how the Court, in *Al-Skeini* (n 2) para 135, quite correctly says that 'where, in accordance with custom, treaty or other agreement, authorities of the Contracting State carry out executive or judicial functions on the territory of another State, the Contracting State may be responsible for breaches of the Convention thereby incurred, *as long as the acts in question are attributable to it rather than to the territorial State*' (emphasis added).

Second, depending on the circumstances, in a single case, there may well be several different active or omissive instances of conduct which can be attributed, expressly or implicitly. There is *jurisdiction-establishing conduct*, ie acts or omissions by which a State, through its organs or agents, establishes control over an area or control over an individual (in our Northern Cyprus example, the deployment of Turkish troops in that part of the island; or in *Ilaşcu,* the provision of vast amounts of military and economic aid by Russia to the Transdniestrian separatists). Then there is the *violation-establishing conduct*, ie the act or omission that can actually constitute a violation of the ECHR (eg failing to investigate in *Al-Skeini* or *Jaloud*; or the killing of the victims, in *Al-Skeini* and *Jaloud*, had the violation of the negative aspect of Article 2 ECHR actually been pleaded). In some cases, especially those that involve the personal conception of jurisdiction, the jurisdiction-establishing conduct and the violation-establishing conduct may actually be one and the same (eg the act of detaining the individual, as in *Hassan*, or of killing them).

Third, this means that an attribution inquiry actually logically precedes the jurisdiction inquiry when it comes to the conduct which is itself constitutive of jurisdiction. Had there been doubts, for example, that Turkey had deployed its troops in Northern Cyprus, the Court would first have had to establish whether the soldiers on the island were, in fact, acting on behalf of the Turkish State.

Fourth, this was exactly the situation in *Jaloud*, since the Netherlands was arguing that the conduct of its soldiers deployed in Iraq was not its own because they were operating under the command of a UK officer. In other words, if the conduct of Dutch soldiers in Iraq was as a general matter no longer attributable to the State of the Netherlands (for whatever reason), the Netherlands could not have exercised jurisdiction under Article 1 either under the personal or under the spatial models.[39]

Fifth, this is also exactly why the Court in *Jaloud* actually resolves an attribution issue in para 151 *before* resolving the jurisdiction issue in para 152 (even though the Court's analysis in preceding paragraphs is not entirely clear in how it is framed):

> That being so, the Court cannot find that the Netherlands troops were placed 'at the disposal' of any foreign power, whether it be Iraq or the United Kingdom or any other power, or that they were 'under the exclusive direction or control' of any other State (compare, *mutatis mutandis*, Article 6 of the International Law Commission's Articles on State Responsibility, see paragraph 98 above; see also *Application of the Convention on the Prevention and Punishment of the Crime of Genocide (Bosnia and Herzegovina v. Serbia and Montenegro), Judgment, I.C.J. Reports 2007*, p. 43, § 406, paragraph 97 above)).
>
> The Court now turns to the circumstances surrounding the death of Mr Azhar Sabah Jaloud. It notes that Mr Azhar Sabah Jaloud met his death when a vehicle in which he was a passenger was fired upon while passing through a checkpoint manned by personnel under the command and direct supervision of a Netherlands Royal Army officer. The checkpoint had been set up in the execution of SFIR's mission, under United Nations Security Council Resolution 1483 (see paragraph 93 above), to restore conditions of stability and security

[39] cf *Behrami and Behrami v France* and *Saramati v France, Norway, and Germany* (Dec) [GC] App nos 71412/01 and 78166/01 (ECtHR, 2 May 2007).

conducive to the creation of an effective administration in the country. The Court is satisfied that the respondent Party exercised its "jurisdiction" within the limits of its SFIR mission and for the purpose of asserting authority and control over persons passing through the checkpoint. That being the case, the Court finds that the death of Mr Azhar Sabah Jaloud occurred within the 'jurisdiction' of the Netherlands, as that expression is to be construed within the meaning of Article 1 of the Convention.[40]

In other words, the Court first establishes that the conduct of Dutch troops in Iraq is still that of the Netherlands; while it does not use the word 'attribution' as such, it clearly invokes two different rules of attribution in the ILC Articles (Articles 6 and 8, the latter via the reference to the *Bosnian Genocide* case). The Court then proceeds to establish that Dutch soldiers exercised authority and control, ie personal jurisdiction, over persons passing through the checkpoint that they set up (this is the jurisdiction-establishing conduct which is attributable to the Netherlands). Finally, after having established jurisdiction, and under a new subheading called 'attribution', the Court establishes the attribution to the Netherlands *of the actual alleged violations*: 'The facts giving rise to the applicant's complaints derive from alleged acts and omissions of Netherlands military personnel and investigative and judicial authorities. As such they are capable of giving rise to the responsibility of the Netherlands under the Convention.'[41]

In sum, *Jaloud* becomes more comprehensible when we see that the case raised not one, *but two,* attribution inquiries, one of which was logically prior to the establishment of jurisdiction. The Court was thus perfectly correct in doing what it did, although it could have expressed itself more clearly. In that regard, the two judges are also correct in saying that the second attribution inquiry does not properly fall within a jurisdiction analysis. It is also correct that, once the Court established that the conduct of Dutch troops in Iraq was still attributable to the Netherlands, the second attribution inquiry that followed was obvious and trivial (the alleged acts and omissions with regard to the investigation were still attributable to the Netherlands). But while its outcome may have been obvious (especially because it was done on the basis of organ status, and because the violation-constitutive conduct was mostly one of omission), this is not to say, as the two judges do, that no such issue existed, or that it was improper for the Court to mention it.

To conclude this section, it is to be hoped that the Court will manage to delineate more clearly the relationship between jurisdiction and responsibility in its future jurisprudence. This will prove to be a pivotal issue in the interstate cases currently pending between Georgia and Russia and Ukraine and Russia. It is one thing to say, for example, that Russia controls the *geographical region* of South Ossetia, another that it controls the *non-State actor* that administers that region, and that hence whatever that actor does is attributable to Russia. Conceptual clarity is also necessary in order to better understand the relationship between Convention-specific rules and those of general international law.

[40] *Jaloud* (n 22) paras 151 and 152.
[41] ibid para 155.

5. The Convention in Armed Conflict

The threshold question of extraterritoriality is conceptually distinct from the relationship between human rights treaties and the law of armed conflict/international humanitarian law (IHL)—extraterritorial application is an issue even outside armed conflict (eg regarding electronic surveillance programs run by the National Security Agency (NSA) and GCHQ), while armed conflict can take place entirely within a State's own territory (eg from the perspective of Ukraine regarding the ongoing conflict there). But the problem of extraterritoriality is particularly acute in situations of armed conflict, and the leading cases on extraterritoriality mainly stem from such situations, attracting both legal and political controversy.

While some human rights bodies, especially in the inter-American system,[42] have a long history of applying IHL, this has not been the case in the European system. The European Court has so far generally avoided relying on IHL; its subject-matter jurisdiction is of course confined to establishing violations of the Convention, and IHL is relevant only insofar as it can affect the interpretation and application of State obligations under the Convention that are at issue in any given case. Even so, the Court has avoided applying IHL even in cases where it was obviously relevant, eg regarding Chechnya, nor has it provided a clear framework on the interaction between the ECHR and IHL.[43]

There are a number of possible explanations for the Court's lack of engagement with IHL: (i) lack of institutional competence or expertise; in particular, most Strasbourg judges today are not international lawyers by training, let alone IHL experts; (ii) unease or general feeling that IHL, with its very different ethos, can somehow dirty or sully the Convention; (iii) factual and evidential uncertainties in politically very controversial cases (eg regarding the targeting decision at issue in *Banković*); (iv) the politics of judicial avoidance—a preference to deal with these cases in a manner that the judges are more comfortable with, while avoiding other tricky issues, say through the device of Article 1 jurisdiction, as in *Banković* in the immediate aftermath of 9/11; (v) genuine uncertainty regarding the scope of the *lex specialis* principle.[44] This is coupled with the general reluctance of States to admit that there is an armed conflict on their territory and to expressly refer to IHL in their pleadings.[45]

But times seem to be changing. While the Court has not been flooded with IHL, its awareness of, and exposure to, IHL issues has grown since 9/11. At the same time, the Article 1 jurisdiction case law—the Court's main avoidance strategy in the past—has been proven to be arbitrary and indefensible, and is thus undergoing

[42] See Cerna, (n 27). See also F Hampson, 'The Relationship between International Humanitarian Law and Human Rights Law from the Perspective of a Human Rights Treaty Body' (2008) 90 IRRC 549.

[43] See, eg W Abresch, 'A Human Rights Law of Internal Armed Conflict: The European Court of Human Rights in Chechnya' (2005) 16 EJIL 741.

[44] See generally Milanovic (n 4) 229ff.

[45] See, eg A Cullen, 'Key Developments Affecting the Scope of Internal Armed Conflict in International Humanitarian Law' (2005) 183 Military Law Review 65, at 85–86.

reorientation. The Court has also had to deal with a number of very difficult cases that are not strictly speaking about armed conflict (eg the hostage-taking at issue in *Finogenov*),[46] while armed conflicts are currently happening even within the once-pristine *espace juridique* of the CoE. The Court thus seems to have had little choice but to start finding its footing regarding the relationship between the Convention and IHL, and this is exactly what it did in *Hassan v The United Kingdom*.

In *Hassan*, the Court 'read down' the categorical list of permitted grounds of detention in Article 5(1) ECHR so as to permit IHL-based detention during international armed conflict (IAC), while at the same time relaxing the requirements of Article 5(4) ECHR so as to permit review of detention even by non-judicial bodies.[47] The Court did so *without* requiring States to derogate from the Convention in IACs but, again, while confining its holding solely to IACs.[48] Most notably, the Court justified its approach by a very robust reliance on Article 31(3)(b) and (c) VCLT, and not on any variant of the *lex specialis* principle.

The parameters of the applicability of the Convention to non-international armed conflicts (NIAC), now much more common, and trickier by far, than IACs, are thus left wide open. We have no way of knowing whether the Court will use the same strong interpretative approach in NIACs as it has done with IACs. But we can safely say that if the Court did not use *lex specialis* for IACs, it will not use *lex specialis* for NIACs either. Similarly, because it is confined to IACs, *Hassan* is also perfectly consistent with the High Court's and Court of Appeal's judgment in *Serdar Mohammed.* We also do not know—though it seems likely—whether the Court will use the same interpretative approach that it applied to detention to the right to life in Article 2 ECHR, reading it down so as to conform (at least in the vast majority of traditional battlefield situations) to the targeting rules of IHL. In *Hassan*, we thus have yet another incremental decision, with the Court deciding only what it absolutely needed to on the facts of the case and providing only limited guidance for the future. This caution makes perfect sense from the standpoint of the Court itself, but it is, of course, of little help to those who have to deal with operational questions on a daily basis.

What then of the interpretative approach that the Court has taken? Whether one agrees with it or not, I do not think it is particularly surprising. It is good, in my view, that the Court did not rely on *lex specialis,* an often confusing and misleading principle, whose supposedly traditional provenance is more fiction than actual tradition.[49] Clearly, the Court chose to do what it did because the majority thought

[46] *Finogenov v Russia* App nos 18299/03 and 27311/03, (ECtHR, 20 December 2011).

[47] See also L Hill-Cawthorne, 'Humanitarian Law, Human Rights Law and the Bifurcation of Armed Conflict' (2015) 64 ICLQ 293.

[48] *Hassan* (n 3) paras 103–7.

[49] See more M Milanovic, 'The Lost Origins of Lex Specialis: Rethinking the Relationship between Human Rights and International Humanitarian Law' in Jens D Ohlin (ed), *Theoretical Boundaries of Armed Conflict and Human Rights* (CUP 2016) 78, draft available at <http://ssrn.com/abstract=2463957> accessed 1 June 2017. But see M Sassòli and L Olson, 'The Relationship between International Humanitarian and Human Rights Law where it Matters: Admissible Killing and Internment of Fighters in Non-International Armed Conflicts' (2008) 90 IRRC 599.

that any alternatives would lead to practically infeasible and unreasonable results, bearing in mind the political context of the day. The Article 31(3)(b) VCLT route that the Court chose to follow is merely a legalistic fig leaf for the policy choice that the Court made (rightly or wrongly). *Hassan* does demonstrate, however, the Court's increasing familiarity with and preparedness to more explicitly rely on IHL. Another confirmation of this point is the Court's readiness to make observations about the definition of the concept of belligerent occupation in the *Sargsyan* case, in which it extensively used and cited IHL scholarship and primary materials.[50] This is, after all, only natural and sensible in a contemporary context in which armed conflicts occur in Europe and cannot be easily ignored—the Court of necessity must acquire a degree of competence in IHL.

6. Conclusion and Outlook

What lessons can then be learned from the European Court's recent jurisprudence? First, it is clear that the applicability of human rights in armed conflict (or post-conflict) is firmly on the agenda and that it will remain so. This is of course, to a significant extent, a function of the wider political context in which it has to operate. On the one hand, the Court is finding it increasingly hard to avoid involving itself in armed conflict situations. On the other, it is conducting its work in an atmosphere of a series of escalating pan-European crises and is wary of pushing member States too hard, lest they push back even harder. Second, the Court has now joined other human rights bodies in setting out a fairly generous and expansive approach to the Convention's extraterritorial applicability. The one big area of uncertainty is kinetic operations in areas not under the relevant State's control but, even there, the expansive trend is likely to continue, at least in the longer term. A further challenge is upcoming cases dealing with electronic surveillance and cyberspace more generally. Third, this means that focus needs to shift to the merits of very hard cases. Wasting precious energies on the threshold applicability issue is a losing strategy in the long run, and has serious repercussions on the Court's appreciation of the merits. Fourth, cases will keep coming. It is crucial to note that these are not simply cases coming from activist, 'ambulance-chasing' law firms against the poor little UK. Interstate cases are especially important, like the pending Georgian and Ukrainian claims against Russia. Even individual cases can have a strong interstate dimension, especially when they come in large numbers—for example, the two recent Nagorno-Karabakh cases both had third party interventions from Azerbaijan and Armenia respectively in the case brought against the other State.

Fifth, the Court and other human rights bodies are starting to become more comfortable in engaging directly with IHL. They are also showing increasing readiness in accommodating IHL and interpreting human rights flexibly in extraordinary situations of armed conflict. However, they are not willing to simply reduce human

[50] *Sargsyan and others v Azerbaijan* [GC] App no 40167/06, (ECtHR, 16 June 2015) paras 93–94, 143–44.

rights in wartime to IHL, or to apply simplistic variants of the *lex specialis* principle. Sixth, human rights in armed conflict can have particular 'bite' with regard to issues *not* expressly regulated by IHL, like the positive obligation to investigate (*Jaloud*), or the human rights of soldiers vis-à-vis their own country.[51] Seventh, this is precisely why a focus on the merits, rather than on extraterritoriality, is, in the long-term, in everybody's interest. The European Court can handle extraordinary situations if it needs to, but it needs properly developed and substantiated argument to do so. Conversely, it also needs to be clearer in the guidance it provides to State Parties and other actors. In doing so, it is now engaging in a meaningful dialogue with domestic courts, especially British courts, with cases like *Serdar Mohammed, Hassan*, and *Al-Saadoon* being clear examples. Finally, States need to seriously consider the option of derogating from the Convention (and other human rights treaties) in extraterritorial situations and in armed conflict, as a means of introducing both clarity and flexibility in the applicable human rights framework.[52]

[51] See *Smith v Secretary of State for Defence* [2010] UKSC 29; *Smith v Ministry of Defence* [2013] UKSC 41.

[52] Extraterritorial derogations are to my mind both available and desirable but should not be seen as some kind of magic bullet. For a more developed argument, see M Milanovic, 'Extraterritorial Derogations from Human Rights Treaties in Armed Conflict' in Nehal Bhuta (ed), *The Frontiers of Human Rights: Extraterritoriality and its Challenges* (OUP 2016) 55, draft available at <http://ssrn.com/abstract=2447183> accessed 1 June 2017. See also Wilde (n 11) 652–56.

6

Extraterritorial Application of the European Convention on Human Rights

Evolution of the Court's Jurisprudence on the Notions of Extraterritorial Jurisdiction and State Responsibility

Işıl Karakaş and Hasan Bakırcı

1. Introduction

States' willingness to limit the scope and effect of human rights instruments is not a new phenomenon. The late Lord Bingham tells us in his book on the rule of law that the first attempt to restrict, or rather to circumvent, the application of a prominent human rights instrument took place in the United Kingdom.[1] Earl Clarendon, who was at the time King Charles II's chief minister, made a practice of dispatching prisoners to outlying parts of the United Kingdom, such as remote islands and garrisons, for the very reason that in those places the writ of *habeas corpus* did not run, because it was at the time a remedy local to England and Wales under the Habeas Corpus Amendment Act 1679. The prisoners were therefore unable to challenge the lawfulness of their detention and were deprived of the protection of the law. This deplorable practice came to an end when Earl Clarendon fell from power and was later impeached. He subsequently fled and died in exile.

However, State authorities' endeavours to find ways to deny individuals their basic human rights, and to escape accountability and responsibility under various laws and treaties, did not end with Clarendon.[2] Some States still send prisoners to detention centres located outside of their countries prompted by the same motive as Clarendon, namely to deny them the right of *habeas corpus* provided in domestic law.[3] Certain States are still able to commit various other types of human rights abuses with near impunity outside their sovereign territories[4] as exemplified by

[1] Tom Bingham, *The Rule of Law* (Penguin Books 2010) 22. [2] ibid 23.

[3] See *El-Masri v The Former Yugoslav Republic of Macedonia* [GC] App no 39630/09 (ECtHR, 13 December 2012); and *Al Nashiri v Poland* App no 28761/11 (ECtHR, 24 July 2014).

[4] Mark Gibney, Katarina Tomaševski, and Jens Vensted-Hansen, 'Transnational Responsibility for Violations of Human Rights' (2004) HHRJ <http://.law.harvard.edu/students/orgs/hrj/iss12/gibney.shtml/> accessed 15 December 2016.

Extraterritorial Application of the European Convention on Human Rights: Evolution of the Court's Jurisprudence on the Notions of Extraterritorial Jurisdiction and State Responsibility. Işıl Karakaş and Hasan Bakırcı. Published 2018 by Oxford University Press.

military operations in Afghanistan, Iraq, Syria, Libya, and Yemen, namely human rights violations which they cannot commit with the same impunity within their national jurisdictions.

In view of these examples, the importance of Article 1 of the European Convention on Human Rights (ECHR)[5] can be better understood, given that this provision defines the scope of the Convention and of the obligations of the Contracting States. In particular, Article 1 imposes positive obligations of 'good government' on each Contracting Party in respect of each person within its jurisdiction. These obligations, however, apply only to those within the jurisdiction of the Contracting Party. Accordingly, a person claiming to be the victim of a violation of the Convention must first demonstrate that s/he was within the jurisdiction of the respondent State at the time of the alleged violation of the Convention. In other words, the issue of jurisdiction is a threshold requirement in the Convention; the question of State responsibility or attribution would arise only after the European Court of Human Rights (ECtHR) is satisfied that the matters complained of are within the jurisdiction of the respondent State.[6]

It is well known that the States Parties to the ECHR are in favour of a more restrictive interpretation of the concept of 'jurisdiction' under Article 1, even more so when it comes to determining the Contracting States' responsibilities for alleged human rights violations occurring outside their home territories in the course of their extraterritorial activities. In this connection, the respondent governments answering to such cases before the Court often argue that the nature of jurisdiction under Article 1 is 'essentially territorial' and that any extension outside the territory of a Contracting State is exceptional. They interpret the Court's previous case law as implying that the notion of jurisdiction should not be allowed to 'evolve' or 'incrementally develop', in the same way as the law in respect of the substantive rights, namely the 'living instrument' doctrine, should not be used in interpreting the concept of jurisdiction under Article 1.[7]

While the Court has so far delivered a significant number of judgments and decisions in cases concerning the extraterritorial activities of the Contracting States, it has received severe criticism for not establishing a consistent and coherent case law with sufficient clarity, 'which speaks with one voice'.[8] In agreement with this criticism, Judge Bonello, in his concurring opinion in the *Al-Skeini* case, described these judgments and decisions as 'a patch-work case-law at best'.[9]

As is clear from the above considerations, the scope of the term 'jurisdiction' used in Article 1 of the Convention is not without controversy. Likewise the

[5] 'The High Contracting Parties shall secure to everyone within their jurisdiction the rights and freedoms defined in Section I of this Convention.'

[6] Michael O'Boyle, 'Comment on Life after Bankovic' in F Coomans and MT Kamminga (eds), *Extraterritorial Application of Human Rights Treaties* (Intersentia 2004).

[7] *Jaloud v The Netherlands* App no 47708/08 (ECtHR, 20 November 2014) para 121.

[8] Lord Alan Rodger, House of Lords opinion in *Al Skeini* [2007] UKHL 26, para 67.

[9] *Al-Skeini and Others v The United Kingdom* App no 55721/07 (ECtHR, 7 July 2011).

boundary between jurisdiction *ratione loci* and attribution *ratione personae* does not lend itself to easy resolution. This chapter will therefore analyse the evolution of the Strasbourg case law on the concept of 'extraterritorial jurisdiction' and will attempt to provide a comprehensive answer to the questions raised. It will also ascertain whether there is any truth in the aforementioned criticism and, most importantly, any room for further development. The chapter will first examine the early jurisprudence of the Convention bodies and explain how they dealt with the difficult question of extraterritorial jurisdiction. It will then discuss the two tests developed by the Court when determining extraterritorial jurisdiction in various case scenarios. Finally, the concluding section of the chapter will summarize these discussions and pose a question for future development of the Court's case law.

2. Extraterritorial Acts that Constitute an Exercise of Jurisdiction under Article 1

Since the Commission's admissibility decision in the case of *X v Federal Republic of Germany* on 25 September 1965,[10] the Strasbourg bodies have dealt with numerous cases involving questions of extraterritorial application of the Convention. While some of these cases were ruled inadmissible, because they failed to meet the formal requirements of admissibility or there was no issue under the Convention, the extensive case law generated both by the Commission and the Court indicates that the Convention bodies have accepted the accountability of the Contracting States for their extraterritorial conduct.

As will be discussed in this chapter, the now defunct Commission and the Court employed several tests to determine whether the extraterritorial conduct of the Contracting States amount to exercise of jurisdiction within the meaning of Article 1. Even though there were some differences in their approach, both institutions have dealt with this question in a logical and methodical way. The experience gained when examining a variety of cases in the last two decades, particularly in the context of the States' global war on terrorism, permitted the Court to clarify the jurisprudence on the interpretation of the word 'jurisdiction' and to create two main tests that are used to establish the exercise of jurisdiction by a Contracting State outside its own territorial boundaries, namely (a) effective control over an area and (b) exercise of authority and control over persons by State agents.[11]

However, before embarking upon an analysis of these tests and how they are used in different case scenarios to establish extraterritorial jurisdiction, we will first look at the early jurisprudence of the Convention bodies, namely the Commission and the former Court, and how they answered this difficult question.

[10] *X v Germany* App no 1611/62 (ECtHR, 25 September 1965) 158.
[11] See Marko Milanovic 'Jurisdiction and Responsibility: Trends in the Jurisprudence of the Strasbourg Court' in this volume.

2.1 The early jurisprudence of the Convention bodies

As already noted, *X v Federal Republic of Germany* is the earliest authority that addressed the question of extraterritorial conduct of the Contracting States. The case concerned a German citizen's complaint that German consular officials in Morocco had asked the Moroccan authorities to expel him. The Commission found the applicant's allegations manifestly ill-founded on the facts and declared the application inadmissible. However, it pointed out that nationals of a Contracting State were within its jurisdiction even when domiciled abroad and that diplomatic or consular representatives of their country of origin performed certain duties with regard to them which, under certain circumstances, might make that country liable under the Convention.[12]

2.1.1 The emergence of the notion of 'authority and responsibility over persons'

In *Cyprus v Turkey*,[13] the Commission examined the applicability of the Convention to northern Cyprus, which had been placed under the control of the Turkish army since 20 July 1974. Considering the object of Article 1, as well as the purpose of the Convention as a whole, the Commission held that the High Contracting Parties were bound to secure the Convention rights to 'all persons under their actual authority and responsibility', whether such authority was exercised within their territory or abroad. It thus ruled that the acts complained of by the Cypriot government fell within the jurisdiction of Turkey and engaged its responsibility under the Convention, despite the fact that the latter had not annexed the territory or established either military or civil government there. The test formulated here to determine the exercise of jurisdiction was not 'territorial' but that of 'authority and responsibility over persons'.

The Commission examined a number of other cases where it had to determine questions of extraterritorial jurisdiction. The cases of *X v Federal Republic of Germany*,[14] *X v The United Kingdom*,[15] and *WM v Denmark*[16] concerned the exercise of jurisdiction on foreign soil through consulates and embassies. In these cases, the Commission held that the responsibility of a Contracting State can be engaged to the extent that the sending State's diplomatic agents affect persons or property on foreign soil. In the northern Cyprus cases, namely *Cyprus v Turkey* and *Chrysostomos et al v Turkey*,[17] the test used by the Commission to determine the 'exercise of jurisdiction' was the exercise of 'power and authority over persons', although this test has been discarded by the Court in favour of the 'effective control over territory' test used in the *Loizidou* judgment.[18] In the *Hess v The United Kingdom* decision,[19]

12 *X v Germany* (n 10) 158.
13 *Cyprus v Turkey* App nos 6780/74 and 6950/75 (ECtHR, 26 May 1975) 2 DR 136.
14 *X v Germany* (n 10).
15 *X v The United Kingdom* App no 7547/76, (ECtHR, 15 December 1977).
16 *WM v Denmark* App no 17393/90 (ECtHR, 14 October 1992) 73 DR 193.
17 *Chrysostomos et al v Turkey* App nos 15299/89, 15300/89, and 15318/89 (ECtHR, 4 March 1991).
18 *Loizidou v Turkey* (Preliminary Objections) App no 15318/89 (ECtHR, 23 March 1995).
19 *Hess v The United Kingdom* App no 6231/73 (ECtHR, 28 May 1975) 2 DR 72.

which was about a prison cooperatively run by Britain and its allies, the Commission considered that the exercise of jurisdiction could be established in respect of persons detained in a prison operated on a foreign soil by a Contracting State. The cases of *Freda*,[20] *Reinette*,[21] *Stocké*,[22] and *Illich Sanchez Ramirez*[23] concerning ad hoc military or police operations in a foreign territory exemplified a Contracting State's exercise of extraterritorial jurisdiction over persons under its power and authority. The *X and Y v Switzerland* case[24] was an example of a State exercising jurisdiction in the territory of another State with the consent of the latter. Finally, in *Mrs W*[25] and *Drozd and Janousek*,[26] the Convention organs examined complaints arising out of acts which had taken place outside the territories of the respondent States and found that there was no action or omission imputable to those States. Accordingly, there was no extraterritorial jurisdiction exercised by those States.

All in all, the early case law indicates that the State's jurisdiction is not limited to its territory but extends to all persons under its 'actual authority and responsibility', whether this authority is exercised on its own territory or abroad. Although the principles quoted in these decisions attribute responsibility to the State when its acts or omissions affect persons on its own territory or abroad, the decisive element in determining whether a person is capable of coming within its jurisdiction is the exercise of authority over that person.

2.1.2 The 'cause and effect' notion of jurisdiction

One of the recognized exceptions to the territorial limitation of the obligation under Article 1 has been established in cases concerning the exclusion of aliens from the territory of Contracting States. In this connection, *Soering v The United Kingdom* was the first case in which the Court considered the question of whether the acts of the Contracting States having effects outside their territories can constitute an exercise of jurisdiction by them and hence engage their responsibility under the Convention.[27]

While the Court affirmed that 'the Convention did not govern the actions of States not Parties to it, or purport to be a means of requiring the Contracting States to impose Convention standards on other states',[28] it considered that this did not discharge the United Kingdom from its responsibilities under Article 3 to ensure that the foreseeable consequences of its extradition did not amount to inhuman and degrading treatment or torture. In other words, the Court ruled that an act by a State within its territory bringing with it adverse extraterritorial consequences could give rise to that State's responsibility under the Convention.

20 *Freda v Italy* App no 8916/80 (ECtHR, 7 October 1980) 21 DR 25.
21 *Reinette v France* App no 14009/88 (ECtHR, 2 October 1989) 63 DR 189.
22 *Stocké v Germany* App no 11755/85 (ECtHR, 19 March 1991), para 24.
23 *Illich Sanchez Ramirez v France* App no 28780/95 (ECtHR, 24 June 1996) 86 DR 155.
24 *X and Y v Switzerland* (1978) 9 DR 71.
25 *Mrs W* App no 9348/81 (ECtHR, 28 February 1983) 32 DR 190.
26 *Drozd and Janousek v France and Spain* App no 12747/ 87 (ECtHR, 26 June 1992).
27 *Soering v The United Kingdom* App no 14038/88 (ECtHR, 7 July 1989).
28 ibid para 86.

The principles enunciated in *Soering* were reiterated by the Court in cases concerning asylum seekers. The Court held that the *Soering* principles equally applied to decisions to expel as well as to extradite.[29]

Nonetheless, in the *Banković* decision,[30] the Court held that expulsion or extradition cases did not concern the actual exercise of a State's jurisdiction abroad since liability was incurred in such cases by an action of the respondent State concerning a person while he or she was on its territory, clearly within its jurisdiction. It further did not agree with the 'cause and effect' approach to jurisdiction asserted by the applicants, which would have resulted in anyone adversely affected by an act imputable to a Contracting State, wherever in the world that act may have been committed or had an effect, being brought within the jurisdiction of the State for the purpose of Article 1. In other words, the Court considered that *Soering* type of authorities did not constitute a true exception to the territorial limitation of Article 1 jurisdiction.

Although the Court qualified the *Soering* line of authorities as demonstrating an exercise of 'territorial' rather than 'extraterritorial' jurisdiction or, at most, a 'limited' extraterritorial application of the Convention rights,[31] this does not mean that a Contracting State's acts or decisions producing effects outside its territory cannot amount to an exercise of extraterritorial jurisdiction and engage its responsibility. The Court has already accepted that Contracting States may be responsible for acts producing effects in third countries.[32]

Accordingly, the conclusion to be drawn from the *Soering* line of authorities is that they do not exemplify a broad principle of extraterritoriality based on effects outside the sphere of jurisdiction.[33] They rather demonstrate the extraterritorial character of certain Convention rights, such as those guaranteed by Articles 2 and 3, and an extension of the Contracting States' obligation under Article 1, so as to cover the duty to ensure that the aliens whom they expel are not exposed to risks outlawed by the Convention in receiving countries.

2.2 Extraterritorial jurisdiction by virtue of effective control

As seen in 2.2.1, the Commission's jurisprudence in the northern Cyprus cases indicates that the exercise of extraterritorial jurisdiction, and the responsibility stemming from such an exercise, depended on the extent to which a State exercised authority and had control over persons or property abroad.

[29] Nuala Mole, *Asylum and the European Convention on Human Rights* (Council of Europe Publishing 1997) 11.

[30] *Banković and Others v Belgium and Others* App no 52207/99 (ECtHR, 12 December 2001) para 68.

[31] *Al-Adsani v The United Kingdom* [GC] App no 35763/97 para 55, para 39 cited in *Mazin Jumaa Gatteh Al Skeini and Others v The Secretary of State for Defence* [2004] EWHC 2911 (Admin) [246].

[32] *Drozd and Janousek* (n 26) para 91 and *Banković* (n 31) para 69 cited in R Lawson, 'Life After Bankovic: On the Extraterritorial Application of the European Convention on Human Rights' in F Coomans and MT Kamminga (eds) (n 6).

[33] *Al Skeini* (n 31) [247].

2.2.1 Loizidou and Cyprus v Turkey

The Court's approach in the *Loizidou v Turkey* (Preliminary Objections) and *Cyprus v Turkey* judgments was different from that of the Commission in the determination of extraterritorial jurisdiction. The former case concerned the inability of Ms Loizidou to gain access to her property in northern Cyprus on account of the Turkish armed forces' control of this territory since 1974. The Turkish government denied liability in respect of Ms Loizidou's complaints and claimed that the mere presence of Turkish armed forces in northern Cyprus was not synonymous with 'jurisdiction' any more than it is with the armed forces of other countries stationed abroad and that their armed forces had never exercised 'jurisdiction' over life and property in northern Cyprus.[34] The Turkish government advanced a further argument claiming that the impugned acts or omissions in question were *not* imputable to Turkey but to the newly set up Turkish Republic of Northern Cyprus (TRNC), which exercised exclusive control and authority over the territory north of the United Nations buffer zone. Nevertheless, the Court dismissed these arguments and held, inter alia, the following:

> Bearing in mind the object and purpose of the Convention, the responsibility of a Contracting Party may also arise when as a consequence of military action—whether lawful or unlawful—it exercises effective control of an area outside its national territory. The obligation to secure, in such an area, the rights and freedoms set out in the Convention derives from the fact of such control whether it be exercised directly, through its armed forces, or through a subordinate local administration.[35]

It appears from the above that the Court's point of reference in determining the exercise of extraterritorial jurisdiction by Turkey was the latter's effective control over the territory of northern Cyprus. It did not matter whether such control was exercised directly, through its armed forces, or through a subordinate local administration, namely through the TRNC. Nor was it necessary to determine whether Turkey actually exercised detailed control over the policies and actions of the TRNC authorities, since overall control of the area was sufficient to engage its responsibility.

The Court's judgment in the inter-state case of *Cyprus v Turkey* has shed further light on the doctrine of effective control over a territory. The Court observed:[36]

> Having effective overall control over northern Cyprus, [Turkey's] responsibility cannot be confined to the acts of its own soldiers or officials in northern Cyprus but must also be engaged by virtue of the acts of the local administration which survives by virtue of Turkish military and other support. It follows that, in terms of Article 1 of the Convention, Turkey's 'jurisdiction' must be considered to extend to securing the entire range of substantive rights set out in the Convention and those additional Protocols which she has ratified, and that violations of those rights are imputable to Turkey.

It transpires from these lines that Turkey's obligation under Article 1 has been extended to cover the duty to secure the entire range of substantive rights guaranteed

[34] *Loizidou* (Preliminary Objections) (n 18) para 56. [35] ibid para 62.
[36] *Cyprus v Turkey* [GC] App no 25781/94 (ECtHR, 10 May 2001) para 77.

by the Convention and its Protocols to individuals who are in the territory of northern Cyprus. Furthermore, taking into account the Cypriot government's inability to exercise its Convention obligations in northern Cyprus, the Court observed that any other finding would result in a regrettable vacuum in the system of human rights protection in northern Cyprus by removing from individuals there the benefit of the Convention's fundamental safeguards.[37]

The Court's above conclusions have been considered to be fully in line with the object and purpose of the Convention.[38] In our opinion, they are also comparable and consistent with the conclusions of the United Nations Human Rights Committee[39] and the International Court of Justice (ICJ) as regards the full application of the International Covenant on Civil and Political Rights to the occupied territories where Israel exercises effective control and assumes responsibility to secure the rights contained therein to the inhabitants of those territories.[40]

2.2.2 The Court's landmark decision: the Banković case

In the *Banković* case,[41] the Court considered the essential question to be whether the applicants and their deceased relatives were, as a result of an extraterritorial act (the aerial strike), capable of coming within the jurisdiction of the respondent States.

The Court ruled that, according to the literal meaning of the words, Article 1 of the Convention must be considered to reflect an ordinary and essentially territorial notion of jurisdiction, as portrayed in public international law, 'other bases of jurisdiction being exceptional and requiring special justification in the particular circumstances of each case'.[42] In other words, in declaring the application inadmissible, the Court considered that the ordinary meaning of the phrase 'within their jurisdiction' would exclude the activities of air forces of a State in another country and that the circumstances of the *Banković* case did not constitute a recognized exceptional situation that could bring the victims of the impugned act within the jurisdiction of the respondent governments. The Court ultimately considered the applicants' submissions to be tantamount to arguing that anyone adversely affected by an act imputable to a Contracting State, wherever in the world that act may have been committed or its consequences felt, was thereby brought within the jurisdiction of that State for the purpose of Article 1 of the Convention. The Court took the view that the wording of Article 1[43] did not provide any support for the applicants' suggestion that the positive

[37] ibid para 78.

[38] Council of Europe, Parliamentary Assembly report on *Areas where the European Convention on Human Rights cannot be implemented*, Doc. 9730 of 11 March 2003, Rapporteur C Pourgourides [35] (11 December 2004) ('Pourgourides report').

[39] Concluding Observations of the HRC: Israel, 18 August 1998, CCPR/C/79/Add.93. <https://unispal.un.org/DPA/DPR/unispal.nsf/0/335F22D5AC5A04FC85256CC50057BE8C> accessed 20 July 2018.

[40] *Legal Consequences of the Construction of a Wall in the Occupied Palestinian Territory (Advisory Opinion)* [2004] ICJ Rep paras 108–11.

[41] *Banković* (n 31) para 68.

[42] ibid para 61.

[43] 'The High Contracting Parties shall secure to everyone within their jurisdiction the rights and freedoms defined in Section I of this Convention.'

obligation under Article 1 could be *divided and tailored* in accordance with the particular circumstances of the extraterritorial act in question.

The Court added a further argument in its reasoning and held that the protection afforded by the Convention was limited to the legal space (*espace juridique*) of the Contracting States.[44] In particular, the Court appeared to have narrowed the 'effective control' exception further by distinguishing between the exercise of 'effective control' of territory within the legal space of the Convention as opposed to territory outside it, and suggested that, in the latter case, the Convention might not impose responsibility for guaranteeing rights that residents of the occupied State had not previously enjoyed.[45]

Moreover, the Court introduced an additional condition into the 'effective control' test: when the respondent State, through the effective control of the relevant territory and its inhabitants abroad as a consequence of military occupat ion or through the consent, invitation, or acquiescence of the government of that territory, 'exercises all or some of the public powers normally to be exercised by that Government.'[46]

The Court's interpretation of jurisdiction in the *Banković* decision has received strong criticism on the grounds that it was restrictive and ill-conceived from the standpoint of international law,[47] as well as in conflict with the Convention organs' earlier decisions on the subject.[48] It was also argued that the concept of jurisdiction in Article 1 was not necessarily identical to the general concept of jurisdiction.[49]

In our view, the Court's 'legal space' argument in the *Banković* decision should not have been interpreted as introducing an additional test for the applicability of the Convention.[50] As argued by some scholars, the 'legal space' argument appeared in a context where the Court was merely responding to the applicants' argument based on the *ordre public* mission of the Convention and, accordingly, was no more than an explanation of the remarks in *Loizidou* concerning the need to fill a vacuum.[51]

[44] *Banković* (n 30) para 73.

[45] See Sarah Miller, 'Revisiting Extraterritorial Jurisdiction: A Territorial Justification for Extraterritorial Jurisdiction under the European Convention' (2009) 20(4) EJIL 1223–26. cf also the chapter by Marko Milanovic in this volume.

[46] *Banković* (n 30) para 71.

[47] A Orakhelashvili 'Restrictive Interpretation of Human Rights Treaties in the Recent Jurisprudence of the European Court of Human Rights' (2003) 14 EJIL 529; and J L Grenier, 'Extraterritorial Applicability of Human Rights Treaty Obligations to United Nations-mandated forces' in *Report on Applicability of Humanitarian Law and Human Rights Law to UN Mandated Forces* (ICRC 2004) 81.

[48] R Lawson, 'Life After Bankovic: On the Extraterritorial Application of the European Convention on Human Rights' in Coomans and Kamminga (eds) (n 6); and Kerem Altiparmak, 'Bankovic: An Obstacle to the Application of the European Convention on Human Rights in Iraq?' (2004) 9(2) Journal of Conflict and Security 213–51.

[49] Martin Scheinin, 'Extraterritorial Effect of the International Covenant on Civil and Political Rights' in Coomans and Kamminga (eds) (n 6); See also Marko Milanovic, 'From Compromise to Principle: Clarifying the Concept of State Jurisdiction in Human Rights Treaties' (2008) 8(3) Human Rights Law Review 435.

[50] Fons Coomans and Menno Kamminga, 'Comparative Introductory Comments on the Extraterritorial Application of Human Rights Treaties' Coomans and Kamminga (n 6).

[51] Michael O'Boyle 'The European Convention on Human Rights and Extraterritorial Jurisdiction: A Comment on Life after Banković' 137, in Coomans and Kamminga (n 6); and Lawson (n 48) 114;

2.2.3 *Effective control over territory outside the legal space*

The *Issa and Others v Turkey*[52] case concerned the alleged killing of six shepherds in the course of three weeks' military operations conducted by the Turkish army in northern Iraq in April 1995. The Court dismissed the case on purely factual grounds. Specifically, it was *not* satisfied that the Turkish army troops were in 'effective control of the area' where the killings took place or that the shepherds had been under the 'authority and control' of the Turkish soldiers prior to their killing. It thus concluded that the deceased had *not* come within the 'jurisdiction' of Turkey for the purposes of Article 1 of the Convention.

However, the Court held that had it been proved that the Turkish army forces were, even temporarily, in effective control of the area in question, it would logically follow that the shepherds were within the jurisdiction of Turkey (and not that of Iraq, which is not a Contracting State and clearly does not fall within the legal space (*espace juridique*) of the Contracting States).[53] Clearly, this dictum was in clear contrast to the Court's conclusion in the *Banković* case, which was declared inadmissible because the Former Republic of Yugoslavia was at the relevant time a non-Convention territory and was not within the legal space of the Contracting States.

The Court's ruling in *Issa* was interpreted as a significant departure from *Banković* and received criticism emanating particularly from the United Kingdom's domestic courts.[54] In our opinion, and as supported by a number of academics,[55] the Court's reasoning in *Banković* and later in *Issa* was reconcilable since the Court was prepared to establish jurisdiction had it been proven that the respondent States exercised effective control over the territories in question or exercised power and authority over the victims. Notwithstanding the 'legal space' argument in *Banković,* the Court was correct in the *Issa* case to hold that the Convention can have extraterritorial application beyond the territories of the Contracting States for their extraterritorial conduct. A contrary conclusion would otherwise be tantamount to arguing that the Contracting States have a *carte blanche* to perpetrate human rights violations

Tobias Thienel, 'The Judgment of the House of Lords in R (Al-Skeini) v. Secretary of State for Defence' (2008) 6 J Int'l Crim Just, 3–4.

[52] *Issa and Others v Turkey* App no 31821/96 (ECtHR, 16 November 2004).

[53] ibid para 74.

[54] *Al Skeini* (n 31) [265]: The High Court judges considered that the *Issa* judgment was inconsistent with the Grand Chamber's view in *Banković*. In particular they held: in our judgment the dicta in Issa do not, for the reasons which we have sought to express, follow any "clear and constant jurisprudence of the Strasbourg court". On the contrary, we think that they are inconsistent with *Banković* and the development of the Strasbourg jurisprudence in the years immediately before *Banković*. In a sense Issa seems to us to look back to an earlier period of the jurisprudence, which has subsequently made way for a more limited interpretation of Article 1 jurisdiction. It may well be that there is more than one school of thought at Strasbourg; and that there is an understandable concern that modern events in Iraq should not be put entirely beyond the scope of the Convention: but at present we would see the dominant school as that reflected in the judgment in *Banković* and it is to that school that we think we owe a duty under section 2(1).

[55] See, for example, Marko Milanovic, 'Al-Skeini and Al-Jedda in Strasbourg' (2012) 23(1) EJIL 124; R Wilde, 'The "Legal Space" or "Espace Juridique" of the European Convention on Human Rights: Is it Relevant to Extraterritorial State Action?' (2005) 2 EHRLR 115–24, para 9.

in non-Convention territories, violations which they cannot perpetrate on their own territory.

2.2.4 Effective control over an autonomous region

In the *Assanidzé* case,[56] the Court had ample opportunity to explain the often-confused relationship between the notions of 'jurisdiction', 'imputability', and 'responsibility' of a Contracting State. The case concerned the applicant's complaint that despite being acquitted by the Supreme Court of Georgia, he had remained in the custody of the authorities of the Adjarian Autonomous Republic (AAR) and that the Georgian authorities had failed in their duty to secure his release. Although the Georgian government accepted that the AAR was an integral part of Georgia, and that the matters complained of were within the jurisdiction of the Georgian State, it claimed that it did not exercise 'effective control' in the region.

The Court found that the central authorities had taken all procedural steps possible under domestic law to secure compliance with the judgment acquitting the applicant, had sought to resolve the dispute by political means, and had repeatedly urged the Adjarian authorities to release him, all to no avail. However, even though it was not inconceivable that States would encounter difficulties in securing compliance with the rights guaranteed by the Convention in all parts of their territory, each State that had ratified the Convention was responsible for events occurring anywhere within its national territory. Consequently, the Court held that the facts were within the 'jurisdiction' of Georgia and that, even though within the domestic system those matters were directly 'imputable' to the local authorities of the AAR, it was solely the 'responsibility' of the Georgian State that was engaged under the Convention.

2.2.5 Extraterritorial effective control over a separatist region

The Court confirmed its earlier jurisprudence in cases concerning separatist regions in Moldova and Nagorno-Karabakh.

2.2.5.1 Moldovan cases

In the cases of *Ilaşcu and Others v Moldova and Russia*[57] and *Catan and Others v the Republic of Moldova and Russia*,[58] the Court examined the question of responsibility of a Contracting State which is unable to exercise effective control over a separatist region which is an integral part of its own territory, as well as the extraterritorial jurisdiction exercised by another Contract State over the same separatist region.

[56] *Assanidzé v Georgia* [GC] App no 71503/01, para 137.

[57] *Ilaşcu and Others v the Republic of Moldova and Russia* [GC] App no 48787/99 (ECtHR, 8 July 2004).

[58] *Catan and Others v the Republic of Moldova and Russia* [GC] App nos 43370/04, 8252/05, and 18454/06 (ECtHR, 19 October 2012).

In the *Ilaşcu and Others* case, the applicants considered that Moldova was responsible for violation of their rights to a fair trial for failing to protect them from inhuman treatment since the Moldovan authorities had not taken adequate measures to cease such treatment. The Russian Federation shared that responsibility as the territory of Transdniestria was *de facto* under Russia's control, owing to the stationing of its troops and military equipment there and the support the Russian Federation gave to the Moldovan Republic of Transdniestria ('MRT'). Both governments claimed that the impugned acts did not come within their jurisdiction and denied responsibility in respect of the applicants' complaints.

The Court first ascertained whether Moldova's responsibility was engaged on account of either its duty to refrain from wrongful conduct or its positive obligations under the Convention. It found that the Moldovan government did not exercise authority over part of its territory, namely that part which is under the effective control of the MRT.[59] Nonetheless, it held that even in the absence of effective control over the Transdniestrian region, Moldova still had a positive obligation under Article 1 of the Convention to take all diplomatic, economic, judicial, or other measures within its power and, in accordance with international law, to secure the applicants' rights guaranteed by the Convention.[60] This positive obligation related both to the measures needed to re-establish its control over the Transdniestrian territory, as an expression of its jurisdiction, and to measures to ensure respect for the applicants' rights.[61] Having found that Moldova had failed to discharge its positive obligation described above, the Court held that it was responsible for the acts complained of.

With regards to the responsibility of the Russian government, the Court noted at the outset the involvement of the Russian troops in the arrest and detention of the applicants. It then considered that the MRT had been set up with the support of the Russian Federation, vested with organs of power and its own administration, and had remained under the effective authority, or at the very least under the *decisive influence*, of the Russian Federation, and in any event that it survived by virtue of the military, economic, financial, and political support given to it by the Russian Federation. For these reasons, and noting the Russian Federation's failure to make any attempt to put an end to the applicants' situation brought about by its agents, the Court held that the applicants came within the 'jurisdiction' of the Russian Federation for the purposes of Article 1 of the Convention and that its responsibility was engaged with regard to the acts complained of.[62]

In the *Catan and Others* case, the Court held that no evidence to discredit its findings in *Ilaşcu* had been adduced, and the ongoing Russian military presence sent a strong signal of continued support for the MRT regime. Therefore the Russian government had not persuaded the Court that the conclusions it reached in *Ilaşcu* were inaccurate, and the applicants fell within Russia's jurisdiction.

However, in contrast to the position in *Ilaşcu*, in which the Court had found that Moldova had not taken all available measures to end the Convention violation, it

[59] *Ilaşcu and Others* (n 57) para 330. [60] ibid para 331.
[61] ibid para 339. [62] ibid paras 393–94.

considered that in the *Catan and Others* case, the Moldovan government had made considerable efforts to support the applicants. The State had thus fulfilled its positive obligations in respect of the applicants.

Two conclusions can be drawn from these rulings. First, even when a Contracting State is unable to control a situation within its territory, resulting from partial military occupation or disobedience by local authorities,[63] the Convention continues to apply and the State concerned must do its utmost to secure the rights and freedoms of the Convention for all with a view to discharging its obligation under Article 1. In other words, a Contracting State 'may not seek refuge behind its inability to control portions of its national territory in order to escape its obligation to do everything which it legally and practically can do in order to secure the rights of the Convention on all its territory'.[64]

Second, as seen in the northern Cyprus cases, a Contracting State can be considered to be exercising Article 1 jurisdiction on foreign soil on account of its overall effective control through a dependent regime which survives there by virtue of its military, economic, political, or other support and which remains under its effective authority, or at the very least under its *decisive influence*. Accordingly, that State's responsibility can be engaged not only for the acts of its own agents but also for the acts, decisions, or omissions of the agents of the dependent regime. Moreover, one of the distinguishing features of the *Ilaşcu* judgment was the new criterion added by the Court in holding Russia responsible for the acts and omissions of the dependent entity, namely Russia's 'decisive influence' on the policies of the MRT.

2.2.5.2 Nagorno-Karabakh cases

In line with its conclusions in its aforementioned Cypriot and Moldovan judgments, the Court reiterated its jurisprudence in the *Chiragov and Others v Armenia* case,[65] which concerned six Azerbaijani applicants' inability to gain access to their homes in a district under the control of the Nagorno-Karabakh Republic (NKR) and, allegedly, the Armenian State.

In the Court's opinion, it was hardly conceivable that Nagorno-Karabakh—an entity with a population of less than 150,000 ethnic Armenians—would have been able, without substantial military support from Armenia, to set up a defence force in early 1992 capable—against Azerbaijan and its population of 7 million—of establishing control of the former Nagorno-Karabakh Autonomous Oblast and of conquering, before the end of 1993, the whole or major parts of seven surrounding Azerbaijani districts.

Relying on numerous reports and public statements, including from current and former members of the Armenian government, the Court found that Armenia, through its military presence and by providing military equipment and expertise,

[63] *Assanidzé* (n 56) para 137.

[64] See Olivier De Schutter, 'Globalization and Jurisdiction: Lessons from the European Convention on Human Rights' (2005) Center for Human Rights and Global Justice Working Paper, NYU School of Law, Number 9, 223.

[65] *Chiragov and Others v Armenia* [GC] App no 13216/05 (ECtHR, 16 June 2015).

had been significantly involved in the Nagorno-Karabakh conflict from an early date. Armenia's military support had continued to be decisive for control over the territories in question. Furthermore, it was evident from the facts established in the case that Armenia had given the NKR substantial political and financial support; its citizens were moreover required to acquire Armenian passports to travel abroad, as the NKR was not recognized by any State or international organization.

The Court concluded, therefore, that Armenia and the NKR were highly integrated in virtually all important matters and the NKR and its administration survived by virtue of the military, political, financial, and other support given to it by Armenia. Armenia thus exercised effective control over Nagorno-Karabakh and the surrounding territories. The Court consequently held Armenia responsible for violation of the applicants' rights to peaceful enjoyment of their possessions and to respect for family and private life and home.

The conclusion to be drawn from the *Chiragov and Others* judgment is that it is a confirmation of the Court's case law in the Cypriot and Moldovan cases, particularly the Court's judgment in the *Loizidou* case.[66] This conclusion has been recently confirmed by the Court in *Mozer v Republic of Moldova and Russia.*[67]

Another judgment, where the Court examined the questions of jurisdiction and responsibility, was rendered in the case of *Sargsyan v Azerbaijan.*[68] The Azeri government argued that since the village of Gulistan was located in a disputed area, surrounded by mines and encircled by opposing military positions, it had only limited responsibility under the Convention. The Court, however, dismissed this argument holding that, in contrast to other cases in which the Court had found that a State had only limited responsibility over part of its territory due to occupation by another State or control by a separatist regime, in the case at hand, it had not been established that Gulistan was occupied by the armed forces of another State. Thus, taking into account the need to avoid a vacuum in the Convention protection, the Court did not consider that the respondent government had demonstrated the existence of exceptional circumstances that would justify limiting its responsibility under the Convention.

The situation in the *Sargsyan* case was more akin to that of the *Assanidzé*[69] case because, from a legal standpoint, the respondent government had jurisdiction as the territorial state and full responsibility under the Convention, even though it might encounter difficulties at a practical level in exercising authority in the area of Gulistan. In particular, the Court ruled that, in cases in which a State is prevented from exercising its authority in part of its territory, its responsibility under the Convention is limited to discharging positive obligations, namely, the state must take judicial, political, or administrative measures.[70]

[66] See, for a different approach, the concurring opinion of Judge Motoc in the *Chiragov* judgment where she argues that the Court came closer to the criterion of the effective control imposed by the ICJ. In her opinion, this case 'represents one of the strongest returns to the general international law or, to put it in a plastic way, to "Oppenheim world" '.

[67] *Mozer v Republic of Moldova and Russia* App no 11138/10 (ECtHR, 23 February 2016) para 98 and 101.

[68] *Sargsyan v Azerbaijan* [GC] App no 40167/06 (ECtHR, 16 June 2015).

[69] *Assanidzé* (n 56).

[70] *Sarsgyan* (n 68) para 131.

2.3 Jurisdiction by virtue of the exercise of power and authority over persons

Another recognized exception to the general rule that the notion of Article 1 jurisdiction is territorial has emerged from cases concerning the exercise of authority or control by a Contracting State over persons on foreign soil. As illustrated by the early jurisprudence of the Convention bodies, a Contracting State is considered to exercise Article 1 jurisdiction wherever its agents—military or civilian—exercise power and authority over persons outside its national territory. The Court has reaffirmed this principle in a number of post-*Banković* judgments, which concerned extraterritorial acts—military or police operations—both within and outside the legal space of the Contracting States.

2.3.1 Exercise of extraterritorial jurisdiction during ad hoc police operations on a foreign territory

In the *Öcalan* judgment,[71] the Court referred to the principles applied in the *Freda, Reinette,* and *Illich Sanchez Ramirez* decisions and held that:

> the applicant was arrested by members of the Turkish security forces inside an aircraft in the international zone of Nairobi Airport. Directly after he had been handed over by the Kenyan officials to the Turkish officials the applicant was under effective Turkish authority and was therefore brought within the 'jurisdiction' of that State for the purposes of Article 1 of the Convention, even though in this instance Turkey exercised its authority outside its territory.

Based on the facts, therefore, the *Öcalan* case represents an exception to the general rule that the concept of jurisdiction in Article 1 is territorial. The justification for the exception is clearly that Turkey was, with the consent of Kenya, exercising effective control over the applicant within the latter's territory.

In the aforementioned *Issa* case, the Court found that it had not been established that Turkey exercised jurisdiction because it was not proven that the applicants were under the authority and control of the Turkish troops before their killing. However, it is clear that the Court would have been prepared to hold Turkey accountable for extraterritorial violation of the Convention if the factual basis of the complaints had been proven.

2.3.2 Exercise of jurisdiction during police or military operations in buffer zones or borders

In the *Isaak v Turkey* case, which concerned a violent demonstration in the UN buffer zone in Cyprus, the Court found that 'even if the acts complained of took place in the neutral UN buffer zone, the Court considers that the deceased was under the authority and/or effective control of the respondent State through its

[71] *Öcalan v Turkey* App no 46221/99 (ECtHR, 12 March 2003) para 93.

agents' and that, accordingly, the matters complained of fell within the 'jurisdiction' of Turkey.[72]

The *Pad and Others v Turkey* case[73] concerned the alleged torture and killing of seven Iranian men in north-west Iran by Turkish soldiers. Although the Court declared the application inadmissible for failure to exhaust domestic remedies, it explicitly rejected the notion of legal space, holding that:

> in exceptional circumstances the acts of Contracting States which are performed outside their territory or which produce effects there ('extraterritorial act') may amount to the exercise by them of jurisdiction within the meaning of Article 1 (see *Issa and Others*, cited above, § 68). Accordingly, a State may be held accountable for violations of the Convention rights and freedoms of persons who are in the territory of another State *which does not necessarily fall within the legal space of the Contracting States*, but who are found to be under the former State's authority and control through its agents operating—whether lawfully or unlawfully—in the latter State.

The Court relied on the government's admission that fire discharged from the Turkish helicopters had caused the killing of the applicants' relatives in concluding that they were under Turkey's jurisdiction regardless of on which side of the border the deaths took place. The Court considered that it would have been entirely arbitrary for the application of the Convention to hinge on the applicants' location within a few hundred metres.[74] This decision was perceived as a move towards accepting a 'cause-and-effect approach' to jurisdiction, comparable to the 'control entails responsibility' understanding of state jurisdiction.[75]

2.3.3 Exercise of extraterritorial jurisdiction over persons in high seas

In the *Medvedyev and Others v France* case,[76] the Court examined the question of exercise of extraterritorial jurisdiction over ships on the high seas. In establishing the exercise of jurisdiction by France, the Court employed the 'authority and control' over persons test. The Court held that, as this was a case of France having exercised full and exclusive control over the vessel and its crew, at least de facto, from the time of its interception, in a continuous and uninterrupted manner until they were tried in France, the applicants were effectively within France's jurisdiction for the purposes of Article 1 of the Convention.[77]

2.3.4 Exercise of extraterritorial jurisdiction on persons detained in overseas prisons

In its admissibility decision in *Al-Saadoon and Mufdhi v The United Kingdom*,[78] the Court held that the UK had jurisdiction over the applicants who had been

[72] *Isaak v Turkey* App no 44587/98 (ECtHR, 28 September 2006).
[73] *Pad and Others v Turkey* App no 60167/00 (ECtHR, 28 June 2007) para 53.
[74] Marko Milanovic (n 55) 124. [75] Lawson (n 48) 84.
[76] *Medvedyev and Others v France* [GC] App no 3394/03 (ECtHR, 29 March 2010).
[77] ibid para 67.
[78] *Al-Saadoon v The United Kingdom* App no 61498/08 (ECtHR, 30 June 2009).

arrested by British forces and detained in a British-run military prison in Iraq. The Court stressed the physical power that the UK agents had over the applicants and used a very similar formulation to that in *Öcalan*, finding that 'the United Kingdom exercised control and authority over the individuals detained . . . solely as a result of the use or threat of military force'. The decisive passage reads as follows:

> The Court considers that, given the total and exclusive *de facto*, and subsequently also *de jure*, control exercised by the United Kingdom authorities over the premises in question, the individuals detained there, including the applicants, were within the United Kingdom's jurisdiction (see *Hess v. the United Kingdom*, no. 6231/73, Commission decision of 28 May 1975, Decisions & Reports vol. 2, p. 72).[79]

The Court's above-cited considerations in the *Al-Saadoon* case confirm its approach in the *Öcalan* case, where factual control over a person is decisive as opposed to legally recognized control, which was heavily emphasized in the exceptions cited in *Banković*.[80] Although the Court also pointed to the United Kingdom government's *de jure* control over the premises, this was not decisive for the case since the Court found that the United Kingdom's de facto control over the premises was only 'reflected in law'.[81] Prisoners in military installations are, therefore, within the State's jurisdiction on the basis of the factual test, just as anyone else who is brought physically within their full effective authority.

In the *Al-Jedda* case,[82] the British government contended that the internment was attributable to the United Nations, not to the United Kingdom, and that the applicant was not, therefore, within the United Kingdom jurisdiction under Article 1 of the Convention. Alternatively, relying on the opinion of the late Lord Bingham at the House of Lords,[83] the government argued that the internment was carried out pursuant to Resolution 1546, which created an obligation on the United Kingdom to detain the applicant which, pursuant to Article 103[84] of the United Nations Charter, overrode its Convention obligations.

The Court first distinguished this case from the *Behrami* and *Saramati* cases,[85] noting that the United Nation's role with regards to security in Iraq in 2004 was quite different from its role in Kosovo in 1999. It then pointed out that the United Nations Security Council (UNSC) resolution after the invasion—Resolution 1483—did not assign any security role to the United Nations. Although Resolution 1511, adopted on 16 October 2003, authorized 'a multinational force under unified command to take all necessary measures to contribute to the maintenance of security and stability in Iraq', the Court did not consider this to mean that the acts

[79] ibid paras 87 and 88.
[80] See Cornelia Janik and Thomas Kleinlein, 'When Soering Went to Iraq . . . : Problems of Jurisdiction, Extraterritorial Effect and Norm Conflicts in Light of the European Court of Human Rights' Al Saadoon Case' (2009) GoJil 1, 3, 487.
[81] ibid. [82] *Al-Jedda v United Kingdom* App no 27021/08 (ECtHR, 7 July 2011).
[83] ibid para 20.
[84] Article 103 states that members' obligations under the UN Charter override their obligations under any other treaty.
[85] *Behrami v France* and *Saramati v France, Germany, and Norway* [GC] App nos 71412/01 and 78166/01 (ECtHR, 2 May 2007).

of soldiers within the multinational force became attributable to the United Nations or ceased to be attributable to the troop-contributing nations.[86] In particular, the United Nations did not assume any degree of control over either the multinational force or any other of the executive functions of the Coalition Provisional Authority. In Resolution 1546, adopted on 8 June 2004, some four months before the applicant was taken into detention, the Security Council had reaffirmed the authorization for the multinational force, but there was no indication that it had intended to assume any greater degree of control or command over the force than it had exercised previously. In sum, the Security Council had neither effective control nor ultimate authority and control over the acts and omissions of troops within the multinational force. The applicant's detention was, therefore, not attributable to the United Nations.

The internment had taken place within a detention facility controlled exclusively by British forces, and the applicant had thus been within the authority and control of the United Kingdom throughout. The decision to hold him in internment had been taken by the British officer in command of the detention facility. The fact that his detention was subject to reviews by committees including Iraqi officials and non-United Kingdom representatives from the multinational force did not prevent it from being attributable to the United Kingdom. The applicant thus fell within the jurisdiction of the United Kingdom for the purposes of Article 1 of the Convention.

The *Al-Jedda* judgment was criticized for not taking a firm position on whether the applicable test was that of 'ultimate authority and control'[87] or effective operational control over the relevant conduct of troops (as suggested by the International Law Commission).[88] It has also led to confusion about the relationship between 'jurisdiction', as a threshold requirement for the applicability of the Convention, and 'attribution', as an element of international responsibility for a breach of the Convention.[89] It was argued by some scholars that the Court's finding on attribution turned into a precondition for a finding on jurisdiction.[90]

In our opinion, the answer lies in the *Catan and Others* judgment, where the Court held that the test for establishing the existence of 'jurisdiction' under Article 1 of the Convention has never been equated with the test for establishing a State's responsibility for an internationally wrongful act under international law.[91]

2.3.5 *Al-Skeini and Others, concerning exercise of extraterritorial jurisdiction on persons held in prisons or fields in occupied territories*

The case of *Al-Skeini and Others v the United Kingdom* concerned the killings of six Iraqi nationals in Basra in 2003 by British troops, where the United Kingdom was

[86] See the chapter by Linos-Alexandre Sicilianos in this volume.
[87] *Behrami* (n 85) paras 133–40.
[88] James Crawford and Simon Olleson, 'The Character and Forms of International Responsibility' in Malcolm D Evans (ed), *International Law* (OUP 2014) 459.
[89] See Marko Milanovic, 'Al-Skeini and Al-Jedda in Strasbourg' (2012) 23(1) EJIL 121–39.
[90] ibid. [91] *Catan and Others* (n 58) para 115.

an occupying power. Five of the victims met their death during military operations involving British soldiers. The sixth applicant, Baha Mousa, died under torture at the hands of British troops in a military base. The families of the victims complained to the Court that the British authorities had not conducted an independent and thorough investigation into the circumstances of the killings.

The Court reiterated its case law that a Contracting State's obligation to secure the Convention rights and freedoms was confined to persons within its 'jurisdiction', a primarily territorial concept. Acts performed or producing effects outside the State's territory could constitute an exercise of jurisdiction only in exceptional circumstances. The Court's case law indicates that such circumstances could exist where State agents exercise authority and control over an individual outside the territory. Exceptional circumstances could also arise when, as a consequence of lawful or unlawful military action, a Contracting State exercised effective control of an area outside the national territory either directly, through its own armed forces, or through a subordinate local administration.

When examining the circumstances of the killings in the applicants' case, the Court observed that, following the removal from power of the Ba'ath regime and until the accession of the interim Iraqi government, 'the United Kingdom (together with the United States) had assumed in Iraq the exercise of some of the public powers normally exercised by a sovereign government'. In particular, it had assumed authority and responsibility for the maintenance of security in south-east Iraq. In these exceptional circumstances, the United Kingdom had, through its soldiers, engaged in security operations in Basra during the period in question and exercised authority and control over individuals killed in the course of such security operations. All the applicants' relatives had died during the relevant period. With the exception of the third applicant's wife, it was not disputed that their deaths were caused by the acts of British soldiers during the course of, or contiguous to, security operations in Basra City. There was thus a jurisdictional link in their cases. Although it was not known which side had fired the bullet that had resulted in the death of the third applicant's wife, she had died in the course of a security operation when British soldiers carried out a patrol in the vicinity of the third applicant's home and joined in the fatal exchange of fire, so there was a jurisdictional link in her case also. The Court then found that the British authorities had failed to carry out an independent and effective investigation into the deaths.

As is clear from the above conclusion, the Court applied the *personal* model of jurisdiction ('authority and control over persons') to the killing of the applicants' relatives in the *Al-Skeini* judgment. The British government were found to have been under an obligation to secure for the victims *only* the rights and freedoms that were relevant to their situation, namely the right to life under Article 2 of the Convention.

The judgment can be considered a real watershed in view of the Court's ruling that the Contracting States have to respect their human rights obligations wherever their agents exercised authority and control over persons, whether in the United Kingdom, Iraq, Yemen, Afghanistan, or elsewhere. It clarified the 'European legal space' concept, which appeared in the *Banković* case, according to which the Convention did *not* only apply within the Council of Europe countries. The judgment clearly showed that human rights are not dependent on the whereabouts of the person but on whether s/he is under the authority and control of agents of the State.

The only drawback in the *Al-Skeini* judgment was the Court's statement that 'the United Kingdom ... exercise[d] some of the public powers normally exercised by a sovereign government'. This statement, which was relied on by the Dutch government in the *Jaloud*[92] case, was perceived as a precondition for application of the personal model of jurisdiction. As Milanovic argues, if the United Kingdom had not exercised such public powers, the personal model of jurisdiction would not have applied. He claims '[w]hile the ability to kill is "authority and control" over the individual if the state has public powers, killing is not authority and control if the state is merely firing missiles from an aircraft. Under this reasoning, drone operations in Yemen or wherever would be just as excluded from the purview of human rights treaties as under *Banković*'.[93]

2.3.6 Exercise of extraterritorial jurisdiction on persons at a military checkpoint

The latest case from Iraq is the aforementioned *Jaloud v The Netherlands*,[94] which concerned the killing of the applicant's son by Netherlands forces at a vehicle checkpoint. As in the above-mentioned Iraqi cases, the applicant complained to the Court that the Dutch authorities had failed to conduct an effective and independent investigation into the killing of the victim by a Netherlands serviceman, a member of the stabilization force in Iraq.

The government disputed that the victim had come within the territorial jurisdiction of the Netherlands. It claimed that the killing could not be attributed to the Netherlands but to the United States and the United Kingdom as the designated 'occupying powers' under United Nations Security Council Resolution 1483, or with the United Kingdom alone as the 'lead nation' in south-eastern Iraq, holding command over the Netherlands contingent of the Stabilization Force in Iraq SFIR. The government further submitted that the Netherlands had never assumed any of the public powers normally exercised by a sovereign government and that there had never been assertion of physical authority or control over the victim before he was shot.

The Court observed that the fact of executing a decision or an order given by an authority of a foreign State was not in itself sufficient to relieve a Contracting State of its obligations under the Convention. It noted that the Netherlands assumed responsibility for providing security in the area where their troops were stationed, to the exclusion of other participating States, and retained *full command* over its contingent there. The Netherlands troops had *not* been at the disposal of any foreign power or under the exclusive direction or control of any other State. The fatal shooting of the applicant's son had taken place at a checkpoint manned by personnel under the

[92] *Jaloud* (n 7). [93] Milanovic (n 89) 130. [94] *Jaloud* (n 7).

command and direct supervision of a Netherlands army officer. The exercise of authority and control over persons passing through the checkpoint thus constituted an exercise of jurisdiction within the meaning of Article 1 of the Convention.

It is therefore clear that the mere exercise of control over a checkpoint is sufficient to establish jurisdiction even in the absence of effective control of the territory concerned.

As in the aforementioned *Al-Jedda* case, the Court's examination of the question of jurisdiction together with attribution and State responsibility caused confusion in *Jaloud*.[95] These concerns have also been raised by certain member States who argue that the concept of 'effective control' as applied by the Court to establish the extraterritorial jurisdiction is not in harmony with the principles of international law.[96]

It is true that the attribution of wrongful acts is necessary to establish responsibility of a State in the context of general international law.[97] In the *Nicaragua* case, the ICJ held that 'to give rise to legal responsibility of the USA, it would in principle have to be proven that that State had *effective control* of the military and paramilitary operations in the course of which the alleged violation was committed'.[98] This 'effective control' test was reaffirmed in the *Bosnian Genocide* case[99] by refusing to apply the broader 'overall control' test[100] of the International Criminal Court for the Former Yugoslavia (ICTY) in the *Tadic* decision.[101]

In the aforementioned cases, the ICJ examined the question of whether the conduct of a group of persons could be attributed to a State, with the result that it could be held responsible under international law for that conduct.[102]

However, the Court's case law clearly shows that the concept of jurisdiction within the meaning of Article 1 is an autonomous one and distinct from the question of attribution. Even when the Court takes into account relevant rules of international law when examining a case, the test for establishing the existence of

[95] Jane M Rooney, 'The Relationship between Jurisdiction and Attribution after Jaloud v. Netherlands' (2015) 62(3) Netherlands International Law Review 407–28; Aurel Sari, 'Untangling Extra-territorial Jurisdiction from International Responsibility in Jaloud v. Netherlands: Old Problem, New Solutions?' (2015) 53 Military Law and the Law of War Review 287–318 <http://ssrn.com/abstract=2554951> accessed 15 December 2016.

[96] See for example the Russian government's view in *Mozer* (n 67) para 93 and also their concern on the quality of some Court judgments when the Court departs from the existing system of international case law which could lead to the fragmentation of public international law expressed at the 2015 Brussels Conference. See H/Inf (2015) 1, 'High-Level Conference on the Implementation of the European Convention on Human Rights, our shared responsibility', Proceedings, Brussels, 26–27 March 2015. Directorate General of Human Rights and Rule of Law, Council of Europe, June 2015, 99.

[97] See *Military and Paramilitary Activities in and against Nicaragua (Nicaragua v United States of America)* [1986] ICJ Rep, para 399.

[98] ibid para 115. In the same line, Article 8 of the Articles on State Responsibility, see James Crawford, *The International Law Commission's Articles on State Responsibility: Introduction, Text and Commentaries* (CUP 2002).

[99] *Application of the Convention on the Prevention and Punishment of the Crime of Genocide (Bosnia and Herzegovina v Serbia and Montenegro)* (Merits) [2007] ICJ Rep 43, paras 402–7.

[100] See Antonio Cassese, 'The Nicaragua and Tadic Tests Revisited in Light of the ICJ Judgment on Genocide in Bosnia' (2007) 18(4) EJIL 650.

[101] *Prosecutor v Tadic* (Judgment) ICTY-91-1-A (15 July 1999).

[102] See *Mozer* (n 67) para 102 on the same matter.

'jurisdiction' under Article 1 of the Convention cannot be equated with the test for establishing a State's responsibility for an internationally wrongful act under general international law.[103]

The question of jurisdiction is, therefore, a preliminary threshold issue before any questions of State responsibility.[104] In other words, if the test for determining State responsibility precedes the test for establishing jurisdiction, this would be putting the cart before the horse.[105]

3. Concluding Remarks

It is clear that significant progress has been made in the protection of human rights and fundamental freedoms since the time of Earl Clarendon. However, recent history has shown that individuals are increasingly vulnerable in the face of State conduct that knows no boundaries. Extensive extraterritorial activity by the Contracting States in the last two decades has led to an influx of a number of cases in which the Court had to examine questions on whether States are responsible for violations of the Convention outside their home territories and, if so, how far the extraterritorial jurisdiction of the Court should extend. In this connection, the Court has generated a coherent body of jurisprudence showing that the meaning of the phrase 'within their jurisdiction' in Article 1 does not reflect an exclusively territorial notion of jurisdiction and that there are exceptions to the territorial limitation of Article 1 jurisdiction.

First, when a State exercises effective control of an area—lawful or unlawful—outside its national territory, that State can be considered to be exercising jurisdiction in that area and its obligation under Article 1 extends to securing the entire range of substantive rights set out in the Convention and those additional Protocols which it has ratified, even if such control is exercised directly, through its armed forces or through a subordinate local administration, as in the cases of northern Cyprus, Transdniestria, and Nagorno-Karabakh.

Second, a Contracting State is considered to exercise its jurisdiction wherever its agents—military or civilian—exercise power and authority over persons on foreign territory, as demonstrated by the cases of *Öcalan, Issa, Al-Jedda, Al-Skeini*, and *Jaloud*.

Third, activities of a State, through its diplomatic or consular agents abroad and on board ships, aircraft, and spacecraft flying its flag, constitute examples of extraterritorial exercise of jurisdiction in accordance with the principles of public international law and within the meaning of Article 1.

Finally, as the above-mentioned exceptions demonstrate, the Court has over the years expanded the notion of jurisdiction and State responsibility in its case law. For the Court, jurisdiction constitutes the threshold question before any questions of State responsibility. International case law has addressed the issue of attribution of

[103] *Catan* (n 58) para 115. [104] *De Schutter* (n 64). [105] O'Boyle (n 6) 131.

international responsibility using different control tests.[106] For its part, the Court looks to the facts of the case in order to determine the jurisdiction of a State within the meaning of Article 1. In other words, the test for establishing jurisdiction has never been equated with the test for establishing a State's responsibility for an internationally wrongful act under general international law. This explains why the threshold of control applied by the Court is lower—in the context of a human rights treaty—than in other international case law.

The Court's interpretation of the Convention as a 'living instrument', as well as a constitutional instrument of the European public order,[107] will help it to deal with new questions[108] beyond the traditional approach of jurisdiction. In view of the object and purpose of the Convention, we consider that the Contracting States must continue to respect the Convention rights of all persons who are found to be under their control, authority, and decisive influence in territories where they carry out extraterritorial activities.

[106] *Military and Paramilitary Activities in and against Nicaragua* (n 97); *Application of the Convention on the Prevention and Punishment of the Crime of Genocide* (n 99) and *Prosecutor v Tadić* (n 101).

[107] *Loizidou* (n 18) para 75.

[108] For example, possible responsibility of the Contracting States for drone strikes outside their legal territories might be brought before the Court as a challenging legal question.

7

Territorial Jurisdiction and Positive Obligations of an Occupied State

Some Reflections on Evolving Issues under Article 1 of the Convention

Ganna Yudkivska

1. Introduction

Professor Philip Allott recently argued that 'there has never been a better time to be an international lawyer', since 're-imagining the one big idea of the international world . . . is a particularly delightful challenge for . . . philosophical idealists'.[1] These days, however, it is quite hard to remain an idealist, even a philosophical one; it could, indeed, be frustrating to be an international lawyer or, even more so, an international judge, in the face of so many challenges when everyone speaks endlessly about international law and tries to find answers in it for the recent threats to peace and stability. It has become a common trend to criticize international law for the failure to change the world for the better.

Nevertheless, it should not be forgotten that, whilst the language of international law is not a solution to international conflict, the courts' interpretation of relevant international obligations does affect international relations to a significant extent: law provides a certain framework for the argumentation of the parties to a conflict in their attempts to solve it.[2]

In this chapter, I would like to elaborate on an unfairly neglected question that is not sufficiently developed in either the doctrine or the practice of international tribunals, including the European Court of Human Rights (ECtHR), but is important and is bound to grow even more so in the coming years. Specifically, this

[1] Philip Allott, 'The Idealist's Dilemma: Re-imagining International Society' address at the Spring Conference of the International Law Association British Branch at the Inner Temple, London (23 May 2014) <http://www.ejiltalk.org/the-idealists-dilemma-re-imagining-international-society> accessed 20 November 2015.

[2] See Christopher J Borgen, 'Public International Law and the Conflict Over Transnistria' in Mensur Akgün (ed), *Managing Intractable Conflicts: Lessons From Moldova and Cyprus* (Istanbul Kültür University 2013) 107–8.

chapter aims to outline the nature and define the scope of the human rights obligations of an *occupied* State, in conjunction with potential concurrent duties and responsibilities of an *occupying* State. Section 2 discusses the posture of international law with respect to the obligations of an injured state. Section 3 draws on the ECtHR's and other international courts' case law to establish that even an occupied State (defined by international law as the 'victim' or the 'injured' State) is subject to human rights obligations. Section 4 proceeds to examine recent developments in the ECtHR's post-*Ilaşcu* jurisprudence. Finally, Section 5 constructs some principles to bring more clarity to the scope of these obligations.

2. What Can Be Expected from an Injured State—The International Law Position

The task of the international law of occupation, as it has developed since the nineteenth century as part of the law of war, is to regulate the conduct of occupying forces. Indeed, it is all about what an occupying power should and should not do. According to the international law of occupation, an occupying power is responsible for the welfare of the population in an occupied area. The duties of such a power are further detailed in the 1907 Hague Regulations,[3] the Fourth Geneva Convention,[4] and the provisions of an Additional Protocol.[5]

In particular, in Eyal Benvenisti's view, Article 43 of the Hague Regulations defines the essence of the occupant's authority and responsibility: 'The authority of the legitimate power having in fact passed into the hands of the occupant, the latter shall take all the measures in his power to restore, and ensure, as far as possible, public order and safety'.[6] Very little is said about the obligations of the State that has lost a part of its territory following a belligerent occupation.

Some situations come under the ECtHR's jurisdiction—Moldova, Ukraine, Georgia, Cyprus, and Azerbaijan claim that they have lost control over parts of their respective territories and consequently cannot guarantee respect for human rights there. The ECtHR has recently recognized that 'the wording of Article 41 [. . .] provides for "afford[ing] just satisfaction to the *injured* party" (in French—"*à la partie lésée*"); a "party" (with a lower-case "p") has to be understood as one of the actual parties to the proceedings before the Court', ie *a State* in an inter-State case *can be*

[3] Hague Convention (IV) respecting the Laws and Customs of War on Land and its annex Regulations concerning the Laws and Customs of War on Land (adopted 18 October 1907) 36 TS No 539.

[4] Geneva Convention (IV) relative to the Protection of Civilian Persons in Time of War (adopted 12 August 1949, entered into force 21 October 1950) 75 UNTS 287.

[5] Protocol Additional to the Geneva Conventions of 12 August 1949, and relating to the Protection of Victims of International Armed Conflicts (Protocol I) (adopted 8 June 1977, entered into force 7 December 1978) 1125 UNTS 3.

[6] Eyal Benvenisti, 'Occupation and Territorial Administration' (2015) Global Trust Working Paper 11/2015, 15 <http://globaltrust.tau.ac.il/publications> accessed 20 November 2015.

an 'injured party'.[7] For the sake of conceptual clarity, we will furthermore refer to a State that has lost control over a part of its territory as an 'injured State'.

Lack of a clearly defined scope of obligations of an injured State at first appears natural—what can one expect from a victim who is already suffering? Is it moral or fair to impose obligations on one who already has lost something, such as, in the case of a State, part of its territory? For instance, international law speaks about a duty to prevent wrongful acts (eg genocide) or a duty to mitigate the consequences of such acts.

The International Law Commission (ILC) has previously examined whether failure to take steps to mitigate damage caused by an internationally wrongful act could be considered a factor affecting the scope of reparation for an injured State. It mentioned that:

> [e]ven a wholly innocent victim of wrongful conduct is expected to act reasonably when confronted by the injury. Although often expressed in terms of a '*duty* to mitigate', this is *not a legal obligation which itself gives rise to responsibility*. It is rather that a failure to mitigate by the injured party may preclude recovery to that extent.[8]

Thus, according to the ILC, lack of positive action cannot trigger the responsibility of an injured State. It referred to the finding of the ICJ in the case concerning the Gabčíkovo-Nagymaros Project:

> Slovakia also maintained that it was acting under a duty to mitigate [...] It stated that 'It is a general principle of international law that a party injured [...] must seek to mitigate the damage he has sustained'.

It would follow from such a principle that an injured State which has failed to take the necessary measures to limit the damage sustained would not be entitled to claim compensation for that damage which could have been avoided. While this principle might thus provide a basis for the calculation of damages, it could not, on the other hand, justify an otherwise wrongful act.[9] It is thus clear that any failure by an injured State to act does not at all exclude or mitigate responsibility of a perpetrator, but can only be relevant to compensation issues.

Even when it comes to countermeasures designed to induce a State responsible for an internationally wrongful act to comply with its obligations, the Draft Articles on Responsibility of States for Internationally Wrongful Acts (ARSIWA)[10] speak about a *right*, but not about an *obligation*, to resort to such measures (measures that would otherwise be contrary to the international obligations of an injured State vis-à-vis the responsible State, if they were not taken by the former in response to an internationally wrongful act by the latter in order to procure cessation and reparation).[11]

In addition, Eyal Benvenisti has specified duties of the ousted government upon return (to refrain from issuing prescriptions that would conflict with some

[7] *Cyprus v Turkey* App no 25781/94 (ECtHR, 12 May 2014).

[8] (2000) II(1) ILC Yearbook 19.

[9] *Gabčíkovo-Nagymaros Project (Hungary/Slovakia)* (Judgment) [1997] ICJ Rep 55, para 80.

[10] ILC, 'Draft Articles on Responsibility of States for Internationally Wrongful Acts' (November 2001) UN Doc A/56/10 chp.IV.E.1 Supplement no 10.

[11] ibid 128.

of the occupant's measures that were in conformity with Article 43 of the Hague Regulations).[12] However, he does not go further than this.

3. The Establishment of Human Rights Obligations of an Injured State—*Ilaşcu v Moldova and Russia*

The ECtHR took a significant step forward in developing some principles in respect to the obligations of an injured State in its landmark judgment in the case of *Ilaşcu v Moldova and Russia*[13] that concerned the responsibility of both Moldova and Russia in respect of acts of the Moldavian Republic of Transdniestria. In this case, Russian-backed separatist forces in the enclave of Transdniestria arrested four Moldovans for 'anti-Soviet activities, fighting by illegal means against the State of Transdniestria and other offences'. These four individuals brought an action against two States, complaining of ill-treatment, unlawful detention, and deterioration of prison conditions following the introduction of their application to the Court. The Court found that 'the Moldovan Government ... does not exercise authority over part of its territory, namely that part which is under the effective control of the [separatists]' but then concluded that 'even in the absence of effective control over the Transdniestrian region, Moldova still has a positive obligation under Article 1 of the Convention to take the diplomatic, economic, judicial or other measures that it is in its power to take and are in accordance with international law to secure to the applicants the rights guaranteed by the Convention'[14].

Thus, for the first time, the Court found that a State which does not have effective control over a part of its territory as a result of occupation by an unlawful separatist regime, and is unable to exercise its jurisdiction there, still has some *positive* obligations deriving from its *de jure* jurisdiction.

The Court's approach represented a new development in international law, according to which human rights obligations are primarily triggered by the effective territorial control.

Let us examine how the Court reached this point. A 1978 decision of the Commission in the case of *Cyprus v Turkey*[15] noted that '[i]t is bound to observe [...] that one High Contracting Party, namely Cyprus, has since 1974 been prevented from exercising its jurisdiction in the northern part of its territory by the presence there of armed forces of another High Contracting Party, namely Turkey'.[16] Based on this fact, the Commission concluded that the presence of Turkey's armed forces in that part of its territory prevented Cyprus from exercising jurisdiction there.

[12] Eyal Benvenisti, *International Law of Occupation* (Princeton University Press 2004) 21–26. In this respect Brad Roth criticizes Benvenisti for ignoring 'entirely the crucial problem of retribution against collaborators' (see Brad R Roth, *Governmental Illegitimacy in International Law* (Clarendon Press 1999) 156).

[13] *Ilaşcu and Others v Moldova and Russia* App no 48787/99 (ECtHR, 8 July 2004).

[14] ibid para 331.

[15] *Cyprus v Turkey* App no 8007/77 (Commission Decision, 10 July 1978).

[16] ibid para 40.

Later, in 1991, in the case of *An and Others v Cyprus*,[17] the applicant brought complaints against Cyprus; the Commission found, referring to the above conclusion in *Cyprus v Turkey*, that '[t]he authority of the respondent Government is in fact still limited to the southern part of Cyprus. It follows that the Republic of Cyprus cannot be held responsible under Article 1 of the Convention for the acts of Turkish Cypriot authorities in the north of Cyprus.'[18] No issue of positive obligations arose that time, and the application was thus declared inadmissible.

Following this line, in 1996 in its key case *Loizidou v Turkey*,[19] the Court accepted the applicant's argument that 'since the Republic of Cyprus cannot be held accountable for the part of the island occupied by Turkey, it must be Turkey which is so accountable. Otherwise the northern part of Cyprus would constitute a vacuum as regards responsibility for violations of human rights',[20] which means that it was clear from the outset that the Republic of Cyprus no longer had any Convention obligation (negative or positive) regarding the occupied territory.[21] It is necessary to note in this respect that Judge Ress, in his separate opinion in the *Ilaşcu* case, distinguished the situation in Northern Cyprus from the one in Transdniestria on the grounds that there was a full military occupation of Northern Cyprus by Turkey, whilst there was no occupation of the Transdniestrian territory by Russia, even though there was a rebel regime and the Russian Federation exercised a decisive influence, and even control, in that territory. This distinction does not appear persuasive from the standpoint of positive obligations, since in both cases we are talking about de facto regimes by self-proclaimed authorities; however, the crucial issue is, as pointed out by Judge Ress, the possibility of influence over such a de facto regime as articulated in the *Ilaşcu* case—an issue to which I will return later.

Next in this progression was the Commission's examination of the case of *Vearncombe v The United Kingdom and The Federal Republic of Germany*, in which Berlin citizens complained about the noise from a military shooting range built and used by the British Army in Berlin. The Commission found that the alleged violation could only be attributed to the United Kingdom and not to the Federal Republic of Germany, because military activities in the British sector of Berlin were based on occupation:

> The shooting range in question is not only used exclusively by the British Army but it was also constructed entirely under the control of the British Military Government. Although the German authorities in Berlin were informed of the plans for constructing the range and certain consultations took place between British and German authorities, the responsibility for the construction and/or use of the range lies solely with the British Military Government.[22]

It would appear that in *Ilaşcu*, the Court departed from the previous jurisprudence and clearly established that, under the Convention, the absence of effective

[17] *An and Others v Cyprus* App no 18270/91 (Commission Decision, 8 October 1991).

[18] ibid para 3.

[19] *Loizidou v Turkey* App no 15318/89 (ECtHR, 18 December 1996) para 49.

[20] ibid.

[21] See Elizabeth Nielsen, 'State Responsibility for Terrorist Groups' (2010) 17.1 Journal of International Law and Policy 151.

[22] *Vearncombe v The United Kingdom and the Federal Republic of Germany* (1987) 59 DR 199.

control over Transdniestria, where separatist forces operated, did not per se exclude the responsibility of Moldova under the Convention. In so holding, the Court relied heavily on positive obligations. It is true that a careful reading of the *Ilaşcu* judgment, together with the annexes on fact-finding and separate opinion of judges who also participated in the fact-finding mission, reveals a very specific circumstance under which the Court was ready to impose positive obligations on the injured state, namely close cooperation between Moldovan and Transdniestrian authorities, which will be mentioned later in this chapter. Still, even in view of this feature, the Court engaged in a rather innovative line of reasoning.

It is relevant in this respect to observe the approach of the International Law Commission (ILC) to the issue of the allocation of responsibility between occupying and occupied States. For instance, in his Eighth Report on State Responsibility,[23] the ILC Special Rapporteur Mr Roberto Ago mentioned that prominent international lawyers disagree on whether or not to recognize a responsibility on the part of an occupying State for an internationally wrongful act committed by the occupied State in a field in which its activity is subject to interference and control by the occupying State. He himself 'definitely believes that it should'.[24] Therefore, not only is an occupying power responsible for its own wrongdoings, it should also be held responsible for the acts of an injured State as long as these acts are within its control. But then, he continued, as long as there are certain areas of activity which do not affect the interests of the occupying State, and thus are left to the free decision of the occupied State, the latter will continue to incur international responsibility for any internationally wrongful acts committed in the areas of activity in question.

The rapporteur illustrated this position with reference to case law. He mentioned, in particular, the judgment rendered on 1 March 1927 by the Alexandria Court of Appeal in the *Fink* case. The applicant claimed compensation from the Egyptian government for damage suffered as a result of the liquidation of his business by the British military authorities occupying Egypt. The liquidation apparently occurred after one of the senior employees had been invited by the Egyptian police to surrender. The Court rejected the claim, stating that the only intervention by the Egyptian government was the invitation by the local police to surrender to the military authorities. And that court stated the following: 'the local authorities, in assisting the occupation forces, have always acted on behalf of the latter in accordance with the principles of international law, [. . .] and the local authorities cannot be held responsible for collaboration imposed by circumstances.'[25] Thus it was clear that 'while the conduct of the Egyptian authorities had been wrongful, it could not have entailed the responsibility of Egypt' since the relevant authorities had been under the control of the occupying State.[26]

[23] Roberto Ago, Special Rapporteur, 'Eighth Report on State Responsibility' (1979) II(1) ILC Yearbook 31. Submitted by the Special Rapporteur to the Commission at its thirtieth session.

[24] ibid para 20.

[25] Journal du Droit International (Paris) 55th year, No 1 (January–February 1928) 196.

[26] Eighth Report on State Responsibility (n 23) para 33.

Another decision referred to by Ago was rendered on 15 September 1951 by the Franco-Italian Conciliation Commission established under the Treaty of Peace with Italy on the claim by the French government calling upon Italy to return property owned by French citizens that had been seized under the decrees issued in 1944–45 by the (Italian) High Commissioner for Sicily, which at that time was under military occupation by the Allied and Associated Powers.[27] The Commission allowed the French claim, stating that the fact that Sicily was under administrative *control* by the Allied and Associated Powers was irrelevant, since no evidence of 'interference either by the commander of the occupation forces or by any allied authority' in respect of the challenged seizure was presented. It follows from this decision that 'the occupied state remains responsible for internationally wrongful acts committed by it without any interference or control by the occupying state'.[28] Vice versa, when any such act occurs under the control of an occupying power, the responsibility for it shifts to the occupying State.

The *Ilaşcu* case was not about wrongful conduct by an occupied State or interference with any right; it was about the obligations of the occupied State, and in this respect it was groundbreaking, even though the jurisprudence on positive obligations had developed significantly in the preceding years. Without providing any further explanation, the Court found that:

> where a Contracting State is prevented from exercising its authority over the whole of its territory by a constraining de facto situation, such as obtains when a separatist regime is set up, whether or not this is accompanied by military occupation by another State, it does not thereby cease to have jurisdiction within the meaning of Article 1 of the Convention over that part of its territory temporarily subject to a local authority sustained by rebel forces or by another State ... [T]he undertaking given by the State under Article 1 must be considered by the Court only in the light of the Contracting State's positive obligations towards persons within its territory.[29]

Whilst a detailed analysis of the Court's evolving jurisprudence on positive obligations goes beyond the scope of the present chapter, we should mention that it is argued that recent case law:

> reflects a new tendency whereby the Court appears systematically to base the positive obligations which it lays down [...] on a combination of the standard-setting provisions of the European text and Article 1 of that text [...] Here there is clearly a change of direction, not unrelated to the reassessment of the overall economy of the Convention that can be seen in some recent decisions. With [the *Ilaşcu* judgment], Article 1 of the Convention is seen more than ever as the cornerstone of the Convention system, to the point that it constitutes an independent source of general obligations—which are also positive obligations—on states.[30]

[27] *Différend Héritiers de S.A.R. Mgr le Duc de Guise* Décision No 107 (1951) 13 RIAA 150.

[28] Eighth Report on State Responsibility (n 23) para 35.

[29] *Ilaşcu and Others v Moldova and Russia* App no 48787/99 (ECtHR, 8 July 2004) para 333.

[30] Jean-François Akandji-Kombe, 'Positive Obligations under the European Convention on Human Rights' *Human Rights Handbook No 7* (Council of Europe 2007).

Criticizing this approach in *Ilaşcu*, a former ECtHR judge, Christos Rozakis, noted that:

> the Court in the case of Ilascu [. . .] incorporate[ed] the issue of positive obligations within the very notion of jurisdiction and [. . .] disregard[ed] the test of effective control as a pre-condition for the establishment of jurisdiction [. . .] It clearly transpires from the *Ilascu* judgment that the Court [. . .] called into question political tactics [of Moldova] in effectively protecting the human rights of the individual applicants.[31]

In other words, for the Court, Article 1 of the Convention does not at all absolve a State which has lost control over its territory from securing for everyone within its *de jure* jurisdiction the rights and freedoms defined in the Convention; to the contrary, the Court has interpreted Article 1 of the Convention as imposing positive obligations, absent effective control, precisely to regain control in order to guarantee full protection of human rights. For Rozakis, this unjustified replacement of the test of effective control with the concept of 'positive obligations' necessitates a very delicate assessment of different political, diplomatic, judicial, and other measures.

A parallel can be drawn to the approach applied by the ICJ concerning the obligation to prevent genocide. In the judgment of *Bosnia and Herzegovina v Serbia and Montenegro*,[32] the Court stressed the obligation of State Parties 'to employ all means reasonably available to them, so as to prevent genocide so far as possible [. . .] [R]esponsibility is [. . .] incurred if the State manifestly failed to take all measures to prevent genocide which were within its power, and which might have contributed to preventing the genocide'. However, having said this, the Court relied on the key concept of due diligence, which 'calls for an assessment *in concreto*';[33] namely it is necessary to evaluate the capacity of the State 'to influence effectively the action of persons likely to commit [. . .] genocide'.[34] This capacity depends on many elements. In the case at issue, the Court stressed the influence that Serbia had over the Bosnian Serbs, due to the strong political, military, and financial ties between them.

In both the *Ilaşcu* and *Bosnia and Herzegovina* cases, the two respective Courts applied rather ambiguous language concerning employment of all available means. In principle, treaties that establish obligations to protect often require States to take appropriate measures, without defining which measures are appropriate. The reasonableness standard is evidently context-specific and there are no sufficient guidelines.[35]

The European Court used the term 'appropriate and sufficient' measures, and also introduced the notion of a 'minimum effort': '[w]hen faced with a partial or total failure to act, the Court's task is to determine to what extent a minimum effort was nevertheless possible and whether it should have been made.'[36] Another important

[31] Christos Rozakis, 'The Territorial Scope of Human Rights Obligations: The Case of the European Convention on Human Rights' in *The Status of International Treaties on Human Rights* (Council of Europe Publishing, 2005) 57–74.

[32] *Application of the Convention on the Prevention and Punishment of the Crime of Genocide (Bosnia and Herzegovina v Serbia and Montenegro)* (Judgment) [2007] ICJ Rep 43.

[33] ibid para 430. [34] ibid.

[35] Monica Hakimi, 'State Bystander Responsibility' (2010) 21 EJIL 341.

[36] *Ilaşcu* (n 29) para 334.

principle recalled by the Court in this case, but unduly ignored in the subsequent cases, is that the State 'has a duty to take all appropriate measures, *which it is still within its power to take*'.[37] It clearly means that the territorial State is relieved of its positive obligations when nothing can practically be done to uphold human rights standards in the territory concerned.

The ECtHR stated that Moldova had an obligation to 're-establish control over Transdniestria'.[38] This appears to be pure political rhetoric with little to do with legal obligations, and also is hardly subject to assessment by legal measures. Moldova was further obliged 'to refrain from supporting the separatist regime'.[39] I find it rather difficult to reconcile positive obligations towards people remaining in occupied territories with the obligation to refrain from supporting the separatist regime. These obligations seem mutually exclusive. If a State engages in negotiations with separatists requesting them to secure human rights of individuals on occupied territories (that was precisely what the Court was expecting to have been done for Mr Ilaşcu), it follows that it would propose something in exchange, such as providing economic support they might need or doing something else. Negotiations by definition suggest some *mutual* profit. Whatever benefit proposed to separatists would inevitably mean support of their regime and postponement of the reintegration of the separated territory. If Moldova was under an obligation to negotiate the release of Mr Ilaşcu and others, it had to propose something to the separatists for *their* benefit in addition to the already ceded territory. Strangely enough, the Court found that economic cooperation with the separatist regime, in view of the resulting improvement of the everyday lives of the people in Transdniestria, cannot be regarded as support for de facto authorities, but on the contrary represents an affirmation by Moldova of its desire to re-establish control over Transdniestria. This finding appears to be confusing, and in any case is not persuasive.

The paradox lies in the fact that the Moldovan authorities, by a somewhat acquiescent attitude of cooperation towards the separatist regime, triggered their positive obligations under the Convention. The judgment mentions, in particular, the fact that persons who had acted as senior officials of the Moldovian Republic of Transdniestria were able to return to Moldova and subsequently assume high office, the signing of agreements on mutual recognition of documents issued by the Moldovan and Transdniestrian authorities and on measures to attract and protect foreign investment (which in itself can amount to de facto recognition of the separatist regime), unofficial relations between the Moldovan and Transdniestrian authorities on judicial and security matters, and even the inclusion of Transdniestrian teams in a national football championship.[40] The consequences of such cooperation were explained by Judge Ress in his concurring opinion: 'In contrast to the situation in Cyprus, relations between the Moldovan constitutional authorities and the authorities of the illegal Transdniestrian regime have never been completely interrupted [. . .] Since the issue is whether Moldova continues to exercise jurisdiction

[37] ibid para 313. [38] ibid para 340. [39] ibid.
[40] ibid paras 168, 174, 177, 185.

over parts of the territory, all these elements of economic relations, political security and other cooperation between the Moldovan and Transdniestrian authorities make it difficult to rebut the responsibility of Moldova in the present case.' He thus concluded that 'Moldova had and still has important means of influence to fulfil its positive obligations'.[41]

Hence, a thoughtful examination of the *Ilaşcu* judgment suggests that positive obligations of an injured State to secure human rights on occupied territory arise *when a connection exists between this State and the occupation regime*, because only in this situation is the State 'still within its power to take' some measures.

But precisely because this was not clearly articulated in the motivation part of the *Ilaşcu* judgment, it is argued among legal scholars that this judgment 'blurs rather than clarifies' the notion of jurisdiction, and 'the concept of positive obligations is brought about in a way that causes puzzlement'.[42]

4. Further Clarification of the Scope of an Injured State's Obligations—A Failed Attempt?

As generally recognized by the Court, any positive obligations of the States under the Convention should be limited by a 'scope of reasonableness', in the sense that they should be directly proportionate to the State's influence over the relevant actors. A State's enjoyment, both *de jure* and de facto, of control over a territory is the precondition for any positive obligations, since only such a control would make the adoption of measures, expected by the Court, reasonable.

In its further practice, the Court seems to disregard the specific feature of cooperation between an occupying power and the injured State, which was present in *Ilaşcu*. In June 2015, two cases related to the Nagorno-Karabakh conflict—*Chiragov and others v Armenia* and *Sargsyan v Azerbaijan*—were examined concurrently by the Grand Chamber. The Court's judgments in these cases have caused serious debate among scholars and practitioners, as well as among the judges of the ECtHR, as it is clear from the number of separate opinions accompanying the judgment.

For the purposes of the present chapter, the judgment in the *Sargsyan v Azerbaijan* case is of interest. The Court held that Azerbaijan, which has been unable to regain control over about twenty percent of territory within its recognized borders for more than twenty years, was fully accountable for the inability of the applicant (who fled in fear for his life in 1992, long before Azerbaijan ratified the Convention) to return to the village Gulistan—uninhabited land situated on a front line, which was under fire from 'NKR' forces subordinated to Armenia.

The *Sargsyan* case differed significantly from the *Ilaşcu* case from the outset, as only one State—the one which had *de jure* jurisdiction over Gulistan—was named

[41] ibid, Partly Dissenting Opinion of Judge Ress, para 5.

[42] Michał Gondek, 'Extraterritorial Application of the European Convention on Human Rights: Territorial Focus in the Age of Globalization?' (2005) 52 Netherlands International Law Review 349, 368.

as the respondent. As was mentioned by my former colleague, Judge Poalelungi, in respect of *Ilaşcu*:

[I]n its ruling, the Court relied on the extent of jurisdiction exercised *proportionally* by each respondent state. Therefore, the Russian Federation was responsible for the substantial violations of the Convention by both its agents (members of the armed forces) and the representatives of the Transdniestrian authorities. It was also established that the concept of jurisdiction in the light of Article 1 had a low implication for Moldova, the latter being held responsible only for failing to fulfil its positive obligations to take legal and diplomatic measures, in respect of its nationals on the territory effectively uncontrolled by it, along with other states and international organizations in order to protect the fundamental rights and freedoms guaranteed by the Convention.[43]

Paradoxically, in the concurrent *Chiragov* judgment, the Court recognized that Armenia exercises effective control over the disputed territory, but Armenia was not named as a respondent State by Mr Sargsyan. Thus, whilst in the *Ilaşcu* case the Court examined the concurrent responsibility of two States—Moldova and Russia—and 'distributed' responsibility between them, in the *Sargsyan* case the claim was lodged against Azerbaijan exclusively.

I stated in my separate opinion that:

[t]he mere fact that the applicant, for obvious reasons, decided to lodge a complaint against only one High Contracting Party involved in the conflict and not both [...] should not automatically engage the full responsibility of Azerbaijan, which is a victim State suffering occupation of a significant part of its territory (as is clear from the *Chiragov* judgment).

Alternatively, although the Court is obviously unable to examine *proprio motu* the issue of responsibility of a State that was not party to the case at hand, the mere existence of a long-standing inter-State conflict should trigger shared responsibility. Evidently, there is no mechanism under the Convention by which to identify a High Contracting Party accountable—partially or fully—for human rights violations complained of if an applicant brings a complaint against a party not responsible or responsible only in part. Nevertheless, it would be deceptive to ignore the factually clearly limited accountability [if any] of the respondent State; and procedural impediments should not turn into substantive wrongs.[44]

Given the findings above on the clear reason for Moldova's partial responsibility for human rights violations in Transdniestria, namely various forms of support for the self-proclaimed regime received from the Moldavian authorities, it is difficult to accept that in the discussed case the entire responsibility was attributed to Azerbaijan without the slightest sign of such cooperation. The Court explained this attribution as follows:

In the above-cited cases concerning Moldova the acceptance that the territorial State had only limited responsibility under the Convention was compensated by the finding that

[43] Mihai Poalelungi, *Positive and negative obligations of the state under the European Convention for the Protection of Human Rights and Fundamental Freedoms* (Iasi, România, Typography Vasiliana 98, 2015) 69.

[44] *Sargsyan v Azerbaijan* [GC] App no 40167/06 (ECtHR, 16 June 2015), Concurring Opinion of Judge Yudkivska.

another Convention State exceptionally exercised jurisdiction outside its territory and thus had full responsibility under the Convention. In contrast, in the present case it has not been established that Gulistan is occupied by the armed forces of another State or that it is under the control of a separatist regime. In such circumstances the Court, taking into account the need to avoid a vacuum in Convention protection, does not consider that the respondent Government has demonstrated the existence of exceptional circumstances of such a nature as to qualify their responsibility under the Convention.[45]

Unable to liken the present situation to the one in the *Ilaşcu* case, the majority of the Grand Chamber furthermore came to, in my view, a strikingly wrong conclusion that this situation was more akin to the situation in *Assanidze v Georgia.*[46] In that latter case, the mayor of the capital of the Ajarian Autonomous Republic in Georgia (a Georgian entity with autonomous status) was convicted by the Ajarian High Court but was later acquitted by the Supreme Court of Georgia, which ordered his immediate release. The central Georgian authorities made repeated unsuccessful attempts through both legal and political channels to have him released. The respondent government fully accepted that the Ajarian Autonomous Republic was an integral part of Georgia, but stressed the difficulties encountered by the central State authorities in exercising their jurisdiction in Ajaria. The Court concluded that the matters complained of 'were within the "jurisdiction" of Georgia within the meaning of Article 1 of the Convention and that, even though within the domestic system those matters are directly imputable to the local authorities of the Ajarian Autonomous Republic, it is solely the responsibility of the Georgian State that is engaged under the Convention'.[47] I find the factual situations in these two cases incomparable. As my colleague, Judge Pinto de Albuquerque, has pointed out:

apart from the case of Mr Assanidze, with its strong political overtones, there was no problem of judicial cooperation between the central authorities and the local Ajarian authorities. Hence, it is rather artificial to compare the situation of direct military confrontation in *Sargsyan* with the situation of the Ajarian Autonomous Republic, which never had separatist aspirations and was not a source of conflict between different States.[48]

The Court thus rejected the government's reliance on the *Ilaşcu* judgment: '[T]he *limitation* of the territorial State's responsibility in respect of parts of its internationally recognized territory which are occupied or under the effective control of another entity'[49] cannot be extended to Gulistan. To hold otherwise, in the absence of the possibility to examine the responsibility of Armenia, would mean 'a vacuum in Convention protection'.[50] In my separate opinion, I expressed the view that in the circumstances of the *Sargsyan* case this legal formula was artificial and led to erroneous and unfair conclusions.

[45] *Sargsyan v Azerbaijan* [GC] App no 40167/06 (ECtHR, 16 June 2015) para 148.
[46] *Assanidze v Georgia* [GC] App no 71503/01 (ECtHR, 8 April 2004).
[47] ibid para 150.
[48] *Sargsyan v Azerbaijan* [GC] App no 40167/06 (ECtHR, 16 June 2015), Dissenting Opinion of Judge Pinto de Albuquerque.
[49] *Sargsyan v Azerbaijan* (n 45) para 149.
[50] ibid para 148.

Interestingly enough, in the case of *Azemi v Serbia*,[51] in which the applicant attempted to engage Serbia's responsibility for the non-enforcement of a decision rendered by a Kosovo court, the ECtHR was satisfied that, as long as Kosovo was placed under an international civil and military presence and Serbia did not exercise any control over the United Nations Mission in Kosovo, Kosovo's judiciary had been established by virtue of this mission's regulations and thus was fully outside Serbia's control. The Court did not forget to note the absence of evidence 'that the Serbian authorities had militarily, economically, financially or politically supported Kosovo's institutions'. The crucial feature for finding Moldova responsible in the *Ilaşcu* case was accordingly missing. Kosovo's declaration of independence 'objectively prevented Serbia from securing the rights and freedoms in Kosovo, over which it had no effective control'. Here the Court was not at all troubled by the existence of 'a vacuum in Convention protection'.

In the *Sargsyan* judgment,[52] the Court examined whether the Azerbaijani authorities had taken sufficient measures to protect the applicant's property in Gulistan. In reply to the government's reliance on their participation in the peace negotiations (as a *minimum effort*), the Court did not find it sufficient for the government 'to fulfil their duty to strike a fair balance between the competing public and individual interests',[53] and stressed that it did not absolve the government from taking other measures. It relied on relevant international standards and the Resolution of 2010 on 'Solving property issues of refugees and displaced persons' of the Parliamentary Assembly of the Council of Europe,[54] which calls on member States (and not only Azerbaijan) to 'guarantee timely and effective redress for the loss of access and rights to housing, land and property abandoned by refugees and IDPs [Internally Displaced People] without regard to pending negotiations concerning the resolution of armed conflicts of the status of a particular territory'.[55] It specified that:

> [P]ending a comprehensive peace agreement, it would appear particularly important to establish a property claims mechanism, which should be easily accessible and provide procedures operating with flexible evidentiary standards, allowing the applicant and others in his situation to have their property rights restored and to obtain compensation for the loss of their enjoyment.[56]

In the absence of a *minimum effort* to even consider the possibility of compensating the applicant and other displaced Armenians for their lack of access to their property, the Court concluded that Azerbaijan had violated both Article 1 of Protocol No. 1 to the Convention, and Article 8 of the Convention.

This type of positive obligation of an injured State significantly differs from what the Court had suggested in *Ilaşcu*—in order to fulfil its obligations, Moldova was required to refrain from supporting the separatist regime and to act through taking

[51] *Azemi v Serbia* (Dec) App no 11209/09 (ECtHR, 5 November 2013).

[52] *Sargsyan* (n 45).

[53] ibid para 236.

[54] Parliamentary Assembly (PA) Resolution 1708 on solving property issues of refugees and displaced persons [2010].

[55] ibid Article 10.1.

[56] *Sargsyan* (n 45) para 238.

all political, judicial, and other measures at its disposal to re-establish its control over the occupied territory.

Azerbaijan can hardly be reproached for any lack of this type of action, as was specified in detail in the dissenting opinion of Judge Hajiyev.[57] Indeed, any attempt by Azerbaijan to re-establish its control over the village of Gulistan is heavily counterbalanced by its obligation to secure the lives and safety of those within its jurisdiction, and may furthermore threaten the maintenance of the ceasefire and endanger peace negotiations. In this judgment, a very limited finding of a violation of positive obligations by Azerbaijan—failure to make any meaningful attempt to consider the possibility of compensating the displaced persons for the lack of access to their property—appears to be justified.

It also echoes a 'duty to mitigate' as developed in international law, which, however, as already mentioned, is not a legal obligation that itself gives rise to an injured State's responsibility.

Nevertheless, the lack of clarity and consistency in the Court's approach is evident. It appears that, at some stage, the Court will have to specify its methodology when it defines the scope of the obligations of an injured State, as well as the procedural rules that will be used to allocate responsibility between a primary responsible State and a victim one. It will also have to identify situations in which an illusory judicial construction—no vacuum in Convention protection is permissible—can lead to substantially unfair results.

To date the Court has only been called upon once, in the case of *Parastayev v Russia*, to determine the extent of the responsibility of both Georgia and Russia, in a situation similar to the Nagorno-Karabakh and Transdniestrian conflicts, for the allegedly unlawful detention of the applicant in South Ossetia, governed by the separatist regime that was presumably subordinate to the Russian authorities.[58] The case was of particular importance for the further development of the 'shared responsibility' problem, and was communicated to both respondent governments but later withdrawn following the applicant's request. Other related cases are lodged either against Georgia or Russia exclusively.

A number of questions are clearly presented in respect of Ukraine's obligations toward the people in Crimea and Donbas, and relevant cases raising such questions are pending before the Court. As in the South Ossetia context, applications are submitted either against Ukraine only, against both Ukraine and Russia, or against Russia only. Several cases have already been declared inadmissible without examining the jurisdictional issue or the scope of positive obligations, since the complaints were wholly unsubstantiated.[59] Apart from that, several inter-state applications have been submitted by Ukraine against Russia. The multitude of the approaches chosen by the applicants should not prevent the Court from reaching equal results in factually and legally-alike situations.

[57] ibid, Dissenting Opinion of Judge Hajiyev.

[58] *Parastayev v Russia and Georgia* (Dec) App no 50514/06 (ECtHR, 13 December 2011).

[59] *Lisnyy and Others v Ukraine and Russia* (Dec) App nos 5355/15, 44913/15, and 50853/15 (ECtHR, 5 July 2016).

In fact, the simultaneous examination of *Sargsyan v Azerbaijan* and *Chiragov v Armenia* was precisely an attempt to see these cases as 'putative inter-State case[s]'[60] but, in my view, the lack of clarity as to the applicable principles of concurrent responsibility as described prevented the Court from achieving equally plausible conclusions. Azerbaijan, which has been trying to regain its control over the whole territory of its recognized borders for more than twenty years, was held fully accountable for the inability to establish a normal life in Gulistan, which is under fire from NKR forces subordinate to Armenia that are clearly outside Azerbaijan's control.

5. Towards Concretizing the Human Rights Obligations of Injured States

As demonstrated above, an injured State is not fully absolved, by the mere fact of occupation, of its obligations to secure for everyone within its still *de jure* jurisdiction the rights and freedoms guaranteed by the Convention. These obligations are limited in the circumstances to 'a positive obligation to take the diplomatic, economic, judicial or other measures that were both in its power to take and in accordance with international law'.[61]

In the Court's interpretation, the positive obligations of an injured State relate both to measures needed (i) to re-establish its control over an occupied territory, and (ii) to ensure respect for individual applicants' rights. As previously mentioned, the obligation to re-establish control requires primarily refraining from supporting the separatist regime and undertaking 'other measures at its disposal' capable of achieving this goal.

Undoubtedly, the necessity to judge the appropriateness and sufficiency of those measures requires the Court to resort to analysis of the efficacy of political options, which is customarily not its role. Thus, for instance, in the Transdniestrian context, the Court has found in several cases that 'from the onset of the hostilities in 1991 and 1992 … Moldova had taken all the measures in its power to re-establish control over Transdniestrian territory'.[62] The Court accepted that 'when confronted with a regime sustained militarily, politically and economically by a power such as the Russian Federation … there was little Moldova could do to re-establish its authority over Transdniestrian territory'.[63] But a number of diplomatic and political measures—adoption of a new Constitution granting a certain amount of autonomy to Transdniestria, signing with the Russian Federation an agreement for the withdrawal of Russian troops from Transdniestria together with several other instruments with a view to settling the Transdniestrian conflict, and meetings and negotiations with the Transdniestrian regime—assured the Court that the Moldovan

[60] *Sargsyan* (n 45).

[61] See, as the most recent authority, *Mozer v The Republic of Moldova and Russia* [GC] App no 11138/10 (ECtHR, 23 February 2016) para 99.

[62] ibid para 152. [63] *Ilaşcu* (n 29) para 341.

authorities had done their best to ensure Transdniestria's return within the Moldovan legal order.

The Court did not examine the Azerbaijani authorities' efforts to re-establish control over Nagorno-Karabakh and seven adjacent regions, since it concluded in the *Sargsyan* case that the village of Gulistan was not occupied, and the *Chiragov* case was lodged against Armenia only. But further cases might raise this issue; also, the cases pending today before the Court in the Georgian and Ukrainian contexts will certainly touch upon this predominantly political side of the positive obligations of an injured State.

The second aspect of positive obligations, namely to ensure respect for the individuals' rights, is about concrete efforts to be made in the particular circumstances of each case. Such efforts might include 'appeals to various intergovernmental organizations and foreign countries [...] asking them to assist in securing the applicant's rights'[64] or 'taking any alternative measures in order to restore [applicants'] property rights or to provide [them] with compensation for [the] loss of their enjoyment'.[65]

The aforementioned requirements to achieve respect for human rights and freedoms in a territory outside a State's control are rather controversial and call for a more nuanced methodology, unavoidably, in upcoming cases. For instance, some clarity is required with respect to the moment when attempts to re-establish control over an occupied territory, and thus grant access to property abandoned there, should be substituted by compensation for the loss of this property (apparently since there is no longer hope that such access can be achieved in the foreseeable future). The scope of the positive obligations of an injured State vis-à-vis the positive obligations of an occupying State, as stressed in the previous section, also needs to be elucidated.

6. Conclusion

Obviously it is very unfortunate that we have cases related to armed conflicts, both pending and frozen, in Europe in the twenty-first century. Given the intensity of human suffering involved in these conflicts, I believe that international judges should demonstrate in these cases the highest degree of sensitivity, wisdom, and discretion.[66]

Indeed, as was mentioned by one of my dissenting colleagues, in the Nagorno-Karabakh cases:

> [l]eft unstated, but implicit in the majority's reasoning, is that the Court will no longer wait for politicians to come to terms with the Nagorno-Karabakh conflict and its human

[64] *Mozer* (n 61) para 153. [65] *Sargsyan* (n 45) para 241.

[66] See, for example, John Cerone, 'Out of Bounds? Considering the Reach of International Human Rights Law' CHRGJ Working Paper (2006) 5. Available at: <http://chrgj.org/wp-content/uploads/2012/07/WPS_NYU_CHRGJ_Cerone_Final.pdf> accessed 5 July 2016.

consequences. If need be, the Court is willing to replace diplomacy, in view of the fact, censured by the majority, that the peace negotiations 'have not yet yielded any tangible results'.[67]

This task is extremely delicate. We should not forget that the ultimate goal of the Convention is to ensure the foundations of peace:

> Every single complaint brought by an individual residing within one of the contracting states is an opportunity to advance and continuously maintain the political culture of democracy, human rights and the rule of law. Every victory won at the individual level is a victory towards an advanced civilised culture and, by extension, a victory towards peace.[68]

A clear guidance as to 'appropriate and sufficient measures' to be undertaken by a territorial State that has lost effective control can undoubtedly be instrumental to the effective protection of human rights. On the other hand, placing an excessive and unrealistic burden on an injured State (also prior to addressing the responsibility of the state directly responsible for the violations complained of) might be seen as counterproductive and as upsetting the fragile structure of State responsibility under international law.

As was argued in respect of the ICJ, the Court can entertain legal disputes despite their political implications; legal disputes are often part of a much broader political dispute dealt with through political and diplomatic means—as long as the judicial function is exercised in a way that achieves the maintenance of peace and security.[69] The same is true for the ECtHR—it has to adjudicate human rights cases against the background of territorial conflicts and the consequent involvement of the concepts of State responsibility, jurisdiction, and attribution that create a Gordian knot, which is to be untied only in a manner that paves the way to 'justice and peace in the world'.

It is worth repeating that 'no legal system can be better than a society, which it serves',[70] as the distinguished ICJ judge Sir Christopher Greenwood used to say. As long as some States show little enthusiasm for general compulsory rules, more and more often only a political choice, and not the judicial process, determines a solution.

[67] *Sargsyan* (n 45).

[68] See Dimitris Xenos, *The Positive Obligations of the State under the European Convention of Human Rights* (Routledge 2011) 15.

[69] See Beatrice Bonafe, 'Territory and Conflicts: Is International Law the Problem?' in Matteo Nicolini, Francesco Palermo, and Enrico Milano (eds), *Law, Territory and Conflict Resolution. Law as a Problem and Law as a Solution* (Brill 2016) 12.

[70] Lecture 'Can International Law Change the World?' presented by Judge Sir Christopher Greenwood, the British Judge at the International Court of Justice at the Residence of the British Ambassador, Sir Geoffrey Adams, 24 February 2015.

PART IV

RESPONSIBILITY

8

Concurrent Responsibilities under the European Convention on Human Rights

The Concurrence of Human Rights Jurisdictions, Duties, and Responsibilities

Samantha Besson *

'The Court has established jurisdiction in respect of the Netherlands. It is not called upon to establish whether the United Kingdom, another State Party to the Convention, might have exercised concurrent jurisdiction.' (*Jaloud v The Netherlands* App no 47708/08 (ECtHR, 20 November 2014) para 153).

1. Introduction

There has been an increase, as of late, in the number of cases in which more than one State at a time exercises effective control over the same people and, hence, in which those numerous States can exercise concurrent jurisdiction over the same human right holders.[1] What this means is that States can increasingly acquire concurrent

* Many thanks to Iulia Motoc for her invitation to participate in the 5th June 2015 Conference at the European Court of Human Rights, Strasbourg, to her, Anne van Aaken, Ganna Yudkivska, Pierre d'Argent, and the other participants for comments and feedback, and to anonymous reviewers for helpful feedback in April 2016 and again in May 2017. I would also like to thank Matthieu Loup and Gaelle Mieli, my former research assistants, for their help with the editing and formal layout of the manuscript. An earlier and shorter version of the argument defended in this chapter, albeit focused on extraterritorial jurisdiction only, was published as: Samantha Besson, 'L'extra-territorialité des Droits de l'Homme Internationaux: Juridictions Concurrentes, Obligations Conjointes et Responsabilités Partagées' in Pierre d'Argent (ed), *Droit des frontières internationales*, Actes des Journées Franco-Allemandes de Droit International 2014 (Pedone 2016).

1 Interestingly, there has been an increase of circumstances in which this has occurred, or can occur, but not necessarily of cases so decided by the ECtHR, for reasons I will explain in this chapter. When the chapter refers to decisions of the ECtHR, therefore, it is often in order to examine their sets of facts and their potential, and not necessarily how they were decided in the end.

Concurrent Responsibilities under the European Convention on Human Rights: The Concurrence of Human Rights Jurisdictions, Duties and Responsibilities. Samantha Besson. © Samantha Besson, 2018. Published 2018 by Oxford University Press.

human rights duties towards the same people and, in turn, concurrent responsibilities in case of violation of their duties.

A first set of cases are those in which one State or more exercises extraterritorial jurisdiction over a territory over which, at the same time, another State exercises territorial jurisdiction. Examples abound in practice, ranging from peace operations abroad[2] to military occupation.[3] The second group of cases derives from the increasingly transnational circumstances of certain people, and in particular from circumstances in which the same people move from the territorial jurisdiction of one State to that of another—physically or virtually. Examples are numerous and include renditions,[4] trafficking,[5] voluntary or forced migration and deportation,[6] and cyberactivity.[7] A third group of cases stems from interstate cooperation and pertains to the coordinated territorial jurisdiction of many States (and sometimes even an international organization) under a common institutional umbrella. These are cases that occur in particular in the context of joint State activities, each over its own territory, under the terms of an international agreement[8] or within an international organization;[9] an example is the European Union (EU)[10] the jurisdiction of which may itself overlap with one or many of its member States.

[2] See, eg *Hassan v The United Kingdom* App no 29750/09 (ECtHR, 16 September 2014); *Jaloud v The Netherlands* App no 47708/08 (ECtHR, 20 November 2014).

[3] See, eg *Loizidou v Turkey* App no 15318/89 (ECHR, 18 December 1996) ECHR 1996-VI 2216; *Ilaşcu and Others v Moldova and Russia* App no 48787/99 (ECtHR, 8 July 2004); *Catan and Others v The Republic of Moldova and Russia* [GC] App nos 43370/ 04, 8252/ 05, and 18454/ 06 (ECtHR, 19 October 2012); *Sargsyan v Azerbaijan* App no 40167/06 (ECtHR, 16 June 2015); *Chiragov and Others v Armenia* App no 13216/05 (ECtHR, 16 June 2015).

[4] See, eg *El-Masri v The Former Yugoslav Republic of Macedonia* [GC] App no. 39630/09 (ECtHR,13 December 2012) *Al Nashiri v Poland* App no 28761/11 (ECtHR, 24 July 2014).

[5] See, eg *Rantsev v Cyprus and Russia* App no 25965/04 (ECtHR, 7 January 2010).

[6] See, eg *MSS v Belgium and Greece* [GC] App no 30696/09 (ECtHR, 21 January 2011).

[7] See, eg *Roman Zakharov v Russia* App no 47143/06 (ECtHR, 4 December 2015). See for a discussion, Marko Milanovic, 'Human Rights Treaties and Foreign Surveillance: Privacy in the Digital Age' (2015) 56 Harvard International Law Journal 81.

[8] See, eg *Drozd and Janousek v France and Spain* App no 12747/87 (ECtHR, 26 June 1992); *Sari and Çolak v Turkey* App nos 42596/98 and 42603/98 (ECtHR, 4 April 2006).

[9] See, eg *Bosphorus Hava Yollari Turizm Ve Ticaret Anonim Sirketi v Ireland* [GC] App no 45036/ 98 (ECtHR, 30 June 2005); *Behrami and Behrami v France* and *Saramati v France, Germany and Norway* App nos 71412/01 and 78166/01 (ECtHR, 2 May 2007); *Al-Jedda v The United Kingdom* [GC] App no 2702/08 (ECtHR, 7 July 2011); *Nada v Switzerland* App no 10593/08 (ECtHR, 12 September 2012); *Al-Dulimi and Montana Management Inc v Switzerland* App no 5809/08 (ECtHR, 26 November 2013).

[10] Because the accession of the EU to the ECHR has now been stalled by the CJEU's negative opinion (Opinion 2/13, *Opinion pursuant to Article 218(11) TFEU* ([CJEU, 18 December 2014]), this chapter focuses on States solely and their jurisdiction, duties, and responsibilities under the ECHR. A lot of what is discussed in the chapter does apply to international organisations, however, once they have what it takes to acquire human rights jurisdiction and human rights duties (see, eg, Samantha Besson, 'The Bearers of Human Rights' Duties and Responsibilities for Human Rights: A Quiet (R)Evolution' (2015) 32 Social Philosophy & Policy 244; Samantha Besson, 'Individual and State Liability for an International Organization's Responsibility—The Challenge of Fairness Unveiled' (2017) VI/1 Italian Journal of Legal Philosophy 51). Then, the issues raised by concurrent human rights jurisdictions, duties, and responsibilities of States and international organizations will most likely become a core concern of international human rights law. On the different types of potential duty-bearers under international human rights law and their concurrence with duty-bearing States, see also Wouter Vandenhole and Willem van Genugten, 'Introduction: An Emerging Multi-Duty-Bearer Human Rights Regime' in Wouter Vandenhole (ed), *Challenging Territoriality in Human*

The recent increase in the number of cases of concurrent jurisdiction raises new questions for international human rights law, and especially for the European Convention on Human Rights (ECHR).[11] In particular, these cases raise questions about how one should articulate the concurrent effective control and hence jurisdictions of different States, how one should specify and allocate their concurrent duties stemming from this concurrence of jurisdiction, and, finally, how one should attribute and then allocate concurrent responsibilities when concurrent duties have been violated.

These three issues arise as consecutive questions in the European Court of Human Rights' (ECtHR's) reasoning in any human rights case implicating more than one State. Of course, concurrent jurisdiction will not necessarily give rise to concurrent duties, on the one hand, and concurrent duties will not necessarily give rise to concurrent responsibilities, on the other. However, in some cases of concurrent responsibilities, the jurisdiction of the States in question and their duties are concurrent, thus making the three questions not only relevant per se, but relevant to address in connection to one another. Understanding how human rights jurisdictions, duties, and responsibilities should be articulated in cases of concurrence is also a pressing issue in terms of global justice more generally.[12] Indeed, what is at stake in these cases are the duties owed to an individual human right holder out of a given set of circumstances, and the remedies that arise from their violation to rectify the situation, and this should be a concern for all the duty-bearing States if there are more than one. More particularly, the specification and allocation of the human rights duties at stake for each State will depend on how many States exercise jurisdiction over the same people at the same time, the threats they pose to the latter's protected interests, and the States' respective capacities to protect the individuals. Subsequently, the responsibilities to cease the violation, and to prevent and remedy it, need to be coordinated among the responsible States to avoid overburdening one of the States with reparations at the advantage of others (unjust enrichment) or, conversely, to the disadvantage of the victim of the human rights violation whose full injury may not be compensated in the end.

Importantly, despite being connected in human rights reasoning, the three issues (jurisdictions, duties, and responsibilities), and the three corresponding albeit distinct

Rights Law—Building Blocks for a Plural and Diverse Duty-Bearer Regime (Routledge 2015); Wouter Vandenhole, 'Obligations and Responsibility in a Plural and Diverse Duty-Bearer Human Rights Regime' in Wouter Vandenhole (ed), *Challenging Territoriality in Human Rights Law—Building Blocks for a Plural and Diverse Duty-Bearer Regime* (Routledge 2015).

[11] This chapter focuses exclusively on ECHR law. It is the international human rights system whose interpretation of the notion of jurisdiction, whether territorial or extraterritorial, is the most advanced, and many analogies can be drawn in other international human rights regimes. See also Samantha Besson, 'The Extraterritoriality of the European Convention on Human Rights: Why Human Rights Depend on Jurisdiction and What Jurisdiction Amounts to' (2012) 25 Leiden Journal of International Law 857, 860–61; Besson, 'The Bearers of Human Rights' Duties and Responsibilities for Human Rights' (n 10).

[12] On this issue, see Samantha Besson, 'La Pluralité d'Etats Responsables—Vers une Solidarité Internationale' (2007) 1 Revue Suisse de Droit International et de Droit Européen 13, 26; Samantha Besson, 'La Responsabilité Solidaire des Organisations Internationales et des Etats—Une Institution Négligée' in Alain Supiot (ed), *La Responsabilité Solidaire* (Collège de France 2018).

roles of 'control' in their respective assessment,[13] should be carefully distinguished conceptually and kept separate as three distinct steps in the analysis. Of course, many primary duties in international law are specified by reference to previous responsibilities (secondary duties), thus blurring the idea that primary duties are necessarily specified *ex ante*. All the same, too often in the past, the issues of jurisdiction, duties, and responsibilities have been conflated in the ECtHR's case law at the price of clarity on the exact implications of concurrent jurisdiction for the allocation not only of human rights duties, but also of responsibilities. This has been the case, for instance, with the conflation between the assessment of the State's control over the individual right holders needed for jurisdiction to be established, and of the control over individual agents required for the attribution of their conduct to the State, whether this occurs when assessing that State's jurisdiction or when establishing its responsibility at a later stage.[14] The same may be said about the conflation between the assessment of the control needed for State jurisdiction to arise and of the control required for the State to acquire positive duties, and hence responsibilities, in the case that these duties are violated.[15] Of course, this can be explained by the ambivalent role of the notion of 'control' in the reasoning pertaining to all three questions or steps. Addressing these three questions together in the present chapter can hopefully contribute to clarifying not only their ties, but also their differences.

This question of concurrent or 'shared' responsibilities[16] is *en vogue* among international lawyers.[17] Studies of the subject in international human rights

[13] Human rights 'jurisdiction' *qua* effective control is to be distinguished from: (i) the competence or title of a State in international law ('jurisdiction' in general international law); (ii) the right to judge of a tribunal or a State; (iii) the effective control necessary to acquire positive duties (of diligence); (iv) the effective control over organs (Articles 4–5 Draft Articles on the Responsibility of States for Internationally Wrongful Acts (ARSIWA)) or private agents (Article 8 ARSIWA) required for the attribution of conduct in the context of international responsibility. See also Besson, 'The Extraterritoriality of the European Convention on Human Rights' (n 11) 866–68.

[14] See, most recently, the confusions in *Chiragov* (n 3) paras 186 and 201 or in *Jaloud* (n 2) paras 154–55. For a critique, see the concurring opinion of Judge Spielmann in *Jaloud* (n 2) paras 3–7; the concurring opinion of Judge Motoc in *Jaloud* (n 2). See also Marko Milanovic, 'Jurisdiction, Attribution and Responsibility in Jaloud' (EJIL: *Talk!* 11 December 2014) <http://www.ejiltalk.org/jurisdiction-attribution-and-responsibility-in-jaloud/> accessed 5 April 2016; Marko Milanovic, 'The Nagorno-Karabakh Cases' (EJIL: *Talk!* 23 June 2015) <http://www.ejiltalk.org/the-nagorno-karabakh-cases/> accessed 5 April 2016; Aurel Sari, 'Untangling Extra-territorial Jurisdiction from International Responsibility in *Jaloud v. Netherlands*: Old Problem, New Solutions?' (2014) 53 The Military Law and the Law of War Review 287; Crawford and Keene, in this volume.

[15] See, eg, *Sargsyan* (n 3) para 140.

[16] 'Concurrent responsibilities' are understood here as stemming from the contribution of many States to the same injury, (i) whether this occurs through the violation of the same duty or not, and (ii) through the same wrongful act or not. When concurrent responsibilities are caused by the same wrongful act, they are usually referred to as 'shared responsibilities' *stricto sensu*, even though the latter term is sometimes used to refer to all kinds of concurrent responsibilities independently of the wrongful act. For reasons of clarity, I will be referring to concurrent responsibilities in this chapter. Note, of course, that the 'responsibilities' at stake in this chapter are remedial responsibilities arising from the breach of an international human rights law duty and not the unallocated *ex ante* 'responsibilities for human rights' that arise from international human rights law: on the distinction, see the discussion in section 3 and Besson, 'The Bearers of Human Rights' Duties and Responsibilities for Human Rights' (n 10).

[17] See, eg, John E Noyes and Brian D Smith, 'State Responsibility and the Principle of Joint and Several Liability' (1988) 13 Yale Journal of International Law 225; Besson, 'La Pluralité d'Etats

law[18] and in ECHR law[19] remain scarce, however. So too does the ECtHR's case law, for it has remained extremely cautious in the matter; this is quite surprising given the number of its cases raising the issue.[20] The aim of this chapter is to consider the conformity of the ECHR regime of concurrent responsibility with the general international law of responsibility.[21] Unlike other areas of international-responsibility law addressed in this volume,[22] however, it is not clear that there is much general international law on concurrent responsibility outside of specific regimes—besides Article 47 Articles on the Responsibility of States for Internationally Wrongful Acts (ARSIWA), of course, which applies to the ECHR *qua* relevant secondary rules on concurrent responsibility, albeit within the limits of the *lex specialis* principle. It may be better, therefore, to turn things the other

Responsables' (n 12); Roger P Alford, 'Apportioning Responsibility Among Joint Tortfeasors for International Law Violations' (2011) 38 Pepperdine Law Review 233; André Nollkaemper and Dov Jacobs 'Shared Responsibility in International Law: A Conceptual Framework' (2013) 34 Michigan Journal of International Law 359; André Nollkaemper, 'Introduction' in André Nollkaemper and Ilias Plakokefalos (eds), *Principles of Shared Responsibility in International Law—An Appraisal of the State of the Art* (CUP 2014); Annemarieke Vermeer-Künzli, 'Invocation of Responsibility' in André Nollkaemper and Ilias Plakokefalos (eds), *Principles of Shared Responsibility in International Law—An Appraisal of the State of the Art* (CUP 2014); Pierre d'Argent, 'Reparation, Cessation, Assurances and Guarantees of Non-Repetition' in André Nollkaemper and Ilias Plakokefalos (eds), *Principles of Shared Responsibility in International Law—An Appraisal of the State of the Art* (CUP 2014); Besson, 'La Responsabilité Solidaire' (n 12).

[18] See, eg, Vandenhole, 'Obligations and Responsibility in a Plural and Diverse Duty-Bearer Human Rights Regime' (n 10); Wouter Vandenhole, 'Obligations Extraterritoriales des Droits de l'Homme: Bilan et Perspectives/Extraterritorial Human Rights Obligations: Taking Stock, Looking Forward' (2013) 5 Journal Européen des Droits de l'Homme/European Journal of Human Rights 804, 827ff; Ashfaq Khalfan, 'Division of Responsibility amongst States' in Malcolm Langford et al (eds), *Global Justice, State Duties—The Extraterritorial Scope of Economic, Social and Cultural Rights in International Law* (CUP 2012).

[19] See, eg, Benedetto Conforti, 'Exploring the Strasbourg Case-Law: Reflections on State Responsibility for the Breach of Positive Obligations' in Malgosia Fitzmaurice and Dan Sarooshi (eds), *Issues of State Responsibility before International Judicial Institutions* (Hart Publishing 2004); Caitlin A Bell, 'Reassessing Multiple Attribution: the International Law Commission and the *Behrami* and *Saramati* Decision' (2010) 42 New York University Journal of International Law and Politics 502; Maarten den Heijer, 'Procedural Aspects of Shared Responsibility in the European Court of Human Rights' (2013) 4 Journal of International Dispute Settlement 361; Maarten den Heijer, 'Shared Responsibility before the European Court of Human Rights' (2013) 60 Netherlands International Law Review 411.

[20] Of course, some of these questions have already given rise to (largely pre-emptive) solutions with respect to the European Union. See, eg, Articles 1(4) and (6) and Article 3(7) of the 2013 Draft Accession Agreement (DAA) between the EU and the ECHR and the *ex ante* exclusion of, respectively, concurrent jurisdiction of the EU and its member States under the ECHR, the joint attribution of conduct to them, and (in part, at least) the allocation of their shared responsibilities by the ECtHR.

[21] See *Banković and Others v Belgium and Others* [GC] App no 52207/99 (ECtHR, 12 December 2001) para 57: 'The Court must also take into account any relevant rules of international law when examining questions concerning its jurisdiction and, consequently, determine State responsibility in conformity with the governing principles of international law, although it must remain mindful of the Convention's special character as a human rights treaty.'

[22] See Crawford and Keene in this volume; Malcolm D Evans, 'State Responsibility and the European Convention on Human Rights: Role and Realm' in Malgosia Fitzmaurice and Dan Sarooshi (eds), *Issues of State Responsibility* (n 19).

way around and consider concurrent-responsibility law under the ECHR itself as developing the general international law of State responsibility on the very particular and controversial issue of concurrent responsibility.[23] In fact, the few basic principles and conditions of concurrent responsibility available in general international law are such that, as I will argue, the ECHR is one of the few contexts in which they could be fulfilled. All this makes it even more important, therefore, for the ECtHR to actively monitor developments on concurrent jurisdictions, duties, and responsibilities in its regime of international responsibility.

The structure of my argument in this chapter is four-pronged. After a few reminders about the notion and role of jurisdiction in international human rights law, the chapter discusses concurrent human rights jurisdictions, concurrent human rights duties arising from concurrent human rights jurisdictions, and concurrent responsibilities in the case of violation of concurrent human rights duties.

2. Human Rights Jurisdiction in a Nutshell

A few reminders about the notion of human rights jurisdiction under Article 1 ECHR are in order because jurisdiction sets the framework in which the concurrence of jurisdictions is conceptualized and, in turn, conditions the emergence of concurrent duties and, possibly, concurrent responsibilities.

Human rights jurisdiction under Article 1 ECHR is pivotal to the application of the ECHR. ECHR rights apply and give rise to duties, provided there is a relationship of jurisdiction between their potential right holders and their potential duty bearers, ie, between some private parties and one (or more) State Party (and perhaps the EU one day).[24] In a nutshell, and based on the ECtHR's case law, jurisdiction may be defined as (i) effective, (ii) regular, and (iii) normative control by the State over a person—whether she is a national, a resident, or neither.[25] [26]

[23] See, on the strategic interpretation of the rules of international-responsibility law by the ECtHR, Evans (n 22) 160; Crawford and Keene in this volume. See also den Heijer, 'Shared Responsibility' (n 19).

[24] Generally, one may consider that the applicability of EU fundamental rights already depends on the jurisdiction of the EU and that the latter can be both territorial and extraterritorial. Of course, the issue is not addressed expressly in the EU Fundamental Rights Charter. It follows, however, indirectly from Articles 1(4) and (6) of the 2013 DAA. See also Besson, 'The Bearers of Human Rights' Duties and Responsibilities for Human Rights' (n 10).

[25] See *Al-Skeini and Others v The United Kingdom* [GC] App no 55721/07 (ECtHR, 7 July 2011) paras 75–76.

[26] See Besson, 'The Extraterritoriality of the European Convention on Human Rights' (n 11) 862–66 and 872–76. See, more generally, Vandenhole, 'Extraterritorial Human Rights Obligations' (n 18); Ralph Wilde, 'Human Rights Beyond Borders at the World Court: The Significance of the International Court of Justice's Jurisprudence on the Extraterritorial Application of International Human Rights Law Treaties' (2013) 12 Chinese Journal of International Law 639; Malcolm Langford, Wouter Vandenhole, Martin Scheinin, and Willem van Genugten (eds), *Global Justice, State Duties—The Extraterritorial Scope of Economic, Social, and Cultural Rights in International Law* (CUP 2012); Marko Milanovic, *Extraterritorial Application of Human Rights Treaties—Law, Principles, and Policy* (OUP 2011); Olivier de Schutter, 'Globalization and Jurisdiction: Lessons from the European Convention on Human Rights' (2006) 6 Baltic Yearbook of International Law 185.

In terms of scope, jurisdiction is 'territorial' when it applies inside the State's national boundaries and on its territory. Its jurisdiction can also be 'extraterritorial', however, when it applies outside of those boundaries and on another State's territory—including territory without an international title and, hence, without jurisdiction in the general international-law sense of the term.[27] Extraterritorial jurisdiction is exercised either through 'personal' control over a certain person or group of people who become human right holders[28] or through 'spatial' control over a territory outside national territory and hence over the people situated on that territory.[29] The overall preference given to personal over spatial jurisdiction in the case law on extraterritorial jurisdiction may be explained by reference to the conceptual and normative complexity of extraterritorial spatial control and, hence, ambivalence about a form of 'territoriality in extraterritoriality'.

Jurisdiction is best understood as a threshold concept: it is not gradual, even if the control that constitutes it can be, so that, once a certain degree of effective control has been reached, there is jurisdiction and ECHR rights apply. Above that threshold, when control varies, the duties and responsibilities may also, but not jurisdiction itself, provided that a minimal degree of effective control was given in the first place—this is even presumed in some cases, as we will see. When that minimal effective control is lost at a later stage, however, two situations should be distinguished. In the case of extraterritorial jurisdiction, the loss of control implies the loss of jurisdiction *tout court* and the loss of the extraterritorial human rights duties it gave rise to. In the case of territorial jurisdiction, however, jurisdiction is not lost through the loss of effective control, but the corresponding human rights duties that arise from it are affected. They are 'limited', according to the ECtHR, to the positive duty to regain effective control so as to be able to bear the other human rights duties again, on the one hand, and to the positive duty to take measures to ensure respect for other individual human rights, on the other.[30]

The evidence needed to establish or disestablish effective control, and hence jurisdiction, varies depending on whether jurisdiction is territorial or extraterritorial. Territorial jurisdiction is presumed: there is a presumption of control of a State over all people situated in its national territory.[31] The degree of evidence it takes to rebut

[27] See Besson, 'The Extraterritoriality of the European Convention on Human Rights' (n 11) 868–70. See, eg, *Jaloud* (n 2) para 142.

[28] See Besson, 'The Extraterritoriality of the European Convention on Human Rights' (n 11) 874–76. See, eg, in the case of a security patrol: *Al-Skeini* (n 25) paras 137 and 142; in the case of detention: *Hassan* (n 2) para 76; or, in the case of a checkpoint: *Jaloud* (n 2) para 152; *Pisari v Moldova and Russia* App no 42139/12 (ECtHR, 19 October 2015).

[29] See Besson, 'The Extraterritoriality of the European Convention on Human Rights' (n 11) 874–76. See, eg, in the case of the Turkish occupation in Cyprus: *Loizidou* (n 3) paras 56–57; and, in the case of the support given by Armenia to the (territorial) administration of the Nagorno-Karabakh Republic on Azerbaijan territory: *Chiragov* (n 3) para 186.

[30] See Besson, 'The Extraterritoriality of the European Convention on Human Rights' (n 11) 862–64. See, eg, *Assanidze v Georgia* App no 71503/01 (ECtHR, 8 April 2004) paras 137–39; *Ilaşcu* (n 3) paras 329–31; *Catan* (n 3) paras 109–10; *Sargsyan* (n 3) paras 130–31 and 139–49.

[31] See Besson, 'The Extraterritoriality of the European Convention on Human Rights' (n 11) 865 on the ambivalent normative *cum* descriptive dimensions of jurisdiction and their implications for the presumption and, arguably, why it is so hard to rebut.

that presumption is also very high in practice.[32] Extraterritorial jurisdiction, by contrast, has to be established positively outside of a State's own territory. Moreover, the practice shows that the threshold of evidence is quite low.[33] This applies both to extraterritorial personal control and to extraterritorial spatial control, the latter being easier to establish comparatively, but more rarely granted for the political reasons mentioned before. The latter implies, indeed, the return of a certain degree of 'territoriality in extraterritoriality', but without reference to official State boundaries this time. Its perpetuation, especially through the protection of a legal institution like human rights jurisdiction, may threaten official State boundaries in the long term.[34] This, in fact, explains why discussions about the potential extension of the rebuttable presumption of jurisdiction to extraterritorial-spatial jurisdiction, especially when territorial control is authorized by international law, are usually met with circumspection.[35]

3. Concurrent Jurisdictions

Concurrent jurisdictions, ie, the concurrence of more than one State's jurisdiction over the same people and, hence, human right holders, can occur in various constellations.

Most of the cases pertain to the concurrence of the territorial and extraterritorial jurisdictions of different States over people who are controlled by those States at the same time, eg, in the case of military occupation.[36] However, one could also conceive of the concurrence of territorial jurisdictions of different States whose distinct control over their territory enables them to control the same people in transnational circumstances in which these people move, either physically or virtually (due, for example, to cyberactivity, renditions,[37] trafficking,[38] or migration).[39] Finally, one could imagine the concurrence of extraterritorial jurisdictions of different States controlling people at the same time in a foreign territory, eg, in the case of multilateral peace operations abroad.[40] As a matter of fact, all three constellations can overlap.[41]

[32] See Besson, 'The Extraterritoriality of the European Convention on Human Rights' (n 11) 876–78. See, eg, *Ilaşcu* (n 3) paras 329–30; *Catan* (n 3) paras 109–10; *Sargsyan* (n 3) paras 130–31 and 139–49.

[33] See, eg, *Chiragov* (n 3) paras 168–86 on the evidence required to establish extraterritorial jurisdiction, especially in contrast with the evidence required to rebut the presumption of territorial jurisdiction in *Sargsyan* (n 3) paras 131, 140, and 148. For a critique, see Milanovic, 'The Nagorno-Karabakh Cases' (n 14), and the partly concurring, partly dissenting opinion of Judge Ziemele in *Chiragov* (n 3) para 5.

[34] Some authors go as far as to refer to 'extraterritorial States' in this context, eg, Vandenhole, 'Extraterritorial Human Rights Obligations' (n 18) 833.

[35] See Besson, 'The Extraterritoriality of the European Convention on Human Rights' (n 11) 877. See also Antal Berkes, 'The Nagorno-Karabakh Conflict Before the European Court of Human Rights: Pending Cases and Certain Forecasts on Jurisdiction and State Responsibility' (2013) 52 The Military Law and the Law of War Review 379, 419–33.

[36] See, eg, *Loizidou* (n 3); *Ilaşcu* (n 3); *Catan* (n 3); *Sargsyan* (n 3).

[37] See, eg, *El-Masri* (n 4); *Al Nashiri* (n 4).

[38] See, eg, *Rantsev* (n 5).

[39] See, eg, *MSS* (n 6).

[40] See, eg, *Hassan* (n 2) paras 78–79; *Jaloud* (n 2).

[41] See, eg *Al-Saadoon and Mufdhi v The United Kingdom* App no 61498/08 (ECtHR, 2 March 2010).

Depending on the degree of control exercised in these different constellations of jurisdiction, the relations between the different States' jurisdictions can vary. In some cases, the control of one State is exercised in the place of another that has lost effective control (one may refer to this as 'complementary jurisdiction'),[42] whereas in other cases the States' respective degrees of control may all be effective on the same territory (one may refer to this as 'joint jurisdiction'), or in their respective territories (one may refer to this as 'competing jurisdiction').[43] The first case is likely to be more common. Indeed, State jurisdiction, like political and legal authority, is in principle exclusive (of that of another State)—at least when it is territorial because of its claim to be legitimate.[44] As a matter of fact, the different States' degrees of control and hence of jurisdiction may be actively coordinated by the respective States so as to complement one another,[45] including through delegation or a lease, for instance.

There are conceptual and practical obstacles barring the road to the recognition and development of concurrent jurisdictions under ECHR law.

Conceptually, the idea of concurrent jurisdictions[46] is in tension with the unicity that is required among the conditions for the legitimate authority of a State and its laws from a human rights perspective and hence from a democratic perspective.[47] The reason lies in the mutual ties between democracy and human rights in the ECHR system. In principle, indeed, ECHR rights are approached as the rights of the members of a democratic community[48] and are the rights that constitute the equal political status of their right holders. What this implies, in turn, is the unicity of the democratic community as a guarantee that its subjects, and by extension their rights, can be equal.[49] This explains why the duality, or even the plurality, of jurisdictions seems to be in contradiction at first with (the unicity of) human rights and democracy.

This democratic and egalitarian dimension of ECHR rights actually explains the importance given to the unicity of jurisdiction in human rights practice. This

[42] See, eg, *Ilaşcu* (n 3) paras 329–30; *Catan* (n 3) paras 109–10.

[43] See, eg, *Hassan* (n 2) para 78; *Jaloud* (n 2) para 153.

[44] See Besson, 'The Extraterritoriality of the European Convention on Human Rights' (n 11) 864–66 and 878.

[45] See, eg, the United Kingdom and the United States in *Hassan* (n 2) paras 78–79; or the Netherlands, the United Kingdom, and Iraq in *Jaloud* (n 2) paras 149–51.

[46] This conceptual unease starts, in fact, with using the plural of 'jurisdiction'.

[47] See Besson, 'The Extraterritoriality of the European Convention on Human Rights' (n 11) 882–23 and 864–66.

[48] See, eg, *Zdanoka v Latvia* [GC] App no 58278/00 (ECtHR, 16 March 2006), para 98. See, on human rights and democracy under the ECHR, Besson, 'The Extraterritoriality of the European Convention on Human Rights' (n 11) 863–64, 866 and 882–83. More generally, the identity between the States' jurisdiction and that of their peoples and the latter's importance in the case of regime change have been confirmed by the United Nations Human Rights Committee in its General Comment no 26 (8 December 1997) UN Doc CCPR/C/21/Rev.1/Add.8/Rev.1 para 4.

[49] See esp *Mathieu-Mohin and Clerfayt v Belgium* App no 9267/81 (ECtHR, 2 March 1987) paras 52–54; *Sejdić and Finci v Bosnia and Herzegovina* [GC] App nos 27996/06 and 34836/06 (ECtHR, 22 December 2009) para 50. On human rights and federalism, see Samantha Besson, 'Le Droit International et Européen des Droits de l'Homme et la Forme Politique Fédérale—*Je t'aime, moi non plus*' in Samantha Besson and Eva Maria Belser (eds), *La Convention Européenne des Droits de l'Homme et les Cantons—Die Europäische Menschenrechtskonvention und die Kantone* (Schulthess 2014).

is, for instance, how one could read the general positive duty of Moldova to regain effective control despite Russia's extraterritorial control and jurisdiction on its territory.[50] This is also how one could explain the possibility for the exceptional limitation of the human rights duties of a State of territorial jurisdiction like Moldova: it is temporarily 'compensated' by the extraterritorial jurisdiction of Russia.[51] Conversely, human rights unicity is also how one could interpret the lack of recognition of Serbia's (apparently extraterritorial) jurisdiction in Kosovo.[52]

Practically, too, there are some obstacles to the recognition of the concurrent jurisdictions of different States under the ECHR. Most of them are related to the procedural requirements for the admissibility of a case before the ECtHR.[53]

First, all States whose jurisdiction is at stake should be parties to the ECHR. This is a first consequence of the indispensable third-party rule.[54] It has been invoked in the cases *Behrami* and *Saadi* regarding non-ECHR States Parties.[55] Interestingly, however, the principle has not been applied too strictly by the ECtHR in Article 3 ECHR extradition or expulsion cases[56] or in international organizations cases.[57] This is because what is at stake is the respect of the ECHR by the main State of jurisdiction and not the actual responsibility of another third-party State or an international organization, thus enabling the Court to assess the lawfulness of the latter's conduct, if it is necessary to establish the responsibility of a State Party to the Convention. Secondly, all States whose jurisdiction is at stake should be parties to the individual procedure before the ECtHR. This is easy to remedy by the applicants, of course. However, in practice, this has not been done often,[58] mainly due to the different admissibility conditions to establish each State's jurisdiction, and especially the effectiveness of the control each of them exercises over the victim.[59] As a result, the main procedural obstacle to

[50] See *Catan* (n 3) paras 109–10 and 145. See also, more recently, *Sargsyan* (n 3) paras 130–31 and 139–49.

[51] See *Sargsyan* (n 3) para 148: '[t]he acceptance that the territorial State had only limited responsibility under the Convention was *compensated* by the finding that another Convention State exceptionally exercised jurisdiction outside its territory and thus had full responsibility under the Convention' (emphasis added).

[52] See *Azemi v Serbia* App no 11209/09 (ECtHR, 5 November 2013) paras 46–49.

[53] See den Heijer, 'Procedural Aspects' (n 19).

[54] See *Case of the monetary gold removed from Rome in 1943 (Italy v France, United Kingdom of Great Britain and Northern Ireland and United States of America)* (Preliminary Question) [1954] ICJ Rep 19, para 32; nuanced in *East Timor (Portugal v Australia)* (Merits) [1995] ICJ Rep 90, paras 102–5.

[55] See, eg, *Behrami* (n 9) para 67; *Saadi v Italy* [GC] App no 37201/06 (ECtHR, 28 February 2008) para 126. See also Besson, 'La Pluralité d'Etats Responsables' (n 12) 15–16; den Heijer, 'Shared Responsibility' (n 19).

[56] See, eg, *Soering v The United Kingdom* App no 14038/88 (ECtHR, 7 July 1989) paras 86–88; *Saadi* (n 55) para 121; *MSS* (n 6) para 342.

[57] See, eg *Behrami* (n 9) para 67; *Banković* (n 21) para 31; *Matthews v The United Kingdom* App no 24833/94 (ECtHR, 18 February 1999) para 33.

[58] Notable exceptions where all States of jurisdiction were put on the stand include: *Banković* (n 21); *Senator Lines GmbH v Austria, Belgium, Denmark, Finland, France, Germany, Greece, Ireland, Italy, Luxembourg, The Netherlands, Portugal, Spain, Sweden and The United Kingdom* App no 56672/00 (ECHR, 10 March 2004) ECHR 2004-IV 331; *Mohammed Hussein and Others v The Netherlands and Italy* App no 27725/10 (ECtHR, 2 April 2013).

[59] See, eg, *Tugar v Italy* (1995) 83-A DR 26; *Aziz v Cyprus, Greece, Turkey and The United Kingdom* App no 69949/01 (ECtHR, 23 April 2002).

the consideration of concurrent jurisdictions in these cases is, once more, the indispensable third-party rule, applied this time with respect to other States Parties to the ECHR.[60]

Independent of these conceptual and practical hurdles, it is easy to observe that the recognition of the concurrent jurisdictions of States by the ECtHR has been rarer in practice than expected, even when it was possible procedurally. More precisely, most cases actually decided on that basis have been cases of competing territorial jurisdictions.[61] Cases of concurrence between territorial and extraterritorial jurisdictions have been much rarer.[62] Finally, there have been no cases of concurrent extraterritorial jurisdictions so far, despite the fact that the Court explicitly entertained the possibility in *Jaloud*.[63] Actually, most cases in which the issue of concurrence of jurisdictions has been explicitly raised recently, albeit to no avail for procedural reasons as explained before, are cases in which, on the one hand, one of the States of jurisdiction was not a State Party to the ECHR[64] or not a party to the procedure before the ECtHR,[65] or, on the other hand, cases involving an international organization, eg, the EU or the United Nations (UN), that is a non-party to the ECHR.[66]

What this means is that many discussions of jurisdiction in the ECtHR's case law could be said to have been unduly biased against a particular State when the concurrent jurisdiction of other States was at play but was not considered. It is not certain that the ECtHR's assessment of the duties and responsibilities of a given State of jurisdiction would have been the same had the duties and responsibilities of other States of jurisdiction been assessed at the same time. The sole State of jurisdiction may be said to have been unfairly burdened by the recognition and allocation of its human rights duties and responsibilities, for it is the only one that could be recognized and allocated those duties and responsibilities ultimately. This may explain, for instance, the generous recognition of the extraterritorial jurisdiction of some States Parties when the State of territorial jurisdiction was not a party to the Convention.[67] One may say the same about the recognition of the territorial or extraterritorial jurisdiction of States Parties that are members of an international organization that cannot exercise jurisdiction and that does not incur duties and responsibilities on that basis under the ECHR.[68]

[60] See, eg, *Hess v The United Kingdom* (1975) 2 DR 72.

[61] See, eg, *MSS* (n 6); *Rantsev* (n 5).

[62] See, eg, *Ilaşcu* (n 3); *Catan* (n 3).

[63] See, eg, *Jaloud* (n 2) para 153: 'The Court has established jurisdiction in respect of the Netherlands. It is not called upon to establish whether the United Kingdom, another State Party to the Convention, might have exercised *concurrent* jurisdiction' (emphasis added).

[64] See, eg, *El-Masri* (n 4); *Al-Jedda* (n 9); *Hassan* (n 2).

[65] See, eg, *Jaloud* (n 2).

[66] See, eg, *Behrami* (n 9); *Al-Jedda* (n 9); *MSS* (n 6).

[67] See, eg, for Macedonia (and not the United States) in the context of extraordinary renditions and black sites: *El-Masri* (n 4); for the United Kingdom (and not the United States) in the context of military prisons: *Hassan* (n 2).

[68] This is how one can explain decisions like *Al-Jedda* (n 9) for the United Kingdom (and not the United Nations) in the context of military intervention.

4. Concurrent Duties

State jurisdiction is the trigger for the application of human rights. Since the jurisdiction of a given State over a certain person gives rise to human rights duties of that State towards that person, one may venture that the concurrent jurisdictions of many States over the same person can give rise to many human rights duties towards that same person. One may then consider the different States of jurisdiction's duties as concurrent too.[69]

It is true that so-called concurrent ECHR duties can arise separately as distinct human rights duties owed by each respective State of jurisdiction to its right holders under their respective relationship of jurisdiction. This is a consequence of the exclusive and, hence, separate nature of political and legal authority in general and, hence, of the different States' jurisdiction even when their respective jurisdictions are concurrent. Human rights duties are unilateral duties owed by each State on its own: they are not owed collectively as multilateral duties.[70] However, because they are owed to the same right holders in the same context, issues pertaining to their relationship in their respective specification and allocation arise in practice. The concurrence of jurisdiction can affect the type and content of human rights duties that arise to the extent that their concurrence implies a concurrence of effective control of the same right holders and, hence, a concurrence of threat to, or impact upon, the right holders' protected interests. This is also true in the case that one of the States of concurrent jurisdictions has lost effective territorial control to another: the former State has positive duties to regain control and to adopt measures to ensure that other human rights duties arise in relation to the human rights duties of the State of extraterritorial jurisdiction exercising effective control over its territory and the same people.[71]

The concurrence of human rights duties can be of three kinds. The first kind of concurrent duties are 'competing duties' arising out of the parallel and distinct (equivalent) effective control and jurisdiction by all States at hand. This will usually be the case when their respective jurisdictions are territorial and each State is exercising it over its own territory.[72] The second kind of concurrent human rights duties are 'joint duties' arising concurrently out of joint effective control and jurisdiction by the States in question. This will usually be the case when one of the States exercises extraterritorial jurisdiction hand in hand with the State of territorial jurisdiction,[73] but also when many States are exercising extraterritorial jurisdiction

[69] For example, the Iraqi, British, and Dutch soldiers in *Jaloud* (n 2) or the British or American soldiers in *Hassan* (n 2).

[70] One should distinguish these duties being owed to all other States (*erga omnes*) from their being owed by all of them (*omnium*). See also Samantha Besson, 'Science without Borders and the Boundaries of Human Rights: Who Owes the Human Right to Science?/Une Science sans Frontière face aux Frontières des Droits de l'Homme—Qui est Débiteur du Droit de l'Homme à la Science?' (2015) 4 Journal Européen des Droits de l'Homme/European Journal of Human Rights, Special issue on the Human Right to Science 462; Samantha Besson, 'The Sources of International Human Rights Law' in Samantha Besson and Jean d'Aspremont (eds), *Oxford Handbook on the Sources of International Law* (OUP 2017).

[71] See, eg, *Ilaşcu* (n 3) para 331; *Catan* (n 3) paras 145–47; *Sargsyan* (n 3) paras 130–31 and 139–49.

[72] See, eg, *MSS* (n 6); *Rantsev* (n 5).

[73] See, eg, *Jaloud* (n 2).

together.[74] Finally, concurrent human rights duties may also be 'complementary duties' arising out of different degrees of effective control and jurisdiction by the States in question. This can be the case when territorial and extraterritorial jurisdictions concur and one State has lost effective control to another State[75] or delegated some of its authority to another State.[76]

Importantly, however, all the usual types of human rights duties, ie, (positive and negative) duties (to respect, protect, and fulfil), can arise in principle from State jurisdiction. These duties merely depend on the type and degree of effective control over the right holders. This applies independently from the territorial or extraterritorial nature of jurisdiction.[77] It would be wrong, therefore, to assume that, in the case of concurrence between territorial and extraterritorial jurisdictions, the latter could only give rise to negative duties. It is true that the kind of effective control needed for positive human rights duties to arise is often more difficult to establish when a State's jurisdiction is extraterritorial, but this eventuality is by no means excluded.[78]

Two questions need to be addressed when facing concurrent human rights duties under the ECHR: first, the allocation of concurrent human rights duties, and second, the democratic legitimacy of the allocation process.

First, with regards to concurrent ECHR duties, depending on whether the human rights duties are the same or not, their allocation raises different questions.

If the duties arising out of concurrent jurisdictions are of different types (eg duties to either respect, protect, or fulfil), the allocation will not be necessary.[79] They will complement each other as they usually do: their allocation can abide by the principles used to allocate them within a single jurisdiction. The duties to respect are complemented by the duties to protect and fulfil.[80] That complementarity[81] is at play, for instance, in the case of the State of (territorial) jurisdiction's general positive duties to regain effective control when it has been lost:[82] these duties fit well with those of the other State of (extraterritorial) jurisdiction due to its generality and institutional content.[83] If, on the contrary, the duties that arise concurrently towards

[74] See, eg, *Hassan* (n 2). [75] See, eg, *Ilaşcu* (n 3) para 331; *Catan* (n 3) paras 145–47.

[76] See, eg, *Jaloud* (n 2) paras 149–51.

[77] See Besson, 'The Extraterritoriality of the European Convention on Human Rights' (n 11) 878–79. See, eg, *Al-Skeini* (n 25) para 137; *Jaloud* (n 2) paras 226–28.

[78] See, eg, *Jaloud* (n 2) paras 226–27.

[79] See also Vandenhole, 'Extraterritorial Human Rights Obligations' (n 18) 827–30.

[80] See Samantha Besson, 'The Allocation of Anti-poverty Rights Duties—Our Rights, but Whose Duties?' in Krista Nadakavukaren Schefer (ed), *Poverty and the International Economic Legal System—Duties to the World's Poor* (CUP 2013), referring to Henry Shue, *Basic Rights* (2nd edn, Princeton University Press 1996) 59, 61, and 173.

[81] See *Sargsyan* (n 3) para 148: '[t]he acceptance that the territorial State had only limited responsibility under the Convention was *compensated* by the finding that another Convention State exceptionally exercised jurisdiction outside its territory and thus had full responsibility under the Convention' (emphasis added).

[82] See, eg, *Catan* (n 3) para 145; *Sargsyan* (n 3) para 131.

[83] See Besson, 'The Extraterritoriality of the European Convention on Human Rights' (n 11) 865–66; Samantha Besson, 'Human Rights and Constitutional Law—Patterns of Mutual Validation and Legitimation' in Rowan Cruft, Matthew Liao, and Massimo Renzo (eds), *Philosophical Foundations of Human Rights* (OUP 2015).

the same people are the same, eg, the same duties to respect, protect, or fulfil, the lack of common institutions or procedures to allocate the duties together makes their respect in practice not only often impossible, but also makes the burden on the single duty-bearing State, or even on each duty-bearing State, difficult to justify as a result. This in turn raises questions about the exact scope and content of these duties unless one can approach their allocation jointly. 'Ought implies can' indeed.

The ECtHR's case law does not provide us with much information about how the allocation of concurrent ECHR duties should take place. The concurrent ECHR duties of every State of jurisdiction are discussed separately and their allocation is not coordinated.[84] When it is coordinated, it has only been by reference to the generality of the positive duty to regain jurisdiction that is treated as a different and complementary kind of duty.[85] The ECHR duties whose allocation comes closer to being coordinated in the ECtHR's case law are actually vested in a single State at a time: each ECHR State indeed bears positive duties to protect right holders against threats to their rights, including against the threats posed by other States of jurisdiction.[86] This makes the latter's duties redundant, therefore, and their concurrent duties irrelevant to settling the case in the end.[87]

Of course, the reasons for the scarcity of case law on the issue are easy to gather. The allocation of ECHR duties is a matter for the internal discretion of States Parties. Even when the ECtHR has the power to review that allocation, its case law pertains to an allocation internal to States, and between its domestic authorities. Indeed, ECHR duties are unilateral (State by State) duties and are not held collectively or multilaterally (together by States).[88] Finally, even if the ECtHR were to review the internal allocation of human rights duties of all States of jurisdiction, subsidiarity would protect the democratic institutional set-up of every State, for the latter belongs to its margin of appreciation.

A ready-made solution to coordinate the allocation of concurrent human rights duties owed by States under the ECHR is to identify a general positive duty of all States of concurrent jurisdiction to allocate human rights duties among themselves. This implies, in particular, a duty to set up institutions and procedures to do this once they have acquired concurrent jurisdiction over the same people. That duty could be derived from States of jurisdiction's general positive duty to allocate human rights duties institutionally among their internal domestic authorities.[89] It applies particularly strongly to the State of territorial jurisdiction, for reasons related to the priority of that form of jurisdiction discussed in the first section, in cases where the concurrence of jurisdiction is effective (eg, in cases of joint jurisdiction), and

[84] See *MSS* (n 6); *Rantsev* (n 5).

[85] See *Ilaşcu* (n 3); *Catan* (n 3).

[86] See *MSS* (n 6).

[87] These positive duties are an important feature of the ECtHR's case law (eg, in *Al Nashiri* (n 4) para 517, by contrast to *El-Masri* (n 4) para 223). In the case of violation, they pre-empt having to work through the attribution of conduct of another State at a later stage in the responsibility reasoning (see also *Costello-Roberts v The United Kingdom* App no 13134/87 (ECtHR, 25 March 1993), paras 150, 157, and 162). See, eg, *Ilaşcu* (n 3) paras 392–93.

[88] See indirectly: *Sari and Çolak* (n 8) paras 91–92 and 96.

[89] See Besson, 'The Allocation of Anti-poverty Rights Duties?' (n 80); Besson, 'The Extraterritoriality of the European Convention on Human Rights' (n 11) 863–65.

especially when the concurrent jurisdiction of other States on its territory is consensual (eg, when it has been acquired through invitation or lease). Finally, when the States of concurrent jurisdictions are acting under an institutional umbrella, such as through an international organization, their positive duties to use that institutional framework, not only to act but also to respect their concurrent human rights duties, are easy to justify based on each State's general positive duty to organize itself institutionally so as to respect human rights. This duty is complemented in this context by the duty of diligence that binds all States that join an international organization whose membership may prevent them from abiding by their ECHR duties.[90] Note that this duty is independent from the existence of human rights duties of the international organization itself.

A further justification for this general positive duty of States of concurrent jurisdiction to coordinate the allocation of concurrent human rights duties among themselves may be found in the democratic and egalitarian dimension of human rights, and the ECHR in particular, as I explained before. Human rights are equal rights of their right holders and should therefore be specified and allocated together and through an egalitarian procedure in which all can participate. This legitimacy concern cuts both ways, however, which brings me to the next point.

Secondly, with regards to the legitimacy of the allocation of concurrent ECHR duties, the institutions or procedures established to coordinate the allocation of concurrent human rights duties can conflict with the democratic institutions and procedures of the State of (territorial) jurisdiction. This applies even when its institutions are weak or non-existent because it has lost effective control. Indeed, each State of territorial jurisdiction has a general positive duty to strengthen its institutions and authority. The existence of competing institutions and procedures to allocate concurrent human rights duties with other States of (extraterritorial) jurisdiction may prevent it, therefore, from respecting its other human rights duties and, accordingly, may be counterproductive in the long run for its democratic development.[91] One may, therefore, argue that priority should be given, in the allocation of concurrent human rights duties, to the duties of the State of (territorial) jurisdiction based on the priority of its democratic duties and the subsidiarity of the other States of jurisdiction's duties.

Finally, it is important to emphasize that the concurrent human rights duties at stake in this section should not be conflated with States' 'responsibilities for human rights'. These are collective or multilateral responsibilities of all States (and other international subjects)[92] that arise from international and European human rights law independently of effective control and jurisdiction.[93] They include

[90] See, eg, *Waite and Kennedy v Germany* ECHR 1999-I 393, para 67; *Al-Dulimi* (n 9) para 114.

[91] See Besson, 'The Extraterritoriality of the European Convention on Human Rights' (n 11) 882–83.

[92] On their allocation among the various responsibility bearers, see Besson, 'The Bearers of Human Rights' Duties and Responsibilities for Human Rights' (n 10); Besson, 'The Allocation of Anti-poverty Rights Duties?' (n 80). See also Monica Hakimi, 'Distributing the Responsibility to Protect' in André Nollkaemper and Dov Jacobs (eds), *Distribution of Responsibilities in International Law* (CUP 2015).

[93] See for a discussion of their differences, Besson, 'Le Droit International et Européen des Droits de l'Homme et la Forme Politique Fédérale' (n 49); Besson, 'The Bearers of Human Rights' Duties and Responsibilities for Human Rights' (n 10).

responsibilities to prevent or protect against human rights violations by other States (of jurisdiction) and, as a result, apply outside of their bearers' territorial jurisdiction, and without requiring extraterritorial jurisdiction of the responsibility-bearing States. Responsibilities for human rights differ from human rights duties in three ways. First, they are grounded in States' capacity to act and not in jurisdiction. Secondly, they are not directed towards, and hence not owed to, the right holders but to all States. Finally, unlike human rights duties of States of jurisdiction, responsibilities for human rights have a content that compels cooperation with those very States of jurisdiction to help them prevent or remedy human rights violations under their jurisdiction.[94] They are, in other words, complementary to human rights duties *stricto sensu* and not concurrent with them. They should not, as a result, be conflated with concurrent human rights duties arising from concurrent jurisdiction.[95] Nor should they be conflated with the secondary duties or remedial responsibilities arising out of the violation of these (primary) concurrent human rights duties. The latter constitute the next point.

5. Concurrent Responsibilities

In the case that many States exercise concurrent jurisdiction and acquire concurrent ECHR duties on that basis, the violation of the latter by some or all the States of jurisdiction could give rise to concurrent responsibilities.

Concurrent responsibilities are understood here as the responsibilities stemming from the contribution of many States to the same injury (i) whether this occurs through the violation of the same duty or not, and (ii) through the same wrongful act[96] or not.[97] When concurrent responsibilities are caused by the same wrongful act, they are usually referred to as 'shared responsibilities' *stricto sensu*, even though the latter term is sometimes applied to refer to all kinds of concurrent responsibilities independently of the nature of the wrongful act.[98] Importantly, if there is no common injury to the same human right holder, responsibilities for the different injuries will arise as well, albeit not *qua* concurrent responsibilities as understood in this section.

[94] See, eg, Articles 55–56 UN Charter; Article 2(1) International Covenant on Economic, Social, and Cultural Rights (ICESCR).

[95] Vandenhole, 'Extraterritorial Human Rights Obligations' (n 18) 825, 828, and 831; Olivier de Schutter et al, 'Commentary to the Maastricht Principles on Extraterritorial Obligations of States in the Area of Economic, Social and Cultural Rights' (2012) 34 Human Rights Quarterly 1084; Margot E Salomon, 'How to Keep Promises: Making Sense of the Duty among Multiple States to Fulfil Socio-Economic Rights in the World' in André Nollkaemper and Dov Jacobs (eds), *Distribution of Responsibilities in International Law* (CUP 2015); Hakimi, 'Distributing the Responsibility to Protect' (n 92).

[96] The same wrongful act is a single, albeit collective, act and not a series of identical but separate acts.

[97] See, eg, Besson, 'La Pluralité d'Etats Responsables' (n 12) 7–11; d'Argent, 'Reparation, Cessation, Assurances and Guarantees of Non-Repetition' (n 17) 211–13.

[98] See, eg, Nollkaemper and Jacobs, 'Shared Responsibility in International Law' (n 17) 366–68; André Nollkaemper and Ilias Plakokefalos, 'Conclusions: Beyond the ILC Legacy' in André Nollkaemper and Ilias Plakokefalos (eds), *Principles of Shared Responsibility in International Law—An Appraisal of the State of the Art* (CUP 2014). See also Besson, 'La Pluralité d'Etats Responsables' (n 12).

In the case of violation of concurrent duties stemming from concurrent jurisdictions, concurrent responsibilities are more likely to arise than in other cases.[99] States of concurrent jurisdiction are indeed more likely to exercise their effective control together and, hence, to cause the same injury. This may be through the same wrongful act or omission and with respect to a violation of the same human rights duties, but not exclusively. In any case, even if the wrongful act and the duty violated are the same, causation can vary greatly between States.[100] Of course, it is important to emphasize again that concurrent responsibilities need not arise at all, and, conversely, they could arise independently of concurrent jurisdictions and/or concurrent duties.

Two implications of the concurrent character of responsibilities in the general law of international responsibility should be discussed: first, the attribution of the illegal conduct and/or responsibility to the different States; and, secondly, the allocation of responsibilities and, in particular, of reparations between them.

First, the attribution of conduct (direct attribution) and/or responsibility (indirect attribution) to many States in cases of contribution to the same injury can lead to the multiplication of responsible States and should be understood accordingly.

The attribution of both conduct (Articles 4–11 ARSIWA) and responsibility (Articles 16–19 ARSIWA) can be either distinct or joint. As a result, one may identify three types of concurrent responsibilities: (i) the attribution of conduct to each of the States can be distinct (Articles 4–5 ARSIWA), as can the attribution of responsibility in cases of assistance of one to the other (Article16 ARSIWA).[101] As a result, concurrent responsibilities by distinct attribution of conduct and/or responsibility may be referred to as 'competing responsibilities'[102] ; (ii) the attribution of conduct may also be 'joint' by reference to the joint dual or plural[103] effective control of the same agents by the States of jurisdiction (Article 8 ARSIWA). Concurrent responsibilities by joint attribution of conduct may therefore be referred to as 'joint

[99] See also Vandenhole, 'Extraterritorial human rights obligations' (n 18) 830–33.

[100] See d'Argent, 'Reparation, Cessation, Assurances and Guarantee of Non-Repetition' (n 17) 211–13.

[101] Note that the reasoning of the ECtHR in *El-Masri* (n 4) para 223 about 'acquiescence or connivance' of the authorities of one State to that of another on the former's territory comes close to fitting the distinct attribution of responsibility under Article 16 ARSIWA, but not quite, and goes further than the International Law Commission had in mind with Article 16 ARSIWA. In *Al Nashiri* (n 4) para 517, however, the Court reverted to an Article 3 ECHR reasoning *à la Soering* (*Soering* (n 56) paras 86–88), without any further reference to the attribution of conduct or responsibility of a State to another and to 'acquiescence and connivance'. On this question, see Crawford and Keene in this volume; André Nollkaemper, 'The ECtHR Finds Macedonia Responsible in Connection with Torture by the CIA, but on What Basis?' (EJIL: *Talk!* 24 December 2012) <http://www.ejiltalk.org/the-ecthr-finds-macedonia-responsible-in-connection-with-torture-by-the-cia-but-on-what-basis/> accessed 5 April 2016.

[102] The distinction between competing, joint, and cumulative responsibilities does not necessarily match that between competing, joint, and complementary duties presented in the previous section. The latter need not all be violated by the same States and the control at stake need not be the same either.

[103] See, eg *Al-Jedda* (n 9) para 84; *The State of the Netherlands v Hasan Nuhanovic* App no 12/03324 (Supreme Court of the Netherlands, 6 September 2013) para 5.9. In contrast, see *Behrami* (n 9) para 140.

responsibilities'. This excludes, for instance, cases of delegation of effective control to another State (Article 6 ARSIWA), in which one State acts for the other; (iii) the attribution of responsibility itself may be regarded as joint in cases of control or coercion exercised by one State upon another State (Articles 17–18 ARSIWA). Concurrent responsibilities by joint attribution of responsibility may be referred to as 'cumulative responsibilities'.

So far, the ECtHR has been reluctant to proceed with the joint attribution of concurrent conduct or responsibilities to many States of jurisdiction at the same time. This is not surprising, for the cases tried have been either situations triggered by competing and distinct wrongful acts,[104] or instances in which there has been a delegation of effective control to one State by the other.[105] To date, as a result, there have been no cases of joint attribution of conduct to two or more States,[106] or of complementary attribution of responsibility to another State.[107] Recent developments in the recognition of joint dual or plural effective control under Article 8 ARSIWA may provide ground for hope regarding the former, however. As to the latter, the Court has not yet referred to the relevant provisions in ARSIWA on the attribution of responsibility and does not formulate these issues clearly along those lines either. Interestingly, in cases in which a joint attribution of responsibility could have been possible, the Court has decided against it by reference to the respective individual duties of the States of concurrent jurisdiction and, albeit unconvincingly, the corresponding need for an individual attribution of conduct to each State.[108]

Secondly, the allocation of responsibilities and, in particular, reparations between many States in the case of contribution to the same injury can prove difficult. Concurrent responsibilities or secondary duties, whether of cessation, reparation, or non-repetition, may be allocated in either a distinct or a joint fashion.[109] This applies whether or not the attribution of conduct and/or responsibility to the different States, as discussed before, was distinct or joint.

The principle for the allocation of responsibilities is individual and distinct (independent) responsibility. Responsibilities are allocated to each responsible

[104] See, eg, *Rantsev* (n 5); *Stojkovic v France and Belgium* App no 25303/08 (ECtHR, 27 October 2011) paras 55–56. See also *Ilaşcu* (n 3) paras 352, 385, and 393.

[105] See, eg, *Drozd and Janousek* (n 8) para 96; *Hassan* (n 2) para 78. For a discussion of the consequences of the exclusive nature of the attribution under Article 6 ARSIWA for concurrent responsibilities, however, see the joint dissenting opinions of Judges Pettiti, Valticos, and Lopes Rocha and of Judges MacDonald, Bernhardt, Pekkanen, and Wildhaber in *Drozd and Janousek* (n 8). See also Sari, 'Untangling Extra-territorial Jurisdiction from International Responsibility' (n 14) for a reading of *Jaloud* (n 2) in the light of Article 6 ARSIWA and Article 7 Articles on the Responsibility of International Organisations (ARIO) and the notion of 'unified command', albeit with respect to the United Nations and not to the United Kingdom in this case.

[106] See, eg, *Hussein* (n 58); *Hess* (60).

[107] See, eg, *Stephens v Malta (no 1)* App no 11956/07 (ECtHR, 21 April 2009) paras 51–52.

[108] See *Sari and Çolak* (n 8) paras 91–92, and 96, despite its reference to 'joint responsibility' of Denmark and Turkey.

[109] This section focuses on the secondary duties or responsibilities of reparation. On the others, see d'Argent, 'Reparation, Cessation, Assurances and Guarantee of Non-Repetition' (n 17) 215–17. Of course, 'just satisfaction' under Article 41 ECHR does not amount to reparation *stricto sensu*. Nor is the existence of an injury *stricto sensu* needed in ECHR responsibility law either. An analogy with reparations in general international law still holds, however.

State in proportion to its share in the contribution to the injury (Article 42 ARSIWA). More specifically, the apportionment can be made according to the causal link between each State's wrongful act and the injury, the stringency of the violated duty, and/or the gravity of the violation.[110] There is an exception, however, in general international responsibility law: joint and several responsibility, ie, a responsibility that is individual but solidary or undivided. According to this principle, each responsible State can be called to remedy the whole injury for all the others (Article 47(1) ARSIWA).[111] This only applies, however, in the case that the injury was caused by the same wrongful act, ie, a single, albeit collective, act and not a series of identical but separate acts, whether this occurs through the joint attribution of conduct or responsibility. The justification for this is, first, the complex causality between single, collective, wrongful acts and the injury, and the argument that it is not easily amenable *ex post* to proportionate allocations of responsibilities[112] and, secondly, the correlation that one can make between being able to act wrongfully together and being able, later on, to coordinate in order to repair the injury together. Provided joint and several responsibility applies, internal rights of recourse should then be available in order to avoid overburdening one of the responsible States and favouring the others (Article 47(2)(b) ARSIWA). There should also be protection against unjust enrichment by the injured State or, by extension, injured individual (Article 47(2)(a) ARSIWA).

In the case of concurrent responsibilities of States under the ECHR, as I have understood them in this section, one could argue for the generalization of the rule of joint and several responsibility.[113] This could, of course, apply to cases in which there has been a single wrongful act, which could often be the case in the context of concurrent human rights jurisdictions and duties, as I explained before. It suffices to think here of the responsibilities incurred through a joint military operation of many States outside their territories,[114] or of the action of the civil administration jointly run by the State of territorial jurisdiction and another State of extraterritorial jurisdiction.[115]

[110] See also d'Argent, 'Reparation, Cessation, Assurances and Guarantee of Non-Repetition' (n 17) 217ff.

[111] On other special and more generous customary or conventional regimes of joint and several responsibility outside of general international law, see Besson, 'La pluralité d'Etats responsables' (n 12) 14–22; d'Argent, 'Reparation, Cessation, Assurances and Guarantee of Non-Repetition' (n 17) 245–46.

[112] In short, causality may be exclusive, parallel, complementary or aggregate, and cumulative or indissociable. The latter is the most difficult when it comes to the apportionment of responsibilities, and the alternative criteria of apportionment are not satisfactory (eg, the 'adequate cause' or 'equivalence principle' discussions). See for further details, d'Argent, 'Reparation, Cessation, Assurances and Guarantee of Non-Repetition' (n 17) 222–32.

[113] Scope precludes addressing the remaining procedural questions, however, that are not addressed under Article 47 ARSIWA and, in particular, the issue of the liberation of other responsible States once one of them has provided a full reparation, and the issue of the grounds for the internal rights of recourse between responsible States if it cannot be causality because it is too complex (potential alternatives are the adequate cause or the equivalence principle but also, arguably, and by analogy to Article 39 ARSIWA, the various grounds of attribution of responsibility in case of joint attribution of responsibilities). See also Besson, 'La Pluralité d'Etats Responsables' (n 12) 24–5.

[114] See, eg, *Banković* (n 21).

[115] See, eg, *Jaloud* (n 2).

However, one may also argue for joint and several responsibility to be extended to all cases of concurrent responsibilities for violations of ECHR rights, even when there is no single wrongful act, provided causality is complex (eg, in cases of cumulative causality).[116] There are three justifications for extending the joint and several responsibility principle in this way.

First of all, as I argued before, there is a general positive duty upon all States of concurrent jurisdiction to set up institutions or procedures in order to coordinate the allocation of their concurrent ECHR duties. This duty to coordinate pertains very well to circumstances of consensual complementary jurisdiction or effective joint jurisdiction. This applies especially when the breach occurs in the institutional context of an international organization like the UN, the EU, or the North Atlantic Treaty Organisation (NATO). In this case, an international institutional framework is already in place and could not only coordinate the implementation of the concurrent human rights duties of States, as I explained before, but also the allocation of their concurrent responsibilities.[117] Secondly, the ECtHR has compulsory jurisdiction to allocate responsibilities *ex post* and, possibly, to set internal rights of recourse between the responsible States if needed. These two arguments actually correspond to the elements missing in other regimes of international law and are usually invoked to limit the generalization of joint and several responsibility despite its greater justice for the victim of violations of international law. What applies in most other cases is indeed, first, the lack of international institutions to coordinate the duties and action on the international plane and, secondly, the absence of international tribunals with compulsory jurisdiction to allocate the responsibilities and internal rights of recourse.[118] Finally, one should note that the victims of the violation of the ECHR are individuals and not States. This makes the justice issue even more pressing for the allocation of human rights responsibilities than it is for interstate responsibilities.

So far, the ECtHR has been reluctant to proceed with the joint allocation of concurrent responsibilities and, especially, of reparations. In most cases, the Court has applied the principle of individual and distinct or independent responsibility.[119] This principle has been used even in the case that the injury was caused by the same wrongful act. The Court addresses the responsibility of each State of jurisdiction independently and by reference to its distinct respective jurisdiction and duties. The ECtHR then proceeds with the ordering of reparations for the distinct injuries constitutive of the single injury,[120] or for proportionate shares of the same injury.[121]

There are various practical reasons one may identify for the Court's reluctance. First, there have been very few cases of recognition of concurrent jurisdictions, as

[116] See, for a similar argument pertaining to 'co-perpetration', d'Argent, 'Reparation, Cessation, Assurances and Guarantee of Non-Repetition' (n 17) 241–4.

[117] See, eg, Article 3(7) DAA. See also Maarten den Heijer and André Nollkaemper, 'A New Framework for Allocating International Responsibility: the EU Accession to the European Convention on Human Rights' (2014) SHARES Briefing Paper <http://www.sharesproject.nl> accessed 4 April 2016.

[118] See Besson, 'La Pluralité d'États Responsables' (n 12) 5–7. See also d'Argent, 'Reparation, Cessation, Assurances and Guarantee of Non-Repetition' (n 17) 244–49.

[119] *Ilaşcu* (n 3) paras 352, 385, and 393; *Stojkovic* (n 106) paras 55–56.

[120] *Rantsev* (n 5) paras 404–11; *MSS* (n 6) paras 341–48.

[121] *Ilaşcu* (n 3) paras 484–90.

I explained before, especially between two or more States of extraterritorial jurisdiction or between a State of territorial jurisdiction and a State of extraterritorial jurisdiction. Those cases, when they were brought to trial, have usually been turned into one single territorial case or into an Article 3 ECHR case *à la Soering*.[122] True, there are still a few test cases to come. These include, in particular, cases in which ECHR States Parties have participated in an international organization's peace mission abroad *à la Jaloud*. As a matter of fact, the EU's accession (and, in particular, Article 3(7) Draft Accession Agreement (DAA) 2013) could have brought another series of test cases had it taken place along the lines of the 2013 DAA. A second reason lies in the broad notion of positive duties developed by the ECtHR. General positive duties of States to protect include, according to the Court and as I explained before, duties to protect against other States' interventions, thus turning potential concurrent duties into a single State's duties.[123] A third explanation may be found, as I indicated before, in the fact that most of the cases tried have been either cases of competing and distinct wrongful acts, or cases of delegation of effective control to one State by the other.[124] Neither of these cases could therefore be submitted *stricto sensu* to the principle of joint and several responsibility.

A fourth explanation is the principle of remedial subsidiarity and, more particularly, the deferral of the *restitutio in integrum* to States Parties (Article 46(1) ECHR). Of course, the Court may grant just satisfactions (Article 41 ECHR), but even these remain subsidiary and based on equity. Generally, the prevalence of non-pecuniary reparations in the individual or general measures issued by the Court makes it difficult to expect more specificity on the allocation of reparations. Finally, one should also mention the lack of procedures before the ECtHR for the organization of internal rights of recourse between responsible States once one of them has provided full reparation for the victim's injury. Arguably, however, other States could file an interstate application,[125] if needed, or raise the issue before the Committee of Ministers.

6. Conclusions

For a long time, the debate about jurisdiction, territorial or extraterritorial, in the ECHR has pertained to its notion, conditions, and related duties. It has now reached the issue of the normative implications for States' duties and responsibilities in circumstances in which many States exercise concurrent jurisdiction.

In response to this new challenge, the present chapter has discussed how one should articulate the concurrent effective control and hence jurisdictions of different States, how one should specify and allocate their concurrent duties stemming from this concurrence of jurisdiction, and, finally, how one should attribute and then allocate their concurrent responsibilities when concurrent duties have been

[122] *Soering* (n 56) paras 86–88. [123] *MSS* (n 6) para 342.
[124] *Rantsev* (n 5); *MSS* (n 6); *Drozd and Janousek* (n 8).
[125] See, eg, *Cyprus v Turkey* [GC] App no 25781/94 (ECtHR, 10 May 2001).

violated. Thereby, the chapter also contributed, hopefully, to the disentanglement of some of these issues whose relationship to the elusive notion of State 'control' has often led the ECtHR to conflation. More generally, it should have shown how much of the ECtHR's practice has promoted, and could promote even further, the development of the still largely underexplored regime of concurrent or 'shared' responsibility in general international law.

The main conclusion one may draw from this chapter's discussion is that the ECtHR's position on these issues is still unsettled. Its largely 'case-by-case' approach needs to be reformed. The concurrent jurisdiction of States is rarely recognized, especially in cases in which two or more States exercise concurrent extraterritorial jurisdiction. Most cases that have been tried so far pertain to the concurrence of territorial jurisdictions and some, more rarely, to the concurrence between territorial and extraterritorial jurisdictions. When concurrent jurisdiction is considered by the Court, however, it is usually in order to identify at least one responding State, the others being usually either non-States Parties or an international organization, at the price arguably of a certain bias. Even when concurrent jurisdiction is recognized, moreover, every single State's jurisdiction is approached as being distinct. In turn, the same may be said about how the Court approaches both the States' respective duties and their respective responsibilities, in cases of violation, as being independent and distinct from one another, even when they have caused the same injury. Sometimes, the Court even eludes the issue by favouring the positive duties of one single State of jurisdiction, usually of territorial jurisdiction, over those of others, thereby pre-empting the question of the concurrence of responsibilities at the same time.

This raises serious issues of justice in the allocation of duties and responsibilities, both for the individual victims of human rights violations and for the States of concurrent jurisdiction. Different States bore concurrent ECHR duties towards the same human right holders in a given context, thereby making their concurrence a key element in a fair and legitimate allocation of duties. Furthermore, different States contributed to the same injury, whether it is through the same wrongful act or not, and whether through a breach of the same ECHR duties or not, thereby making their concurrent responsibilities a central feature of a fair allocation of responsibilities and especially of reparations. This chapter's argument has been that, because ECHR States Parties are parties to the same human rights instrument, they have a positive duty to coordinate institutionally in order to allocate not only their concurrent duties but also, later on, their concurrent responsibilities. Because they are submitted to the compulsory jurisdiction of the ECtHR, moreover, the latter can help them in doing that and then allocate internal rights of recourse if needed *ex post*. This last point actually strengthens the argument for applying the principle of joint and several responsibilities to the responsibilities of States of concurrent jurisdiction.

Of course, some of the issues raised by concurrent jurisdictions, duties, and responsibilities in the human rights context are not easy to solve. How, for instance, should we reconcile the unicity of the democratic subject and human right holders protected by the ECHR with the duality or plurality of effective jurisdictions, human rights duty-bearers, and legitimacy providers?[126] How, in a next step, should we work out the deterritorialization of democracy itself induced by the extraterritoriality of human rights? Hence, most probably, the pockets of resistance in favour of territorial jurisdiction one observes in the ECtHR's extraterritoriality case law, ie, what I have called remnants of 'territoriality in extraterritoriality'. One should mention, in particular, the priority given to personal over spatial control in the establishment of extraterritorial jurisdiction, the greater weight given to the State of territorial jurisdiction over the State of extraterritorial jurisdiction in the evidentiary process, the priority given to the general (positive) duties of the State of territorial jurisdiction over the specific duties of the State of extraterritorial jurisdiction including in case of loss of effective control, and the priority of the responsibilities of the State of territorial jurisdiction over those of the State of extraterritorial jurisdiction.

Clearly the issue of concurrent jurisdictions, duties, and responsibilities in the ECHR will not go away, and certainly not by *fiat* as the Court tried to do in *Jaloud*. The increase of extraterritorial activity, transnational circumstances, and interstate institutional cooperation will create many new cases to come. Furthermore, as I have argued in this chapter, due to its compulsory jurisdiction the ECtHR is by far best situated to address them.

[126] See, eg, Besson, 'The Extraterritoriality of the European Convention on Human Rights' (n 11) 882–84.

9

The Structure of State Responsibility under the European Convention on Human Rights

*James Crawford and Amelia Keene**

1. Introduction

The International Law Commission (ILC) Articles on the Responsibility of States for Internationally Wrongful Acts (ARSIWA)[1] purport to express the general law of State responsibility, and they are clearly conceived as applying—subject to the *lex specialis* rule—to human rights treaties such as the European Convention on Human Rights (ECHR). By contrast, Malcolm Evans makes the bold claim that the character of the ECHR as a human rights treaty 'makes the international principles of State responsibility *irrelevant* to its operation, so it is not clear why they should be referred to at all'[2] while others have argued that the ECHR 'goes beyond what is traditionally envisaged under the law of international responsibility' since individuals have direct access to the Court.[3]

For its part, the Court in *Banković* said that:[4]

> The Court must take into account any relevant rules of international law when examining questions concerning its jurisdiction and, consequently, determine State responsibility in conformity with the governing principles of international law, although it must remain mindful of the Convention's special character as a human rights treaty.

The question is whether, in truth, the Court has departed from the rules, and whether those departures are necessary given the special character of the Convention. Is

* Thanks to Paul Mertenskötter for research assistance.

[1] International Law Commission, 'Articles on the Responsibility of States for Internationally Wrongful Acts' YBILC 2001 II/2, 26 [ARSIWA].

[2] Malcolm Evans, 'State Responsibility and the ECHR' in Malgosia Fitzmaurice and Dan Sarooshi (eds), *Issues of State Responsibility before International Judicial Institutions* (Hart 2004) 159 (emphasis in original).

[3] Melanie Fink, 'The European Court of Human Rights and State Responsibility' in Christina Binder and Konrad Lachmayer (eds), *The European Court of Human Rights and Public International Law: Fragmentation or Unity* (Nomos 2014) 93.

[4] *Banković and Others v Belgium and Others* (Admissibility), App No 52207/99, 12 December 2001; (2007) 44 EHRR SE5.

it using the rules as 'a malleable instrument' to achieve its own ends,[5] or have the rules so far held up within the case law of the Court? Alternatively, has the Court shown the ARSIWA to be inadequate, such that new rules are necessary?

At least four general trends of the Court are discernible. First, the Court has had to fill gaps in the rules on State responsibility, both in the cases decided before the adoption of the ARSIWA[6] and, more recently, in the context of Member-State responsibility for international organizations (IOs). Cases in this vein, such as *Bosphorus*,[7] have in turn influenced the drafting of the Draft Articles on the Responsibility of International Organisations (ARIO). Second, the Court has broadly interpreted many ECHR rights as giving rise to positive or primary obligations of the State, avoiding the need to engage in the secondary rules of State responsibility, as in *Costello-Roberts*.[8] In some cases involving actions by a private entity, such as *Kotov*,[9] the Court has attempted to frame these developments in State responsibility terms. In others, it has pulled back from a more radical rule of third State responsibility by instead emphasizing the primary Article 3 obligation on the State.[10] The third trend is the explicit departures from the general principles on State responsibility in certain special cases, namely UN peacekeeping missions, where an 'ultimate authority' rule has been applied rather than the 'effective control' rule;[11] and in the case of extraordinary rendition, where the Court has developed an 'acquiescence or connivance' rule to hold a third State responsible for the acts of another State on its territory.[12] Fourth, the Court has failed to clarify the relationship between attribution and jurisdiction, which arises acutely in cases involving extraterritorial acts.[13] Thus the Court seeks faithfully to apply the rules in some contexts, but not in others.

[5] Evans (n 2) 160.

[6] For an account of the rules of attribution applied by the ECtHR before the ARSIWA, see: Haritini Dipla, *La Responsabilité de l'Etat pour Violation des Droits de L'Homme: Problèmes d'Imputation* (Pedone 1994). See also the accompanying Foreword by Luigi Condorelli noting on the relationship between the ILC and the ECtHR that: 'Le constat de depart était que, d'une part, la Commission du droit international élabore son projet (qui se veut applicable à tous les domaines) sans prendre véritablement en consideration la matière des droits de l'homme et, en particulier, la jurisprudence des organes de la Convention européenne; d'autre part, que ces derniers organes ne semblent pas avoir à l'esprit, dans leur activité quotidienne, les travaux qui se déroulent à la CDI.' In the event, the jurisprudence of the ECtHR was influential in the drafting of the ARSIWA, as is evident from the frequent references to it in the Commentary: International Law Commission, 'Draft Articles on Responsibility of States for Internationally Wrongful Acts with Commentaries' YBILC 2001 II/2.

[7] *Bosphorus v Ireland*, App No 45036/98, 30 June 2005; (2006) 42 EHRR 1, para 156.

[8] *Costello-Roberts v United Kingdom* App no 13134/87 (ECtHR, 25 March 1993).

[9] *Kotov v Russia* App no 54522/00 (ECtHR, 3 April 2012).

[10] *Al Nashiri v Poland* App no 28761/11 (ECtHR, 24 July 2014).

[11] *Behrami and Behrami v France* and *Saramati v France, Germany and Norway* (Admissibility) App nos 71412/01 and 78166/01 (ECtHR, 2 May 2007) paras 28–34.

[12] *El-Masri v The Former Yugoslav Republic of Macedonia* [GC] App no 39630/09 (ECtHR, 13 December 2012).

[13] For example, *Jaloud v The Netherlands* App no 47708/08 (ECtHR, 20 November 2014).

2. Attribution

2.1 A procedural/substantive distinction

We begin by addressing and rejecting a method some commentators have argued that the Court employs to avoid applying the general law on responsibility: by application of a procedural/substantive distinction. Evans argues that this has instanced divergence from the ARSIWA in the case of attribution, in particular the 'direction or control' test in Article 8, which provides:[14]

> The conduct of a person or group of persons shall be considered an act of a State under international law if the person or group of persons is in fact acting on the instructions of, or under the direction or control of, that State in carrying out the conduct.

The commentary to the ARSIWA suggests that Article 8 should be interpreted strictly, whereby the conduct may be attributed to the State only where it directed or controlled the specific operation and the conduct complained of was an integral part of the operation.[15]

Evans argues that the ECtHR has broadened the test, holding States responsible for those who are not its agents or acting pursuant to its direction or control. He points to cases such as *Tepe v Turkey*,[16] where, although it was not possible to attribute the conduct directly to the State, it was held responsible for procedural failings, in particular the failure to carry out a proper investigation into the kidnapping and death of the applicant's son, in violation of the right to an effective remedy in Article 13 of the ECHR. The Court reached this conclusion despite noting the lack of proof beyond a reasonable doubt supporting the substantive claim that agents of the State were implicated in the killing itself.[17]

Rather than viewing this case as representing a broadening of State responsibility rules, it can be seen as an orthodox application of the ARSIWA. Turkey was held liable for a procedural breach which was attributable to it, but not a substantive breach which was not. The principle of attribution was applied to the question of procedural failings—State agents had failed to investigate. The same distinction between procedural and substantive obligations is also made by the International Court of Justice (ICJ).[18] The distinction between procedural/substantive obligations is not a way of avoiding the rules of state responsibility.

[14] Evans (n 2) 157. [15] ILC commentary, 47–49.
[16] *Tepe v Turkey*, App No 27244/95, 9 May 2003; [2003] 39 EHRR 29.
[17] ibid para 196.
[18] See, eg, *Whaling (Australia v Japan)* [2014] ICJ Rep 226, holding that Japan was not liable for procedural breaches, but that it had failed to meet its substantive obligations under the International Convention for the Regulation of Whaling.

2.2 Governmental authority and attribution of the acts of private individuals

The issue of attributing the acts of private individuals carrying out a governmental function first arose in the ECtHR in 1991 and has raised much more difficult issues of the application of ARSIWA. In *Costello-Roberts*, the Court held Ireland responsible for the acts of teachers that denied ECHR-derived rights.[19] It emphasized the role of the State in providing education and that this fell within the State's regulatory function. Subsequently, it has confirmed that the obligation of protection is particularly important in the field of education.[20] This approach has continued to influence post-ARSIWA decisions. The Court in *O'Keeffe* held Ireland responsible for failing to protect the applicant from sexual abuse occasioned while at primary school in the 1970s.[21] It held that Ireland had breached its positive obligation in Article 3 of the Convention to take measures to ensure that individuals are not subjected to mistreatment, as the mechanisms it put in place for detection and reporting of ill-treatment were not effective. There was no discussion of whether the conduct was attributable to the State. Instead, the Court relied on *Costello-Roberts* as affirming the principle that a State could not avoid its protective obligations under the ECHR by delegating primary education to a private entity.[22] This was so despite the finding that, at the time, education in Ireland was owned and managed by, and in the interests of, non-State actors (largely religious organizations) to the exclusion of State control.[23] The Court characterized this as the relinquishing of governmental control to a non-State actor,[24] implying that education is an inherently government function.

This line of cases is not restricted to the context of education. The Court has found that positive obligations arise in the context of the organization of the labour market,[25] the regulation of bar associations,[26] and private psychiatric treatment.[27] In *Storck v Germany*, the Court held that the wrongful detention under Article 5 of the ECHR was 'imputable' to the State on the basis that police officers were used to force her to return to a private clinic in circumstances in which she had neither consented to the treatment nor had it been legally certified. So far, this is an orthodox application of ARSIWA Article 4 as police officers are clearly government agents. The Court went on to hold that there had also been a breach of the positive obligations of the State under Articles 5 and 8 of the ECHR. Its reasoning highlighted a number of factors that could also be seen as supporting an argument that there was an element of governmental authority being delegated, noting that:[28]

[19] *Costello-Roberts v United Kingdom* (1991) (Report of the European Commission of Human Rights), emphasizing the regulatory function; *Costello-Roberts* (n 8), where the Court instead emphasized the right to education.

[20] *Ilbeyi Kemaloğlu and Meriye Kemaloğlu v Turkey* App no 19986/06 (ECtHR, 10 April 2012) para 35.

[21] *O'Keeffe v Ireland* App no 35810/09 (ECtHR, 28 January 2014).

[22] ibid para 150.

[23] ibid para 157.

[24] ibid para 162.

[25] *Evaldsson and Others v Sweden* App no 75252/01 (ECtHR, 13 February 2007) para 63.

[26] *Buzescu v Romania* App no 61302/00 (ECtHR, 24 May 2005) para 78.

[27] *Storck v Germany* App no 61603/00 (ECtHR, 16 June 2005) para 103.

[28] ibid para 103–06.

> [w]ith regard to persons in need of psychiatric treatment in particular [...] there are hospitals run by the State which coexist with private hospitals. The State cannot completely absolve itself of its responsibility by delegating its obligations in this sphere to private bodies or individuals.

But at no point was the analysis put in terms of the ARSIWA. Instead, the Court held that Germany had breached its positive obligations. The same reasoning that could be used to support an attribution under Article 5 of the ARSIWA is instead being used to support a conclusion on positive obligations, following *Costello-Roberts*.

In assessing whether this line of jurisprudence is consistent with ARSIWA, it could be said that these cases fall squarely within Article 5, which provides:

> The conduct of a person or entity which is not an organ of the State under article 4 but which is empowered by the law of that State to exercise elements of the governmental authority shall be considered an act of the State under international law, provided the person or entity is acting in that capacity in the particular instance.

Providing education, detaining psychiatric patients, regulating the legal profession or the labour market: all are governmental functions that may have been delegated to private entities but for which the State ultimately remains responsible according to the ECtHR. But the Court does not reach its conclusions on Article 5 terms. There is no mention of Article 5 in its judgments and no discussion as to the sphere of 'governmental authority', nor any analysis of the relevant legal framework empowering the delegation of power. Rather than holding the State directly responsible for the failures of the private entity under the ARSIWA rules, the Court has bypassed this step by reading into Article 3 of the ECHR a positive obligation of protection for which the State is directly responsible.

More recently, in *Kotov v Russia*,[29] the Court can be seen attempting to reconcile its jurisprudence with the ARSIWA. The case involved a private creditors' body that chose to create a category of privileged creditors who were entitled to be paid first in the event of a liquidation, with the result that the applicant, not a privileged creditor, failed to recover most of what was owed to him. The Court held that the liquidator had not acted as a State agent, and that Russia could not be held directly responsible for his wrongful acts, before going on to find that Russia had also not breached its own positive obligation to provide a mechanism to protect the applicant's rights under Article 1 of Protocol No. 1.

The case could herald a new strategy of engagement by the Court with the ARSIWA. Rather than going directly to the question of positive obligations, the Court extensively quoted from the relevant ILC Articles and Commentary.[30] Moreover, it drew an important distinction between attributing acts of a private body to a State pursuant to Article 5 of ARSIWA and the positive obligations that separately accrue to the State under the ECHR, rather than between the two as it had done in the past. However, it remains to be seen how the Court will deal with a case that is factually closer to *Costello-Roberts*. Although the *Kotov* judgment

[29] *Kotov v Russia* App no 54522/00 (ECtHR, 3 April 2012).

[30] ibid paras 30–32.

cited this jurisprudence, perhaps suggesting that it now ought to be viewed in light of Article 5 of ARSIWA, it did not attempt to reconcile the cases or even point out the tension. Nevertheless, the structure of *Kotov* suggests that there may now be two alternative routes to hold a State responsible for an act such as that which occurred in *Costello-Roberts*, either by attributing conduct to the State pursuant to Article 5 of ARSIWA, or by holding it directly liable for breaches of its own positive obligations under Article 3 of the ECHR.

This period of engagement with ARSIWA may have been short-lived. In two more recent cases against Russia following *Kotov*—*Liseytseva and Malov*—the Court again struggled with its application of ARSIWA.[31] The cases involved debtor companies who were responsible for water and heating supplies,[32] and for public transportation services,[33] and were required to carry out 'social tasks' under the relevant legislation. Their assets could not be privatized and the relevant tariffs were paid by the government.[34] The companies were liquidated because the tariffs were not paid, and two of their employees succeeded in bringing proceedings for unpaid wages through the Russian courts, which were not able to be enforced since the companies had no assets. Russia challenged the proceedings on the basis that the debts of the companies were not attributable to it, and thus the Court had no jurisdiction *ratione personae*.

The Court ultimately concluded that Russia should be held responsible for a breach of Article 6 of the Convention, since enforcement is a critical aspect of the fair-trial right. Russia had effectively decided to liquidate the companies, not to pay the salaries of the employees, and to ignore the judgments while setting up new companies to perform the same functions. The Court cited both Articles 5 and 8 of ARSIWA earlier in the judgment, implicitly recognizing that both might be relevant. But in its dispositive reasoning, it referred only to Article 8 as confirming its conclusion, stating that its reasoning 'is consistent with the ILC's interpretation of the aforementioned Article 8 of the Articles on State Responsibility'.[35] There is no mention of Article 5 and the reference to Article 8 seems cosmetic. In holding the State's responsibility engaged, the Court reasoned that to 'determine the issue of State responsibility for the debts of unitary enterprises the Court must examine whether and how the extensive powers of control provided for in the domestic law were actually exercised by the authorities in a given case'.[36] It is not clear why the Court did not apply Article 5, neither is it clear that it correctly applied Article 8. Its reasoning is closer to Article 5, in that it focuses on the public function being carried out by the companies. Finally, it is curious that the Court does *not* consider positive obligations, since it did so in every other case in this context.

Our objection is not to the Court's development of the idea of positive obligations as such. As with the procedural/substantive distinction, the distinction between positive and negative obligations does not avoid the application of the ARSIWA. Our concern is that the development of positive obligations may have prevented the Court from asking the logically prior question as to whether the respondent State is

[31] *Liseytseva and Maslov v Russia* App nos 39483/05 and 40527/10 (ECtHR, 9 October 2014).
[32] ibid para 208. [33] ibid para 215. [34] ibid paras 203–4, 209, 216.
[35] ibid para 205. [36] ibid paras 128, 205–6.

directly responsible for the commission of the wrongful acts, rather than for a failure to prevent them only. In many of the cases outlined above, the Court has relied on the type of factors that would be relevant in considering whether Article 5 of the ARSIWA applied in finding that the State has positive obligations. Thus, although *Costello-Roberts* was decided before the ARSIWA was concluded, it continues to overshadow the question of State responsibility in the ECHR context. Perhaps *Kotov* signals that the Court is now willing to take the question of attribution more seriously in this context.

3. State Responsibility for Acts of International Organizations (IOs)

3.1 Member States of IOs

Another area in which there is potential divergence from the rules on State responsibility in the jurisprudence of the ECtHR is in the context of Member-State responsibility for apparent violations of the ECHR on the part of IOs. This arises in particular in relation to the possibility of holding a Member State liable for a failure to provide an effective remedy in relation to staff disputes within an IO to which it is party. Ryngaert notes a conflict between two competing principles: the principle that IOs have individual legal personality and can be held responsible for their wrongful acts, and the principle that States have a duty to provide an effective remedy.[37]

The leading case is *Waite & Kennedy*.[38] This case stems from a broader line of cases beginning with *Bosphorus*, whereby the Court presumes that IOs provide equivalent rights protection to that which the State has an obligation to provide, unless that protection is shown to be 'manifestly inadequate'.[39] The Court has not been entirely clear about what a State must do in order to incur responsibility in this context. Some cases, including *Bosphorus*, have emphasized that there must be State action, so that where a State has not intervened directly or indirectly in an international administrative dispute, it cannot be held to be liable.[40] However, the threshold for what constitutes State action appears to be very low, such that a State asking an IO's administrative tribunal for a preliminary ruling on a point of law could be said to have intervened in the procedure, thus engaging its responsibility for any failures in the proceedings.[41]

Furthermore, in *Gasparini*, the Court stated that a 'structural lacuna' in the internal dispute-resolution system of an IO would suffice for it to hold a Member State responsible, perhaps for a breach of the right to a fair trial or of the right to an

[37] Cedric Ryngaert 'The European Court of Human Rights' Approach to the Responsibility of Member States in Connection with Acts of International Organisations' (2011) 60 ICLQ 997, 998.

[38] *Waite and Kennedy v Germany*, App No 26083/94, 18 February 1999; (2000) 30 EHRR 261.

[39] *Bosphorus v Ireland*, App No 45036/98, 30 June 2005; (2006) 42 EHRR 1, para 156.

[40] *Boivin v 34 Member States of the Council of Europe* App no 73250/01 (ECtHR, 9 September 2008) 7.

[41] Ryngaert (n 37) 1004; *Cooperatieve Producentenorganisatie van de Nederlandse Kokkelvisserij UA v The Netherlands* App no 13645/05 (ECtHR, 20 January 2009).

effective remedy.[42] This would suggest that, in order for State responsibility to be engaged, there must be a certain threshold level of severity in the primary breach, rather than focusing on the actors involved and their relationship with the State.

The jurisprudence of the Court on the circumstances in which a State would be held responsible for the failure by an IO to provide a sufficient remedy remains somewhat unclear since no breach by a State has yet been found.[43] It is not easy to determine the extent to which the cases comply with the general rules on State responsibility. Moreover, the law of the responsibilities of IOs remains somewhat unsettled, with the ARIO having faced considerable criticism.[44] There also remains ambiguity about the relationship between the ARIO and ARSIWA and the responsibilities of States in this context.[45] This is a matter on which ARSIWA are deliberately silent, and the ECtHR has sought to develop its own set of rules, which have in turn influenced the drafting of the Articles in the ARIO on multiple responsibility and the responsibilities of a Member State for acts of an IO.[46] Allocating responsibility between an IO and a State will become particularly significant if, and when, the European Union finally accedes to the ECHR.[47]

3.2 Attribution in peacekeeping operations

Separating out the strands of State and IO responsibility has proved particularly difficult in cases involving United Nations and North Atlantic Treaty Organization (NATO) peacekeeping or security operations. In *Behrami and Saramati,* the Court rejected the liability of France for acts of French troops carrying out a NATO operation in Kosovo.[48] It cited Article 5 of the ARIO[49] and Article 6 of the

[42] *Gasparini v Italy and Belgium* (Admissibility) App no 10750/03 (ECtHR, 12 May 2009) 7.

[43] Ryngaert (n 37) 998.

[44] Many of these criticisms are collated in: Maurizio Ragazzi (ed), *Responsibility of International Organizations: Essays in Memory of Sir Ian Brownlie* (Martinus Nijhoff 2013). But see Michael Wood, '"Weighing" the Articles on Responsibility' 59, in the same book, noting that although many States and international organizations had been highly critical of the Articles, 'to a considerable degree these criticisms had been addressed by the time the Commission came to adopt the final articles in 2011'.

[45] Ryngaert (n 37) 998; see also José Alvarez, 'Misadventures in Subjecthood' (2010) EJIL: *Talk!* <http://www.ejiltalk.org/misadventures-in-statehood/> accessed 11 May 2018, arguing that the assumption that States are presumptively responsible for the acts of IOs is not clearly established as a matter of international law.

[46] ARIO 2011, Articles 48 and 61, see in particular the reference to the jurisprudence of the Court at paras 3–8 of the commentary to Article 61.

[47] Fink (n 3) 117; The legality of accession has thus far been rejected by the European Court of Justice: *Accession by the Community to the European Convention for the Protection of Human Rights and Fundamental Freedoms* Opinion 2/94, European Court of Justice, 28 March 1996; *Accession of the European Union to the European Convention for the Protection of Human Rights and Fundamental Freedoms—Compatibility of the draft agreement with the EU and FEU Treaties* Opinion 2/13, European Court of Justice, 18 December 2014.

[48] *Behrami* (n 11) paras 28–34.

[49] Article 5 of the ILC Draft ARIO 2004 is substantially the same as Article 7 of the ILC Draft ARIO 2011, which reads: 'The conduct of an organ of a State or an organ or agent of an international organization that is placed at the disposal of another international organization shall be considered under international law an act of the latter organization if the organization exercises effective control over that conduct.'

ARSIWA,[50] noting the relevant excerpt from the commentary on Article 5 of the ARIO, which, in so far as relevant, provides:

> When an organ of a State is placed at the disposal of an international organization, the organ may be fully seconded to that organization. In this case the organ's conduct would clearly be attributable only to the receiving organization [. . .] Article 5 deals with the different situation in which the lent organ or agent still acts to a certain extent as organ of the lending State or as organ or agent of the lending organization. This occurs for instance in the case of military contingents that a State placed at the disposal of the [UN] for a peacekeeping operation, since the State retains disciplinary powers and criminal jurisdiction over the members of the national contingent. In this situation the problem arises whether a specific conduct of the lent organ or agent has to be attributed to the receiving organization or to the lending State or organization [. . .]
>
> Practice relating to peacekeeping forces is particularly significant in the present context because of the control that the contributing State retains over disciplinary matters and criminal affairs. This may have consequences with regard to attribution of conduct [. . .]
>
> Attribution of conduct to the contributing State is clearly linked with the retention of some powers by that State over its national contingent and thus on the control that the State possesses in the relevant respect.
>
> As has been held by several scholars, when an organ or agent is placed at the disposal of an international organization, the decisive question in relation to attribution of a given conduct appears to be who has effective control over the conduct in question.

The commentary seems to contemplate that the contributing State could be jointly or solely responsible for the acts of its troops in a UN peacekeeping operation.

The Court held that the acts were not attributable to the respondent States. In fact, rather than deal with the case as a question of attribution and extraterritorial jurisdiction, it instead characterized it as a question of whether the Court was competent to determine the responsibility of the UN organs involved. It stated that the:[51]

> [. . .] question raised by the present cases is, less whether the respondent States exercised extra-territorial jurisdiction in Kosovo but far more centrally, whether this Court is competent to examine under the Convention those States' contribution to the civil and security presences which did exercise the relevant control of Kosovo. Accordingly the first issue to be examined by this Court is the compatibility *ratione personae* of the applicant's complaints with the provisions of the Convention.

It held that the conduct in question—the failure by the UN Mission in Kosovo (UNMIK) to carry out demining in *Behrami* and the detention by the Kosovo Force (KFOR) in *Saramati*—was directly attributable to the UN, which was acting pursuant to Chapter VII of the UN Charter.[52] Accordingly, it concluded that it did not have jurisdiction *ratione personae* over the respondent States. Its judgment could be read as broadly consistent with Article 5 of the ARIO if it were essentially a finding on the facts that the relevant UN entities retained effective control. Instead, having established that the acts were attributable to the relevant UN entities and thus to the Security Council, the Court seemed to assume that this precluded attribution

[50] *Behrami* (n 11) paras 28–34.
[51] ibid paras 71–72.
[52] ibid para 121, 127, 141.

to NATO and/or to the respondent States. This was so despite its conclusion in *Saramati* that NATO had effective control over detention.[53]

The most troubling aspect of the reasoning came where the Court emphasized that the decisive factor was whether 'the United Nations Security Council retained ultimate authority and control so that operational command only was delegated'.[54] In focusing on ultimate authority, it ignored the degree to which NATO and the respondent States in fact had effective control. It is not clear whether, in doing so, the Court was intending to reject the applicability of Article 5 of ARIO, but its 'ultimate authority and control' test is a clear departure from Article 5. Moreover, it raises the troubling possibility that a State might create an IO that retains 'ultimate authority and control' for any operations carried out under its aegis to avoid responsibility for the actions of its armed forces, even where effective control rests with the State.[55] As Brownlie has explained, States 'cannot avoid responsibility by creating an international organization'.[56]

The Court has been criticized for its failure to apply the correct rules on responsibility. Gaja's ILC report concluded that: 'had the Court applied the criterion of effective control set out by the Commission, it would have reached the different conclusion that the conduct of national contingents allocated to KFOR had to be attributed either to the sending State or to NATO.'[57] Arguably the Court should also have considered whether multiple responsibility was a possibility. At least one commentator suggests that the Court was alive to this, but intended to create an exception to multiple attribution in a case in which the UN Chapter VII peacekeeping operations were at play,[58] an exception not borne out in the ARIO. Possibly the Court was being over-deferential for fear of stepping on the United Nations' mandate. Others have argued that, by implicitly excluding the possibility of multiple responsibility, the Court 'has created a loophole in which Convention-Contracting States acting under UN authority are not held liable for their Convention obligations'.[59]

The Court might then have been expected to clarify the position in *Al-Jedda*,[60] which involved the internment of an Iraqi-British man on suspected terrorism affiliations for three years by United Kingdom armed forces carrying out security missions in Iraq as part of the multinational force the Court held was authorized by the United Nations Security Council (UNSC).[61] It did not, even though it appeared to be common

[53] ibid para 140. [54] ibid para 133.

[55] James Crawford, *State Responsibility: The General Part* (CUP, 2013) 199–200; Marko Milanovic and Tatjana Papić, 'As Bad as it Gets: The European Court of Human Rights' *Behrami* and *Saramati* Decisions and General International Law' (2009) 58(2) ICLQ 267, 268.

[56] Ian Brownlie, 'The Responsibility of States for the Acts of International Organizations' in Maurizio Ragazzi (ed), *International Responsibility Today. Essays in Memory of Oscar Schachter* (Martinus Nijhoff 2005) 361.

[57] ILC, Giorgio Gaja, Special Rapporteur, 'Seventh Report on Responsibility of International Organizations' (27 March 2009) 26 UN Doc A/CN.4/610.

[58] Kjetil Mujezinovic Larsen, 'Attribution of Conduct in Peace Operations: The 'Ultimate Authority and Control' Test' (2008) 19 EJIL 509, 528.

[59] Caitlin A Bell, 'Reassessing Multiple Attribution: The International Law Commission and the *Behrami* and *Saramati* Decision' (2011) 42 Int L & Pol 501, 533–34.

[60] *Al-Jedda v The United Kingdom*, App No 27021/08, 7 July 2011; (2011) 53 EHRR 23.

[61] UNSC Res 1511 (16 October 2003); UNSC Res 1454, 8 June 2004.

ground between the parties that the effective control test from Article 5 applied.[62] Instead the Court concluded that both the effective control and ultimate authority test were satisfied on the facts, without treating them individually or stipulating which one was properly applicable:[63]

> For the reasons set out above, the Court considers that the United Nations Security Council had neither effective control nor ultimate authority and control over the acts and omissions of troops within the Multinational Force and that the applicant's detention was not, therefore, attributable to the United Nations.

The Court went on to conclude that the requirement of State jurisdiction under Article 1 was satisfied[64] and that the applicant's detention constituted a breach of Article 5(1).[65] Its conclusions are not easily reconcilable with *Behrami*. As Larsen argues, in both cases, actual control could be or was in fact exercised by the Security Council, such that, in *Behrami* terms, the conduct in *Al-Jedda* ought not to have been attributable to the UK.[66] In both cases, the respondent State was contributing forces to a security force acting under Security Council authorization. The UN did not have a role when the UK and US first took action in Iraq but, by the time of the applicant's internment, the ECtHR considered their presence had been confirmed by UNSC resolutions pursuant to Chapter VII. Perhaps the different conclusions can be explained by the fact that the different history of UN involvement continued to impact on the chains of control on the ground in Iraq.

Fink argues that the distinction drawn by the Court between the cases on a factual basis in *Al Jedda* 'clearly demonstrates the ECtHR's wish for conformity with general international law'.[67] This assessment is too strong. The Court did not expressly over-rule *Behrami* and applied both tests in holding that the conduct was not attributable to the Security Council. It had an opportunity to clearly disavow its 'ultimate authority' test, which has no foundation in the law of State responsibility, but it did not do so.

4. Third-State Responsibility

A further category of cases where the ECtHR pushed the boundaries of ARSIWA involves (the non-application of) Article 16, dealing with the responsibility of a State for providing '[a]id or assistance in the commission of an internationally wrongful act'.[68] As Nollkaemper notes, this question of third-State responsibility proved problematic for the Court in *El-Masri v The Former Yugoslav Republic of Macedonia*.[69] The

[62] *Al-Jedda* (n 60) para 84; see also *R (Al-Jedda) v Secretary of State for Defence* [2007] UKHL 58, [2008] 1 AC 332.

[63] *Al-Jedda* (n 60) para 84. [64] ibid para 86. [65] ibid para 110.

[66] Larsen (n 58) 357. [67] Fink (n 3) 117.

[68] See: *El-Masri* (n 12); *Al Nashiri* (n 10) paras 207, 451–58, 517–19, 530–32, 568–69.

[69] André Nollkaemper, 'The ECtHR Finds Macedonia Responsible in Connection with Torture by the CIA, but on What Basis?' (2012) EJIL: *Talk!* <http://www.ejiltalk.org/the-ecthr-finds-macedonia-responsible-in-connection-with-torture-by-the-cia-but-on-what-basis/> accessed 11 May 2018.

case involved the participation of Macedonia in a case of extraordinary rendition, where it was responsible for handing over suspects to CIA agents.

The Court stated that:[70]

> [. . .] the acts complained of were carried out in the presence of officials of the respondent State and within its jurisdiction. Consequently, the respondent State must be regarded as responsible under the Convention for acts performed by foreign officials on its territory with the acquiescence or connivance of its authorities.

It ultimately found that Macedonia was directly responsible for a violation of Article 5 of the ARSIWA for the entire period of Mr El-Masri's captivity, suggesting that his detention by the CIA was attributable to Macedonia.[71] Nollkaemper[72] argues that:

> The general law of responsibility by its conception of responsibility-based-on-wrongfulness, prefers determinations that one is responsible for the handing over of a person or for its inaction, not for the resulting torture itself. In contrast, the Court's approach may allow us to say that if a state hands over a person to another state in the knowledge that the person is tortured, and stands by when that torture happens, it bears responsibility for the torture itself.

What we see again in *El-Masri* is a broadening of the rules on the responsibility of a third State for violations carried out on its territory but not by it. The case is not far from the *Costello-Roberts* context. Indeed, at times, the Court seems to be suggesting that the responsibility of Macedonia arises from breaches of its positive obligations under Article 3 of the ECHR, stating that Macedonia's responsibility arises from the transfer into custody of the applicant and his eventual transfer to Afghanistan, despite the existence of a real risk that he would be subjected to further mistreatment contrary to Article 3 of the ECHR.[73] But the Court clearly goes beyond this. Rather than expanding the substantive obligations of the ECHR to avoid engaging with the ARSIWA as it did in *Costello-Roberts*, the Court instead develops its own jurisprudence on State responsibility for conspiracy, or 'connivance', in a way which has no basis in the ARSIWA.

Subsequently, in another extraordinary rendition case, *Al Nashiri v Poland*, the Court cited *El-Masri* and quoted the 'acquiescence or connivance' standard, but then seemed to place greater emphasis on Poland's responsibility for its own breaches of Article 3, rather than holding that the CIA's actions can be attributed to it.[74] Thus it pulls back slightly from the connivance standard.

5. Jurisdiction

A fourth category of cases involve State jurisdiction for extraterritorial acts. It is relevant to spend longer on this topic as there are a series of cases that implicate State responsibility to varying degrees. Unravelling the relationship between State

[70] *El-Masri* (n 12) para 206. [71] ibid paras 235, 240. [72] Nollkaemper (n 69).

[73] See ibid para 223.

[74] *Al Nashiri* (n 10) para 517. See also *Husayn (Abu Zubaydah) v Poland* App no 7511/13 (ECtHR, 24 July 2014) para 512, to the same effect.

jurisdiction, the Court's jurisdiction, and State responsibility in the jurisprudence is no easy task, particularly in cases involving the extraterritorial application of the ECHR. The Court in *Catan and Others v Moldova and Russia*[75] stated that the existence of jurisdiction is not to be equated with the test for responsibility in extraterritorial cases.[76] Yet overlapping terminology and a lack of clarity in the Court's reasoning has given rise to much academic debate and considerable confusion. The Court's misunderstanding of the interactions between jurisdiction and attribution has the potential to threaten both the coherence of the secondary rules on State responsibility and the Court's own jurisprudence. In this part we will deal with some of the recent case law in order to establish the circumstances in which questions of attribution properly arise at the jurisdictional phase of a proceeding.

Some commentators have argued that 'the notion of jurisdiction merely is a shorthand expression for certain elements of the first question on attribution'.[77] Others conceptualize a three-part analysis for State responsibility in the human rights context: (i) attribution, (ii) breach, and, only then, (iii) 'whether victims of human rights violations are within the "jurisdiction" of a State'.[78] The most extensive discussion of the question is that of Milanovic.[79] He adopts a number of important distinctions in an effort to understand the Court's approach to extraterritorial jurisdiction.

First, he points out that the term 'jurisdiction' in Article 1 means the physical jurisdiction of the State (which we term 'State jurisdiction'), not jurisdiction of Court.[80] He explains:

> Of course, if a particular human rights treaty does not apply in the absence of a state's jurisdiction, this would automatically lead to the treaty body in question lacking jurisdiction *ratione materiae*, in the same way that the treaty body would lose jurisdiction *ratione personae* if it found that the wrongful act complained of was not attributable to the defendant state. In other words, since the subject-matter jurisdiction of the European Court [...] is limited to interpreting and applying the ECHR [... it] will invariably lack jurisdiction if the treaty itself does not apply. Nonetheless it is not [its] jurisdiction which is the object of inquiry for the purposes of Article 1 ECHR.[81]

It is understandable why this line is often confused, since without State jurisdiction under Article 1, the ECtHR cannot have competence to hear the case against the State. By contrast, State jurisdiction is necessary to the Court's jurisdiction

[75] *Catan and Others v Moldova and Russia* App nos 43370/04, 8252/05, and 18545/06 (ECtHR, 19 October 2012) para 115.

[76] See also: *Jaloud* (n 13); *Loizidou v Turkey* (Preliminary Objections) App no 15318/89 (ECtHR, 23 March 1995).

[77] Martin Scheinin, 'Just Another Word? Jurisdiction in the Roadmaps of State Responsibility and Human Rights' in Malcolm Langford et al (eds), *Global Justice, State Duties: The Extraterritorial Scope of Economic, Social and Cultural Rights in International Law* (CUP 2013) 214–15.

[78] Maarten den Heijder and Rick Lawson, 'Extraterritorial Human Rights and the Concept of "Jurisdiction"' in Malcolm Langford et al (eds), *Global Justice, State Duties* (n 77) 154.

[79] Marko Milanovic, *Extraterritorial Application of Human Rights Treaties: Law, Principles, and Policy* (OUP 2011). See also: Marko Milanovic, 'Jurisdiction, Attribution and Responsibility in Jaloud' (2014) EJIL: *Talk!* <http://www.ejiltalk.org/jurisdiction-attribution-and-responsibility-in-jaloud/> accessed 11 May 2018.

[80] Milanovic, *Extraterritorial Application* (n 79) 19.

[81] ibid 20.

but not concomitant with it, as other conditions may also have to be met for the Court to have jurisdiction. The question is where attribution fits in relation to these two concepts.

Second, Milanovic explains the different types of State jurisdiction that arise in Article 1. For an extraterritorial act, State jurisdiction can arise either within a territory under its effective control (the spatial sphere),[82] or because the State has exercised control over an individual outside an area under its effective control (the personal sphere).[83] The personal sphere of State jurisdiction has been explained by the Court as follows: '[i]t is clear that, whenever the State, through its agents, exercises control and authority over an individual, and thus jurisdiction, the State is under an obligation under Article 1 to secure to that individual the rights and freedoms under Section I of the Convention that are relevant to the situation of that individual.'[84]

Third, Milanovic distinguishes between '*jurisdiction-establishing conduct*, i.e. acts or omissions by which a State, through its organs or agents, establishes control over an area or control over an individual' and '*violation-establishing conduct*, i.e. the act or omission that can actually constitute a violation of the ECHR'.[85] He suggests that the 'attribution inquiry actually logically precedes the jurisdiction inquiry when it comes to conduct which is itself constitutive of jurisdiction'.[86] So he argues the attribution question must be resolved before getting to that Article 1 State jurisdiction question, which is what the Court appears to do in the *Jaloud* case.[87]

While we would adopt Milanovic's distinctions as helpful, it seems problematic to treat attribution as conceptually distinct from jurisdiction. To understand why this is so, it is necessary to have regard to the close relationship between State jurisdiction and the Court's jurisdiction. Attribution establishes the link between the extraterritorial act and the State. Such a link is needed to establish personal or spatial jurisdiction.

We suggest that the correct analysis for determining State jurisdiction is:

The spatial sphere

1. Did the act occur in a territory under the effective control of the State? Attribution is relevant here because effective control of a territory can only be established by an organ or agent acting on behalf of the State.

The personal sphere

2. If not, did the State, through its organ or agent, exercise control over an individual? Attribution is relevant here because the State can only exercise such control over an individual through its organ or agent.

[82] *Al-Skeini v United Kingdom*, App No 55721/07, 7 July 2011; (2011) 54 EHRR 18, para 131; as the ICJ observed in the *Wall* opinion, jurisdiction is primarily territorial: *Legal Consequences of the Construction of a Wall in the Occupied Palestinian Territory* (Advisory Opinion) [2004] ICJ Rep 136, para 109.

[83] *Al-Skeini* (n 82) paras 149–50.

[84] ibid para 137.

[85] Milanovic, 'Jurisdiction, Attribution and Responsibility in Jaloud' (n 79).

[86] ibid.

[87] *Jaloud* (n 13) paras 140–52.

On this analysis, whether the basis for State jurisdiction is spatial or personal, it will be necessary to establish that the act of the organ or agent is attributable to that State. In some cases, a separate attribution analysis will also have to be carried out at the merits stage, where the jurisdiction-establishing conduct and the violation-establishing conduct are not identical. This may be more common in cases where the jurisdiction relied on is territorial, rather than personal.

Our suggested nuance on Milanovic's framework is to be preferred as it better reflects the role of the rules on State responsibility as secondary rules. The attribution question here is necessarily grounded in the facts that give rise to State jurisdiction, so it should be considered as part of this analysis. It also better reflects how the Court approaches the question in practice, as it may not always be necessary to make a separate finding of attribution in cases where the act in question was obviously attributable to the State, as in *Al-Skeini* or *Banković*. Finally, isolating the attribution question may also risk confusing the question of attribution at the merits and jurisdiction stages.

Turning then to the cases, we would endorse the approach adopted in an early case on attribution and extraterritoriality: *Drozd and Janousek v France and Spain*, which involved two men convicted of a jewellery robbery in Andorra by an Andorran court comprising a French and a Spanish judge.[88] The Court first determined that Andorra was not within the territory of Spain or France, but noted that this did not dispose of the question, since 'their responsibility can be involved because of acts of their authorities producing effects outside their own territory'.[89] It went on to decide that the acts of the judges in question could not be attributed to France or Spain, because they were acting as Andorran judges and not sitting in their capacity as French or Spanish judges.[90] It thus upheld the preliminary objection to the Court's jurisdiction *ratione personae* on the Article 6 claim. The question of attribution was an integral step to finding jurisdiction over an extraterritorial claim. Without attributable conduct, the Court could not establish that the act was within the State's jurisdiction under Article 1, Andorra not being part of the European Union, and the acts not falling within either the spatial or personal sphere of the jurisdiction of France or Spain. Therefore, it did not have competence to determine the dispute.

In *Behrami/Saramati*, the Court denied jurisdiction on the basis that 'the impugned acts and omissions of KFOR and UNMIK cannot be attributed to the respondent States and, moreover, did not take place on the territory of those States or by virtue of a decision of their authorities'.[91] This was despite the fact that the Court had held that the territory was 'under the effective control of the international presences which exercised the public powers normally exercised by the Government of the FRY [Federal Republic of Yugoslavia]'.[92] The problem was that the States involved were operating under a UNSC resolution and the Court did not have a mandate to review United Nations compliance with the ECHR or determine whether the acts were attributable to the UN.[93] We have already criticized the rules of attribution applied in *Behrami*. Here we make a different point, namely that the Court was correct to the extent that

[88] *Drozd and Janousek v France and Spain* App no 12747/87 (ECtHR, 26 June 1992).
[89] ibid paras 90–91. [90] ibid paras 96–97. [91] *Behrami* (n 11) para 151.
[92] ibid para 70. [93] ibid para 71.

it incorporated this attribution question into the jurisdiction analysis, finding that there could not be State jurisdiction if the acts were not attributable to the States before the Court because this was the way in which State jurisdiction was sought to be established.

This may be compared to *Loizidou v Turkey*, where the Court took the opposite approach, avoiding asking a specific attribution question as to whether Turkey exercised control over the actions of the Turkish Republic of Northern Cyprus (TRNC). At the preliminary objections stage, it stated as follows:[94]

> The Court would emphasise that it is not called upon at the preliminary objections stage of its procedure to examine whether Turkey is actually responsible under the Convention for the acts which form the basis of the applicant's complaints. Nor is it called upon to establish the principles that govern State responsibility under the Convention in a situation like that obtaining in the northern part of Cyprus. Such questions belong rather to the merits phase of the Court's procedure. The Court's enquiry is limited to determining whether the matters complained of by the applicant are capable of falling within the 'jurisdiction' of Turkey even though they occur outside her national territory.
>
> [. . .]
>
> Bearing in mind the object and purpose of the Convention, the responsibility of a Contracting Party may also arise when as a consequence of military action—whether lawful or unlawful—it exercises effective control of an area outside its national territory. The obligation to secure, in such an area, the rights and freedoms set out in the Convention derives from the fact of such control whether it be exercised directly, through its armed forces, or through a subordinate local administration.

The Court reasoned that in order to find there was State jurisdiction, it was sufficient that Turkey exercised effective control of the area outside its national territory. It went on to note that Turkish troops were occupying Northern Cyprus and had prevented the applicant from accessing her property.[95] Such conduct by Turkish troops would be prima facie attributable to Turkey and constitutes jurisdiction-establishing conduct that might be relevant to the question as to whether Turkey was in fact exercising effective control, even if the Court expressly said that the question of attribution was irrelevant to jurisdiction. Thus the Court at least implicitly considered the attribution question at the jurisdictional phase.

At the merits phase, the Court determined that it was not necessary for it to determine whether Turkey had effective control over the policies and actions of the authorities of the TRNC for the purposes of attribution, since '[i]t is obvious from the large number of troops engaged in active duties in northern Cyprus [. . .] that her army exercises effective overall control over that part of the island. Such control, according to the relevant test and in the circumstances of the case, entails her responsibility for the policies and actions of the "TRNC" '.[96] The error the Court made at the merits stage was to rely on its conclusion that there was State jurisdiction to conclude that Turkey was responsible for the particular conduct that gave rise to breach. In the process, it failed to apply the rules of State responsibility, which would instead

[94] *Loizidou* (n 76) paras 61–63. [95] ibid para 63.
[96] *Loizidou v Turkey* (Merits) App no 15318/89, (ECtHR, 18 December 1996).

have depended on the fact that it was Turkish troops who had denied the applicant access to her home.

The Court again grappled with this question of the relationship between jurisdiction and attribution in the parallel merits judgments in *Sargsyan v Azerbaijan*[97] and *Chiragov v Armenia*.[98] These cases are two of more than a thousand arising from the Nagorno-Karabakh conflict that are pending before the Court, slightly more than half of them against Armenia, the remainder against Azerbaijan.[99] Both respondent States contested the question of State jurisdiction under Article 1 of the ECHR at an earlier admissibility hearing, but the Court left these issues to the merits.[100] Both cases involved an autonomous province landlocked within Azerbaijan, the Nagorno-Karabahk Autonomous Oblast (NKAO). In 1991, the majority Armenian population of the province purported to secede from Azerbaijan to form the Nagorno-Karabahk Republic (NKR). By 1993, NKAO had come under the control of local Armenian forces. The *Chiragov* case concerned a number of displaced minority Azeri who had fled from the NKAO. Similarly, the *Sargsyan* case was filed by a displaced Armenian man who had fled his village of Gulistan, in Azerbaijan, during the conflict. The judgments follow the same general structure and reasoning, but the more interesting is *Chiragov*, where the attribution question arose most acutely. In particular, could Armenia be held responsible for the acts of NKR armed forces of Armenian ethnicity in Nagorno-Karabahk who were occupying Azerbaijani territory?

The Court in *Chiragov* began by dealing with jurisdiction. It noted that, formally, the territory remained part of Azerbaijan. Therefore, it was necessary to apply the *Catan* exception from the requirement for territoriality under Article 1, that of 'effective control'.[101] The Court restated the exception as being a question as to 'whether the Republic of Armenia exercised and continues to exercise effective control over the mentioned territories and as a result may be held responsible for the alleged violations'.[102]

The problem is that this 'effective control' test looks and sounds like an attribution analysis, but it actually concerns the question of what spatial control the State has over the territory in question for the purposes of determining jurisdiction. Thus in *Al-Skeini*, the Court explained that:[103]

> Another exception to the principle that jurisdiction under Article 1 is limited to a State's own territory occurs when, as a consequence of lawful or unlawful military action, a Contracting

[97] *Sargsyan v Azerbaijan* (Merits) App no 40167/06 (ECtHR, 16 June 2015).

[98] *Chiragov and Others v Armenia* (Merits) App no 13216/05 (ECtHR, 16 June 2015).

[99] *Sargsyan* (n 97) para 216.

[100] *Sargsyan v Azerbaijan* (Admissibility) App no 13216/05, (ECtHR, 14 December 2011); *Chiragov and Others v Armenia* (Admissibility) App no 13216/05 (ECtHR, 14 December 2011). For an account of these cases, see Antal Berkes, 'The Nagorno-Karabakh Conflict Before the European Court of Human Rights: Pending Cases and Certain Forecasts on Jurisdiction and State Responsibility' (2013) 52(2) Military Law and the Law of War Review 379.

[101] *Catan* (n 75) para 106: 'Where the fact of such domination over the territory is established, it is not necessary to determine whether the Contracting State exercises detailed control over the policies and actions of the subordinate local administration.'

[102] *Chiragov* (n 98) paras 167–69.

[103] *Al-Skeini* (n 82) para 138.

State exercises effective control of an area outside that national territory. The obligation to secure, in such an area, the rights and freedoms set out in the Convention, derives from the fact of such control, whether it be exercised directly, through the Contracting State's own armed forces, or through a subordinate local administration.

The difficulty with the Court's analysis in *Chiragov* is that it conflates this effective control question with the attribution question. In some cases, as in *Al-Skeini*, where the United Kingdom was clearly in control of the area in Iraq through its armed forces, there will be no attribution issue. In *Chiragov*, that issue arose because it was not clear that the armed forces occupying the NKAO were part of the Armenian national army.

In its analysis, the Court said the answer will depend primarily on military involvement. It noted that the Armenian armed forces were 'highly integrated' with those of the NKR and had been 'significantly involved' in the conflict. It undertook only a very limited analysis of the financial element (noting in passing that the United States also provided financial support to the NKR) and no analysis of the control structures.[104]

Notwithstanding the Court's frequent recitation that the test for jurisdiction is different to attribution, it employs an 'effective control' test.[105] But this is the test for State jurisdiction, not for attribution. It is much looser than that set out for attribution by the ICJ in *Nicaragua*,[106] as reaffirmed in the *Bosnia-Genocide* case.[107] In the *Bosnia-Genocide* case, neither the fact that the Federal Republic of Yugoslavia (FRY) was providing significant financial support nor the 'powerful' military and logistical ties between Belgrade and the Bosnian Serbs was sufficient to find the FRY responsible for the genocide at Srebrenica in the absence of clear evidence of control.

Having carried out a quasi-attribution analysis, the Court does not then turn to ask whether the NKR troops were in effective control of the NKAO. It makes no attribution finding comparable to that in *Al-Skeini* that:[108]

[. . .] the United Kingdom (together with the United States of America) assumed in Iraq the exercise of some of the public powers normally to be exercised by a sovereign government. In particular, the United Kingdom assumed authority and responsibility for the maintenance of security in south-east Iraq. In these exceptional circumstances, the Court considers that the United Kingdom, *through its soldiers engaged in security operations in Basra during the period in question*, exercised authority and control over individuals killed in the course of such security operations, so as to establish a jurisdictional link between the deceased and the United Kingdom for the purposes of Article 1 of the Convention.

[104] *Chiragov* (n 98) para 180.

[105] ARSIWA, Article 8, see also ARSIWA Commentaries, Article 8, para 8.

[106] *Military and Paramilitary Activities in and against Nicaragua (Nicaragua v United States of America)* (Merits) [1985] ICJ Rep 64 and 65, para 115.

[107] *Application of the Convention on the Prevention and Punishment of the Crime of Genocide (Bosnia and Herzegovina v Serbia and Montenegro)* [2007] ICJ Rep 43, 204–6, paras 396–413. A looser 'overall control' test was applied in the *Tadić* case, but this applies in the context of individual criminal liability only, not in the State responsibility context: *Prosecutor v Tadić* ICTY-94-1-A (15 July 1999) 38(6) ILM 1518 and 1541, para 117.

[108] *Al-Skeini* (n 82) para 149 (emphasis added).

Instead, the Court applies an attribution-like test at the jurisdiction phase, only to completely bypass attribution at the merits phase of the case,[109] holding Armenia directly responsible for its positive obligations under Articles 1, 8, and 13 of Protocol No. 1.

Likely it did so to keep the reasoning consistent with the parallel case of *Sargsyan*. Factually, this case differed in that the territory from which the applicant had fled remained part of Azerbaijan but was effectively a no-man's land. In determining jurisdiction, the Court applied a presumption of competence:[110]

> Even in exceptional circumstances, when a State is prevented from exercising authority over part of its territory, due to military occupation by the armed forces of another State, acts of war or rebellion or the installation of a separatist regime within its territory, it does not cease to have jurisdiction within the meaning of Article 1 of the Convention.

But in the next paragraph, still under the heading of jurisdiction, it went on to state that in such a case where the State was prevented from exercising its authority in part of its territory, its responsibility would be limited to discharging positive obligations under the ECHR.[111] The dispositif records in one line that the Court dismissed the preliminary objection on jurisdiction and responsibility. The Court found that Azerbaijan had 'effective control' over the territory even though it 'may encounter difficulties at a practical level' in exercising that authority.[112] This might have given rise to a finding of State jurisdiction. But instead the Court relied on the presumption of competence to determine jurisdiction only for positive obligations. It went on to find, as in *Chiragov*, that Azerbaijan was directly responsible for breach of its positive obligations under Articles 1, 8, and 13 of Protocol No. 1.

Studying the two cases together, it is curious that one—*Sargsyan*—essentially relies on the idea of positive obligations as limiting a State's responsibility, whilst the other—*Chiragov*—relies on quasi-attribution rules to found the State jurisdiction but then deals only with positive obligations when it comes to the merits with little discussion of responsibility. *Chiragov* should have engaged with the secondary rules of attribution at its merits phase, and more clearly separated out the attribution and 'effective control' analysis when determining jurisdiction. The reliance in both cases on the positive obligations of States appears to be a continuation of *Costello-Roberts*, where broad interpretations of the ECHR obligations are invoked to avoid engaging with the rules of State responsibility. Yet this has a detrimental result, as positive obligations restrict the extent of the State's responsibility.

This issue of the relationship between (ultimately) the Court's jurisdiction and attribution is not unique to the ECtHR. The ICJ has struggled with a similar issue as to whether a preliminary objection raised on the grounds that the act in question was not attributable to the respondent State is properly a jurisdictional or admissibility challenge. In the first *Bosnia and Herzegovina Genocide* case, attribution was not

[109] *Chiragov* (n 98) Dissenting Opinion of Judge Gyulumyan.
[110] *Sargsyan* (n 97) para 127. [111] ibid para 131.
[112] ibid para 150, Dissenting Opinion of Judge Yudkivsky: 'Can anyone exercise authority, in any sense of the word, over heavily mined territory which lies either side of a frontline, surrounded by armed forces from both sides and which, consequently, no one can even enter?'

raised at the preliminary objections phase.[113] The Court could have raised it *proprio motu*, but it did not do so. Instead, attribution became a key issue at the merits phase in relation to the genocide at Srebrenica.[114] In *Croatia v Serbia (Genocide)*, attribution was raised as a preliminary objection.[115] The *Croatia v Serbia* jurisdiction judgment did not clarify whether the issue of attribution was a question of admissibility or jurisdiction, simply noting that it was 'presented by Serbia as a matter of admissibility rather than of jurisdiction' and that it was closely bound up with the question of the Court's temporal jurisdiction.[116] The Court held that neither the *ratione temporis* issue nor admissibility had an exclusively preliminary character and left both questions to be decided after the merits had been argued.[117] At the merits phase, the Court avoided pronouncing on attribution since it held that there had been no prima facie breach of the Convention.[118] Thus, at least substantively, both cases treated attribution as a merits issue, not a jurisdiction question.

There is a key procedural difference between ICJ and ECtHR preliminary objections. While the ICJ rules include a presumption that any preliminary objection will be heard in a separate proceeding,[119] the ECtHR rules presume that any preliminary objection will be heard along with the merits.[120] This means that it is more likely that the facts will have been fully argued by the time that the ECtHR comes to determine a question of jurisdiction, making it easier to determine attribution then, where it may be required. As the ICJ's experience demonstrates, it is not always easy to separate attribution from the merits.

To return to our main point, in a case involving extraterritorial acts, the ECtHR ought to apply the same ARSIWA rules of attribution at both the jurisdiction and merits phases, and should be transparent about its application of those rules. It should also ensure that it includes a separate finding on attribution as part of its jurisdiction analysis where this is called into question. Since the merits and jurisdictional phases are usually heard together in the ECtHR, the Court should have the necessary facts to enable it to do so.

6. Conclusion

Evans' claim that the human rights character of the ECHR 'makes the international principles of State responsibility *irrelevant* to its operation', although no doubt attractive to human rights advocates, should be rejected as anarchic. One might as well

[113] *Application of the Convention on the Prevention and Punishment of the Crime of Genocide (Bosnia-Herzegovina v Yugoslavia)* (Preliminary Objections) [1996] ICJ Rep, 595.

[114] *Application of the Convention on the Prevention and Punishment of the Crime of Genocide (Bosnia-Herzegovina v Serbia and Montenegro)* (Merits) [2007] ICJ Rep 43, paras 377–415.

[115] *Case concerning Application of the Convention on the Prevention and Punishment of the Crime of Genocide (Croatia v Serbia)* (Preliminary Objections) [2008] ICJ Rep 412.

[116] ibid para 124. [117] ibid para 129.

[118] *Case concerning Application of the Convention on the Prevention and Punishment of the Crime of Genocide (Croatia v Serbia)* (Merits) [2015] ICJ Rep 3, paras 118, 442.

[119] Rules of the International Court of Justice 1978 (as amended), Article 79.

[120] Rules of the European Court of Human Rights, Article 48(2).

suggest that the customary law rules reflected in the Vienna Convention on the Law of Treaties do not apply to human rights treaties. The ILC rules on State responsibility operate on the contrary assumption that they fully apply in the human rights context as the relevant secondary rules on State responsibility. States remain States, even when recognizing and affirming human rights.

The jurisprudence of the ECtHR sits somewhere between these two positions and, in consequence, presents a rather ragged and unsystematic appearance. In some cases, the State responsibility rules have not been applied. The Court developed a novel 'acquiescence or connivance' rule to hold a third State responsible for the acts of another State on its territory (*El-Masri*), a rule that has no place in Article 16 of the ARSIWA. It also refused to apply the ARIO in finding that an 'ultimate authority' test was to be preferred to the 'effective control' rule set out in what is now Article 7 of the ARIO (*Behrami*). Moreover, the Court has broadly interpreted Article 3 of the ECHR so as to engage States' direct responsibility for the acts of private actors without reference to the attribution rules under the ARSIWA (*Costello-Roberts*). More recently, the Court relied heavily on positive obligations under the ECHR to avoid difficult State responsibility questions in the *Sargsyan* and *Chiragov* cases. But there are other indications that the Court has more fully applied the rules on State responsibility and has pulled back from some of its earlier departures. It is also making its own contribution to the rules on the responsibility of States for the acts of IOs, influencing the drafting of the ARIO. We suggest that the Court should consciously make an effort to cite and apply the ARSIWA rules, both at the jurisdictional and merits phases, thus promoting systemic consistency.

10

The ECHR and Responsibility of the State: Moving Towards Judicial Integration

A View from the Bench

Iulia Motoc and Johann Justus Vasel

1. Introduction

The concept of State responsibility[1] has taken a very distinct form within the European Convention of Human Rights (ECHR). It is reflected in—though certainly not equated with—the notion of 'jurisdiction' enshrined in Article 1 of the ECHR. The term 'jurisdiction' appears fairly straightforward, yet it may be one of the most important notions in the Convention. It decides the reach of European human rights law and determines whether a case is heard or not, and whether the machinery and its substantive guarantees grant protection or not.

While the member States of the Convention favour a rather restrictive understanding of the notion of 'jurisdiction'—in particular regarding the extraterritorial application of the Convention—the Court tends to expand the meaning of it. The Court sees 'jurisdiction' as a power-centric ('effective control') threshold-concept, which is not limited by (territorial) boundaries.[2] Accordingly, 'jurisdiction' is the subject of much academic debate.[3] Apart from a wide spectrum of interpretations of the concept and a confusing, as well as intricate, bulk of cases of the ECtHR, which arguably lacks a coherent approach and conflates several paradigms and criteria,[4]

[1] Pioneer in this area, Ian Brownlie, *System of the Law of Nations: State Responsibility, Part I* (Oxford Clarendon Press 1983); see, for a fundamental analysis subsequent to the adoption of the International Law Commission Articles, James Crawford, Alain Pellet, Simon Olleson (eds), *The Law of International Responsibility* (OUP 2010); René Provost (ed), *State Responsibility in International Law* (Ashgate Publishing 2002); James Crawford, *State Responsibility* (CUP 2014).

[2] See Michael O'Boyle, 'The European Convention on Human Rights and Extraterritorial Jurisdiction: A Comment on "Life After Bankovic"' Fens Coomans and Menno T Kamminga (eds), *Extraterritorial Application of Human Rights Treaties* (Intersentia 2004) 125.

[3] See, for an extensive examination, Marko Milanovic, *Extraterritorial Application of Human Rights Treaties: Law, Principles, and Policy* (OUP 2011). See also Kristen E Boon, 'Are Control Tests Fit for the Future? The Slippage Problem in Attribution Doctrines' (2014) 15(2) Melb J Int Law 329.

[4] Further developing the argument of a confusion between jurisdiction and responsibility reflected in the Court's jurisprudence (from the earlier case *Loizidou* to *Ilaşcu and Others, Catan* and *Jaloud*, and now *Chiragov*), see Milanovic (n 3); see also, Marko Milanovic, 'Jurisdiction and Responsibility: Trends

there is wide consensus that the Court considers and applies 'jurisdiction' as a somewhat autonomous concept.[5] While the use of this autonomous concept is in line with the unavoidable, generally accepted, and even appreciated, autonomous interpretation by the ECtHR,[6] autonomy that fails to take any account of general international law bears the risk of abetting the process of fragmentation.

However, no matter what reading one takes of the controversial, ambiguous, and thus rather mystifying, if not obscure, concept of self-contained regimes,[7] it is clearly attributed with a connotation and normative intent of seclusion and insularity, which is in stark contrast to the structure, spirit, and task of the ECHR. The object and purpose of the Convention is to create a regional system which admittedly requires its own—but nevertheless not self-contained—structures, standards, and mechanisms. Although the ECHR has set up its own 'internal' system for reacting to violations, this does not amount to qualifying as a self-contained regime as asserted in the early *SS Wimbledon* case (1923) or the later *Hostages* case (1980).[8] Rather, the ECtHR aims at a high degree of judicial or systemic integration, which is in line with Article 32(3)(c) of the Vienna Convention on the Law of Treaties of 1969.[9] The approach taken in the *Banković* decision in 2001 still holds true today:

> The Court must also take into account any relevant rules of international law when examining questions concerning its jurisdiction, and consequently, determine State responsibility in conformity with the governing principles of international law, although it must remain mindful of the Convention's special character as a human rights treaty.[10]

The Court reiterated that in the judgment relied upon by the government of the Russian Federation, the International Court of Justice (ICJ) had been concerned with determining when the conduct of a person, or group of persons, could be

in the Jurisprudence of the Strasbourg Court' in this volume; Marko Milanovic, '*Al-Skeini* and *Al-Jedda* in Strasbourg' (2012) 23 EJIL 121.

[5] Christoph Grabenwarter, *European Convention on Human Rights. Commentary* Article 1, para 13 (Hart 2014). See also partly dissenting opinion of Judge Bratza, joined by Judges Rozakis, Hedigan, Thomassen, and Pantiru, para 8, *Ilaşcu and Others v Moldova and Russia* [GC] App no 48787/99 (ECtHR, 8 July 2004).

[6] See George Letsas, 'The Truth in Autonomous Concepts: How to Interpret the ECHR' (2004) 15 (2) EJIL 279.

[7] An early analysis is undertaken by Bruno Simma, 'Self-Contained Regimes' (1985) 16 NYIL 111; see also Bruno Simma and Dirk Pulkowski, 'Of Planets and the Universe: Self-Contained Regimes in International Law' (2006) 17 EJIL 483. See also Axel Marschnik, *Subsysteme im Völkerrecht* (Duncker & Humblot 1997) 74–79. An overview is provided by Eckart Klein, 'Self-Contained Regime' *Max Planck Encyclopedia of Public International Law* (last updated November 2006, OUP 2006).

[8] These examples are used in the International Law Commission, 'Draft Articles on Responsibility of States for Internationally Wrongful Acts' (November 2001) UN Doc A/56/10 chp.IV.E.1 Supplement no 10, adopted by the International Law Commission at its fifty-third session (2001). Report of the Study Group of the International Law Commission 'Fragmentation of International Law: Difficulties Arising from the Diversification and Expansion of International Law' 58th Session (1 May–9 June and 3 July–11 August 2006) UN Doc A/CN.4/L.682 (finalized by Martti Koskenniemi) hereinafter 'the ILC Report'. The commentary (5) to Article 55 defines a self-contained regime as a 'strong form' of *lex specialis*.

[9] Magdalena Forowicz (ed), *The Reception of International Law in the European Court of Human Rights* (OUP 2010) 13.

[10] *Banković and Others v Belgium and Others* [GC] App no 52207/99 (ECtHR, 12 December 2001), para 57.

attributed to a State, so that the State could be held responsible under international law in respect of that conduct. In *Banković*, however, the Court was concerned with a different question, namely, whether the facts complained of by an applicant fell within the jurisdiction of a respondent State within the meaning of Article 1 of the Convention. As the summary of the Court's case law set out above demonstrates, the test for establishing the existence of 'jurisdiction' under Article 1 of the Convention has never been equated with the test for establishing a State's responsibility for an internationally wrongful act under international law.

This integrative approach is rendered tangible in its rulings by using interpretative tools, like the *lex specialis* principle, to align regional human rights law with general international law. Thus, the Court implements, specifies, and reaffirms the understanding of the relationship between general international law and regional law that is already set out in the preamble to the ECHR[11]: Having regard to general international law, the governments of European countries have taken the first steps to implement and enforce certain rights. The fact that the relationship between general international law and the Convention system is marked by mutual participation, rather than by exclusion, and that the ECHR can be characterized as an interrelated subsystem, also becomes apparent in the references to international law in certain provisions of the Convention, namely, Article 7 §§ 1 and 2, Article 15 § 1, Article 35 § 1 and Article 1 of Protocol No. 1.

This chapter takes as its starting point two of my separate opinions and will try to demonstrate, following the line of thought contained in those opinions, that there is a tendency towards convergence between the approach taken by the European Court of Human Rights (ECtHR) in matters of jurisdiction and responsibility and general international law.

After analysing the notion of *lex specialis* with regard to the question of responsibility and jurisdiction as (implicitly) proposed by the ECtHR in the *Catan* judgment, this chapter considers the question of the attribution of conduct introduced for the first time in the *Jaloud* judgment.[12] The article draws a parallel between the notion of effective control used in the ICJ's *Nicaragua* case[13] and the *Chiragov* case. It argues that the Court's ruling in *Chiragov*[14] is closer to the criterion of effective control imposed by the ICJ. The analysis will show that in both recent decisions, *Jaloud* and *Chiragov*, the Court is moving towards a judicial integration in the sense of a reasoned difference between responsibility in human rights and general international law. Although, in future judgments, the ECtHR will have to offer even

[11] Preamble to the Convention: 'The Governments signatory hereto, being members of the Council of Europe, Considering the Universal Declaration of Human Rights proclaimed by the General Assembly of the United Nations on 10th December 1948; [. . .] Being resolved as the governments of European countries which are like-minded and have a common heritage of political traditions, ideals, freedom and the rule of law, to take the first steps for the collective enforcement of certain of the rights stated in the Universal Declaration.'

[12] *Jaloud v The Netherlands* [GC] App no 47708/08 (ECtHR, 20 November 2014).

[13] *Case Concerning Military and Paramilitary Activities in and Against Nicaragua (Nicaragua v United States of America)* [1986] ICJ Rep 14.

[14] *Chiragov and Others v Armenia* [GC] App no 13216/05 (ECtHR, 16 June 2015).

more consistent legal reasoning to maintain this trend, it is evident that the ECHR is not a self-contained regime but contributes to greater judicial integration.

2. The *Catan* Case—*Lex Specialis* Principle

The *Catan*[15] judgment of 2012, which dealt once again with Russia's continued control of a separatist region in Moldova, serves as a prime example to illustrate the aforementioned intricacies related to the controversial notion of 'jurisdiction'. While the subject matter of the case dealt with complaints by the Moldovan community in Transdniestra about the effect of a language policy adopted by the separatist regime in the early 1990s, it particularly caught attention on account of complex questions regarding 'jurisdiction' (Article 1 of the ECHR) in the context of extraterritoriality. Maintaining its previous findings in the *Ilaşcu* judgment,[16] the ECtHR found that the separatist regime could not have survived without the continued military, economic, and political support of Russia,[17] and accordingly held that Russia had incurred responsibility under the Convention.[18] To rebut Russia's quite convincing and substantial argument that the ECtHR's approach in *Ilaşcu* was not in line with general international law, namely the ILC's Articles on the Responsibility of States for International Wrongful Acts[19] and the case law of the ICJ concerning the attribution of non-State action to a State,[20] the Court famously stated:

> the test for establishing the existence of 'jurisdiction' under Article 1 of the Convention has never been equated with the test for establishing a State's responsibility for an internationally wrongful act under international law.[21]

Prima facie, this statement could be qualified as a step taken by the ECtHR to dismiss general international law: While the latter requires 'complete control' over the non-State actor or 'effective control' over the specific conduct in question,[22]

[15] *Catan and Others v the Republic of Moldova and Russia* [GC] App nos 43370/04, 8252/05, and 18454/06 (ECtHR, 19 October 2012).

[16] *Ilaşcu* (n 5). [17] *Catan* (n 15) paras 120–21. [18] ibid paras 149–50.

[19] ibid para 74. [20] ibid paras 75, 76, and 115.

[21] ibid para 115. In line with Milanovic (n 3) 41–45, sharply differentiating State responsibility and jurisdiction.

[22] The 'complete control test' and the 'effective control test' were both established in the *Case Concerning Military and Paramilitary Activities in and against Nicaragua* (n 13) paras 109 and 115. A comprehensive overview is provided in Crawford (n 1) 146–56. For an analysis of the various 'control tests', see Stefan Talmon, 'The Responsibility of Outside Powers for Acts of Secessionist Entities' (2009) 58 ICLQ 493. Specifically on the Nicaragua case, see Thomas M Franck, 'Some Observations on the ICJ's Procedural and Substantive Innovations' (1987) AJIL 81(1) 116; Fred L Morrison, 'Legal Issues in the Nicaragua Opinion' (1987) 81(1) AJIL 160; Antonio Cassese, 'The Nicaragua and Tadić Tests Revisited in Light of the ICJ Judgment on Genocide in Bosnia' (2007) 18(4) EJIL; Rafael Nieto-Navia, 'State Responsibility in Respect of International Wrongful Acts of Third Persons: The Theory of Control' in *The Global Community Yearbook of International Law And Jurisprudence: Global Trends: Law, Policy & Justice Essays in Honour of Professor Giuliana Ziccardi Capaldo* (OUP 2013); Valentina Zambrano, 'State Responsibility for Human Rights Violations: The Ultimate Control Test and the Interpretation of UN Security Council Resolutions (2013) 2 EHLR 180.

the ECtHR created and applied its own standards. Applying such an autonomous concept,[23] irrespective of general international law, could thus be seen as pointing towards a self-contained regime.

A closer analysis and critical evaluation of the *Catan* judgment reveals that the decision is an example of how the Court uses the principle *lex specialis derogat legi generali* as a tool to integrate the Convention into general international law and coalesce both legal fields. As a precondition, it is of importance to understand what is meant when we refer to the *lex specialis* principle in this context. The spectrum of 'specialness' ranges from 'self-contained regimes' as the maximal extreme (excluding general international law altogether) to weaker forms of limited deviation.[24] It is this latter confined and selective form of specialness that we have in mind when we refer to the *lex specialis* rule. It is crucial to understand that this concept of *lex specialis* is inspired by complementarity.[25] It is not marked by rivalry and hierarchy but characterized by a symbiotic relationship providing mutual stabilization and reciprocal supplementation. The special norm is more a concretization and elaboration of the general norm and thus does not aim to overrule or set aside the general law. The verb *derogat* from the *lex specialis derogat legi generali* maxim neither means 'devaluate' nor 'diminish' but allows the Court to 'deviate', 'diverge', 'depart', or 'digress'. Thus, the general norm remains as a valid background norm. It is this limited form of deviation which ultimately aims at achieving the further development of general international law[26] rather than the fragmentation of it that can be seen in the Court's ruling in *Catan*. Indeed, as the ILC report makes clear, some relationships between norms promote harmonization. One such relationship is between special and general law.[27]

While the ECtHR neither refers to this principle explicitly nor explains its implicit application in any respect, the *lex specialis* maxim serves as the underlying rationale for the Court's ruling. This is apparent when the ECtHR, while applying its own threshold test, reiterates the 'obligation to take account of the relevant rules and principles of international law and to interpret the Convention so far as possible in harmony with other rules of international law of which it forms part'.[28] This implicit use of the *lex specialis* doctrine enables the Court to use its own standards and at the same time avoids a contradiction with international law. Thus, the ruling illustrates the harmonizing and reconciling effect of the *lex specialis* principle. This lies in the fact that while it gives priority to the special norm, the more general norm

[23] Grabenwarter (n 5) Article 1 §13.

[24] In this we draw on Simma and Pulkowski (n 7) 490.

[25] Dorata Marianna Banaszewska, 'Lex specialis' *Max Planck Encyclopedia of Public International Law* (last updated November 2015 OUP) para 8.

[26] Frédéric Vanneste, *General International Law Before Human Rights Courts: Assessing the Specialty Claims of International Human Rights Law* (Intersentia 2010) 577.

[27] ILC report (no 8) pp 30–115; other relationships of norms that promote harmonization can be found in the relationships between prior and subsequent law, between rules that operate on different hierarchical levels, and between each norm operating in a broader international system. See, for instance, Sean D Murphy, 'Deconstructing Fragmentation: Koskenniemi's 2006 ILC Project' [2013] Temple International and Comparative Law Journal 293.

[28] *Catan and Others* (n 15) para 136.

will continue to exist in the 'background' and complement it.[29] It certainly does not eliminate the general norm, but it does eliminate the conflict.

However, this reading of the *Catan* judgment raises the question of why the Court did not refer explicitly to the *lex specialis* concept if it functions so well as a harmony enhancer. The answer to this question is threefold.

First, it should be noted that a narrow understanding of the *lex specialis* principle requires, as a prerequisite for its application, a normative conflict and this could be called into question. At first sight, the test for establishing responsibility in general international law and the approach of the ECtHR seem to be neither contradictory nor opposing in a strict logical sense and, thus, the precondition of an antinomy appears to be missing. They appear to be different, but have concurring concepts or standards. However, a closer, consequential analysis shows that the application of these standards would, in fact, result in a certain incompatibility: According to the standards of State responsibility derived from general international law, Russia would not be accountable while, under the jurisdiction test of the ECtHR, it is held responsible. In other words, similarity may still mean disparity and this disparity, this reasoned differentiation, can be justified in the light of the *lex specialis* maxim.

A second reason why the ECtHR has refrained from explicitly referring to the *lex specialis* maxim might be that the use of this principle in the realm of international law is contested. From the standpoint of legal history, as well as legal theory, it has been argued that the widely used application of *lex specialis* in international law appears questionable if not flawed.[30] These doubts and criticism of the *lex specialis* principle in international law are certainly not unsound. However, one has to take into account that the maxim is a highly abstract principle. Its legal nature is ambiguous[31] and its meaning is neither precisely defined nor definite. Consequently, its content is not irrevocable and remains open for development and transplantation.

Third, the ECtHR might have been hesitant to explicitly invoke the *lex specialis* principle due to its affiliation with the concept of self-contained regimes—the very opposite of what the Court has wanted to imply and, as pointed out above, is actually obliged to do. According to the commentary to Article 55 on the Responsibility of States for Internationally Wrongful Acts, 'weaker' and 'stronger' forms of *lex specialis* can be distinguished and the subcategory of the latter is held to be a self-contained

[29] Banaszewska (n 25) para 8.

[30] Most criticism is concerned with the *lex specialis* rule and the relationship between human rights law and international humanitarian law but the majority of the analysis also questions the use of the principle as a whole; see, inter alia, Silvia Borelli, 'The (Mis)-Use of General Principles of Law: Lex Specialis and the Relationship Between International Human Rights Law and the Laws of Armed Conflict' L Pineschi (ed), *General Principles of Law: The Role of the Judiciary* (Springer 2015) 265–93; Bill Bowring, 'Fragmentation, *Lex Specialis* and the Tensions in the Jurisprudence of the European Court of Human Rights' (2010) 14 (3) Journal of Conflict & Security 485; Marko Milanovic, 'The Lost Origins of *Lex Specialis*. Rethinking the Relationship between Human Rights and International Humanitarian Law' in Jens David Ohlin (ed), *Theoretical Boundaries of Armed Conflict and Human Rights* (CUP 2016) 78–117; Nancie Prud'homme, '*Lex Specialis*: Oversimplifying a More Complex and Multifaceted Relationship?' (2007) 40(2) Israel Law Review 356.

[31] Erich Vranes, 'Lex Superior, Lex Specialis, Lex Posterior—Zur Rechtsnatur der "Konfliktlösungsregeln"' (2005) 65 Zeitschrift für ausländisches öffentliches Recht und Völkerrecht 391.

regime.[32] In order to prevent any unjustified speculation as to the ECHR being a self-contained regime, the Court may have avoided alluding to the *lex specialis* maxim at the outset.

Be this as it may, the implicitness does not challenge the conclusion that the *Catan* decision is informed by the *lex specialis* maxim. This very principle serves as an underlying rationale to create a complementary relationship between the general and the specific and at the same time justifying a diverging standard from international law.

3. Aligning the ECHR with General International Law—The *Jaloud* Case

Closely linked to (and sometimes even conflated with) the issue of 'jurisdiction' is the criterion of 'attribution of conduct', which is also a feature of the conflict between general international law standards and the allegedly 'heretic' standards applied by the Strasbourg Court. The pivotal judgment, which introduced this concept of imputing human conduct to a State in the sphere of European human rights law and sparked much debate,[33] was the case of *Jaloud v The Netherlands.*[34]

A patrol of Dutch soldiers, sent to Iraq to investigate a previous shooting incident, had opened fire on a car which had failed to comply with the orders to stop at a checkpoint. This resulted in the death of the front passenger (on behalf of whom the application was made) from multiple gunshot wounds. As is customary, the use of lethal force by a soldier of a Member State of the ECHR automatically triggered an international investigation, following which the authorities reached the conclusion that the use of force had been justified in the circumstances. After that, the victim's family argued before both the domestic courts and the ECtHR, relying on Article 2 of the ECHR protecting the right to life, that the Dutch State had failed to meet its obligations to properly investigate the death of their son with a view to bringing the person responsible to justice.[35]

As many commentators have said, '*Jaloud* does not disappoint. The extraterritorial plot thickens and certainty remains in suspense'.[36]

[32] ILC's Articles on Responsibility of States for Internationally Wrongful Acts with Commentaries, see Commentary on Article 55 (n 8) para 5: 'Article 55 is designed to cover both "strong" forms of *lex specialis*, including what are often referred to as self-contained regimes, as well as "weaker" forms such as specific treaty provisions on a single point, for example, a specific treaty provision excluding restitution. PCIJ referred to the notion of a self-contained regime in the *S.S. 'Wimbledon'* case with respect to the transitional provisions concerning the Kiel Canal in the Treaty of Versailles, as did the ICJ in the *United States Diplomatic and Consular Staff in Tehran* case with respect to remedies for abuse of diplomatic and consular privileges.' See also Simma (n 7).

[33] Marko Milanovic, 'Jurisdiction, Attribution and Responsibility in Jaloud' [2014] *Blog of the European Journal of International Law* <https://www.ejiltalk.org/jurisdiction-attribution-and-responsibility-in-jaloud/> accessed on 11 August 2017.

[34] *Jaloud* (n 12)

[35] ibid.

[36] Aurel Sari, '*Jaloud v Netherlands*: New Directions in Extra-Territorial Military Operations' [2014] Blog of the European Journal of International Law <https://www.ejiltalk.org/jaloud-v-netherlands-new-directions-in-extra-territorial-military-operations/> accessed 25 April 2017.

In answering the first question before it, the Court addressed the core of the interpretation of the doctrine of jurisdiction, here concerning that of the Netherlands in the Iraqi State, in which the Dutch State was not an occupying power as envisaged by Resolution 1483.[37] By balancing the allegations of the applicant and those of the Dutch government, what the ECtHR actually did was settle the relationship between the concepts of 'occupation' and 'control' in the context of military operations. Thus, the Court took an important step in facilitating judicial integration and ensuring coherence and harmony in the interpretation of the Convention in line with the provisions of the various international laws.

Accordingly, the Court lay down a set of principles which led to its interpretation of attribution of conduct. It is established that neither conduct nor jurisdiction is automatically (and in a blanket manner) attributed on grounds of an 'occupying power' status[38] but also that attribution of conduct cannot be circumvented simply on account of following orders given by authorities[39] and that jurisdiction must be subject to a more detailed and fact-specific analysis. This led to the conclusion that, as no indication was given in the circumstances that the Dutch troops were placed at the disposal of any foreign power, the respondent party exercised its jurisdiction within the limits of its mission in Iraq.[40]

What the Court said next stands as proof that the Court holds dear the principles of international law in regard to determination of jurisdiction which it had previously established in the *Catan* case.[41] Thus, in paragraph 154, the majority distinguished the concept of jurisdiction from the attribution of conduct, repeating that the former did not in any way automatically imply the latter. Referring to *Al-Skeini*,[42] and emphasizing its own standards while still replacing them in the broader framework of the principles of international law, the Court here managed to align the ECHR with general international law.

What makes *Jaloud* particularly important in this matter is stated in Marko Milanovic's commentary as follows: 'the judges of the Grand Chamber found the question of the relationship between the Article 1 ECHR concept of state jurisdiction, and general international law concepts such as attribution of conduct and responsibility for wrongful acts, to be particularly vexing. Judging by the language used, there must have been quite the internal debate.'[43] Thus, Judges Spielmann and Raimondi expressed a separate opinion identifying the need for a clearer differentiation between 'jurisdiction' and 'attribution' if international law principles were to be understood in line with the Convention:

> The concept of 'attribution' is indeed to be distinguished from that of 'jurisdiction' as the latter has been interpreted in the Court's case-law […] 'jurisdiction' essentially refers to

[37] UN Security Council Resolution 1483 (22 May 2003) [on the situation between Iraq and Kuwait] UN Doc S/RES/1483.

[38] *Jaloud* (n 12) para 142. [39] ibid para 143. [40] ibid para 152.

[41] *Catan* (n 15) para 19.

[42] *Al-Skeini and Others v The United Kingdom* [GC] App no 55721/07 (ECtHR, 7 July 2011). See also *Al-Jedda v The United Kingdom* [GC] App no 27021/08 (ECtHR, 7 July 2011).

[43] Marko Milanovic, 'Jurisdiction, Attribution and Responsibility in Jaloud' (2014) Blog of the European Journal of International Law <https://www.ejiltalk.org/jurisdiction-attribution-and-responsibility-in-jaloud/> accessed 25 April 2017.

the territorial principle [...] the concept of 'attribution' essentially concerns the sensitive issue of the 'imputability' of internationally wrongful acts. The 'codicil' of paragraphs 154 and 155, along with the unnecessary references to the case-law of the International Court of Justice (see paragraphs 95–97) and to the International Law Commission's Articles on State Responsibility in the part of the judgment setting out the relevant international law, is ambiguous, subsidiary and incomprehensible.[44]

Regardless of the alleged lack of clarity of the majority's assessment, from the point of view that concerns us, *Jaloud* explains the attribution of conduct by appealing to the need for further judicial integration and the importance of the ECHR in doing so. As stated in Judge Motoc's concurring opinion in *Jaloud*:

Firstly, at the pre-interpretive stage the Court very clearly expresses its position on the International Law Commission's Articles on State Responsibility (see paragraph 98 of the judgment) and the case-law of the International Court of Justice (see paragraphs 95–97). Above all, however, for the first time in this case the Court specifies that it is ruling on the imputability resulting from application of the relevant Articles on State Responsibility of the International Law Commission. Thus, with regard to responsibility under international law, it states that "the alleged acts and omissions of Netherlands military personnel and investigative and judicial authorities" are such as to be capable of "giving rise to the responsibility of the Netherlands under the Convention". Imputability was necessary in order to complement the legal logic arising from general international law, particularly State responsibility, with all the consequences that are entailed.[45]

The Court's clear move away from a fragmented international legal system has also been observed by scholars.[46] The *Jaloud* case thus conveys multiple messages from a legal perspective. 'Firstly, it ascertains that when operating in theatre, armed forces and their legal advisors should generally work on the assumption that the Convention applies rather than on the assumption that it does not apply.' Even more importantly for our purposes, '*Jaloud* confirms the general trend in the European Court's case law towards a more expansive approach to the extraterritorial application of the ECHR', which is intended to be in line with the principles perpetuated by general international law and human rights law alike.[47]

4. Parallels between the ICJ and ILC—Moving Towards the Notion of 'Effective Control' in the *Chiragov* Case

We can see from *Jaloud* that the principles residing in international law have become widely used by the ECtHR, but the analysis does not stop there. The decision in *Chiragov and Others v Armenia*[48] also demonstrates how cases concerning the

[44] Concurring opinion of Judge Spielmann, joined by Judge Raimondi, *Jaloud* (n 12) paras 3–5.
[45] Concurring opinion of Judge Motoc, *Jaloud* (n 12) para 3.
[46] See, for an overview, Philippa Webb, *International Judicial Integration and Fragmentation* (OUP 2013) Introduction and 145 et seq; Magdalena Forowicz, *The Reception of International Law in the European Court of Human Rights* (OUP 2010) 13.
[47] Milanovic (n 33). [48] *Chiragov* (n 14).

extraterritorial reach of the ECHR reflect the legal reality of judicial integration, as it closely follows the criteria of the principle of 'effective control' established in respect of the jurisdiction of the ICJ. While *Jaloud* focuses on the differences between jurisdiction and attribution of conduct, as an issue raised by extraterritoriality, the *Chiragov* decision raises arguments regarding jurisdiction and effectiveness in the exercise of control. *Jaloud* and *Chiragov* thus reflect the movement of the court towards judicial integration by enhancing the Court's willingness to respect two important concepts of international law which are greatly interdependent, as effective control is a legal standard which applies in attribution of conduct.[49]

Chiragov and Others, from a factual perspective, deals with the aftermath of the Nagorno-Karabakh conflict, in the sense that it brings before the Court the right of persons displaced by the conflict to access their property (under Article 1 of Protocol No. 1 to the Convention), rather than with the conflict itself as this was outside the Court's temporal jurisdiction.

Central to this case was the question of whether the government of Armenia had effective control over the area concerned. The doctrine of 'effective control' is significant in cases such as this with an extraterritorial component, as 'the exercise of jurisdiction is a necessary condition for a Contracting State to be able to be held responsible for acts or omissions imputable to it which give rise to an allegation of the infringement of rights and freedoms set forth in the Convention'. In case of extraterritoriality, effectiveness in the exercised control is a precondition for jurisdiction. Thus, if a State causes human rights violations outside its territory, unless it exercises effective control, it bears no responsibility.[50]

In settling this question, the Court has reiterated an established principle in its jurisprudence according to which 'the exercise of extra-territorial jurisdiction by a Contracting State occurs when this State, through the effective control of the relevant territory and its inhabitants abroad as a consequence of military occupation … exercises all or some of the public powers normally to be exercised by that Government'.[51] Thus, the Court recognizes that 'jurisdiction' under Article 1 is not limited to a State's own territory when, on account of military action, a Contracting State exercises effective control of an area outside that national territory.[52]

The Grand Chamber in *Chiragov* re-examined the criteria for determining effective control, which it had established before, and adopted a more nuanced approach, underlining the importance of having in every case of that type a new and fact-specific inquiry.

When assessing the question of effective control of a Convention State, the Court will look on a case-by-case basis at the degree of control, the effect the control has

[49] Vassilis P Tzevelekos, 'Reconstructing the Effective Control Criterion in Extraterritorial Human Rights Breaches: Direct Attribution of Wrongfulness, Due Diligence, and Concurrent Responsibility' (2014) 36(1) Michigan Journal of International Law 129.

[50] ibid. [51] *Chiragov* (n 14) para 168.

[52] On this point, see in particular for an analysis of *Chiragov,* together with *Sargsyan v Azerbaijan* [GC] App no 40167/06 (ECtHR, 16 June 2015), Marko Milanovic, 'The Nagorno-Karabakh Cases' (2014) Blog of the European Journal of International Law <https://www.ejiltalk.org/the-nagorno-karabakh-cases/> accessed 28 April 2017.

on the occupied State's local administration, the strength of the occupying State's presence in the area, and the extent to which its military, economic, and political support for the local subordinate administration provides it with influence over the region. More importantly, the Grand Chamber stresses that effective control over an area outside a State's own territory is primarily a factual question. [53]

A careful assessment of all those factors led the Court to dismiss the Armenian government's objection that the State did not have effective control over the territory (and that it thus lacked jurisdiction). The judges were satisfied on the facts of the case that Armenia had been significantly involved in the conflict from an early date, having a strong military presence, providing a large quantity of military equipment and expertise, and being highly integrated in the territory.[54]

In order to explain the rationale underpinning the Court's decision in this case, it must be specified that various branches of international law have provided different legal answers as to the interpretation of 'effective control'. An analysis of the ICJ's view of the matter inevitably involves consideration of the famous *Nicaragua*[55] case, in which the United States, on account of its support in the rebellion against the Nicaraguan government and by mining Nicaragua's harbours, was found to be 'in breach of its obligations under customary international law not to use force against another State', 'not to intervene in its affairs', 'not to violate its sovereignty', 'not to interrupt peaceful maritime commerce', and 'in breach of its obligations under Article XIX of the Treaty of Friendship, Commerce and Navigation between the Parties signed at Managua on 21 January 1956'.[56]

'Effective control' was one of the main issues in that case as the ICJ held that 'for this conduct to give rise to legal responsibility of the United States, it would in principle have to be proved that that State had effective control of the military or paramilitary operations in the course of which the alleged violations were committed'.[57] Thus, a form of dependence needed to be established between the United States and the rebellion group.

The ICJ established in that case that no less than complete dependency on the external power would satisfy as identification criteria for determining effective control. 'In its view, the fact that the external power had conceived, created and organised the secessionist entity, or the armed opposition group which created the secessionist entity, appeared to establish a strong presumption that the secessionist entity was completely dependent on the external power and was none other than its instrument or agent [. . .] In other words, the secessionist entity is completely dependent on the

[53] For a discussion on the facts, see Aeyal Gross, *The Writing on the Wall: Rethinking the International Law of Occupation* (OUP 2017) 110–12.

[54] ibid para 186: 'All of the above reveals that the Republic of Armenia, from the early days of the Nagorno-Karabakh conflict, has had a significant and decisive influence over the "NKR", that the two entities are highly integrated in virtually all important matters and that this situation persists to this day. In other words, the "NKR" and its administration survives by virtue of the military, political, financial and other support given to it by Armenia which, consequently, exercises effective control over Nagorno-Karabakh and the surrounding territories, including the district of Lachin. The matters complained of therefore come within the jurisdiction of Armenia for the purposes of Article 1 of the Convention'.

[55] *Nicaragua* (n 13). [56] ibid para 292. [57] ibid para 115.

external power if it can only carry out its activities with the various forms of support supplied by that power, so that withdrawal of that assistance would result in the cessation of the entity's activities.'[58]

On a close examination, similar formulations of standards can be seen in *Chiragov*. In that decision, the Court considered that Armenia's military support had been 'decisive for the conquest of and continued control over the territories in issue', and that 'the evidence, not least the 1994 military co-operation agreement, convincingly show[ed] that the armed forces of Armenia and the "NKR" [were] highly integrated'[59] in the area. The Court in *Chiragov* used for the first time, in its extensive jurisprudence on the matter, a term such as 'highly integrated' to describe the relationship between the Armenian government and the territory's local administration.[60] This standard appears to be very similar to the one established by the ICJ in the *Nicaragua* case, more so than to the one which can be found in the Court's previous relevant case law. It can be said then that, through the *Chiragov* decision, the ECtHR staged a return to the general principles of international law.

To sum up:

> It is true that in the present case the Court did not examine the question of attribution of the acts on account of which the applicants have been deprived of their possessions. However, the situation under general international law is not the same as in the earlier cases. Here, the Court has already established the existence of a high degree of integration between the two entities. A State may perhaps have been able to prove the involvement of the Armenian armed forces in the acts of the authorities of the "NKR" but for an individual wishing to assert their fundamental rights that would have been very difficult, if not impossible. That is why this *lex specialis* was introduced.[61]

5. Conclusion: Fragmentation, Constitutionalization, and Judicial Integration of International Law

Taking the above analysis of the Court's rulings into consideration, it becomes evident that one would be fundamentally mistaken to view the ECHR as a self-contained regime distancing itself from general international law.[62] This perspective would be both erroneous and detrimental. Similarly to Rudolf Carnap's finding in 'Pseudoproblems of Philosophy', the debate on whether the ECtHR's jurisprudence is in conflict with, or starkly deviates from, general international law might be qualified as a mere 'pseudoproblem of international law'. Just as Carnap sought to eliminate metaphysics, much of the discourse on different standards amounts to hyperbolically construing a conflict between the ECHR and general international

58 *Chiragov* (n 14) Concurring opinion of Judge Motoc.

59 ibid para 180.

60 ibid: 'The evidence [...] convincingly shows that the armed forces of Armenia and the "NKR" are highly integrated.'

61 ibid.

62 This finding is in line with Vanneste (n 26) pointing out that, although some human rights tendencies can be identified, overall the case law of the ECtHR points towards harmony, not autonomy.

law, which should equally be eliminated. This understanding is supported by the finding of the ILC Report of Fragmentation that there is an 'omnipresence of general law'.[63] Accordingly, the Report not only qualified the self-contained regime as a 'misnomer' but denied its sheer existence.[64]

In line with this, the ECHR neither can nor intends to escape this encompassing legal universe of which it forms a part. Consequently, the remaining question is simply one of how to align the ECHR with, and integrate it into, the omnipresent realm of international law. As shown, the *lex specialis* principle may—among other techniques—serve as a helpful tool in accomplishing this task and creating a dynamic and harmonious mobile structure or web architecture[65] between the general and the specific.

By doing so, the ECtHR takes part in a more general development. It contributes to overcoming the antipodean perspectives on the development of international law that have been dominating the discourse of public international law for more than two decades: fragmentation or constitutionalization.[66] Instead, the case law of the ECtHR represents and reflects the broader phenomenon of judicial integration. This approach aims to stabilize the fragile and fragmented international legal system by providing and ensuring compatibility among the different strata and bodies of law, but also claims a certain degree of flexibility and variation, which is a *conditio sine qua non* for the international legal system. While uniformity is an unrealistic end result given the complexity and variety of international courts and the legal issues that come before them, similar factual scenarios and similar legal issues are treated in a consistent manner and any disparity in treatment is explained and justified. The desired outcome is harmony and compatibility, which simultaneously allow for different solutions in particular cases. Multiple solutions in various international courts may allow for legal innovation and the eventual adoption of the most appropriate solution.

[63] See 'Fragmentation of International Law' (n 8). [64] ibid paras 192–93.

[65] See, to this effect, Andreas Voßkuhle 'Metaphors for this New Inter-judicial Relationship: Pyramid or Mobile—Human Rights Protection by the European Constitutional Courts' (Opening of the Judicial Year 2014 at the European Court of Human Rights Strasbourg, 31 January 2014).

[66] On the debate surrounding the fragmentation of international law, see Benedetto Conforti, 'Unité et Fragmentation du Droit International: Glissez, mortels, n'appuyez pas!"' (2007) 111 Revue Générale de Droit International Public; Pierre-Marie Dupuy, 'A Doctrinal Debate in the Globalisation Era: On the "Fragmentation" of International Law' (2007) 1 European Journal of Legal Studies; Bruno Simma, 'Universality of International Law from the Perspective of a Practitioner' (2009) 20 EJIL 265; Sahib Singh, 'The Potential of International Law: Fragmentation and Ethics' (2011) 24 Leiden Journal of International Law 23; Anne-Charlotte Martineau, 'The Rhetoric of Fragmentation: Fear and Faith in International Law' (2009) 22 Leiden Journal of International Law; Alexandra Khrebtukova, 'A Call to Freedom: Towards a Philosophy of International Law in an Era of Fragmentation' (2008) 4 Journal of International Law and International Relations 51; Martti Koskenniemi, *From Apology to Utopia: the Structure of International Legal Argument* (CUP 2005, reissue of 1989 edition with a new epilogue); David Kennedy, 'The Last Treatise: Project and Person (Reflections on Martti Koskenniemi's From Apology to Utopia)' (2006) 7 German Law Journal 982; Mireille Delmas-Marty, *Ordering Pluralism* (Hart Publishing 2009); Webb (n 46); I Motoc, 'Conception of Pluralism and International Law' in H Ruiz Fabri, E Jouannet, and V Tomkivitz (eds), *Select Proceedings of the European Society of International Law* (Hart 2008).

This conclusion sheds light on the fact that the diverse and pluralist structure constituted by the variety of legal regimes and judicial decision-making bodies may not only be threatening coherence and thus have *caused* fragmentation, but simultaneously may *resolve* it: fragmentation is tackled by judicial integration such as that undertaken by the ECtHR. In the end, we should not worry about fragmentation[67] (any more) and may even say 'farewell'[68] to the pejorative term depicting the diverse and pluralistic structure that once arose out of the post-Cold War era.[69]

[67] Alain Pellet in forum 'Should we (still) worry about Fragmentation?' European Society of International Law, 11th Annual Conference: The Judicialization of International Law—A Mixed Blessing? Oslo, 10–12 September 2015.

[68] Mads Andenas and Eirik Bjorge, *A Farewell to Fragmentation: Reassertion and Convergence in International Law* (CUP 2016).

[69] Anne Peters, 'Fragmentation and Constitutionalization' in Anne Orford and Florian Hoffman (eds), *The Oxford Handbook of the Theory of International Law* (OUP 2016).

11

The UN Security Council, State Responsibility, and the European Court of Human Rights

Towards an Integrated Approach?

Linos-Alexandre Sicilianos

1. Introduction

The question of the responsibility of States acting in execution of a Security Council resolution has repeatedly arisen in the case law of the European Court of Human Rights (ECtHR), from the 2005 *Bosphorus* judgment[1] to the *Al-Dulimi* case,[2] with a number of significant steps along the way, in particular: the *Behrami and Saramati* decision,[3] concerning the activities of UNMIK (United Nations Mission in Kosovo) and KFOR (Kosovo Force) in Kosovo, the *Al-Skeini*[4] and *Al-Jedda v The United Kingdom* judgments,[5] concerning the activities of the United Kingdom forces in Iraq, the *Nada v Switzerland* judgment,[6] concerning Security Council blacklists, and two important cases against the Netherlands, namely the *Stichting Mothers of Srebrenica* decision,[7] concerning the conflict in Bosnia, and the *Jaloud* judgment,[8] adopted more recently by the Grand Chamber.

Beyond the technical issues arising in these cases, the central question they raise concerns the relationship between the United Nations (UN) system and that of the European Convention on Human Rights (ECHR),[9] and consequently the Court's

[1] *Bosphorus Hava Yolları Turizm ve Ticaret Anonim Şirketi v Ireland* [GC] App no 45036/98 (ECtHR, 30 June 2005).

[2] *Al-Dulimi and Montana Management Inc v Switzerland* [GC] App no 5809/08 (ECtHR, 21 June 2016).

[3] *Behrami and Behrami v France* and *Saramati v France, Germany and Norway* (Dec) [GC] App nos 71412/01 and 78155/01 (ECtHR, 2 May 2007).

[4] *Al-Skeini and Others v The United Kingdom* [GC] App no 55721/07 (ECtHR, 7 July 2011).

[5] *Al-Jedda v The United Kingdom* [GC] App no 27021/08 (ECtHR, 7 July 2011).

[6] *Nada v Switzerland* [GC] App no 10593/08 (ECtHR, 12 September 2012).

[7] *Stichting Mothers of Srebrenica and Others v The Netherlands* (Dec) App no 65542/12 1(ECtHR, 1 June 2013).

[8] *Jaloud v The Netherlands* [GC] App no 47708/08 (ECtHR, 20 November 2014).

[9] For an overall analysis of the judicial control of Security Council resolutions by international, regional, and national courts, see Institute of International Law, 'Judicial Control of Security Council Decisions (UNO)' Rapporteur: Rüdiger Wolfrum, (2015) 76 Yearbook of the Institute of

role in this vast geopolitical framework and, at the same time, its function in guaranteeing the fundamental values of European public order.

A retrospective examination of the cases cited above may sometimes give the impression that the Court oscillates between a somewhat reserved, or even self-effacing, attitude, and a significantly more assertive approach, at times showing reverence towards the Security Council and at other times a form of defiance towards it. It is therefore important to take a step back from this often sensitive dispute and to attempt to conceptualize this issue as a whole.

To do so, we need to make a distinction between Security Council resolutions that involve, or could potentially involve, the use of armed force and those which impose economic or targeted sanctions. First of all, the two types of resolutions have a different legal basis: economic sanctions are imposed on the basis of Article 41 of the UN Charter, whereas military operations are based mainly on Article 42[10] or—better still, at least in the case of authorized operations—on Chapter VII of the Charter as a whole.[11] The two series of resolutions also, and above all, differ as regards the means and procedure for their implementation: the latter involves the deployment of military troops abroad, while the former requires the establishment of a legal and regulatory framework to enforce the economic sanctions within the territory of the forum State—corresponding to the respondent State before the Court.

2. Execution of Resolutions Involving Use of Force

2.1 Extraterritorial application of the ECHR

The execution of resolutions involving the use of armed force will almost inevitably raise the question of the extraterritorial application of the ECHR. While the UN member States wishing to contribute to the implementation of Security Council resolutions of this kind may offer logistical support or decide to cover part of the expenses of the operation concerned, such forms of contribution do not, in principle, raise any issues in terms of human rights protection. Problems of this nature normally arise, however, when the participating State contributes military troops—either as part of a multinational force, or as part of a UN peacekeeping operation—to be deployed within the territory of the State in which the crisis calling for resolution by the Security Council is taking place.

International Law, 413ff; ibid vol 77-I, 11ff. See also, Antonios Tzanakopoulos, *Disobeying the Security Council. Countermeasures against Wrongful Sanctions* (OUP 2011); Antonios Tzanakopoulos, 'Sharing Responsibility for UN Targeted Sanctions' (2015) 12 International Organizations Law Review 427; David Leary, 'Balancing Liberty and the Security Council: Judicial Responses to the Conflict between Chapter VII Resolutions and Human Rights Law under the Council's Targeted Sanctions Regime' in James A Green and Christopher PM Waters (eds), *Adjudicating International Human Rights: Essays in Honour of Sandy Ghandhi* (Brill/Martinus Nijhoff 2015) 69–98.

[10] See Olivier Corten, *Le Droit Contre la Guerre* (2nd edn, Pedone 2014) 520f, 531.

[11] On this point see Linos-Alexandre Sicilianos, 'Entre Multilatéralisme et Unilatéralisme: l'Autorisation par le Conseil de Sécurité de Recourir à la Force' (2008) 339 Recueil des Cours de l'Académie de Droit International 9, 166.

Much has been written about the extraterritorial application of the ECHR,[12] and it is not the purpose of this chapter to dwell on this subject in detail. It may simply be observed in this connection that the decision in the *Banković* case[13] was somewhat case-specific and that, since then, the Court has clearly nuanced and refined important aspects of it. The *Al-Skeini*,[14] *Al-Jedda*,[15] and *Jaloud*[16] judgments, among others, testify to this development.

The principle established in the Court's case law in this sphere is that, while being essentially territorial in its application, the ECHR may be applicable outside the territory of the State concerned in a range of specific situations, including—and especially—when that State's armed forces are operating abroad. This position is corroborated by the case law of the International Court of Justice (ICJ) and the practice of the Human Rights Committee and other international human rights protection bodies.[17] It is noteworthy that the approach pursued by these international bodies is now unequivocal on this point, reflecting the principle of general international law that '[e]very internationally wrongful act of a State entails the international responsibility of that State',[18] irrespective of where the act was perpetrated or the source of the obligation breached. The distinction—admittedly not always very clear—drawn by the ECtHR between attribution and jurisdiction[19] cannot call into question this fundamental principle.

It must also be acknowledged that the extraterritorial scope of the ECHR is taking on greater importance nowadays, given that the States Parties to the ECHR are increasingly active in the context of military operations abroad, usually on the basis of Security Council resolutions. To insist on the 'regional' nature of the ECHR would sit ill with this significant development for maintaining and restoring international peace and security, while also leaving a 'black hole' in human rights protection and double standards in its application.

[12] See, among many other sources, Michal Gondek, 'Extraterritorial Application of the European Convention on Human Rights: Territorial Focus in the Age of Globalization' [2015] NILR 349; Marko Milanovic, *Extraterritorial Application of Human Rights Treaties. Law, Principles and Policy* (OUP 2011); Vassilis P Tzevelekos, 'Reconstructing the Effective Control Criterion in Extraterritorial Human Rights Breaches: Direct Attribution of Wrongfulness, Due Diligence, and Concurrent Responsibility' (2014) 36 Michigan Journal of International Law129–78; Nehal Bhuta (ed), *The Frontiers of Human Rights: Extraterritoriality and its Challenges* (OUP 2016); Lea Raible, 'The Extraterritoriality of the ECHR: Why *Jaloud* and *Pisari* Should be Read as Game Changers' (2016) 2 EHRLR 161.

[13] *Banković and Others v Belgium and Others* (Dec) [GC] App no 52207/99 (ECtHR, 12 December 2001).

[14] *Al-Skeini* (n 4) paras 130 et seq.

[15] *Al-Jedda* (n 5) paras 74f.

[16] *Jaloud* (n 8) paras 140f.

[17] See in particular *Legal Consequences of the Construction of a Wall in the Occupied Palestinian Territory* (Advisory Opinion) [2004] ICJ Rep 136, para 111; *Armed Activities on the Territory of the Congo (Democratic Republic of the Congo v Uganda)* (Judgment) [2005] ICJ Rep 168, para 216; *Application of the International Convention on the Elimination of all Forms of Racial Discrimination (Georgia v Russian Federation)* (Provisional Measures) [2008] ICJ Rep 353, paras 108f; Human Rights Committee, General Comment no 31, 'Nature of the General Legal Obligation on States Parties to the Covenant' (29 March 2004) UN Doc CCPR/C/21/Rev.1/Add.13; and Committee on the Elimination of Racial Discrimination, Concluding Observations on Israel, UN Doc A/62/18, paras 225ff.

[18] Article 1, International Law Commission (ILC) Draft Articles on Responsibility of States for Internationally Wrongful Acts, (2001) II(2) ILC Yearbook 32 and related commentary.

[19] *Jaloud* (n 8) paras 154–55.

2.2 Multinational and UN operations

Another question that needs to be clarified regarding the responsibility of States acting in execution of Security Council resolutions involving the use of force concerns the distinction between multinational military operations—authorized by the Security Council—and the UN's peacekeeping, peacemaking, or peace-enforcement operations.

The latter are UN operations in that their name refers to that organization: they use the UN flag and emblems; they are generally funded from the UN budget; their personnel are treated as UN personnel; and, above all, they are placed under UN command. On the basis of these factors, UN peacekeeping operations constitute subsidiary bodies of the Security Council.

The situation is entirely different for multinational forces. Their designation does not refer to the UN, they do not use UN emblems, their budget is funded by the participating States, their personnel are not treated as UN personnel, and, above all, they are placed under the command of either a State or a regional organization, but not the UN. Unlike UN peacekeeping operations, multinational forces are not subsidiary bodies of the UN.[20]

That being so, these two types of operations should not be placed on the same footing. To maintain that UN operations (such as UNMIK) and multinational operations (such as KFOR) are both placed under the 'ultimate authority and control' of the Security Council—to use the phrase employed by the Court in its *Behrami and Saramati* decision—and that their acts are attributable to the UN[21] would appear to be an over-simplistic approach.[22] It is significant that, in the commentary on its Draft Articles on the Responsibility of International Organizations, the International Law Commission (ILC) made a clear distinction between the two situations by noting that, unlike in the case of UN peacekeeping operations, 'conduct of military forces of States or international organizations is not attributable to

[20] For a more detailed analysis of the differences between authorized operations and UN peacekeeping operations, see Sicilianos (n 11) 141–62.

[21] *Behrami* (n 3) in particular paras 133ff.

[22] For a criticism of this approach, see in particular Pierre Klein, 'Responsabilité pour les faits Commis dans le Cadre d'Opérations de Paix et Étendue du Pouvoir de Contrôle de la Cour Européenne des Droits de l'Homme: Quelques Considérations Critiques sur l'Arrêt *Behrami* et *Saramati*' (2007) 53 Annuaire Français de Droit International 55; Philippe Lagrange, 'Responsabilité des États pour actes accomplis en application du Chapitre VII de la Charte des Nations Unies' (2008) 112 Revue Générale de Droit International Public 94–95; Caroline Laly-Chevalier, 'Les Opérations Militaires et Civiles des Nations Unies et la Convention Européenne des Droits de l'Homme' (2007) 40 Revue Belge de Droit International 642–44; Kjetil Mujezinović Larsen, 'Attribution of Conduct in Peace Operations: The "Ultimate Authority and Control" Test' (2008) 19 European Journal of International Law 521–22; Paolo Palchetti, 'Azioni di Forze Istituite o Autorizzate dalle Nazioni Unite davanti alla Corte Europea dei Diritti dell'Uomo: i casi *Behrami* e *Saramati*' (2007) 90 Rivista di Diritto Internazionale 689–90; Aurel Sari, 'Jurisdiction and International Responsibility in Peace Support Operations: The *Behrami* and *Saramati* Cases' (2008) 8 Human Rights Law Review 164; Linos-Alexandre Sicilianos, 'L'(ir)Responsabilité des Forces Multilatérales?' in Laurence Boisson de Chazournes and Marcelo Kohen (eds), *International Law and the Quest for its Implementation, Liber Amicorum Vera Gowlland-Debbas* (Brill 2010) 98; ILC, 'Report of the International Law Commission on the Work of its 63rd Session' (26 April–3 June and 4 July–12 August 2011) UN Doc A/66/10, commentary on Article 7, paras 10 et seq.

the United Nations when the Security Council authorizes States or international organizations to take necessary measures outside a chain of command linking those forces to the United Nations'.[23] In such circumstances, the conduct at issue is attributable to the entity that exerts effective control over it, that is, a State participating in the multinational force or the international organization that assumes command over the operation, or both (in the case of shared responsibility).

In line with this approach, the *Al-Jedda v The United Kingdom* judgment, adopted by the Grand Chamber, set matters straight by finding that the Security Council had 'neither effective control nor ultimate authority and control' over the acts and omissions of troops within the multinational force operating in Iraq under Security Council Resolution 1546 (2004) and that the applicant's detention was therefore not attributable to the UN[24] but to the respondent State. Admittedly, the Court was careful to distinguish the situation in Kosovo in the context of the *Behrami and Saramati* cases from the situation prevailing in Iraq at the time of the facts relating to the *Al-Jedda* case. The geopolitical background to these cases was indeed very different. From a strictly legal viewpoint, however, it must be acknowledged that the Security Council did not have any more control over KFOR, which was set up under Resolution 1244 (1999), than it had over the multinational force authorized to operate in Iraq by Resolution 1546 (2004). Both cases involved multinational forces acting outside the chain of command linking them to the UN. In other words, the Grand Chamber was right to shift its approach as regards the attribution of the acts of multinational forces to the participating States and not the UN.

The more recent judgment in *Jaloud v The Netherlands* confirms this approach. While mentioning the Security Council's authorization by means of Resolution 1511 (2003), the Court emphasized that the Netherlands had 'retained full command over its contingent',[25] which was decisive for establishing the Netherlands' 'jurisdiction' within the meaning of Article 1 of the ECHR.[26]

2.3 Non-applicability of Article 103 of the UN Charter

The *Al-Jedda* judgment also set matters straight on another important point, namely Article 103 of the UN Charter and its applicability to operations authorized by the Security Council. It will be recalled that Article 103 provides: 'In the event of a conflict between the obligations of the Members of the United Nations under the present Charter and their obligations under any other international agreement, their obligations under the present Charter shall prevail.' Contrary

[23] ibid Chapter II (Attribution of conduct to an international organization), introduction, para 5. See also Institute of International Law, 'L'Autorisation du Recours à la Force par les Nations Unies', Rapporteur: Raúl Emilio Vinuesa, (2011) 74 Yearbook of the Institute of International Law 365, 384–85.

[24] *Al-Jedda* (n 5) para 84.

[25] *Jaloud* (n 8) para 149.

[26] It is significant that the Court left open the question whether the United Kingdom—which was not a party to the proceedings—had 'exercised concurrent jurisdiction' as one of the 'lead nations' of the operation in question (ibid para 153).

to the *Behrami and Saramati* decision, in which Article 103 was invoked,[27] the *Al-Jedda* judgment avoided relying on that provision—for good reason, since Article 103 does not apply to operations that have simply been authorized by the Security Council.[28] Authorizations of this kind amount to an invitation or an encouragement for member States to take part in a particular military operation. They do not create any legal obligation to do so.

Furthermore, the wording of a Security Council authorization is generally fairly flexible—referring to maintaining order and security, for example—and as a result, it always leaves considerable discretion to the States participating in the operation concerned. As the Court noted in the *Al-Jedda* judgment, 'the terminology of [...] Resolution [1546] appears to leave the choice of the means to achieve this end to the member States within the Multinational Force'.[29] In these circumstances, the presumption must be that the Security Council intended States within the multinational force to contribute towards maintaining security in Iraq while complying with their obligations under international human rights law.[30] This is a strong presumption—or indeed a premise—given that the Security Council is supposed to act in accordance with the purposes of the UN as set forth in Article 1 of the Charter, including 'respect for human rights and for fundamental freedoms' (Article 1, para 3).

As the Court observed on the basis of a detailed analysis of the terms used by the Security Council, nothing in Resolution 1546 (2004) or any other subsequent resolutions could be construed as imposing any obligation on the United Kingdom to place an individual whom its authorities considered to constitute a risk to the security of Iraq 'in indefinite detention without charge'. On the contrary, both the UN Secretary-General and the United Nations Assistance Mission for Iraq (UNAMI), likewise set up by the Security Council, had criticized this practice of internment. In these circumstances, 'in the absence of a binding obligation to use internment, there was no conflict between the United Kingdom's obligations under the Charter of the United Nations and its obligations under Article 5 § 1 of the Convention'.[31]

Similar considerations apply *mutatis mutandis* to all operations authorized by the Security Council. Since 1990, the Security Council has authorized more than thirty operations, in each case according to the same logic: the Council notes the existence of a threat to peace, gives the go-ahead for the setting up of a multinational force, lays down the general mandate for the operation and the objectives to be achieved, and then carries out an extremely limited, or indeed nominal,[32] supervision of the conduct of the operations, leaving considerable discretion to the participating States. In these circumstances, the problem of a direct conflict

[27] *Behrami* (n 3) in particular para 147.

[28] See Sicilianos (n 11) 180, and contrast Robert Kolb, 'Does Article 103 of the Charter of the United Nations Apply only to Decisions or also to Authorizations Adopted by the Security Council?' [2004] ZaöRV21, 26.

[29] *Al-Jedda* (n 5) para 105. [30] ibid. [31] ibid para 109.

[32] See Théodore Christakis and Karine Bannelier, 'Acteur Vigilant ou Spectateur Impuissant? Le Contrôle Exercé par le Conseil de Sécurité sur les États Autorisés à Recourir à la Force' (2004) 2 RBDI 498; Sicilianos (n 11) 155ff.

between the obligations flowing from the Charter, and more specifically from the resolution authorizing the multinational operation concerned, and the respondent State's human rights obligations does not even arise in practice. To maintain the contrary would be to disregard the hybrid legal nature, the particularities, and the profile of authorized operations.

2.4 UN peacekeeping operations

Beyond the question of authorized operations, it is important to consider the further issue of the responsibility of States Parties to the ECHR that supply troops to a UN peacekeeping operation. In the *Behrami and Saramati* decision, the Court held that the acts or omissions of UNMIK were attributable to the UN.[33] More recently, in the *Stichting Mothers of Srebrenica* decision, the Court found that the Netherlands courts had rightly refused to consider the application on the merits by referring to the UN's immunity from jurisdiction in relation to the activities of the United Nations Protection Force (UNPROFOR) in Bosnia.[34]

Both solutions are correct in principle. Contrary to authorized operations, peacekeeping operations are—as noted in section 2.2—subsidiary bodies to the UN, and on that account their actions generally engage the responsibility of that organization (which in principle enjoys immunity from jurisdiction before the domestic courts). This principle has long been accepted by the UN. As the UN Legal Counsel has observed, '[a]s a subsidiary organ of the United Nations, an act of a peacekeeping force is, in principle, imputable to the Organization, and if committed in violation of an international obligation entails the international responsibility of the Organization and its liability in compensation'.[35]

However, as the ILC has rightly observed, this position is based on the assumption that the UN has 'exclusive control' of the deployment of national contingents in a peacekeeping force.[36] It should nevertheless be borne in mind that contributing States retain a certain degree of control over members of their contingents, particularly in disciplinary and criminal matters. Depending on the facts of the case, this aspect may have a bearing on the attribution of the conduct in question to the State concerned.[37]

There have also been cases where national contingents have continued to seek and receive orders from their national authorities. As was found by the Commission of Inquiry, established to investigate armed attacks on the personnel of the United Nations Operation in Somalia (UNOSOM II), the force commander was not in 'effective control' of several national contingents which had persisted in seeking orders from their home authorities. There were even operations undertaken under the UN flag, and in the context of UNOSOM's mandate, which 'were totally outside the

[33] *Behrami* (n 3) paras 142f. [34] *Stichting Mothers* (n 7) in particular paras 146ff.

[35] Letter of 3 February 2004 from the United Nations Legal Counsel to the Director of the Codification Division (A/CN.4/545, sect II.G).

[36] ILC (n 22) commentary on Article 7, para 6.

[37] See the example mentioned by the ILC, ibid para 7.

command and control of the United Nations'.[38] Clearly, in such circumstances, it is virtually impossible to attribute the actions of the national contingents concerned to the UN.

There have also been certain cases where a multinational (or regional) force and a UN mission have carried out a joint operation.[39] In such cases, international responsibility for the conduct of the troops lies with the entity in which operational command and control is vested according to the terms of the cooperation arrangements between the State or States providing the troops and the UN. In the absence of such arrangements, responsibility will be determined in each case according to the degree of 'effective control' exercised by either party in the conduct of the operation.[40]

This reasoning applies *mutatis mutandis* to all UN peacekeeping operations, 'insofar as it is possible to distinguish in their regard areas of effective control respectively pertaining to the United Nations and the contributing State'.[41] In other words, where, and to the extent that, the State in question retains effective control over the conduct at issue, its responsibility may also be engaged. The criterion of 'effective control' on the ground is a factual element[42] which is decisive for the purposes of attributing the conduct to the UN or the contributing State, or both simultaneously.[43]

That being so, instead of simply adopting an abstract or indeed dogmatic approach, it is important for the ECtHR to look at each case in rather greater depth, by examining whether the respondent State had effective control over the conduct at issue. The Court will have to determine each individual case on the basis of the particular facts.

The issue of the responsibility of the States Parties to the ECHR in enforcing the economic sanctions adopted by the Security Council has certain similarities, but also a number of differences, in relation to the issue discussed above.

3. Execution of Resolutions Imposing Economic Sanctions

3.1 From global to targeted sanctions

In considering the case law of the ECtHR against the general background of economic sanctions in international law,[44] it is important to remember that during

[38] Security Council, 'Report of the Commission of Inquiry Established Pursuant to Security Council Resolution 885 (1993) to Investigate Armed Attacks on UNOSOM II Personnel which Let to Casualties Among Them' (1 June 1994) UN Doc S/1994/653, 37, paras 243f.

[39] The example of KFOR and UNMIK in Kosovo, established pursuant to UNSC Res 1244 (10 June 1999) UN Doc S/RES/1244, is certainly the best known. However, there are a number of others, such as the 'hybrid operation' between the UN and the African Union in Darfur, the deployment of which was authorized by Resolution UNSC Res 1769 (31 July 2007) UN Doc S/RES/1769. For further examples, see Sicilianos (n 11) 290ff.

[40] According to the UN Secretary-General, UN Doc A/51/389, 7, paras 17f.

[41] According to the ILC, ibid para 9.

[42] See Tzanakopoulos (n 9) 40.

[43] As regards the question of attributing conduct to two subjects of international law simultaneously, see Francesco Messineo, 'Attribution of Conduct' in André Nollkaemper and Ilias Plakokefalos (eds), *Principles of Shared Responsibility in International Law* (CUP 2014) 60.

[44] With regard to this question, see in particular Vera Gowlland-Debbas (ed), *United Nations Sanctions and International Law* (Kluwer 2001); Laura Picchio Forlati and Linos-Alexandre Sicilianos (eds), *Les Sanctions Économiques en Droit International/Economic Sanctions in International Law* (Martinus Nijhoff 2004).

the 'sanctions decade' (the 1990s), the Security Council generally adopted global economic sanctions. These were measures taken against a State, and hence an entire people, such as the economic sanctions against Iraq (following its invasion of Kuwait), the former Yugoslavia, or Haiti. The famous *Bosphorus* case related to this generation of sanctions.

In 2000, the then UN Under-Secretary-General for Political Affairs did not hesitate to describe these sanctions as 'blunt' instruments[45] which had a devastating impact on the economy of the State affected, including—above all—on the economic and social rights of its population, without necessarily achieving the aim pursued. Neighbouring States (such as Greece in the case of the sanctions against the former Yugoslavia) suffered significant 'side-effects'.[46] The Interlaken and Bonn/Berlin processes led to a reform of this system and the introduction of 'smart' or 'targeted' sanctions,[47] aimed directly at the decision-makers and their immediate or less immediate circles and seeking to spare, as far as possible, the population of the State concerned. The issue of Security-Council (and European-Union) 'blacklists' relates mainly to this second generation of sanctions.

It should not be forgotten that this reform process led to a significant improvement, or even a certain humanization, in the Security Council's power to impose sanctions. However, although the overall effects of this new generation of measures were relatively limited since they affected a more or less specific number of people, targeted sanctions managed to raise a range of other problems, relating in particular to civil rights and traditional freedoms. It was not long before the measures attracted the ire of the Council of Europe's Parliamentary Assembly, which expressed the view that the procedural and substantive standards applied by the Security Council and the Council of the European Union (EU) 'violate the fundamental principles of human rights and the rule of law'.[48] The *Kadi I* case[49] and subsequent cases concerning blacklists—including, for example, *Nada* and *Al-Dulimi* as far as the ECHR is concerned—are to be seen against this overall background.

Following this brief summary of the historical context, it is important to note that cases concerning economic sanctions do not raise any issues in terms of 'jurisdiction' within the meaning of Article 1 of the ECHR. The measures in question are applied in the territory of the respondent State by means of acts at national level, attributable to the organs of that State.[50] Contrary to the execution of Security Council

[45] Security Council 'Overview of Security Council Meeting Record' (17 April 2000) UN Doc S/PV. 4128, 2.

[46] See Djacoba Liva Tehindrazanarivelo, *Les Sanctions des Nations Unies et leurs Effets Secondaires* (PUF 2005).

[47] For further information about this reform process, see Linos-Alexandre Sicilianos, 'Sanctions Institutionnelles et Contre-mesures: Tendances Récentes' in Picchio Forlati and Sicilianos (eds) (n 44) 3, 61ff. On targeted sanctions see also Rüdiger Wolfrum (n 9) vol 76, 444ff, vol 77-I, 62ff.

[48] Parliamentary Assembly of the Council of Europe, Resolution 1597 (2008), 'United Nations Security Council and European Union blacklists', para 6.

[49] Joined cases C-402/05 P and C-415/05 P *Kadi and Al Barakaat International Foundation v Council and Commission* (ECJ, 3 September 2008) (*Kadi I*). For a critical analysis of this judgement, see among others Luis M. Hinojosa Martínez, 'Bad Law for Good Reasons: The Contradictions of the *Kadi* Judgment'(2008) 5 International Organizations Law Review 339.

[50] *Bosphorus* (n 1) para 121.

resolutions involving the use of force, the implementation of resolutions imposing economic sanctions does not raise the issue of the extraterritorial application of the ECHR. However, the questions arising in connection with economic sanctions differ according to whether or not the State enforcing the sanctions is a member of the European Union.

3.2 Enforcement of sanctions by EU Member States

In principle, the EU member States do not act on the basis of the Security Council resolution as such. They act pursuant to an EU regulation implementing the economic sanctions imposed by the Security Council. Such regulation creates a kind of screen. Its existence was what caused the European Court of Justice (ECJ), in the *Kadi I* case,[51] to find that there had been a violation of a series of fundamental rights, without calling into question—at least in formal terms—the legality of the Security Council's actions. The dispute focused on the procedure for the implementation of the Council's resolution, and not the act of imposing sanctions as such.

The same is true, *mutatis mutandis*, in the case law of the Strasbourg Court. The *Bosphorus* judgment, which constitutes a *locus classicus* in this area, puts forward the well-known 'equivalent protection' criterion, according to which, if the international organization concerned provides equivalent protection—that is, comparable to that afforded by the ECHR, the presumption will be that a State satisfies the requirements of the ECHR when it does no more than implement legal obligations flowing from its membership of the organization. However, the presumption in question is rebuttable.[52] It can be rebutted if it is considered that the protection of ECHR rights was 'manifestly deficient'. In such cases, the Court considers that the ECHR, as a 'constitutional instrument of European public order', should prevail over the interests of international cooperation.[53]

The facts of the *Bosphorus* case, as summarized in the Strasbourg Court's judgment, made it clear that the procedure for executing Security Council Resolution 820 (1993) – the relevant resolution in the case—was dictated by the UN Sanctions Committee in New York. However, the Community regulation implementing the UN sanctions formed the legal basis for the impoundment of the aircraft at issue and acted as a shield leaving the Security Council safe from any reproach. The Strasbourg Court's attention was focused on the guarantees of human rights

[51] *Kadi I* (n 49).

[52] For a more in depth analysis of the concept of equivalent protection see, among others, Paul De Hert and Fisnik Korenica, 'The Doctrine of Equivalent Protection: Its Life and Legitimacy before and after the European Union's Accession to the European Convention on Human Rights' (2012) 13 GLJ 874; Florence Benoît-Rohmer, 'Bienvenue aux Enfants de Bosphorus: la Cour Européenne des Droits de l'Homme et les Organisations Internationales' [2010] *Revue Trimestrielle des Droits de l'Homme* 19; Cathryn Costello, 'The Bosphorus ruling of the European Court of Human Rights: Fundamental Rights and Blurred Boundaries in Europe' (2006) 6 HRLR 87; Cedric Ryngaert, 'The European Court of Human Rights' Approach to the Responsibility of Member States in Connection with Acts of International Organization' (2011) 60 ICLQ 997.

[53] *Bosphorus* (n 1) para 156. See also, Vera Gowlland-Debbas, 'The Security Council and Issues of Responsibility under International Law' (2011) 353 Recueil des Cours 185.

protection in Community law, which were held to be 'equivalent' to those provided by the ECHR. The Court also considered that there was generally a presumption of equivalence—albeit a rebuttable one—between human rights protection within the Community system and the protection afforded under the ECHR.[54]

Once the Court has found that EU law does afford equivalent protection, the respondent State, where it has correctly applied that law, is likewise safe from criticism and its responsibility cannot be engaged. In other words, if the Court considers that the presumption is applicable in the case before it and has not been rebutted, the conclusion is inevitable: there must be a finding of no violation. Accordingly, caution is required before the 'equivalent protection label' can be awarded.

Indeed, it is worth recalling the remarks made in the joint concurring opinion of Judges Rozakis, Tulkens, Traja, Botoucharova, Zagrebelsky, and Garlicki appended to the *Bosphorus* judgment, pointing out the limits of human rights protection within the EU and calling on the Strasbourg Court to apply the equivalent-protection criterion cautiously, on a case-by-case basis. While stating that they were convinced of the growing role of fundamental rights and their integration into the Community legal order—a finding borne out in the light of the Lisbon Treaty, which made the Charter of Fundamental Rights a binding instrument—the aforementioned judges regretted the general and abstract review under the Community system.

In that context, they highlighted in particular the importance of the right of individual application as the keystone of the protection system set forth in the ECHR.[55] This right is one of the basic obligations assumed by States on ratifying the ECHR. It is, therefore, difficult to accept that the effectiveness of this remedy could be reduced as a result of the transfer of powers to the EU. Notwithstanding the existence of a plurality of appeals, individual access to the EU courts remains limited. Despite its value, a reference for a preliminary ruling as an internal means of prior review cannot replace the external, *ex post facto* supervision carried out by the ECtHR on the basis of an individual application. This is all the more true as a reference to the Luxembourg Court for a preliminary ruling does not constitute an appeal but a request for interpretation. Furthermore, the competent national court retains a certain discretion in applying the ECJ's ruling in the dispute before it. In other words, leaving it to the EU judicial system to ensure 'equivalent protection', without retaining a means of verifying on a case-by-case basis that the protection afforded is indeed comparable, would be tantamount to consenting tacitly to substitution, in the field of EU law, of the ECHR standards with the EU's own standards.

The concurring opinion also emphasizes the 'relatively undefined' nature of the criterion of 'manifestly deficient' used, as noted above, to rebut the presumption of 'equivalent protection'.[56] It is true that the criterion in question establishes a relatively low threshold, contrasting with the nature and scope of the supervision carried out under the ECHR. It should also be borne in mind that in accordance with

[54] *Bosphorus* (n 1) paras 159–65.

[55] Joint concurring opinion of Judges Rozakis, Tulkens, Traja, Botoucharova, Zagrebelsky, and Garlicki, appended to *Bosphorus* (n 1) para 3.

[56] ibid para 4.

Article 53, the ECHR guarantees a minimum level of protection. Admittedly, the EU Charter of Fundamental Rights provides: 'In so far as this Charter contains rights which correspond to rights guaranteed by the Convention for the Protection of Human Rights and Fundamental Freedoms, the meaning and scope of those rights shall be the same as those laid down by the said Convention [. . .]' (Article 52, paragraph 3). However, abstract application of the equivalent-protection criterion cannot have the effect of lowering the minimum level of protection afforded by the ECHR. As the authors of the aforementioned concurring opinion noted at the time, 'the Union has not yet acceded to the European Convention on Human Rights and [. . .] full protection does not yet exist at European level'.[57]

This reserved attitude is even more appropriate today, it would seem, following opinion 2/13, adopted by the ECJ in December 2014.[58] Without wishing to recapitulate the criticisms expressed on this subject by various authors,[59] it has to be acknowledged that the opinion in question renders the prospect of EU accession to the ECHR more remote. Everyone loses out in this situation, but most of all the citizens of the EU. The ECtHR, for its part, should apply the equivalent-protection doctrine vis-à-vis the EU in the spirit mentioned above. An attentive examination on a case-by-case basis will be needed if the Strasbourg Court is to discharge its duty properly. Such an approach has been recently confirmed by the judgment in *Avotiņš v Latvia*.[60] As the Grand Chamber put it:

> The Court carries out this assessment [. . .] in order to determine whether it can apply the presumption of equivalent protection to the decision complained of, a presumption which the Court applies in accordance with conditions which it has itself laid down. The Court thus considers that the question whether the full potential of the supervisory mechanisms provided for by European Union law was deployed [. . .] should be assessed *in the light of the specific circumstances of each case*.[61]

Having highlighted this development, we still need to address the questions relating to the implementation of Security Council sanctions by the States Parties to the ECHR that are not EU member States.

3.3 Implementation of sanctions by non-EU Member States

While the practical difference between this scenario and the one discussed above may appear purely formal, in legal terms the distinction between the two situations is considerable. A non-member State of the EU that adopts measures for the implementation of a Security Council resolution imposing economic sanctions is a direct

[57] ibid para 3.

[58] ECJ, Opinion 2/13—Opinion pursuant to Article 218, para 11, TFEU, 18 December 2014.

[59] See, among many others, Jean-Paul Jacqué, 'L'avis 2/13 de la CJUE. Non à l'Adhésion à la Convention Européenne des Droits de l'Homme?'(2014) Droit de l'Union Européenne <http://www.droit-union-europeenne.be/412337458> accessed 11 May 2018; Denys Simon, 'Deuxième (ou second et dernier?) Coup d'Arrêt à l'Adhésion de l'Union à la CEDH: étrange avis 2/13' (2015) 2 Europe 4.

[60] *Avotiņš v Latvia* [GC] App no 17502/07 (ECtHR, 23 May 2016).

[61] ibid paras 110–11 (emphasis added).

agent in the enforcement of the resolution. In such circumstances, there is no EU regulation and, hence, no screen or shield between the national legal system and the system of the UN Charter. This means that, if we are to apply the equivalent-protection criterion here, we will need to compare the guarantees provided by the ECHR with those afforded by the procedure before the Security Council and its sanctions committees.[62]

It is true that following the virulent criticisms of the blacklisting process, the Security Council set up the Office of the Ombudsperson[63] to help the Al-Qaeda Sanctions Committee[64] to examine delisting requests. More recently, this procedure has been extended and reinforced.[65] It must be acknowledged, however, that despite these developments, the proceedings before the Ombudsperson are essentially diplomatic in nature and lead at most to a recommendation to the sanctions committee, which accordingly has the final say as to whether the person concerned should be delisted. This being so, the procedure in question clearly does not offer comparable guarantees to those afforded by the judicial system established by the ECHR.

One might, therefore, wonder whether the equivalent-protection criterion is relevant in this context. Admittedly, the criterion was formulated in general terms in the *Bosphorus* case. In theory, it can be applied in respect of any international organization to which the States Parties to the ECHR decide to transfer powers potentially touching upon human rights protection. It is true that in the case of *Gasparini v Italy and Belgium*, for example, the Court applied the equivalent-protection test outside the EU context, in respect of NATO, the subject matter there being the rights of NATO officials and their compatibility with Article 6 ECHR.[66]

The application of the equivalent-protection doctrine in relation to NATO has been possible, however, because NATO's constitutive treaty—the North Atlantic Treaty of 4 April 1949[67]—contains no clause that is comparable to Article 103 of the UN Charter. In fact, no other constitutive instrument of an international organization contains such a clause. The UN Charter and its Article 103 are unique in that regard. The provision in question constitutes the cornerstone of the international legal order because it contains a key element of that order's hierarchical structure. The United Nations and other international organizations cannot therefore be placed on the same plane. This means that the equivalent-protection test

62 See the Chamber judgment in the case of *Al-Dulimi v Switzerland* App no 5809/08 (ECtHR, 26 November 2013) paras 115ff.

63 UNSC Res 1904 (17 December 2009) UN Doc S/RES/1904

64 This committee was set up by UNSC Res 1267 (15 October 1999).

65 See UNSC Res 1989 (17 June 2011) UN Doc S/RES/1989 and UNSC Res 2083 (17 December 2012) UN Doc S/RES/2083. On the importance of the changes introduced in the sanctions against Al-Qaeda, see Luis M. Hinojosa Martínez and Carmela Pérez-Bernárdez, 'El Derecho a La Tutela Judicial Efectiva En El Derecho Europeo Y Las Sanciones Contra Al Qaeda' in Jorge Cardona Llorens et al (eds), *Estudios de Derecho Internacional y Derecho Europeo en Homenaje al Profesor Manuel Pérez González* (Tirant lo Blanch 2012) 1569, at 1576ff. It has to be noted, however, that the mandate of the Office of the Ombudsperson is limited to the Al-Qaida Sanctions List (see UNSC Res 2083 (17 December 2012) UN Doc S/RES/2083, paras 19ff).

66 See *Gasparini v Italy and Belgium* (Dec) App no 10750/03 (ECtHR, 12 May 2009).

67 UNTS vol 34.

does not simply apply to all international organizations alike. To the extent that Article 103 is applicable to economic sanctions adopted by the Security Council, UN law itself contains a rule which governs any conflict between obligations arising from the Charter and from any other international agreement.

More specifically, when it comes to the implementation of the Security Council's (binding) economic sanctions by non-members of the EU, there are two sides to the equation: either there is no real conflict of obligations for the respondent State, in which case the equivalent-protection test does not even come into play; or there is a conflict of obligations, but then it will be governed by Article 103 of the UN Charter. In both cases—and *tertium non datur*—the equivalent-protection test is inapplicable to a situation such as the present. It is, moreover, significant that in the *Nada v Switzerland* judgment[68]—concerning the applicant's inclusion on a Security-Council blacklist by the Swiss authorities—and more recently in *Al-Dulimi*,[69] the Grand Chamber carefully avoided relying on that test.

In the same cases, the Court also skirted around the application of Article 103 of the UN Charter. On the face of it, that provision *is* indeed applicable in this context because economic sanctions are, in principle, imposed by binding Security Council resolutions based on Article 41 of the Charter (and not simply 'authorized'). It should be borne in mind, however, that Article 103 does not concern a conflict of norms *in abstracto*. It is aimed at resolving *in concreto* a potential conflict of obligations.[70] This means that the Court must determine in each individual case whether such a conflict is indeed present.

In so doing, the Court takes as its starting point a strong presumption, or indeed a premise, that the obligations flowing from the UN Charter should be harmonized as far as possible with those deriving from the ECHR. In other words, in its most recent case law in this area, the Court has adopted an approach that seeks to reconcile States' obligations under the ECHR and the Charter. As the Grand Chamber has aptly noted:

> [I]n interpreting its resolutions, there must be a presumption that the Security Council does not intend to impose any obligation on member States to breach fundamental principles of human rights. In the event of any ambiguity in the terms of a United Nations Security Council resolution, the Court must therefore choose the interpretation which is

[68] *Nada* (n 6).

[69] *Al-Dulimi* (n 2) para 149. For a commentary on this judgment see Anne Peters, 'The New Arbitrariness and Competing Constitutionalisms: Remarks on ECtHR Grand Chamber Al-Dulimi' (2016) EJIL: *Talk!* <https://www.ejiltalk.org/?s=The+New+Arbitrariness+and+Competing+Constitutionalisms%3A+Remarks+on+ECtHR+Grand+Chamber+Al-Dulimi> accessed 29 July 2018; Marko Milanovic, 'Grand Chamber judgment in Al-Dulimi v. Switzerland'(2016) EJIL: *Talk!* <https://www.ejiltalk.org/?s=Grand+Chamber+judgment+in+Al-Dulimi+v.+Switzerland> accessed 28 July 2018; Vassilis P Tzevelekos, 'The *Al-Dulimi* Case before the Grand Chamber of the European Court of Human Rights: Business as Usual? Test of Equivalent Protection, (Constitutional) Hierarchy and Systemic Integration' (2017) 38(6) QIL 5–34. See also the critical approach by Judges Ziemele and Nußberger in their partly dissenting and dissenting opinions respectively, appended to *Al-Dulimi* (n 2), as well as the concurring opinion of Judge Pinto de Albuquerque, joined by Judges Hajiyev, Pejchal, and Dedov, and the concurring opinions of Judges Keller, Kūris, and Sicilianos.

[70] See Robert Kolb, 'L'article 103 de la Charte des Nations Unies' (2013) 367 Recueil des Cours 9, 145f.

most in harmony with the requirements of the Convention and which avoids any conflict of obligations.[71]

To put it another way, having regard to the normative framework governing the Security Council's activities, there is a presumption whereby its resolutions do not create any obligations that are incompatible with those undertaken by the member States in the domain of human rights. The presumption in question is, admittedly, rebuttable. Nevertheless, any doubt must be dispelled in favour of an interpretation of the relevant Security Council resolutions which avoids a conflict of obligations. This idea of presumption was used in *Nada*[72] and has been developed in the *Al-Dulimi* judgment.[73]

The ECtHR first reiterates the findings of its case law according to which, in view of the UN's important role in promoting and encouraging respect for human rights, 'it is to be expected that clear and explicit language would be used were the Security Council to intend States to take particular measures which would conflict with their obligations under international human rights law'.[74] The ECtHR thus assumes the logical consequence of that idea: in the absence of any clear or explicit wording excluding or limiting respect for human rights in the context of the implementation of sanctions against individuals or entities at national level, 'the Court must always presume that those measures are compatible with the Convention'.[75]

The words 'must always presume' do not mean that the presumption in question suddenly becomes irrebuttable. It is certainly not in dispute that, except in respect of norms of *jus cogens*, the Security Council has the possibility of provisionally departing from specific human rights provisions. This is what transpires, moreover, from the judgments given in the context of the *Al-Dulimi* case by the Swiss Federal Court, and the ECtHR shares its conclusions on that point.[76] However, the presumption of human rights compliance by Security Council resolutions is a strong presumption, in the sense that only 'clear and explicit' language is capable of rebutting it. Any vague, ambiguous, or implicit terms would not have that effect.

As a rule, although Security Council resolutions may be binding, as are resolutions that impose economic sanctions, they leave States a certain degree of latitude as to the procedure for their implementation. This applies in particular to the means to be employed or the possibility of derogations or exceptions on humanitarian grounds, for example.[77] By making use of this latitude—which is 'admittedly limited but nevertheless real'[78]—States must find appropriate solutions in order to harmonize their obligations. Only if such harmonization proves impossible will Article 103 of the Charter be applicable. In other words, according to the Court's

[71] *Al-Jedda* (n 5) para 102. See also *Nada* (n 6) para 171 and *Al-Dulimi* (n 2) para 140.

[72] *Nada* (n 6) paras 171ff.

[73] *Al-Dulimi* (n 2) paras 139–40.

[74] *Al-Jedda* (n 5) para 102 and *Nada* (n 6) para 171.

[75] *Al-Dulimi* (n 2) para 140.

[76] ibid para 136.

[77] See Sicilianos (n 47) 82ff (also for further references).

[78] *Nada* (n 6) para 180. See, however, the critical remarks of Jean-Paul Jacqué, 'A propos de *Nada contre Suisse*: les Résolutions du Conseil de Sécurité devant la Cour Européenne des Droits de l'Homme' (2013) European Yearbook on Human Rights 303, at 308.

approach, this Article applies only as a last resort, once all other possible means of harmonizing the States' obligations have been exhausted.

Applying this methodology in *Al-Dulimi*, the Court finds that the relevant Security Council resolution, namely Resolution 1483 (2003),[79] did not expressly prohibited access to a court—guaranteed by Article 6 of the ECHR—and thus the possibility for the national courts to verify, in terms of human rights, the (blacklisting) measures taken at national level pursuant to this resolution. Nor does the ECtHR detect any other legal factor that could legitimize such a restrictive interpretation.[80]

Consequently, the ECtHR considers that 'the fact that it has remained totally impossible for [the applicants] to challenge the confiscation measure for many years is hardly conceivable in a democratic society'.[81] The ECtHR thus seems to be suggesting that such a drastic restriction on the right of access to a court would impair the essence of that right. On the other hand, the ECtHR takes account of the nature and legitimate aim of the impugned measures, namely the protection of international peace and security. In order to strike a 'fair balance' between the necessity of ensuring respect for human rights and the imperatives of the protection of international peace and security, the ECtHR takes the view that the courts of the respondent State should have exercised 'sufficient scrutiny so that any arbitrariness [could] be avoided'.[82]

The ECtHR reiterates in this connection that '[o]ne of the fundamental components of European public order is the principle of the rule of law, and arbitrariness constitutes the negation of that principle'.[83] Moreover, in the context of such scrutiny—admittedly minimal, but nevertheless important—the applicants should have been afforded 'at least a genuine opportunity to submit appropriate evidence to a court, for examination on the merits, in order to show that their inclusion on the impugned lists had been arbitrary'.[84] This means that, at least at the outset, the burden of proof is on the applicants, who should have sufficient evidence at their disposal to enable them, if appropriate, to prove that the measures taken against them are arbitrary in nature.

As thus defined, the scrutiny intended by the ECtHR in *Al-Dulimi* does not seem to place an excessive burden on the national judicial authorities, while taking into account, in a balanced manner, the imperatives of the protection of international peace and security—and, accordingly, the responsibilities of the Security Council under the Charter, on the one hand, and the rights at the heart of the Convention system, on the other.

In my opinion, this is a wise approach. It has the merit of avoiding a systemic conflict, or even the fragmentation of the international legal order. Instead, it seeks to promote a coherent view of international law. The Court scrupulously avoids calling into question the Security Council's decisions as such or encouraging States to engage in a form of 'disobedience'[85] towards the body with primary responsibility for maintaining international peace and security. At the same time, the Court assumes its role in guaranteeing the values enshrined in the ECHR and the Protocols thereto.

[79] UNSC Res 1483 (22 May 2003) UN Doc S/RES/1483.
[80] *Al-Dulimi* (n 2) para 143. [81] ibid para 152. [82] ibid para 146.
[83] ibid para 145. [84] ibid para 151.
[85] To use the expression employed by Tzanakopoulos (n 9).

4. Concluding Remarks

In conclusion, it will be noted that the Court is in the process of refining its conceptual tools for determining the responsibility of the States Parties to the ECHR acting in execution of a Security Council resolution. Where the implementation of resolutions involving the use of force is concerned, the Court's recent case law has shown a shift towards systematic acceptance of the extraterritorial scope of the ECHR. The distinction—not always very clear—between the concepts of jurisdiction and attribution cannot call into question the fundamental principle that every internationally wrongful act of a State entails its international responsibility, irrespective of the place where the act was perpetrated.

As to whether the conduct in issue should be attributed to the States Parties or to the UN, the Court now makes a clear distinction between operations authorized by the Security Council and UN peacekeeping operations. The former are placed under national command and control authorities, and consequently the question of the UN's responsibility does not even arise. In the case of UN operations, however, it is important to undertake a more detailed examination of the question of shared responsibility between the UN and States contributing troops.

The question of the responsibility of the States Parties to the ECHR in the implementation of resolutions imposing economic sanctions will be addressed differently according to whether or not the respondent State is a member of the EU. The criterion of 'equivalent protection' is only applicable in the former scenario. And in any event, it needs to be applied cautiously on a case-by-case basis, bearing in mind that the prospect of EU accession to the ECHR has receded following the ECJ's opinion 2/13, and that, as a result, the protection of human rights is still not complete in Europe.

As regards the enforcement of economic sanctions by non-EU member States, the Court tends to interpret Security Council resolutions in a manner consistent with the obligations deriving from the ECHR. Without ruling out the applicability of Article 103 of the Charter in the circumstances of each individual case, such an approach seeks to avoid a conflict of obligations, and thus tension between the UN and ECHR systems. The Court favours an integrated and harmonized interpretation and application of (potentially conflicting) obligations of States under the two systems. In other words, the Court's approach is oriented towards systemic harmonization rather than towards normative conflict. At the same time, the Security Council should continue to improve the sanctions process through greater observance of the principles of the rule of law. The Court, for its part, can only affirm and consolidate its role in guaranteeing the fundamental values of European public order.

12

Punitive Damages in Strasbourg

Paulo Pinto de Albuquerque and Anne van Aaken

1. Introduction

'Punitive damages' have long been a controversial topic of discussion in national as well as in international law.[1] This is no different for the European Court of Human Rights (ECtHR or the Court). 'Punitive damages' is the preferred expression in the United States, Canada, and continental Europe, while the term 'exemplary damages' is used in other Commonwealth countries; however, they both refer to the same concept, just as 'aggravated damages' do. Punitive or exemplary damages are understood as being established with the purpose of atoning for the deeds of the wrongdoer and preventing repetition of the wrongful act by the offender, or emulation by third parties, without being limited to mere compensation for the pecuniary and non-pecuniary losses caused to the claimant, including loss of profit.

The Court's Practice Directives of March 2007 and January 2016 on 'Just Satisfaction'[2] state that '[t]he purpose of the Court's award in respect of damage is to compensate the applicant for the actual harmful consequences of a violation. It is not intended to punish the Contracting Party responsible. The Court has therefore, *until now*, considered it inappropriate to accept claims for damages with labels such as "punitive", "aggravated" or "exemplary" '. One would thus expect that punitive damages are not used by the Court. But is this really the case?

The purpose of this chapter is, first, to argue that this Practice Directive is no longer up to date[3] in that the Court uses punitive damages implicitly, and, second, that there are well-established social-science reasons why punitive damages should be used.

[1] Henry Brooke, 'A Brief Introduction: The Origins of Punitive Damages' in Helmut Koziol and Vanessa Wilcox (eds), *Punitive Damages: Common Law and Civil Law Perspectives* (Springer 2009) 2.

[2] Para 9, Practice Directive issued by the President of the Court in accordance with Rule 32 of the Rules of Court on 28 March 2007 and with the same wording, Para 9, *Practice Directive, Just Satisfaction* of 1 January 2016, available at <http://www.echr.coe.int/Documents/PD_satisfaction_claims_ENG.pdf> accessed 29 September 2017 (emphasis added).

[3] cf in the same vein Dinah Shelton, *Remedies in International Human Rights Law* (3rd edn, OUP 2015) 412–13.

The chapter proceeds as follows: The first part establishes that the Court has already changed its course and uses punitive damages, albeit rather implicitly (2). The second part shows that punitive damages are on the rise and not necessarily prohibited in international and European Law (3). The third part provides the social-science rationale why punitive damages should be used in certain cases. The idea of 'punitive damages' is strongly connected to the effectuation of law. Whenever enforcement might be weak, eg, because victims tend not to bring claims for different reasons, 'punitive damages' can set the correct incentives for following the law. This assumption has most explicitly been discussed in the economic analysis of law, on which we will draw (4). The last part concludes (5).

2. Establishing Punitive Damages in the ECtHR

'Just satisfaction' under Article 41 of the European Convention on Human Rights (ECHR or the Convention) means mostly monetary compensation for the damage suffered by the victim of a human rights violation. It may include pecuniary, as well as non-pecuniary (moral or immaterial), damage, as well as costs and expenses.[4] We argue that there are instances in which the damages awarded include, implicitly, punitive damages in its calculation.

Let´s go step by step. The Court clearly endorsed a position in favour of punitive damages in the recent case of *Nagmetov v Russia.*[5] In view of the fact that it had found a double violation in respect of the fundamental right under Article 2 of the ECHR on account of the use of firearms by the police causing the death of the applicant's son, the shortcomings in the investigation, and that over nine years had passed after the events without any monetary award having been made at the domestic level, the Court considered that the applicant must have suffered anguish and distress which cannot be compensated for by a mere finding of a violation. Having regard to the above considerations, the Court found it appropriate and necessary in the particular circumstances of the case to award the applicant, on an equitable basis, a sum of 50,000 euros (EUR), in respect of non-pecuniary damage, plus any tax that may be chargeable to him, in spite of the fact that the applicant had not submitted a claim for just satisfaction on account of non-pecuniary damage, and the respondent government had acknowledged, before the Court, the violation under the material limb of Article 2 of the Convention. The Court could not have taken a more explicit position in favour of punitive damages.

[4] cf Szilvia Altwicker-Hámori, Tilman Altwicker, and Anne Peters, 'Measuring Violations of Human Rights: An Empirical Analysis of Awards in Respect of Non-Pecuniary Damages under the European Convention on Human Rights' (2016) 76 Heidelberg Journal of International Law 1 for an empirical assessment of the Court's awards in respect of non-pecuniary damages.

[5] *Nagmetov v Russia* App no 35589/08 (ECtHR, 5 November 2015) confirmed by the Grand Chamber on 30 March 2017, paras 69 and 73: '[D]amage occurred as a result of a breach of a fundamental human right and reflect in the broadest of terms the severity of the damage'; para 81: 'Where the Court envisages of its own motion a just-satisfaction award on account of non-pecuniary damage, it is appropriate to take into account the particular gravity and the particular impact of the violation of the Convention (for instance, on account of its nature or degree)'.

In fact, punitive damages had already been established previously by the Grand Chamber in the case of *Cyprus v Turkey* (Just Satisfaction).[6] According to the claimant State, just satisfaction should be provided to the lawful heirs of 1,456 missing persons and to all the Greek Cypriots living in the Karpas region between 1974 and the date of the Grand Chamber judgment on the merits in May 2001. The respondent State disputed these figures as merely 'hypothetical', maintaining that the number of missing persons may have varied over time, some of them might have left no lawful heirs, and it was simply impossible to identify all the residents of the Karpas region since 1974. The Grand Chamber found that it was not necessary to establish the exact number of individual victims of human rights violations, and fixed two lump sums for the benefit of each of these groups of persons, with the obligation for the claimant State to distribute the monetary amounts to the victims or their lawful heirs. In fact, the number of missing persons has decreased in view of the exhumations carried out in recent years, and the victims in the Karpas region are neither identified nor identifiable solely on the basis of the evidence in the file. The Court did not even require, as the claimant State had proposed, that the number of Karpas residents be agreed between the parties or, in the absence of agreement, established by the President of the Court 'on the basis of written evidence and submissions as to the number and location of residents and their heirs'. Furthermore, the Court did not establish any criteria, practical arrangements, or rates governing the distribution of the compensation among the victims or their lawful heirs according to their individually differing circumstances (eg, wives, mothers, children), and most importantly it did not impose any condition regarding the devolution of the compensation in cases where the victims and their lawful heirs are not found. In this event, the claimant State will be the final beneficiary of the amounts paid by the respondent State.

The punitive nature of this compensation is flagrant. In spite of the fact that the identity of the victims of the respondent State's actions and omissions and the ensuing massive and gross human rights violations committed in the Karpas enclave could not be established, that the missing-persons claims would have been time-barred if lodged individually by their respective families, and that there can be no certainty that the indemnities obtained will devolve to the individuals concerned, the Court punished the respondent State for its unlawful actions and omissions and their harmful consequences.

There is nothing new about this procedure. As a matter of fact, the practice of the Court shows that punitive damages have been applied in seven types of cases. First, the Court has ordered compensation without any claim for just satisfaction being lodged by the applicant at all. On the basis of the 'absolute character' of the violated right,[7] the 'particularly serious character of the

[6] *Cyprus v Turkey* (Just Satisfaction) [GC] App no 25781/94 (ECtHR, 12 May 2014).

[7] *Chember v Russia* App no 7188/03 (ECtHR, 3 July 2008) para 77 (10,000 euros); *X v Croatia* App no 11223/04 (ECtHR, 17 July 2008) para 63 (8,000 euros); *Igor Ivanov v Russia* App no 34000/02 (ECtHR, 7 June 2007) para 50 (5,000 euros); *Mayzit v Russia* App no 63378/00 (ECtHR, 20 January 2005) paras 87–88 (3,000 euros); and *Nazarenko v Ukraine* App no 39483/98 (ECtHR, 29 April 2003) para 172 (2,000 euros).

violations',[8] the 'gravity of the violations',[9] or the 'fundamental importance of that right',[10] the Court is ready to order compensation for violations of Articles 3 and 5 without any claim being made for specific damages. In other cases, the applicant asks the Court to be compensated but does not specify the amount, and the Court orders what it finds to be fair in the particular case.[11] We submit that in those cases 'fairness' includes the same considerations as described above. There are also cases in which the applicant makes a claim for just satisfaction specifying a particular amount for non-pecuniary damage, but in which the Court awards a higher amount.[12] When the Court awards compensation for an amount higher than the alleged damage, or even independently of any allegation of damage, the nature of the just satisfaction is no longer compensatory; instead, we deem it punitive since it surpasses the amount claimed, ie, the harm suffered by the victim. The inherent purpose of that remedy is not to place the injured party in the position in which he or she would have been had the violation not taken place, since the injured party claims to have suffered lesser damage or does not even claim to have sustained any damage. The fundamental purpose of that remedy is, hence, to punish the wrongdoing State and prevent a repetition of the same pattern of wrongful action or omission by the respondent State and other Contracting Parties to the Convention.

Secondly, the Court has in some cases established a 'symbolic' or 'token indemnity',[13] with the obvious purpose of blaming and shaming the respondent State, thus making the punishment an example for other States.

Thirdly, the Court has also awarded just satisfaction in cases in which the applicant complained about the domestic law without indicating any personal specific damage other than the distress caused by the existence of the law itself.[14] It is clear that the just satisfaction award is then an exemplary punishment of the respondent State for having legislated in a way incompatible with the Convention.

[8] *Bursuc v Romania* App no 42066/98 (ECtHR, 12 October 2004) para 124 (10,000 euros). This criterion is also coded by Altwicker et al (n 4) 25–40 finding that violations of 'life, physical and mental integrity' receive the highest amount of damages.

[9] *Gorodnitchev v Russia* App no 52058/99 (ECtHR, 24 May 2007) para 143 (10,000 euros).

[10] *Rusu v Austria* App no 34082/02 (ECtHR, 2 October 2008) para 62 (3,000 euros); *Crabtree v The Czech Republic* App no 41116/04 (ECtHR, 25 February 2010) para 60 (2,000 euros); and *Khudyakova v Russia* App no 13476/04 (ECtHR, 8 January 2009) para 107 (5,000 euros).

[11] For example, *Celik and Yildiz v Turkey*, App no 51479/99 (ECtHR, 10 November 2005) paras 30–31, and *Davtian v Georgia* App no 73241/01 (ECtHR, 27 July 2006) para 70.

[12] For instance, *Stradovnik v Slovenia* App no 24784/02 (ECtHR, 13 April 2006), paras 23–25, in which the Court awarded 6,400 euros for the excessive length of the proceedings, when the applicant had asked for 5,000 euros.

[13] For example, *Engel and Others v The Netherlands* (Article 50) App nos 5100/71, 5101/71, 5102/71, 5354/72, and 5370/72 (ECtHR, 23 November 1976) para 10 (100 Dutch guilders); and *Vaney v France* App no 53946/00 (ECtHR, 30 November 2004) para 57 (one euro).

[14] For instance, in *SL v Austria* App no 45330/99 (ECtHR, 9 January 2003), the Court made an award for non-pecuniary damage, even though the impugned provision of the Austrian Criminal Code had already been repealed and the applicant had therefore 'achieved in part the objective of his application'.

Fourthly, the Court has ordered just satisfaction for a 'potential violation' of the Convention.[15] Here again, the purpose of just satisfaction is to censure and punish the respondent State's conduct rather than to compensate for damage, which has not yet occurred.

Fifthly, the Court has not even excluded the possibility that the applicant suffered, as a result of the 'potential effects of the violation found', a loss of real opportunities of which account must be taken 'notwithstanding the fact that the prospects of realisation would have been questionable'.[16] In these particular cases, just satisfaction does not even remedy a virtual harm done to the applicant, since it is doubtful that it would ever have materialized. It is the fault-based conduct of the respondent State that the Court wants to punish.

Sixthly, the Court sometimes even awards compensation in spite of the lack of supporting documents, and contradictions in the statements made by the applicants regarding the losses claimed.[17] When no evidence of the alleged damage is produced, the award of damages lies entirely at the discretion of the Court. In these circumstances of total lack of evidence and discretionary award of damages, just satisfaction has an inherent element of punishment, since it does not remedy a proven damage, which remains speculative, but instead punishes the respondent State's wrongful conduct.

Seventhly, in cases of general interest, the Court determines just satisfaction taking into account its exemplary effect.[18]

In other words, the existence of punitive or exemplary damages under the Convention is an indisputable fact in the Court's practice, with the Court, both in its Grand Chamber and Chamber formations, having overcome step by step the classical paradigm of the Draft Articles on State Responsibility which indicate that the purpose and scope of reparation are limited to remedial measures, thus excluding punitive damages.[19]

As Shelton holds, the Court 'has a stronger textual basis for awarding punitive damages, as there is clear precedent for punitive damages in the arbitral decisions on state responsibility for injury to aliens. The term "satisfaction" has a broader meaning than is reflected in the judgments of the European Court'.[20] Since just satisfaction is only to be awarded when the domestic legal order has not provided full reparation, Article 41 ECHR excludes any compensation exceeding

[15] For example, *Mokrani v France* App no 52206/99 (ECtHR, 15 July 2003) para 43, and *Gürbüz v Turkey* App no 26050/04 (ECtHR, 10 November 2005) para 75 (see the critical opinion of Judges Caflisch and Türmen).

[16] *Sporrong and Lönnroth v Sweden* (Article 50) (1984) Series A no 88, para 25; *Bönisch v Austria* (Article 50) (1986) Series A no 103, para 11 App no. 8658/79; and *Sara Lind Eggertsdóttir v Iceland* App no 31930/04 (ECtHR, 5 July 2007) para 59.

[17] For example, *Barberà, Messegué and Jabardo v Spain* (Article 50) (1994) Series A no 285-C, paras 18–20, App no 10588/83; 10589/83; 10590/83 (leave in Art. 50); despite the fact that the decisions of the Spanish courts subsequent to the principal judgment had already afforded the applicants reparation for non-pecuniary damage.

[18] For example, *Xenides-Arestis v Turkey* (Just Satisfaction) App no 46347/99 (ECtHR, 7 December 2006) and *Ananyev and Others v Russia* App nos 42525/07 and 60800/08 (ECtHR, 10 January 2012).

[19] See the Commentary to Articles 36 and 37 of the Draft Articles on State Responsibility.

[20] Shelton (n 3) 417.

full reparation, but 'full' reparation can only be achieved if and when the need for prevention and punishment in the specific circumstances of the case has also been satisfied. Only then is satisfaction 'just'.[21] Compensation for quantifiable losses may not be sufficient and the obligation of full reparation may include punitive damages that go beyond remedying the pecuniary and non-pecuniary damage caused to identified persons.

3. Punitive Damages in International and European Law

Punitive damages are still controversial in international law. In the following, we will analyse punitive damages in treaty and case law in general international law (3.1), in European Union Law (3.2), by the Council of Europe (3.3), and other human rights bodies[22] (3.4). This will show that the use of punitive damages is gaining ground.

3.1 General public and private international law

The Court's case law is not isolated within the framework of international law. Early cases in international law were qualified as rewarding punitive damages, especially for wrongdoing against foreigners.[23] As Whiteman holds: 'At times, the excess in the amount of damages awarded over the actual loss or injury may [...] be accounted for in part by the fact that the [...] persons making the award were influenced by the seriousness of the part taken by the respondent state in the incident out of which the claim arose. Such damages might well be considered punitive in their nature, although they are not so denominated.'[24] Nevertheless, it is impossible to say that they were generally accepted,[25] not even in cases of international crimes and human rights violations.[26]

The International Law Commission (ILC) also discussed punitive damages. In the First Report on State Responsibility of 1956 the then-Special Rapporteur, Garcia-Amador, stated: 'The purpose of reparation is not necessarily solely restitution or compensation for material damage. "Reparation" measures may also have a punitive function. In such cases the measures in question should be regarded as a penalty, applicable to the party guilty of the act giving rise to responsibility.' He continued

[21] The question of how damages should be measured is still unclear, but financial just satisfaction can be made under three headings: pecuniary loss, non-pecuniary loss, and costs and expenses. Robin CA White and Clare Ovey, *The European Convention on Human Rights* (5th edn, OUP 2010) 44.

[22] UN Treaty bodies have not discussed punitive damages—the issue has arisen mostly in regional human rights courts.

[23] For a discussion of the cases, see Nina HB Jørgensen, *The Responsibility of States for International Crimes* (OUP 2000) 187 et seq.

[24] Marjorie M Whiteman, *Damages in International Law* (US Government Printing Office 1937) 628.

[25] Jørgensen (n 23) 200 et seq: 'Despite the fact that none of the tribunals in these cases spoke of punitive damages, most commentators at the time agreed that the idea of punishment could be part of the concept of damages.'

[26] Eg, *Corfu Chanel case (UK v Albania)* [1949] ICJ Rep 4, 23.

by saying that: 'The character and measure of reparation should be determined by reference to the extent of the damage caused and to the seriousness of the act giving rise to responsibility, and also by reference to the purpose which the reparation is to serve.'[27] The second Report on State Responsibility of 1989 by Special Rapporteur Arangio-Ruiz also referred to punitive damages:

> To confine the consequences of any international delict (let alone an international crime) to restitution in kind and pecuniary compensation would mean to overlook the necessity of providing some specific remedy—having a preventive as well as a punitive function—for the moral, political and juridical wrong suffered by the offended state or states in addition to, or instead of, any amount of material damage.[28]

In contrast, the final Articles on State Responsibility (ARSIWA)[29] hold in the commentary to Article 36 that '[c]ompensation corresponds to the financially assessable damage suffered by the injured State or its nationals. It is not concerned to punish the responsible State, nor does compensation have an expressive or exemplary character.'[30] The ILC also states that 'just satisfaction' under Article 37 is 'not intended to be punitive in character, nor does it include punitive damages'.[31]

To sum up: It seems that, currently, punitive damages are awarded rather covertly so that they are indistinguishable from compensation in its narrow sense, although the degree of wrongfulness of the act in question is likely to be a relevant factor in determining the quantum of damages.[32] As Jørgensen holds: '[T]he idea that pecuniary reparation can exceed the limits of restitution, and in some instances go beyond even moral damages and amount to punishment, would seem to be a general principle of law, and it could be that practice is simply lagging behind principle.'[33] This would be in line with taking a more public law approach to international responsibility, and moving away from the private law, purely interstate paradigm.[34]

27 (1956) II ILC Yearbook, 220.

28 (1989) II(1) ILC Yearbook, 41.

29 Articles on the Responsibility of States for Internationally Wrongful Acts, (2001) II(2) ILC Yearbook.

30 ibid para 4.

31 ibid, para 8. Similarly, Stephan Wittich, 'Compensation', *Max Planck Encyclopedia of Public International Law* (online edn, 2008) para 10 <http://legal.un.org/ilc/texts/instruments/english/draft_articles/9_6_2001.pdf> accessed 11 July 2018: 'In particular, compensation does not have the purpose of punishing the responsible State, nor does it have an expressive, vindictive, or exemplary character by deterring blameworthy conduct.' See also para 44 for an assessment of punitive damages in international law. Nevertheless, he states that for the calculation of compensatory damages several factors can be taken into account, including 'the conduct of the parties before, during, and even after the breach [which] may have a significant influence on the amount of compensation [. . .] Finally, all the (other) circumstances of the breach will have to be taken into account when assessing the amount of compensation due—eg whether the breach is a continuing one, whether the wrongdoing State has repeatedly acted unlawfully, the gravity of the breach, or the concern to reach an equitable and acceptable outcome' (para 13).

32 Jørgensen (n 23) 206.

33 ibid.

34 See for a discussion, André Nollkaemper and Dov Jacobs, 'Shared Responsibility in International Law: A Conceptual Framework' (2013) 34 Michigan Journal of International Law 359, 401 et seq. They hold that international 'responsibility traditionally has served the interests of individual states (rather than the public interest)'. Under a public law concept as followed in ARSIWA, responsibility 'thus is not contingent upon a showing that a disputed act has caused injury to a state or other person to

In the field of private international law,[35] neither the New York Convention on the Recognition and Enforcement of Foreign Arbitral Awards of 10 June 1958, nor the Hague Convention on the Recognition and Enforcement of Foreign Judgments in Civil and Commercial Matters of 1 February 1971, make reference to punitive damages as a ground for refusing recognition and enforcement of an arbitral award or a foreign judgment. Furthermore, Article 29 of the Montreal Convention for the Unification of Certain Rules for International Carriage by Air of 28 May 1999 provides that punitive damages shall not be recoverable. Article 11(1) of the Hague Convention on Choice of Court Agreements of 30 June 2005[36] provides that recognition or enforcement of a judgment may be refused if, and to the extent that, it awards punitive damages. This provision is not linked to the *ordre public* clause contained in Article 9(e), which prohibits the use of this clause to deny recognition of punitive damages awards. Article 74 of the United Nations Convention on Contracts for the International Sale of Goods of 11 April 1980 also provides that damages for breach of contract by one party may not exceed the loss, which the party in breach foresaw or ought to have foreseen at the time of the conclusion of the contract, in the light of the facts and matters of which he then knew or ought to have known, as a possible consequence of the breach of contract. Nonetheless, the United Nations Commission on International Trade Law (UNCITRAL) Digest of Case Law on the United Nations Convention on Contracts for the International Sale of Goods affirms that '[d]omestic law may also apply to issues such as punitive damages. In one case a court seemingly accepted the validity of a claim for punitive damages in the context of a CISG damages claim, although the determination of the amount of damages was left open'.[37] Punitive damages are inter alia allowed in England, South Africa, and the United States and common law systems are generally more open to them. They are neither new nor limited to a few countries only; on the contrary, they are found in legal systems throughout the world.[38] Even those systems which do not expressly allow them, and even deny them, sometimes covertly use them.[39] Whereas they are still rare in international commercial arbitration, there are legal developments, especially concerning the enforcement of awards under the New York Convention, leading to their rise.[40]

whom an international obligation is owed, but rather is premised on the notion of an illegal act. In this construction, the law of international responsibility does not only protect the rights of injured parties but protects the international legal order as such against acts that violate international law' (footnotes omitted).

[35] For an overview, see Marta Requejo Isidro, 'Punitive Damages From a Private International Law Perspective' in Helmut Koziol and Vanessa Wilcox (eds), *Punitive Damages: Common Law and Civil Law Perspectives* (Springer 2009) 237–55.

[36] Entry into force 1 October 2015; 44 ILM 1294 (2005).

[37] 2012 edn, 346.

[38] Shelton (n 3) 403.

[39] For an overview, see Koziol and Wilcox (n 35); Shelton (n 3) 403–4; and Melvin M Belli, Sr, 'Punitive Damages: Their History, Their Use and Their Worth in Present-Day Society' (1980) 49 UMKC L R 1.

[40] Markus A Petsche, 'Punitive Damages in International Commercial Arbitration: Much Ado about Nothing?' (2013) 29 Arbitration International 89.

3.2 Punitive damages in European Union law

The 'position of the European Union regarding punitive damages is not only ambivalent, but also clearly self-contradictory', according to Gerhard Wagner.[41] While punitive damages may not be required, it nevertheless seems clear that they may be acceptable in some instances.[42] In some legal areas of the European Union, like the regulation of the agricultural and the securities markets, there has been a policy of punitive civil claims being allowed. Article 18 of Regulation No 1768/95 refers to 'special civil law claims' and Article 28 of Directive 2004/109/EC refers to 'civil and/or administrative penalties'.[43] This trend has been endorsed by the Court of Justice in both *Von Colson and Kamann v Land Nordrhein Westfalen*[44] and *Harz v Deutsche Tradax GmbH*,[45] in which the Court of Justice considered that compensation must be sufficient to act as a deterrent against sex discrimination in employment. In *Manfredi v Lloyd Adriatico et al*,[46] the Court of Justice went even further, establishing that, in accordance with the principle of equivalence, national courts could award punitive damages for breaches of then-EC competition law if, and when, such damages were also available for breaches of national law. Punitive damages somehow sneaked into the concept of 'effective, proportionate and dissuasive' sanctions.[47] In particular, the 'dissuasive' aspect hints to the possibility of sanctions, including damages, which deter future undesired behaviour. We will discuss the rationale for this in section 4.

Furthermore, it can be argued that, within the European Union, there has been an acknowledgment of the extra-compensatory purposes of civil liability and, consequently, of the legitimacy of punitive damages when they are not excessive. Regulation (EC) No 864/2007 of the European Parliament and of the Council of 11 July 2007 on the law applicable to non-contractual obligations (Rome II)[48] states that:

> The application of a provision of the law designated by this Regulation which would have the effect of causing non-compensatory exemplary or punitive damages of an excessive nature to be awarded may, depending on the circumstances of the case and the legal order of the Member State of the court seized, be regarded as being contrary to the public policy (*ordre public*) of the forum.[49]

[41] Gerhard Wagner, 'Neue Perspektiven im Schadensersatzrecht—Kommerzialierung, Strafschadensersatz, Kollektivschaden, Gutachten für den 66. Deutschen Juristentag' in *Verhandlungen des 66. Deutschen Juristentages* (Vol 1, Part A Stuttgart 2006) A 71.

[42] cf Shelton (n 3) 418.

[43] See for further issue areas and an overview, Bernhard A Koch, 'Punitive Damages in European Law' in Koziol and Wilcox (n 35) 197–209.

[44] Case 14/83 *Von Colson and Kamann v Land Nordrhein Westfalen* [1984] ECR 1892.

[45] Case C-79/83 *Dorit Harz v Deutsche Tradax GmbH* [1984] ECR 1922.

[46] Joined cases C-295/04 to C-298/04 *Vincenzo Manfredi v Lloyd Adriatico et al* [2006] ECR I-6641.

[47] This 'boiler-plate' language has since then often been used. It first appeared in Case C-68/88 *Commission v Hellenic Republic* [1989] ECR 2965 (no 24). The matter concerned measures member States have to take in order to respond to Community law infringements.

[48] OJ C 289/3, 28 November 2006.

[49] Recital 32 of the preamble to the Rome II Regulation.

Yet it is relevant to note that the provision of Article 24 of the proposal for the Rome II Regulation[50] stated that 'application of a provision of the law designated by this Regulation which has the effect of causing non-compensatory damages, such as exemplary or punitive damages, to be awarded shall be contrary to Community public policy'. With the new wording, proportionate punitive damages were incorporated into European Union law.

In addition, neither Council Regulation (EC) No 44/2001 of 22 December 2000 on jurisdiction and the recognition and enforcement of judgments in civil and commercial matters, nor Council Regulation (EC) No 2201/2003 of 27 November 2003 concerning jurisdiction and the recognition and enforcement of judgments in matrimonial matters and the matters of parental responsibility refer to punitive damages as a ground for refusing recognition and enforcement of a foreign judgment.

Furthermore, the question of deterrence was clearly incorporated into the primary law of the EU in Article 260(2) and (3) of the Treaty on the Functioning of the European Union (TFEU). The provisions provide for imposing financial sanctions on member States for non-compliance with the judgments of the EU Court of Justice or the failure to transpose directives.

3.3 The Council of Europe view on punitive damages

In the Council of Europe, the Committee of Ministers noted that:

> the setting up of a merely compensatory or acceleratory remedy may not suffice to ensure rapid and full compliance with obligations under the Convention, and [. . .] further avenues must be explored, e.g. through the combined pressure of various domestic remedies (punitive damages, default interest, adequate possibility of seizure of state assets, etc), provided that their accessibility, sufficiency and effectiveness in practice are convincingly established.[51]

This clear stance in favour of punitive damages taken by the highest political body of the Council of Europe was not an isolated statement. In 2000, the Parliamentary Assembly of the Council also considered the introduction of fines to be imposed on States that persistently fail to execute the judgments of the Court, with a view to introduce more effective measures in the face of non-compliance.[52] As Shelton holds: 'Article 46 may give the Court the implied competence to condemn the state to pay exemplary damages when the state refuses to abide by a judgment.'[53] Furthermore, the Explanatory Report to the Civil Law Convention on Corruption notes that State Parties whose domestic law provides for punitive damages are not required to exclude their application in addition to full compensation.[54] In the field of social rights, the European Committee of Social Rights monitors the requirement for the damages awarded in practice to be sufficiently dissuasive to prevent future infringements.[55]

[50] COM (2003) 427. [51] Interim Resolution CM/ResDH (2008) 1 of 6 March 2008.
[52] For a discussion, see Shelton (n 3) 414. [53] ibid. [54] ETS No 174, para 36.
[55] Second Report submitted by the Government of Hungary, covering the period from 1 January 2007 until 31 December 2010, 83.

3.4 Punitive damages in the Inter-American system of human rights

In the Inter-American human rights protection system, opinions are still divided.[56] Article 63(1) of the American Convention on Human Rights[57] refers to the award of 'fair compensation'. While the Inter-American Commission has expressed itself in favour of punitive damages, or at least of a punitive aim to compensation,[58] the Inter-American Court initially had a more reserved position.[59] More recently, in the *Myrna Mack Chang* case, the Inter-American Court came close to the Commission's position by ordering the payment of aggravated damages based on the extreme seriousness of the respondent State agents' conduct.[60] It held that it 'must order payment of a compensation for non-pecuniary damages, in fairness'.[61] Since the Inter-American Court in its majority was not that explicit, it is worth quoting from the separate opinion of Judge Cançado-Trindade to a fuller extent:

> The viewpoint, espoused by the Inter-American Court of Human Rights in the past, according to which compensations "with exemplarizing or dissuasive purposes" have no place in international law, has been completely surpassed. It is in accordance with a reactionary vision, shaped by the precepts of juridical positivism, that until recently (whether consciously or not) held back development regarding this matter, and which no longer reflects [. . .] the current stage of evolution of international law in this regard. Furthermore, in my view, realization of the exemplarizing or dissuasive purposes can—and must—be sought not only through compensations, but also through other (non-pecuniary) forms of reparation. Irrespective of the civil or criminal elements of the international responsibility of the State, I believe it is undeniable that reparations can adopt a punitive or repressive nature, to ensure the realization of justice and to put an end to impunity. It is also necessary to bear in mind that, while reparations (both pecuniary and moral) benefit the injured party directly, punishment (or repressive action against the State found in violation), in turn, benefits the human community itself as a whole; not to admit this would be to allow the State found in violation to remove itself from the Law.[62]

As held by Shelton: 'The idea of "aggravated" violations is now accepted by the Inter-American Court and can be the avenue for various forms of non-pecuniary

[56] See for an overview that is critical of punitive damages, Agostina Noelia Chichero and Sebastián A Green Martínez, 'Punitive Damages and the Principle of Full Reparation in the Case Law of the Inter-American Court of Human Rights' in Yves Haeck, Oswaldo Ruiz-Chiriboga, and Clara Burbano Herrera (eds), *The Inter-American Court of Human Rights: Theory and Practice, Present and Future* (Intersentia 2015) 337–54.

[57] OAS Treaty Series no 36, 1144 UNTS 123 entered into force 18 July 1978.

[58] See Scott Davidson, *The Inter-American Human Rights System* (Dartmouth Publishing Company 1997) 217. See also the request for punitive damages in *Velasquez Rodriguez v Honduras* (Reparations and costs) judgment of 21 July 1989, para 37.

[59] *Velasquez Rodriguez* (n 58) para 38; *Godinez Cruz v Honduras* (Reparations and costs) judgment of 21 July 1989, para 36; and *Garrido and Baigorria v Argentina* (Reparations and costs) judgment of 27 August 1998, paras 43–44.

[60] *Myrna Mack Chang v Guatemala* (Merits, reparations and costs) judgment of 25 November 2003, para 246–86, and especially the separate opinion of Judge Cançado Trindade. See also Shelton, *Remedies* (n 3) 411–13 for a discussion of the case.

[61] *Myrna Mack Chang* (n 60) para 260.

[62] ibid (n 60) separate opinion of Judge Cançado Trindade, paras 36–38 (footnotes omitted).

damages.'[63] As again held by Cançado Trindade: 'Once aggravated responsibility has been accepted, its juridical consequences must be established'[64]—be they monetary or not.

4. A Social-Science Rationale for Using Punitive Damages

The primary purpose of a damages award is certainly to compensate the claimant for the harm done to her or him. The rationale of punitive damages goes further: deterrence of others and the defendant, including punishment for especially outrageous behaviour.[65] Whenever a purpose of a norm is stated, a need for a social analysis arises in order to verify whether the purpose will be fulfilled in reality. This induces analysis of the effects of law in order to put it on a better evidential base. This analysis can be based on theoretical assumptions or—even better—on empirical research. Given that there are, to our knowledge, no empirical studies in international law concerning punitive damages,[66] we base our analysis on social-science theory only. We will use the economic analysis of law concerning punitive damages as a first step and extend the analysis to behavioural economics.[67]

The classical economic analysis of law, as well as huge parts of international-relations scholarship, assume rational actors. Legal scholarship often uses this assumption implicitly. Thus, it is assumed that actors, including States, pursue their goals rationally under constraints (eg, law).[68] This means that the primary incentives are set by external constraints and behaviour adjusts accordingly. Human rights law, in this view, is an instrument that can provide behavioural incentives for the State not to engage in human rights violations. The threat of being held liable induces the State to incorporate the losses for the victims into their decision on whether, and how, to engage in certain activities. This line of reasoning implies that damages should be high enough for the State to internalize the externalities it has caused. In the case that the probability of being held liable is 100 per cent, full compensation of the harm done would, in principle,[69] be enough to deter a State from engaging in

63 Shelton (n 3) 417.

64 *Myrna Mack Chang* (n 60) separate opinion of Judge Cançado Trindade, para 41.

65 For a legal theoretical discussion, see Dorsey D Ellis, Jr, 'Fairness and Efficiency in the Law of Punitive Damages' (1982–83) 56 California Law Review 1.

66 But see for international law generally: Gregory Shaffer and Tom Ginsburg, 'The Empirical Turn in International Legal Scholarship' (2012) 106 American Journal of International Law 1.

67 A similar approach is taken by Shelton (n 3) 406, when she says: 'Punitive damages may also deter, influencing the behavior of the particular wrongdoer and all others who might be tempted to act in the same way in the future, because rational actors are assumed to weigh the anticipated costs of wrongdoing against the anticipated prospective benefit.' See also ibid 403.

68 For international law, see Andrew Guzman, *How International Law Works: A Rational Choice Theory* (OUP 2008) and Joel P Trachtman, *The Economic Structure of International Law* (Harvard University Press 2008) as well as Anne van Aaken and Joel Trachtman, 'Political Economy of International Law: Towards a Holistic Model of State Behavior' in Alberta Fabricotti (ed), *The Political Economy of International Law: A European Perspective* (Edward Elgar 2016) 9–43.

69 It might though be the case that compensation does not equal the 'gain' from the violation for the State. In that case, in order to have optimal incentives, the sanction needs to be higher than the amount of compensation.

the harmful activity.[70] There are two basic reasons in the economic analysis of law to have damages equal harm (under a strict liability rule).[71] The first is the level of precaution[72] taken by the potential violator. The second is the level of activity of a potentially harmful activity.[73] In both cases, if damage equals harm, the socially correct incentives are set.

However, there are many reasons why the probability of being held liable falls below 100 per cent and, thus, the socially desired level of precaution and level of activity is not achieved, since damages do not equal harm.[74] First, it might be difficult and costly for victims to reach the Court; many victims will never bring a case for reasons of access to justice. Secondly, victims may suffer from what is known in economic analysis of law as 'rational apathy'. Even if they might have a meritorious claim, they might find it too costly to bring a complaint when comparing the costs (not only legal costs) to the expected compensation.[75] This reasoning may apply especially if there are widespread violations which are not too grave and victims may wait for others to bring a claim (especially if a decision has a de facto *inter omnes* effect). Here, the total losses might be substantial overall, so that it would be socially advantageous if the State were to be held liable. Systemic and widespread violations are a case at hand. The idea of punitive damages, thus, also serves to overcome the problem of rational apathy. Victims who claim damages serve the social goal of deterrence.[76] Since, however, bringing a claim is costly and those costs are borne privately, not enough claims might be brought. Increasing the expected damages may solve this problem.[77] Thirdly, there might be especially

[70] The assumed calculation of the State (or any tortfeasor) is as follows: the State engages in a violation if and only if benefits outweigh the costs: B > P (H). B is the benefit of the activity for the State, P is the probability of Harm (H) which equals the compensation due. This is of course simplified in that the State is not a unitary actor (ie, those committing the violation are not necessarily those who pay) and harm done does not necessarily equal compensation, for many reasons. Furthermore, one may question whether States (entities in general) react to incentives as individuals and whether they are rational, but we rely here on a long tradition in international law and international-relations scholarship assuming rational States. After all, law is presumed (even if often implicitly) to cause reactions in its addressees. On the problem of the rationality assumption, see Anne van Aaken, 'Behavioral International Law and Economics' (2014) 55 Harvard International Law Journal 421.

[71] Since fault is not required for finding a human rights violation, the ECHR can be equated to a strict-liability regime, as in some areas of national tort law.

[72] According to economic theory, the level of precaution taken by the tortfeasor is independent from the liability regimes (strict or fault), also in a strict-liability regime, eg, product liability in some countries. A product can still be produced with more or less caution, leading accordingly to more or less damage caused.

[73] The level of activity means that a certain activity, eg, car driving, can be reduced so that it causes less harm. The same applies for human rights violations—the State can engage more or less in human rights violating activity.

[74] See for a discussion in the realm of private law Louis T Visscher, 'Economic Analysis of Punitive Damages' in Koziol and Wilcox (n 35) 219–36.

[75] cf Anne van Aaken, 'Making International Human Rights Protection More Effective: A Rational-Choice Approach to the Effectiveness of Ius Standi Provisions' in Stefan Voigt, Max Albert, and Dieter Schmidtchen (eds), *International Conflict Resolution, Conferences on New Political Economy 23* (Siebeck/Mohr 2006) 29–58.

[76] The idea that a person who fights for his rights also fights for the (rule of) law is an old one, see Rudolf von Jhering, *Der Kampf ums Recht* (6th edn, Manz 1880).

[77] cf Visscher (n 74) 224 et seq.

outrageous violations which were committed intentionally. If society views certain violations as especially unacceptable, the deterrence function of punitive damages demands stronger incentives through the imposition of higher than expected damage payments.[78] Fourthly, if the State has taken steps to avoid detection and verifiability in order to lower the probability of being convicted,[79] punitive damages can compensate that by imposing higher damage payments. Fifthly, many times, there are hard-to-measure components of harm (such as non-pecuniary losses), which are often excluded from damages, and thus damages do not equal the harm done.[80]

In all those cases, the probability of being convicted would fall under 100 per cent and, thus, the State no longer weighs the cost of violating human rights correctly—the deterrence purpose is impacted. Economic analysis is thus primarily concerned with under-detection and under-enforcement.[81] But it also takes into account systematically insufficient compensatory damages, eg, in cases of death or serious bodily injury.[82] Thus, the factor by which compensatory damages should be multiplied in those cases is the reciprocal of the probability of being held liable.[83] If, for example, the probability is 50 per cent, compensatory damages should be doubled to provide correct incentives. This reciprocal is termed the 'total damage multiplier'.[84] The punitive part then consists of total damages minus the compensatory part.

A further argument for punitive damages arises from behavioural economics, a rather new branch of economics based on psychological insights tested in lab experiments and field studies. In contrast to the rational choice assumption, people have cognitive biases, are fairer on the one hand and more spiteful on the other hand, and have only bounded willpower.[85] The economic analysis of law has traced the incentive effects of punitive damages on potential wrongdoers based on the assumption

[78] As held in *Myrna Mack Chang* (n 60) separate opinion of Judge Cançado Trindade, para 30: 'Reaction to grave and systematic violations of human rights and of International Humanitarian Law became, in our days, a legitimate concern of the international community as a whole.'

[79] cf Visscher (n 74) 223.

[80] This is not to say that there are not good reasons for the latter problem, which arises in all legal systems: cf A Mitchell Polinsky and Steven Shavell, 'Punitive Damages' in Michael Faure (ed), *Tort Law and Economics Encyclopedia of Law and Economics* (vol 1, 2nd edn, Edward Elgar 2009) 232 et seq; as well as Visscher (n 74) 225.

[81] Catherine M Sharkey, 'Economic Analysis of Punitive Damages: Theory, Empirics and Doctrine' in Jennifer H Arlen (ed), *Research Handbook on the Economics of Tort* (Edward Elgar 2013) 491.

[82] Joni Hersch and Kip Viscusi, 'Saving Lives Through Punitive Damages' (2010) 83 Southern California Law Review 229.

[83] Robert Cooter, 'Punitive Damages for Deterrence: When and How Much?' (1998) 40 Alabama Law Review 1143.

[84] AM Polinksy and S Shavell, 'Punitive Damages' in P Newman (ed), *The New Palgrave Dictionary of Economics and the Law* (1998) 193.

[85] For an overview, see Christine Jolls, Cass R Sunstein, and Richard H Thaler, 'A Behavioral Approach to Law and Economics' (1998) 50 Stanford Law Review 1471; Russell B Korobkin and Thomas S Ulen, 'Law and Behavioral Science: Removing the Rationality Assumption from Law and Economics' (2000) 88 California Law Review 1051; Cass R Sunstein (ed), *Behavioral Law and Economics* (CUP 2000); Eyal Zamir and Doron Teichman (eds), *Handbook on Behavioral Economics and the Law* (OUP 2014).

that they pursue their material advantage. Behavioural economics focuses inter alia on social norms. As Cooter holds:

> The institution of punitive damages allows judges [. . .] to express righteous anger through speech and punishment. Expression of emotions by the court demonstrates the strength of its commitment to the law in question. Perception of this commitment shapes the expectations of citizens [in our case: States] and changes their behavior.[86]

This is not the place to expand on that approach,[87] but what can be safely said is that punitive damages express a special verdict on the shamefulness of conduct. It is well established that honour, stigma, and social norms influence behaviour. Changing people's perceptions of what constitutes 'normal' behaviour or values among their peers also influences their behaviour (notwithstanding material incentives).[88] We may assume that this holds also for States.[89]

There has been a long discussion on the expressive law theory, holding that the law is more than a set of prices but also serves to convey a society's norms of behaviour.[90] This discussion has largely been theoretical, focusing on the symbolic content of legislation on drinking or smoking in public, religious displays, etc, and of course upon the question of whether a certain behaviour should be regulated by administrative or rather criminal law (the latter expressing stronger repudiation of the behaviour in question). Recently, this theory has been tested empirically and is largely confirmed.[91]

The theory of expressive adjudication focuses this research on the role of courts and their decisions.[92] The theory provides an additional explanation for adjudicative compliance that is distinct from both the court's threat of sanctions and its institutional legitimacy. It holds that 'there are certain circumstances in which adjudicative expression can, by itself, influence the behaviour of existing disputants and of future potential disputants. Here, the account of adjudication is non-coercive and "expressive" in that it focuses on what law says rather than the sanctions that law threatens'[93] (as rational choice approaches would) in order to induce compliance. This is especially important in international law. But it also leads us to stress the importance of the expressive function of punitive damages—expressing clear

[86] Robert Cooter, 'Punitive Damages, Social Norms and Economic Analysis' (1997) 60 Law and Contemporary Problems 73, 74.

[87] See extensively van Aaken (n 70).

[88] Roland Benabou and Jean Tirole, 'Law and Norms' NBER Working Paper 17579 (2011) <www.nber.org/papers/w17579> accessed 29 September 2017.

[89] For a discussion of caveats of transposing individual behavioural insights to collective actors such as states, see van Aaken (n 70).

[90] Elizabeth Anderson and Richard H Pildes, 'Expressive Theories of Law: A General Restatement' (2000) 148 University of Pennsylvania Law Review 1503; Robert D Cooter, 'Expressive Law and Economics' (1998) 27 Journal of Legal Studies 585; Richard H McAdams, 'A Focal Point Theory of Expressive Law' (2000) 86 Virginia Law Review 1649; Richard H McAdams, 'The Expressive Power of Adjudication' (2005) 5 University of Illinois Law Review 1045; Richard H McAdams, 'An Attitudinal Theory of Expressive Law' (2000) 79 Oregon Law Review 339.

[91] For an overview, see Benabou and Tirole (n 88).

[92] McAdams, 'The Expressive Power of Adjudication' (n 90).

[93] ibid 1046.

signals to the respondent State but also all other member States of the Council of Europe on the disapproval of the State's behaviour. Thus, also from a behavioural-economics point of view, punitive damages have a function which should even enhance the arguments brought forward by traditional rational choice theory.

5. Conclusion and Outlook

Summing up, the ECtHR has been at the forefront of an international trend, using just satisfaction to prevent further violations of human rights and to punish wrongdoing governments. In all the cases described, there was no explicit and exact calculation of the harm suffered by the victim, but rather an add-on to the amount awarded which is not otherwise explicable. The acknowledgment of punitive, or exemplary damages, under the Convention is essential in at least three cases: (i) gross violations of human rights protected by the Convention or the additional Protocols, especially when there are multiple violations at the same time, repeated violations over a significant period of time, or a single continuing violation over a significant period of time (eg, the killing of a political opponent or the silencing of a critical TV channel could justify such punitive damages); (ii) prolonged, deliberate non-compliance with a judgment of the Court delivered with regard to the recalcitrant Contracting Party (eg, the prolonged indifference of a State Party to a judgment of the Court, which had found it in breach of the Convention, in spite of repeated efforts of the Committee of Ministers and the injured party to have the judgment complied with); and (iii) the severe curtailment, or threat thereof, of the applicant's human rights with the purpose of avoiding, impairing, or restricting his or her access to the Court, as well as the Court's access to the applicant (eg, the use of some grave tactics to silence the applicant, such as directly or indirectly threatening his life or that of his loved ones or initiating arbitrary criminal proceedings against the applicant, like in *Oferta Plus SRL v Moldova* (Just Satisfaction)).[94] In all these three cases, the underlying premise for punitive damages is not only causality between the wrongful conduct and the harm, but also intention or recklessness (gross negligence) by the wrongdoing State—that is to say, by its organs and agents. All three instances described above (gross violations, deliberate non-compliance, and curtailing access to court) are in conformity with the social-science insights regarding when punitive damages should be used for deterrence.

Furthermore, the Court's legal and moral authority and the practical solvency of the entire European human rights protection system are particularly at stake here. The gravity of such breaches engages the interests of all Contracting Parties to the Convention, the Council of Europe as an institution, and Europe as a whole. The principle of State sovereignty cannot, in the light of Article 26 of the Vienna

[94] *Oferta Plus SRL v Moldova* (Just Satisfaction) App no 14385/04 (ECtHR, 12 February 2008), para 76.

Convention on the Law of Treaties, be invoked to justify such gross wrongdoing. As Lauterpacht put it:

> [A] violation of international law may be such that it needs, in the interest of justice, an expression of disapproval that goes beyond material reparation. To place limits on liability within the State to *restitutio in integrum* would be to abolish the criminal law and a major part of the law of torts. To abolish these aspects of liability between States would be to adopt, on the grounds of sovereignty, a principle that is repugnant to justice and carries with it an encouragement to wrongfulness.[95]

The Court correctly applies punitive damages when the general rule of law is at stake, using both, the positive incentives of punitive damages for the applicants overcoming rational apathy as well as the negative incentives for States violating the Convention. It does so presumably to set a signal also for other member States, and thus to strengthen its own authority and with it human rights protection in Europe. Following behavioural insights, using punitive damages may also send strong signals to other States that a certain behaviour is highly reproachable, and thus induce better compliance even without strong sanctioning mechanisms, which is especially important in international law.

Whereas, between sovereign nations, the question of the power to impose penalties is political rather than legal in nature, if there is no court adjudicating the case, the conclusion is different between nations bound by a human rights treaty, such as the Convention, which confers rights on natural and legal persons and imposes negative and positive obligations on the Contracting Parties enforceable by an international court through binding judgments. Within this framework, just satisfaction by means of punitive damages does not entail a sanction applied by one State against another, but instead corresponds to an authoritative and indispensable response by an international court to the wrongdoing State. The Court speaks then on behalf of all the Contracting Parties, acting as the ultimate defender of a Europe rooted in the rule of law and faithful to human rights. This is in line with the object and purpose of the Convention. To overlook the need for such a response would in turn encourage States, especially the most powerful ones, to assume that human rights violations can easily be made good by mere pecuniary compensation. Moreover, in determining punitive damages the Court acts, as we have identified, within the boundaries established by the principle of proportionality and with full regard to such factors as the objective gravity of the wrongful conduct, the degree of reprehensibility of the intention or recklessness of the wrongdoer, the extent of the harm caused to the applicant and third parties, the consequential gains obtained by the wrongdoer and third parties, and the probability of non-enforcement of the breached right. Therefore, punitive damages are an appropriate and necessary instrument for fulfilling the Court's mission to uphold human rights in Europe and to ensure the observance of the engagements undertaken by the Contracting Parties in the Convention and the Protocols thereto.

[95] Hersch Lauterpacht, 'Règles Générales du Droit de la Paix' (1937) 62 Recueil des Cours de l'Academie de Droit International 350.

Furthermore, this direction might be the way international law is moving. Is the 'private law' approach in international law, holding on to the principle of reparation of harm done that must be compensated, still adequate? Or can the other goal of deterrence be captured by other incentives for norm conformity of States? The ARSIWA have on the whole moved in this direction. Pellet talks about a 'revolution' in international law.[96] Damage is not a prerequisite for responsibility; rather it is necessary and sufficient under Articles 1 and 2 of the ARSIWA that only two elements are present: breach and attribution. This imposes a responsibility of conduct, not result (as in administrative law, in which a fine can be imposed for crossing a red light without injuring anyone). This move towards an 'objectification'[97] of international responsibility (or the public law dimension)[98] that stresses the second goal: the deterrence or incentive function. In times of increasing global public goods, including human rights as a normative public good, those functions might become more important. Punitive damages may serve to effectuate the *inter omnes* obligations of States, as well as the human rights of the peoples of the Council of Europe.

[96] Alain Pellet, 'The Definition of Responsibility in International Law' in J Crawford et al (eds), *The Law of International Responsibility* (OUP 2010) 9.

[97] ibid 8, 15, and 9: '[I]nternational law must be respected independently of the consequences of a violation and any breach entails the responsibility of its author.'

[98] Nollkaemper and Jacobs (n 34) 401 et seq. See also George Abi-Saab, 'The Uses of Article 19' (1999) 10 European Journal of International Law 339, 350–51: '[T]o defend the normative integrity of the legal system itself against patterns of behaviour which go against its most fundamental principles and thus undermine its regular functioning and credibility [. . .] It can legitimately be feared that setting aside the dual regime of responsibility would be widely perceived as a reversal of the evolution of general international law from a community-oriented system back to a purely intersubjective one.'

PART V
IMMUNITY

13

A Moving Target

The Approach of the Strasbourg Court to Immunity

*Philippa Webb**

1. Introduction

The law of immunity is dynamic. The last 50 years have seen significant changes in the doctrine and practice. The European Court of Human Rights (ECtHR) has, over the past fifteen years in particular, played an influential role in the law applicable to this 'moving target'. It has decided cases on the invocation of immunity in proceedings relation to territorial torts, employment disputes, enforcement of judgments and awards, international organizations, and damages for grave violations of human rights.[1]

The ECtHR has expressly acknowledged that State immunity is a concept of international law and part of the body of relevant international law that its interpretation of the European Convention of Human Rights (ECHR) must take into account.[2]

In this chapter, I will discuss three approaches of the ECtHR to the identification of general international law in cases involving the immunities of States, officials, and international organizations: the ECtHR looking to the International Court of Justice (ICJ); the ECtHR looking to national practice; and the ECtHR looking to the work of the International Law Commission (ILC) and the provisional application of treaties.

I argue that although the ECtHR strives to locate itself within general international law, it necessarily approaches questions of immunity through the lens of Article 6 ECHR (section 2 of this chapter). This has, at times, taken the Court down a different

* I am grateful to Lady Hazel Fox QC and Andrew Sanger for insightful conversations about this topic, and to the conference participants, the editors of this volume, and the reviewers for their valuable feedback. I thank Freya Foster and Rishi Gulati for research assistance.

[1] T Schilling, 'The Case-Law of the European Court of Human Rights on the Immunity of States' in Anne Peters et al (eds), *Immunities in the Age of Global Constitutionalism* (Brill Nijhoff 2015) 267 at 270–1.

[2] *Al-Adsani v The United Kingdom* [GC] App no 35763/97 (ECtHR, 21 November 2001) 123 ILR 24, para 54; *Kalogeropoulos v Greece and Germany* App no 59021/00 (ECtHR, 12 December 2002) 129 ILR 537.

path to other judicial bodies. In the specific field of the employment exception to immunity, we can identify the emergence of a 'European approach' (part 3).

The chapter concludes with some brief reflections on the evolution of the law of immunity at the ECtHR, including whether the Court's concepts of 'alternative measures of compliance' and 'reasonable alternative means of redress' may infiltrate general international law to provide a route to greater accountability (part 4). Accountability is understood not in the narrow legal sense of gaining access to court and an enforceable remedy, but in a broad sense of receiving some measure of redress and acknowledgment, including outside of the courtroom, for violations of rights.

2. Approaches of ECtHR to Identifying General International Law

The ECtHR is mindful of the Convention's 'special character as a human rights treaty' and has sought to interpret it in harmony with general international law.[3] To this end, it pays attention to the case law of the ICJ and national courts, as well as the work of the ILC, in seeking to identify the general international law applicable to a case.

2.1 Looking to the ICJ

The ICJ and the ECtHR have in recent years been looking to each other's jurisprudence. President Spielmann and former ICJ President Rosalyn Higgins have observed that courts of The Hague and Strasbourg could 'be perceived as partners for the protection of human rights'.[4] This is true across a range of topics, including immunity. In most cases this symbiotic relationship is to be welcomed—it enhances the coherence of international law, providing certainty to applicants and States. But there may be situations where this partnership may sometimes be misplaced or go too far, given the different mandates, applicable law, and membership of the two courts.

In *Jones v The United Kingdom* (2014),[5] the fourth section of the ECtHR referred to the ICJ judgments in *Arrest Warrant*,[6] *Djibouti v France*[7] and, most importantly,

[3] *Loizidou v Turkey* App no 15318/89 (ECtHR, 18 December 1996) para 43.

[4] Speech given on the occasion of the opening of the judicial year, 30 January 2009, by Rosalyn Higgins, President of the ICJ, 'The International Court of Justice and the European Court of Human Rights: Partners for the protection of human rights' in *Dialogue between Judges* (European Court of Human Rights, Council of Europe 2009) 99–113. Cited by Dean Spielmann, President of the ECtHR, in 'Fragmentation or Partnership? The Reception of ICJ case-law by the European Court of Human Rights' in Andenas and Bjorge (eds), *A Farewell to Fragmentation. Reassertion and Convergence in International Law* (CUP 2015) 173.

[5] *Jones v The United Kingdom* App nos 34356/06 and 40528/06 (ECtHR, 14 January 2014).

[6] *Arrest Warrant of 11 April 2000 (Democratic Republic of the Congo v Belgium)* (Judgment) [2002] ICJ Rep 3.

[7] *Certain Questions of Mutual Assistance in Criminal Matters (Djibouti v France)* (Judgment) [2008] ICJ Rep 177.

Jurisdictional Immunities of the State.[8] The Chamber acknowledges[9] that the ICJ emphasized in the *Jurisdictional Immunities* judgment that it was addressing 'only the immunity of the State itself from the jurisdiction of the courts of other States; the question of whether and to what extent immunity might apply in criminal proceedings against an official of the State is not in issue in the present case'.[10] Yet, the ECtHR followed the ICJ's judgment with respect to the immunity of State officials, as well as that of the State. In the *Jurisdictional Immunities* judgment, the ICJ had been silent as to immunity of a State official from civil proceedings, but it was clear that the judgment was focused on the State itself and, arguably, even limited to 'acts committed on the territory of the forum State by the armed forces of a foreign State [. . .] in the course of conducting an armed conflict'.[11]

The ICJ's earlier judgment in the *Arrest Warrant* case had only addressed the immunity of high-ranking officials (immunity *ratione personae*) so the *Jones v The United Kingdom* judgment was an opportunity for the ECtHR to consider the immunity *ratione materiae* of lower ranking officials in civil proceedings. The Chamber took the 'general international law' to be that pronounced by the ICJ. As others have pointed out, the Chamber did not conduct a substantive proportionality assessment, including considering whether alternative means of redress existed.[12] The ECtHR's judgment in *Jones* was welcomed by the UK government, but caused dismay for civil society.[13] Constituencies engaged in human rights litigation will have to reassess and reorient their strategies by, for example, bringing criminal instead of civil proceedings, using non-judicial methods such as publicity or negotiation, or encouraging a willing third State to bring a case in an international court.[14]

In *Stichting Mothers of Srebrenica v The Netherlands*,[15] the third section also relied on the ICJ *Jurisdictional Immunities* judgment, as well as *Bosnia v Serbia*[16] and the *Cumaraswamy* advisory opinion.[17] This time the Chamber extended the ICJ's reasoning in *Jurisdictional Immunities* from States to the United Nations, finding that a civil claim should not override immunity from suit for the sole reason that it was based on an allegation of a particularly grave violation of a norm of international law, even a peremptory norm.[18] The *Mothers of Srebenica* have pursued their claims

[8] *Jurisdictional Immunities of the State (Germany v Italy: Greece intervening)* (Judgment) [2012] ICJ Rep 99.

[9] *Jones* (n 5) para 92.

[10] *Jurisdictional Immunities* (n 8) para 91.

[11] ibid para 65.

[12] See the chapter by Riccardo Pavoni in this volume.

[13] See, eg, L McGregor, 'Jones v UK: A Disappointing End' (2014) EJIL: *Talk!* <http://www.ejiltalk.org/jones-v-uk-a-disappointing-end/> accessed 23 May 2018.

[14] See, eg, *Questions relating to the Obligation to Prosecute or Extradite (Belgium v Senegal)* [2012] ICJ Rep 422.

[15] *Stichting Mothers of Srebrenica v The Netherlands* App no 65542/12 (ECtHR, 11 June 2013).

[16] *Application of the Convention on the Prevention and Punishment of the Crime of Genocide (Bosnia and Herzegovina v Serbia and Montenegro)* (Judgment) [2007] ICJ Rep 43.

[17] *Difference Relating to Immunity from Legal Process of a Special Rapporteur of the Commission on Human Rights* (Advisory Opinion) [1999] ICJ Rep 62.

[18] *Stichting Mothers of Srebrenica* (n 15) para 158.

against The Netherlands, as a national State of the battalion of peacekeepers who were at Srebrenica. They have met with some success in the Dutch courts.[19]

The applicants in *Stichting Mothers of Srebrenica* had argued that there was an absence of an alternative remedy if the Dutch courts did not set aside the United Nations' immunity.[20] The agreement on the status of the United Nations Protection Force in Bosnia and Herzegovina of 15 May 1993[21] required that a claims commission be set up, but this had not been done. In fact, no UN peacekeeping mission has ever established a claims commission even though this is a standard provision in peacekeeping agreements.[22] The applicants argued that domestic proceedings thus represented their only opportunity for redress.

In this situation, the ECtHR had a choice between two approaches to determining the availability of immunity: (i) its own jurisprudence in cases involving international organizations or (ii) the ICJ's holding on State immunity in the *Jurisdictional Immunities* Judgment. Under the first approach, the ECtHR had held in *Waite and Kennedy*[23] and *Beer and Regan*[24] that a 'material factor', in determining whether granting an international organization immunity from domestic jurisdiction was permissible under the ECHR, was whether the applicants had available to them 'reasonable alternative means' to protect effectively their Convention rights. This involved consideration of the availability and quality of an internal justice system for resolving disputes between employees or contractors and the international organization.

Under the second approach, in *Jurisdictional Immunities* the ICJ had firmly rejected conditioning the entitlement to State immunity on the availability of an effective alternative remedy.

> Neither in the national legislation on the subject, nor in the jurisprudence of the national courts which have been faced with objections based on immunity is there any evidence that entitlement to immunity is subjected to such a precondition. States also did not include any such condition in either the European Convention or the United Nations Convention.[25]

The Chamber in *Stichting Mothers of Srebrenica* chose to follow the ICJ and somewhat cryptically dismissed the first approach by saying, '[a]s regards international organisations, this Court's [ECtHR] judgments in *Waite and Kennedy* and *Beer and*

[19] In July 2014, the Hague District Court ordered The Netherlands to compensate the families of more than 300 men who had been turned over to Bosnian Serb forces and later killed. It held that Dutch UN peacekeepers should have known that the men, deported from the Dutch compound by Bosnian Serb forces on 13 July 1995, would be killed. Case 195247 HA ZA 07-2973 *Mothers of Srebrenica v State of the Netherlands*, 16 July 2014.

[20] *Stichting Mothers of Srebrenica* (n 15) paras 161–63.

[21] 1722 UNTS 77, Article 48.

[22] M Zwanenberg, 'UN Peace Operations Between Independence and Accountability' (2008) 5 IOLR 23, 27. See also Bruce Rashkow, 'Remedies in response to harm caused by UN peacekeeping activities' (2014) AJIL Unbound <https://www.asil.org/blogs/remedies-harm-caused-un-peacekeepers> accessed 23 May 2018. Instead, the UN tends to establish 'local claims review boards' which consist entirely of members of the peacekeeping operation. Their impartiality is therefore open to question.

[23] *Waite and Kennedy v Germany* [GC] App no 26083/94 (ECtHR, 18 February 1999) para 68.

[24] *Beer and Regan v Germany* [GC] App no 28934/95 (ECtHR, 18 February 1999) para 58.

[25] *Jurisdictional Immunities* (n 8) para 101.

Regan cannot be interpreted in such absolute terms either'.[26] The Chamber went on to observe that Article 6 of the ECHR did not require the Netherlands to step into the vacuum left by the UN's failure to set up a dispute-settlement system for such cases.[27] Notably, the Strasbourg court has applied the 'reasonable alternative means' or 'equivalent protection' test in other international-organization cases involving targeted sanctions.[28]

As evidence emerges of the UN's alleged complicity in human rights violations with respect to cholera in Haiti or sexual assault in the Central African Republic, calls for accountability have grown stronger,[29] but they have not resulted in the setting aside of immunity in the courtroom. Thousands of Haitians filed a class action against the UN in the United States for, among other things, its failure to screen Nepalese peacekeepers who introduced cholera to Haiti. US courts held that the UN enjoys immunity from jurisdiction under Section 29 of the General Convention.[30]

The UN has the option of responding to claims by waiving its immunity, or through impartial assessment by standing claims commissions, or another mechanism. It has refused to pursue these options in the Haiti cholera case. Instead, in August 2016, UN Secretary-General Ban acknowledged 'moral responsibility' and stated he was putting together a compensation package for Haitian victims.[31] This

[26] *Stichting Mothers of Srebrenica* (n 15) para 164.

[27] ibid para 165.

[28] *Al-Dulimi And Montana Management Inc v Switzerland* App no 5809/08 (ECtHR, 26 November 2013). In the Grand Chamber decision of 23 June 2016, the Court rejected the equivalent-protection test in the circumstances of the case, finding that Switzerland was not faced 'with a real conflict of obligations capable of engaging the primacy rule in Article 103 of the UN Charter. This finding makes it unnecessary for the Court to determine the question of the hierarchy between the obligations of the States Parties to the Convention under that instrument, on the one hand, and those arising from the UN Charter, on the other [...] The Court's finding similarly renders nugatory the question whether the equivalent protection test should be applied [...] Consequently, the respondent State [...] should persuade the Court that it has taken—or at least has attempted to take—all possible measures to adapt the sanctions regime to the individual situation of the applicants, at least guaranteeing them adequate protection against arbitrariness' (para 149).

[29] *Report of an Independent Review on Sexual Exploitation and Abuse by International Peacekeeping Forces in the Central African Republic* (17 December 2015) recommends, inter alia, that when a troop-contributing country 'initiates proceedings with a view to prosecuting sexual offenses by one of its peacekeeping troops, the UN should facilitate these processes [... I]mmunity should not be a bar to UN officials and experts on mission when they are called to testify as witnesses to crimes of sexual violence. In particular, where the UN has itself referred the alleged incident of sexual violence to the responsible national authorities for investigation or prosecution, there should be a presumption that UN staff will cooperate in the legal proceedings. The Office of Legal Affairs should adopt an approach to immunity that presumes cooperation and active participation of UN staff in accountability processes; immunity should stand only in circumstances where the UN has determined that disclosure of information by staff members could result in a security threat to the victims or witnesses, or where the victim did not provide his or her informed consent to the disclosure of the information' (at xii).

[30] *Georges and Others v United Nations and Others*, US District Court, Southern District of New York, 9 January 2015; upheld on appeal, *Georges v United Nations*, No 15–455 (2d Cir 2016). Approximately 9,500 Haitians have died from cholera since the outbreak and over 800,000 have been ill.

[31] The statement followed a report by Philip Alston, Special Rapporteur on Extreme Poverty and Human Rights, that stated: 'The United Nations was clearly responsible and it must now act accordingly [... W]hat is at stake is the Organization's overall credibility in many different areas. Its existing position on cholera in Haiti is at odds with the positions that it espouses so strongly in other key policy areas. It has a huge amount to gain by rethinking its position and a great deal to lose by stubbornly maintaining

acknowledgment of moral responsibility is a first step, but without legal backing it may prove to be an empty promise. As of August 2017, the UN Haiti Cholera Response Multi-Partner Trust Fund has raised less than 1 per cent of its target amount.[32]

In the absence of adequate remedies, victims and their supporters are likely to continue to seek justice before national, regional, and international courts. The ECtHR may well find more such cases on its docket in the future.

2.2 Looking to national courts

When the ECtHR looks to national courts, it often has to assess whether their decisions constitute 'international custom, as evidence of a general practice accepted as law'.[33] In *Al-Adsani* and *Jones*, careful attention has been paid to national practice (both cases and legislation). In *Jones*, the Chamber explored practice in the US, Canada, New Zealand, Australia, Italy, Greece, Poland, France, and Slovenia, finding that 'State practice on the question [of an exception to immunity of State officials when accused of torture] is in a state of flux, with evidence of both the grant and the refusal of immunity *ratione materiae* in such cases'.[34] Despite this 'state of flux'—this moving target—the Chamber was 'satisfied that the grant of immunity to the State officials in the present case reflected generally recognised rules of public international law'.[35]

One could say that this was a missed opportunity to engage in the type of in-depth analysis and 'reflection' that the Chamber acknowledged was still 'required' regarding the relationship between civil and criminal immunity, and the question of whether torture can be committed in an 'official capacity' for immunity purposes.[36]

One important aspect of the law in which the ECtHR has taken a different approach to national courts is the relationship between Article 6 of the ECHR, immunity and jurisdiction.

The ECtHR has held that the right of access to a court is an inherent part of the right to a fair trial under Article 6(1) of the ECHR.[37] Different approaches have emerged to the question of whether State immunity is actually a restriction on the right of access to a court:[38]

1. The ECtHR has treated immunity as prima facie interfering with the right of access to court.

its current approach': (2016) UN Doc A/71/367, para 73. On 1 December 2016, Secretary-General Ban offered an apology to Haitians on behalf of the UN and acknowledged the UN's moral, if not legal, responsibility. He said he was 'profoundly sorry' and urged member States to raise up to US$400 million to treat and cure Haiti's cholera victims. Boon, 'The United Nations as Good Samaritan: Immunity and Responsibility' (2016) 16 Chicago JIL 341.

[32] <http://mptf.undp.org/factsheet/fund/CLH00> accessed 23 May 2018.

[33] Article 38(1)(b) of the ICJ Statute.

[34] *Jones* (n 5) para 213.

[35] ibid para 215.

[36] ibid para 212; C Keitner, '*Jones v United Kingdom*' (2014) 108 AJIL 302.

[37] *Golder v The United Kingdom* App no 4451/70 (ECtHR, 21 February 1975) para 36.

[38] Andrew Sanger, 'State Immunity and the Right of Access to a Court under the EU Charter of Fundamental Rights' (2016) 65 ICLQ 213, 221.

2. Some UK courts have opined that the right of access to a court is *not* engaged where international law requires States to grant immunity because the grant of immunity deprives the court of jurisdiction *ab initio*.[39] Lord Hoffmann in *Jones v Saudi Arabia* explained that 'there is not even a *prima facie* breach of Article 6 if a State fails to make available a jurisdiction which it does not possess'.[40] Lord Bingham agreed: 'I do not understand how a state can be said to deny access to its court if it has no access to give.'[41]

The significance of this divergence in practice was highlighted in *Benkharbouche and Janah v Embassy of Sudan and Libya*,[42] a case on employment decided in 2015 by the UK Court of Appeal and upheld by the Supreme Court in 2017. Lord Justice Lloyd Jones in the Court of Appeal favoured the approach taken by other UK courts:

> Article 6 cannot have been intended to confer on Contracting States a jurisdiction which they would not otherwise possess, nor could it have conferred a jurisdiction denied by general international law in such a way as to be binding on non-Contracting States. It is unfortunate that in none of its many decisions in which the point has been raised has the Strasbourg court grappled with these considerations.[43]

It may be true that the ECtHR has not expressly grappled with these issues, but its jurisprudence has been constant in finding that Article 6 is prima facie engaged in immunity cases.

It has held, time and again, that:

1. 'the grant of sovereign immunity to a State in civil proceedings pursues the legitimate aim of complying with international law to promote comity and good relations between States through the respect of another State's sovereignty',[44] and
2. 'measures taken by [States] which reflect generally recognized rules of public international law on State immunity cannot *in principle* be regarded as imposing a disproportionate restriction on the right of access to a court as embodied in Article 6(1).'[45]

[39] ibid 221.

[40] *Jones v Saudi Arabia* [2006] UKHL 26, (2007) 1 AC 270, 2006 2 WLR 1424, para 64.

[41] ibid para 14.

[42] *Benkharbouche & Anor v Embassy of the Republic of Sudan (Rev 1)* [2015] EWCA Civ 33; *Benkharbouche v Secretary of State for Foreign and Commonwealth Affairs* [2017] UKSC 62 .

[43] ibid para 16.

[44] *Al-Adsani* (n 2) 40, para 54. See also *Kalogeropoulou and Others v Greece and Germany* App nos 3456/06 and 40528/06 (ECtHR, 14 January 2014) 546; *Fogarty v United Kingdom* [GC] App no 37112/97 (ECtHR, 21 November 2001) 123 ILR 53, 65, para 34; *McElhinney v Ireland* [GC] App no 31253/96 (ECtHR, 21 November 2001) 123 ILR, 85, para 35; *Cudak v Lithuania* [GC] App no 15869/02 (ECtHR, 23 March 2010) para 60; *Sabeh El Leil v France* [GC] App no 34869/05 (ECtHR, 29 June 2011) para 52; *Wallishauser v Austria* [First Section] App no 156/04 (ECtHR, 17 July 2012) para 64; *Oleynikov v Russia* [First Section] App no 36703/04 (ECtHR, 14 March 2013) para 60; *Jones v Saudi Arabia* UKHL para 188.

[45] *Fayed v UK* App no 17101/90 (ECtHR Chamber, 21 September 1994) para 65, cited in *Al-Adsani* (n 2) para 47. *Kalogeropoulou* (n 44).

This separation of the questions of immunity and jurisdiction accords with the general international law position set out by the ICJ in its *Arrest Warrant* judgment:

> [R]ules governing the jurisdiction of national courts must be carefully distinguished from those governing jurisdictional immunities: *jurisdiction does not imply absence of immunity, while absence of immunity does not imply jurisdiction.*[46]

As Sanger observes, the right of access to a court in Article 6 does not confer jurisdiction on a national court: it requires that the court exercise jurisdiction that it already possesses, but might not have chosen to exercise pursuant to a rule of international law.[47]

In the event, the English Court of Appeal in *Benkharbouche* held that it was 'not necessary for [it] to choose between these competing approaches',[48] and that the grant of immunity to Libya and Sudan conflicted with the applicants' right of access to a court: the relevant provisions of the UK State Immunity Act were found to be incompatible with Article 6 ECHR and were disapplied pursuant to Article 47 of the EU Charter on Fundamental Rights, insofar as the claims concerned rights under European law.

2.3 Looking to the work of the International Law Commission and the provisional application of treaties

The ECtHR has also looked to the work of the ILC and the application of treaties of limited membership (eg, European Convention on State Immunity 1972 (ECSI)) or treaties not yet in force (2004 UN Convention on the Jurisdictional Immunities of States and their Property (UNCSI)) as part of its desire to locate itself within general international law.

UNCSI only has twenty-one of the thirty required ratifications to enter into force,[49] but the ECtHR has held that it reflects customary international law applicable to any State that:

1. Has not objected to the UN Convention's adoption;[50]

[46] *Arrest Warrant* (n 6) para 59 (emphasis added).

[47] Sanger (n 38) 224–25. The right is a limitation on the national courts' discretion on the exercise of jurisdiction.

[48] The approach of the Strasbourg court would not result in a Contracting State being held to be in breach of Article 6 simply because it gave effect to a rule of international law requiring the grant of immunity. In any such case, the grant of immunity would be held to be a proportionate means of achieving a legitimate aim. Under the Strasbourg jurisprudence, any debate as to what are the applicable rules of international law is transferred to a later stage of the analysis and addressed in the context of Article 6 (*Benkharbouche* (n 42) para 16).

[49] As of 1 July 2016.

[50] *Cudak* (n 44) paras 66–67. See also *Naku v Lithuania And Sweden* App no 26126/07 (ECtHR, 8 November 2016) Section IV, holding that the access to court of a former employee of the Swedish Embassy in Vilnius had been violated by Lithuanian courts upholding the immunity of Sweden. Lithuania did not vote against the adoption of the text of Articles 5, 6 and 11 of UNCSI but has not ratified the Convention either (para 60).

2. Has not objected to the adoption of a specific rule in the ILC Draft Articles;[51]
3. Signed the UN Convention;[52] or
4. Was in the process of ratifying the UN Convention.[53]

In *Cudak*, the Court quoted the ILC commentary to Article 11 which stated that 'the rules formulated in Article 11 appeared to be consistent with the emerging trend in the legislative and treaty practice of a growing number of states'.[54] The Court then made the leap from the 1991 Draft Articles to the 2004 UN Convention, and from an 'emerging trend [. . .] in a growing number of States',[55] to widespread and representative State practice accompanied by *opinio juris*.[56]

According to the ECtHR, a State's participation in the negotiation or adoption of UNCSI makes it 'possible to affirm that [a draft article] applies to the respondent state under customary international law'.[57] In the *Oleykinov* judgment, the Court held that Russia appears to have accepted restrictive immunity as a principle of customary international law even prior to its signature of the UN Convention by not (persistently) objecting to the 1991 ILC Draft Articles.[58]

The Court's approach to the identification of custom has been labelled as 'casual'.[59] Professor Pavoni, writing in this volume, also raises this critique. The embrace of the UNCSI, either in whole or in part, is somewhat surprising when contrasted with the extensive surveys of State practice and *opinio juris* by the Strasbourg Court in *Jones v The United Kingdom* and the ICJ in *Jurisdictional Immunities*. Even then, both courts acknowledged the 'flux' in practice and apparently left the door open to future developments.

At the other end of the spectrum, we have the position of the Office of the Commissioner of the Ministry of Foreign Affairs of China in the *FG Hemisphere* case (Hong Kong Court of Final Appeal), arguing that the fact China signed the UN Convention was merely 'to express China's support of the [. . .] coordination efforts made by the international community' and could not provide evidence of the adoption of the restrictive doctrine by China.[60]

[51] *Wallishauser v Austria* [First Section] App no 156/04 (ECtHR, 17 July 2012) para 69. The ILC Draft Article 11 (1991) and Article 11 of UNCSI (2004) are not identical. No finality on the formulation of the exception to immunity for employment in Article 11(2)(a) had been reached in 1991 and the eventual UNCSI Article 11 'is the product of the later extensive deliberations in the Working Group of the UN's Sixth Committee': H Fox and P Webb, *The Law of State Immunity* (3rd rev edn, OUP 2015), 452. See also Riccardo Pavoni's chapter in this volume.

[52] *Oleynikov* (n 44) para 67.

[53] *Sabeh El Leil* (n 44) para 58.

[54] *Cudak* (n 44) paras 66–67.

[55] ibid para 66.

[56] *North Sea Continental Shelf (Federal Republic of Germany/Netherlands)* (Judgment) [1969] ICJ Rep 3, para 73.

[57] *Cudak* (n 44) para 67.

[58] *Oleykinov* (n 44) paras 67–68.

[59] R Van Alebeek, 'Oleynikov Judgment on State Immunity' (2013) ECHR Blog<http://echrblog.blogspot.co.uk/2013/03/oleynikov-judgment-on-state-immunity.html> accessed 19 October 2015. See also Case C-154/11 *Mahamdia v People's Democratic Republic of Algeria* [2012] ECR I-309, Opinion of AG Mengozzi.

[60] *Democratic Republic of Congo and others v FG Hemisphere Associates LLC*, Hong Kong Court of Final Appeal (CFA) 8 June 2011, 147 ILR 376, para 46.

3. A 'European Approach' to Employment Cases

As discussed in the previous part, the ECtHR has endorsed Article 11 of UNCSI (and Article 11 of the ILC Draft Articles before that) as part of general international law. This part will show how this has resulted in the emergence of a distinct 'European approach' to employment disputes involving both States and international organizations.

The ECtHR has applied the right of access to court to the public service and to State employees pursuant to ECHR, Article 6(1).[61] It has expressly referred to Article 11 of UNCSI and Article 5 of ECSI.

While the Court upheld State immunity regarding an employment claim in the *Fogarty* case, the claim was for reinstatement of an employee in a post in its diplomatic mission. This fell within the 'three Rs' (recruitment, renewal, and reinstatement), which remain within the sovereign domain of States in employment disputes, as recognized in Article 11(2)(c) of UNCSI. The ECtHR noted the absence of 'any trend towards the relaxation of the rule of immunity as regards issues of recruitment'.[62]

In other cases, however, the Court has set aside State immunity to clear the way for aggrieved employees to bring domestic proceedings. In *Cudak v Lithuania, Sabeh El Leil v France, Wallishauser v Austria*, and *Naku v Lithuania and Sweden*, the Court adopted the wording of Article 11 of UNCSI in determining whether the retention of immunity by the foreign State employer or its security interest barred a claim brought by an employee in a court of the forum State in the territory where employment takes place.

The increasing engagement of the Strasbourg Court in the regulation of employment disputes has been criticized as channelling the international rules of State immunity into a regional approach that is not necessarily accepted elsewhere, including in the US. Such criticisms concern not only the courts taking little account of the merits of internal, alternative dispute-resolution procedures, but also the lack of recognition of the flexibility of contract as a method of providing a fair allocation of the conflicting interests of all parties.[63]

The European approach has been followed by national courts. In *Benkharbouche*, the UK Court of Appeal removed the immunity of Sudan and Libya in what has been called a 'dramatic extension of the principle of effectiveness of EU law'.[64] It seems to offer potential claimants the chance to directly enforce EU fundamental rights both (i) in spite of State immunity and (ii) against non-EU states.[65]

[61] *Vilho Eskelinen v Finland* [GC] App no 63235/00 (ECtHR, 19 April 2007).

[62] *Fogarty* (n 44) para 38.

[63] Fox and Webb (n 51) 447. This of course is subject to the power imbalance that exists between a State and its employee.

[64] L Rodgers, 'Immunity and the Public/Private Boundary in EU Employment Law' (2015) 6(1) European Labour Law Journal 48, 63.

[65] ibid. Sanger observes that this may also lead to an 'arbitrary distinction' in the UK between human rights claims that involve EU law, where the conflicting domestic law will be disapplied, and human rights claims that 'only' come within the ECHR, where the remedy would be a declaration of

Moreover, in the international organizations context, European host States may find themselves in a 'catch-22':[66] if the host State denies access to courts by upholding the immunity of the international organization, it violates Article 6 ECHR. If the host State does grant access to court, it potentially violates the provision of the headquarters agreement on recognizing the international organization's immunity. Krieger suggests viewing Article 6 ECHR as an obligation to renegotiate the headquarters agreement,[67] but it is more likely that international organizations will weigh the risks and perhaps decide to relocate their headquarters outside of Europe.

Having said that, in a 2015 case on international organization immunity, the ECtHR noted that while there is a current trend in international law towards a relaxation of the rule of state immunity as regards a State's employment disputes with staff, particularly in diplomatic missions abroad, it is 'not aware of any such trend in international law in relation to the jurisdictional immunity of international organizations, as opposed to that of States'. Moreover, the case involved recruitment, which remains protected by State immunity.[68]

Any claim to the development of a 'European approach' must also take into account what is happening in Luxembourg. The Court of Justice of the European Union (CJEU) has not yet faced the question of state immunity head-on. In the *Mahamdia* judgment the CJEU looked at the issue from the perspective of Regulation 44/2001 on jurisdiction in civil matters. The Advocate-General was sceptical of the ECtHR's finding that UNCSI Article 11 is customary international law:[69]

> [I]t must also be acknowledged that no theory of State immunity from jurisdiction has really emerged. Returning to the State as an employer, national approaches are very varied and national courts sometimes give preference to the nature of the functions performed, sometimes the purpose of those functions and sometimes the nature of the contract. [...] These national differences are so pronounced that any codification at international level is very difficult and may even cast doubt on the actual existence of a rule of customary international law in this regard which is any more than an undeniable tendency [...] The case-law of the European Court of Human Rights does not offer a much more convincing answer.

4. The Evolution of the Law on Immunity at the ECtHR

The ECtHR occupies a special place in the evolving law on immunity. On the one hand, it decides complex immunity cases using the standard of 'generally recognized rules of public international law' as the determining factor for decision. It has a higher throughput of such cases than the ICJ or CJEU, issuing approximately 1000

incompatibility with the UK Human Rights Act: A Sanger, 'The State Immunity Act and the Right of Access to a Court' (2014) 73 Cambridge Law Journal 1, at 4.

66 Krieger, 'Immunität: Entwicklung und Aktualität als Rechtsinstitut' (2014) 46 Berichte der Deutschen Gesellschaft für Völkerrecht 233, at 252–53.

67 ibid.

68 *Klausecker v Germany* [Fifth Section] App no 415/07 (ECtHR, 6 January 2015) para 75.

69 *Mahamdia* (n 59) paras 23–25; see also para 26 for specific comments on *Cudak*.

judgments per year since 2011.[70] It has become the 'de facto court of appeal' on controversial immunity issues.[71]

On the other hand, the ECtHR is required to judge all immunity cases through the lens of Article 6 of the ECHR—the right of access to a court. This can restrict and perhaps distort its ability to consider all the legal aspects of a case. In *Jones v The United Kingdom*, for example, the Chamber did not engage in a close examination of the 'official' nature of torture or the differences, if any, between civil and criminal proceedings. The right in Article 6 calls for regulation by the state. The right is subject to limitations and the ECtHR has developed principles which allow a margin of appreciation to the Contracting State in respect of such limitations, but not where it does not pursue a legitimate aim and does not have a relationship of proportionality between the means employed and the aim to be achieved.[72]

In immunity cases involving human rights violations, the ECtHR has accepted that the restriction on the right of access to court imposed by immunity is *proportionate* as long as it respects generally recognized rules of public international law.[73] But in other cases, such as those involving the immunity of international organizations, the Strasbourg Court has assessed *proportionality* in terms of whether there are alternative means of redress.[74]

The ECtHR's requirements of legitimate aim and proportionality when applied to the bar of immunity in human rights violations cases may have too readily been assumed to be satisfied and incapable of any review. Nevertheless, the possibility of two other approaches is already present in the Court's case law: (i) alternative measures of compliance and (ii) reasonable alternative means of redress.

The first approach comes from the *Nada* case, where the ECtHR ruled that, where a question arises as to the hierarchy between the obligations under the ECHR on the one hand and under the UN Charter on the other, 'for a measure to be regarded as proportionate and as necessary in a democratic society, *the possibility of recourse to an alternative measure that would cause less damage to the fundamental right at issue whilst fulfilling the same aim must be ruled out*'.[75] In that case, the applicant was the subject of a sanctions regime that Switzerland interpreted as preventing him not only from entering Switzerland but also from leaving the enclave of Campione d'Italia, even to travel to any other part of Italy, the country of which he was a national.[76] The Court held that Switzerland should have allowed some alleviation of the sanctions regime, having regard to the realities of the applicant's nationality, age, and health.[77]

The *Nada* decision has potential relevance to assessing whether State immunity is an acceptable bar to human rights complaints. The ECtHR ruled that reliance on the overriding effect of a Security Council Chapter VII Resolution did *not*

[70] European Court of Human Rights, Annual Report 2014, 171.
[71] Van Alebeek (n 59). [72] Fox and Webb (n 51) 69.
[73] *Al-Adsani* (n 2); *Jones* (n 5); T Schilling (n 1) 281.
[74] *Waite and Kennedy* (n 23) paras 68–70; *McElhinney* (n 44) para 39. This is explored in the chapters by Vice-President Raimondi and Professor Pavoni in this volume.
[75] *Nada v Switzerland* [GC] App no 10593/08 (ECtHR, 12 September 2012) para 183 referring to *Ahmed and Others v HM Treasury* [2010] UKSC 2, 2 WLR 378. Emphasis added.
[76] ibid para 189. [77] ibid para 195.

exempt Switzerland from seeking alternative ways of compliance to accommodate the applicant's claim. One could argue by analogy that immunity's requirement of respect for another State's sovereignty may be accommodated by proof that immunity's legitimate aim has not been exceeded by the making of a complaint in respect of human rights.[78]

The second approach—reasonable alternative means of redress—comes from *Waite and Kennedy* and *Beer and Regan*. In these cases the Court balanced the granting of jurisdictional immunity against the availability of other dispute settlement mechanisms: 'reasonable alternative means to protect effectively [the applicants'] rights under the Convention'.[79] Peters has seen such language as an indication that the 'balancing-approach' is gaining ground in international and domestic case law.[80] If this balancing approach was applied in cases like the Haiti cholera litigation, it would be apparent that victims have no 'reasonable alternative means' of redress. In those circumstances, the ECtHR's own jurisprudence (which it did not apply in the *Mothers of Srebrenica* case, discussed earlier) endorses the setting aside of immunity in order to uphold the right of access to court of the victims.

Both of these approaches depart from that taken by the ICJ in *Jurisdictional Immunities*, but they enhance the possibility of accountability for human rights violations. The ECtHR has to examine whether its desire to locate itself in general international law requires it to follow the principal judicial organ of the UN in these matters. As the emerging de facto court of appeal on immunity, the ECtHR has the potential to lead us into an age of greater accountability for human rights violations balanced by the certainty and coherence that states and international organizations need to function at the highest level.

[78] Fox and Webb (n 51) 47.

[79] *Waite and Kennedy* (n 23) para 68.

[80] Anne Peters, 'Immune against Constitutionalisation?' in Peters et al (n 1) 1, 14.

14

The Myth of the Customary Nature of the United Nations Convention on State Immunity: Does the End Justify the Means?

*Riccardo Pavoni**

1. Introduction

According to the European Court of Human Rights (ECtHR), questions of foreign State immunity are governed by customary international law, 'the codification of which is enshrined'[1] in the not-yet-in-force 2004 UN Convention on Jurisdictional Immunities of States and Their Property[2] (UNCSI). Perhaps, this statement is meant to be qualified to the effect that the UNCSI as a whole may, *in principle*, be regarded as a reflection of customary law. This qualification would imply a case-by-case review of the actual customary status of the various provisions in the UNCSI.

Yet in all relevant decisions so far,[3] the ECtHR has upheld the customary character of the UNCSI norms at play, namely the employment exception in Article 11,[4] the rules on service of process on foreign States in Article 22,[5] and the commercial

* This chapter reviews developments in case law and State practice up to 1 October 2017.

[1] *Sabeh El Leil v France* App no 34869/05 (ECtHR, 29 June 2011) para 18; *Wallishauser v Austria* App no 156/04 (ECtHR, 17 July 2012) para 30; *Wallishauser v Austria (No 2)* App no 14497/06 (ECtHR, 20 June 2013) para 39; *Radunović and Others v Montenegro* App nos 45197/13, 53000/13, and 73404/13 (ECtHR, 25 October 2016) para 41.

[2] General Assembly Res 59/38, annex, 2 December 2004, not yet in force. As of 15 July 2018, 22 States have ratified or acceded to the Convention, whereas, under Article 30, the deposit of 30 instruments of ratification or accession is necessary for its entry into force.

[3] For the sake of accuracy, in *Wallishauser (No 2)* (n 1) para 72, the Court refrained from addressing the customary status of Part IV (Articles 18–21) UNCSI relating to State property immunity from execution ('even if it were established that the content of Articles 18 to 21 of the 2004 Convention were applicable as rules of customary international law . . . ').

[4] *Cudak v Lithuania* App no 15869/02 (ECtHR, 23 March 2010) paras 66–67; *Guadagnino v Italy and France* App no 2555/03 (ECtHR, 18 January 2011) para 70; *Sabeh El Leil* (n 1) paras 54, 57, 58; *Wallishauser* (n 1) para 71; *Radunović* (n 1) paras 69, 73; *Naku v Lithuania and Sweden* App no 26126/07 (ECtHR, 8 November 2016) para 89.

[5] *Wallishauser* (n 1) para 69.

exception in Article 10.[6] This position has paved the way for findings of violation of the right of access to a court under Article 6 of the European Convention on Human Rights (ECHR), as the respondent States had granted immunity inconsistently with the UNCSI. Whereas, on the strength of the existing case law, the ECtHR has confirmed that such grants of immunity are a *legitimate* means 'of complying with international law to promote comity and good relations between States',[7] it has nonetheless held them *disproportionate* restrictions on the right to a court for being at variance with the 'generally recognised rules of public international law'[8] purportedly contemplated by the UNCSI.

Sections 2 and 3 critically discuss the ECtHR's jurisprudence based on the UNCSI in order to shed light onto its problematic aspects from both a methodological and interpretative viewpoint. It is submitted that the ECtHR's approach to the identification of customary law in this area is superficial, that its wholesale recognition of the customary status of the UNCSI is mistaken, and that a number of its interpretations of the relevant UNCSI provisions are questionable.

Yet the chapter seeks to enquire into the unprofessed reasons which may lie behind this jurisprudence. One may argue that this bold jurisprudence, which finds against States that have acted upon the 'holy' doctrine of State immunity, is a *means* for the Strasbourg Court to vindicate its role as a human rights champion in an area where it has frequently been accused of unwarranted deference and timidity towards national bodies. It is well known that several consistent decisions of the ECtHR, such as *Al-Adsani* and *Jones*, have dismissed a general human rights exception to State immunity, even when the most serious violations of international law were at stake. In the ECtHR's opinion, denials of individual justice arising from grants of immunity to foreign States accused of torture or war crimes do not violate the ECHR. Unsurprisingly, UNCSI's silence on this issue has been a significant factor in reaching those decisions.

By contrast, faced with a set of norms contained in a treaty authoritatively arising from the UN system and restricting State immunity in areas such as labour, commerce, or property, the ECtHR may have favoured a consequentialist posture. In other words, it may have taken the view that the ultimate *end* of safeguarding individual rights impaired by controversial—ie, inconsistent with the UNCSI as read by the ECtHR itself—grants of immunity would justify every legal *means*, however questionable, such as a lenient approach to customary law. Rigour and accuracy would significantly get lost in the process, but the final balance struck between human rights

[6] *Oleynikov v Russia*, App no 36703/04 (ECtHR, 14 March 2013) paras 61, 66, 68.

[7] See, eg, *Jones and Others v United Kingdom* App nos 34356/06 and 40528/06 (ECtHR, 14 January 2014) para 188.

[8] *Jones* (n 7) para 189. This controversial approach to the test for justifying restrictions on ECHR rights arising from grants of State immunity goes back to a well-known trio of cases adjudicated by the ECtHR in 2001: see *Al-Adsani v United Kingdom* App no 35763/97 (ECtHR, 21 November 2001) paras 54–56; *McElhinney v Ireland*, App no 31253/96 (ECtHR, 21 November 2001) paras 35–37; *Fogarty v United Kingdom* App no 37112/97 (ECtHR, 21 November 2001) paras 34–36. Whereas in these, and subsequent cases, the test benefited the impugned national decisions because they were deemed in line with general international law and could not thus, *in principle*, be viewed as disproportionate restrictions on the right to a court, it struck back against respondent States in the context of the UNCSI jurisprudence discussed in the text.

and State immunity may turn out to be reasonable. Obviously, the ECtHR cannot undertake such an operation in a (perceived) vacuum. It is precisely for this reason that the UNCSI becomes a reputable written text coming to the rescue of the Court, ie, a sort of fetish to be invoked, albeit rather loosely, in order to show the soundness of the decisions handed down in State immunity cases. However, it is not to be taken for granted that the ECtHR's calculus has been accurate in this area, ie, that the Court has carefully pondered the pros and cons of its UNCSI jurisprudence. The dilemma remains as to whether the end justifies the means. Thus, section 4 seeks to go beyond issues of form and process, and assesses instead the extent to which the ECtHR's decisions at stake should be endorsed for substantive reasons relating to their practical implications for the protection of human rights adversely affected by grants of foreign State immunity. A few final remarks follow (section 5).

2. Outsourcing the Identification of Customary Law on State Immunity to the International Law Commission: The *Cudak* Jurisprudence

Cudak[9] represents the leading judgment of the ECtHR's UNCSI jurisprudence. It involved a complaint under Article 6 brought by a former switchboard operator of the Polish embassy in Vilnius on account of the immunity granted to Poland in compensation proceedings relating to her dismissal. The Court declared that the employment exception to State immunity formulated in 'Article 11 of the International Law Commission's 1991 Draft Articles, on which the 2004 Convention was based, applie[d] to the respondent State under customary international law'.[10] The underlying suit was found to be within the terms of that exception, because none of the several counter exceptions contemplated in the provision at stake was relevant.[11] The respondent State's decision to uphold immunity was disproportionate to the legitimate aim pursued and, therefore, amounted to a violation of the right of access to a court.[12] As a matter of fact, *Cudak* bestowed the status of *rule of decision* on the UNCSI and related texts of the International Law Commission[13] (ILC) for all immunity cases concerning legal

[9] *Cudak* (n 4). [10] ibid para 67. [11] ibid paras 69–72.
[12] ibid paras 74–75.
[13] See especially 'Draft Articles on Jurisdictional Immunities of States and Their Property and Commentaries Thereto' (1991) II(2) ILC Yearbook, 13. The juxtaposition of the ILC Draft Articles and UNCSI provisions, as the texts where the alleged customary rules would be located, is confusing. It is not clear what the purpose is in insisting on the customary status of the 1991 Draft Articles in the face of a subsequent treaty embodying those rules. Perhaps with a view to dispelling any uncertainty over the *ratione temporis* application of the pertinent customary norms to the proceedings at issue, the Court's intention might be to merely draw attention to the critical date (ie 1991) when, in its opinion, such customary norms were crystallized into a written text. At any rate, as later recalled in the present chapter, this approach becomes particularly problematic when the provisions of the Draft Articles are significantly dissimilar from those set out in the UNCSI. *Guadagnino* constitutes the single decision where the foregoing ambiguity is absent, *Guadagnino* (n 4) para 70 ('Les principes inscrits dans l'article 11 de la Convention de 2004 faisant partie intégrante du droit coutumier international, ils engagent l'Italie bien qu'elle n'ait pas ratifiée ladite Convention').

situations *covered*[14] by their provisions. This approach has been endorsed, with some cosmetic amendments, by all pertinent subsequent decisions.

What is clear is that the involvement of the ILC in the drafting process leading up to the adoption of the UNCSI in 2004 has been pivotal to the Court's affirmation of the Convention's customary nature. As to the employment exception in Article 11, the Court found support[15] in a statement in the ILC commentary on the 1991 Draft Articles, according to which that provision 'appear[ed] to be consistent with the emerging trend in the recent legislative and treaty practice of a growing number of States'.[16] Of course, this formulation is wholly at odds with the hypothesis that the ILC intended to codify a pre-existing customary norm arising from the interplay of a general, consistent, and constant State practice with the belief that such a practice reflects rules of law (*opinio juris*). It also seems inconsistent with the hypothesis that the ILC Draft Articles were regarded as crystallizing an emerging customary norm, when one considers that the ILC was in fact referring to the practice of a very limited number of States, ie, those few which had enacted ad hoc laws on State immunity and/or were parties to the 1972 European Convention on State Immunity (ECSI).[17] Moreover, the ILC's statement in question did not mention what can be regarded as the most significant—if only on a purely quantitative basis—manifestation of State practice in the area of State immunity, ie, judicial decisions of national courts.

Be that as it may, from a methodological viewpoint the ECtHR is certainly not alone when it heavily relies on the ILC's findings about customary international law. Most prominently, outsourcing[18] the identification of custom to the ILC is a technique commonly employed by the International Court of Justice (ICJ).[19] After all, a thorough survey of State practice is at the basis of the ILC's activities relating to the topics in its programme of work. The technique may be reasonable for a host of further reasons. These include the epistemological challenges relating to the determination of customary law, the elaborate and inclusive procedures pursuant to which ILC's texts are finalized through a constant interaction with States and other actors, the fine reputation undeniably enjoyed by the ILC within the international

[14] This does not mean that the UNCSI and its preparatory work are insignificant with regard to issues not covered by its provisions. Indeed, the absence of a given exception to State immunity in the UNCSI is regarded as an important factor militating against the customary status of that exception. This point is confirmed by the ECtHR's case law involving the alleged human rights exception to the immunity of foreign States and their officials, see *Jones* (n 7) paras 79–80, 205, 209; cf already *Al-Adsani* (n 8) paras 23–24, 62–63, 65. Nonetheless, what crucially distinguishes these cases from those discussed in the text is that, short of any guidance from written norms of international law, the ECtHR *did* undertake a wide-ranging review of State practice and developments at the international level; see, albeit only with respect to the immunity of State *officials* for torture, *Jones* (n 7) paras 59–154, 202–15; cf *Al-Adsani* (n 8) paras 22–31, 60–66.

[15] *Cudak* (n 4) paras 29, 66.

[16] ILC Commentary, Draft Article 11, para 14.

[17] Basel, 16 May 1972, in force 11 June 1976, ETS No 74, 1495 UNTS 182. As of 1 September 2017, only 8 States (out of 47 Council of Europe members automatically entitled to ratify or accede) are parties to this Convention.

[18] This expression is borrowed from S Talmon, 'Determining Customary International Law: The ICJ's Methodology between Induction, Deduction and Assertion' (2015) 26 EJIL 417, 437.

[19] For exhaustive references including reliance on codification conventions, see A Pellet, 'Article 38' in A Zimmermann, C Tomuschat, K Oellers-Frahm, and CJ Tams (eds), *The Statute of the International Court of Justice: A Commentary* (2nd edn, OUP 2012) 731, 822–34 (nn 635–38, 643); cf Talmon (n 18) 437–38 (nn 141–42, 145–49).

community, and the generally good quality of the documents arising from ILC's processes.[20]

Yet, for one thing, it should be noted that, in *Jurisdictional Immunities of the State*,[21] the ICJ's attitude towards the customary nature of the UNCSI was restrained,[22] thus profoundly different from the ECtHR's *Cudak* jurisprudence, which unsurprisingly was not cited in that judgment. The ICJ even showed sympathy for the argument that a key exception in the UNCSI, namely the territorial tort exception in Article 12, was not in fact representing customary law insofar as it was also meant to apply to *jure imperii* activities of foreign States.[23]

Regardless of that, and more fundamentally, scholars have frequently highlighted the dangers arising for courts when they relinquish their power to autonomously identify customary rules in favour of the ILC. Lately, Stefan Talmon has considered blind reliance on ILC's findings as nothing else than a technique of assertion, ie, one through which custom, far from being established in an inductive or deductive manner, ends up corresponding to the law as the ICJ (or any other court, for that matter) sees fit.[24] Without necessarily sharing this view, there is however more than a grain of truth in the proposition that abrupt, uncritical assertions as to what the law is, as the ECtHR has basically done in its *Cudak* jurisprudence, are a hotspot for judicial lawmaking, hence for accusations of unwarranted activism, lack of legitimacy, and arbitrariness.[25]

Therefore, the ECtHR should be very cautious when assessing whether it is appropriate to defer to the ILC's materials as evidence of customary law. It should handle those materials with care by critically examining their genesis, quality, and reliability. This is precisely what has *not* been done with respect to the 1991 ILC Draft Articles on State immunity and related commentary. The commentary in particular largely constitutes an obstacle to a correct understanding of the UNCSI.[26] Frequently, its contents do not reflect either the text of the Draft Articles as adopted on second reading in 1991, or, more importantly, the provisions of the UNCSI as concluded in 2004.[27] The latter is squarely the case with Article 11 on the employment exception

[20] See F Lusa Bordin, 'Reflections of Customary International Law: The Authority of Codification Conventions and ILC Draft Articles in International Law' (2014) 63 ICLQ 535, 549–58; P Tomka, 'Custom and the International Court of Justice' (2013) 12 The Law and Practice of International Courts and Tribunals 195, 202–4.

[21] *Jurisdictional Immunities of the State* [2012] ICJ Rep 99.

[22] ibid especially paras 64–65, 117; cf Tomka (n 20) 212–14; Lusa Bordin (n 20) 544.

[23] *Jurisdictional Immunities of the State* (n 21) para 64: 'Germany has not, however, been alone in suggesting that, in so far as it was intended to apply to *acta jure imperii*, Article 12 was not representative of customary international law' (with *controversial* citations to supporting statements from China and the United States). Such consideration was unnecessary given that, as later pointed out by the ICJ itself, the issue to be decided was different, namely, whether a subset of *jure imperii* activities (military activities in the context of armed conflicts) were caught by the tort exception under customary international law.

[24] Talmon (n 18) 434.

[25] cf ibid 441–42.

[26] R O'Keefe and CJ Tams, 'General Introduction' in R O'Keefe and CJ Tams (eds), *The United Nations Convention on Jurisdictional Immunities of States and Their Property: A Commentary* (OUP 2013) xxxvii, xxxvix.

[27] See also the warning contained in the Statement of the Chairman of the Ad Hoc Committee on Jurisdictional Immunities of States and Their Property introducing to the Sixth Committee the Draft Convention on Jurisdictional Immunities of States and Their Property, GAOR, '59th Session, Sixth Committee, 13th meeting' (25 October 2004) UN Doc A/C.6/59/SR.13, para 35: 'Generally, it must

to State immunity, which differs considerably from the corresponding provision of the 1991 draft and dilutes that exception in several respects, thus making it more difficult to lift immunity in labour disputes. In short, the ILC commentary cannot be regarded as 'formally authoritative, let alone conclusive, as to the correct interpretation and application of the Convention'.[28]

However, as recalled earlier, the *Cudak* judgment not only accepted the customary status of the employment exception in the ILC Draft Articles, it also acknowledged that the same was true for the corresponding norm in the UNCSI. In doing so, the ECtHR was seemingly unaware or, at best, unduly dismissive of the textual divergences between the two provisions. Leaving this problem aside for the moment and focusing on methodological matters, it is apparent that no caution at all was dictated to the ECtHR by the fact that the UNCSI was not in force (as continues to be the case). At the time of the judgment (that is, some five years and a half after its adoption), it had been ratified by eight States only, not including the respondent State, which had (and still has) neither ratified nor signed the Convention. Clearly, in and of themselves, these circumstances are not fatal to the customary character of a multilateral treaty potentially codifying the law and to its opposability *in casu*, but they do constitute relevant indicators which invite prudence. Not in the eyes of the ECtHR, however, which merely recalled that a norm expressed in a conventional provision may bind States which have not ratified the treaty in question 'in so far as that provision reflects customary international law, either "codifying" it or forming a new customary rule'.[29]

Here, the Court cited paragraph 71 of the *North Sea Continental Shelf* judgment by the ICJ.[30] With respect, this is an incredibly unfortunate quotation. First, that judgment is well known as one of the rare occurrences where the ICJ ruled out the customary status of a norm included in a treaty purportedly codifying the law and concluded on the basis of work carried out by the ILC, namely the principle of equidistance for the delimitation of the continental shelf between adjacent States under Article 6(2) of the 1958 Geneva Convention on the Continental Shelf. After an accurate review of the pertinent ILC's activities,[31] the ICJ found that that principle 'was proposed by the Commission with considerable hesitation, somewhat on an experimental basis, at most *de lege ferenda*, and not at all *de lege lata* or as an emerging rule of customary international law'.[32] Secondly, paragraph 71 is located in the section of the judgment enquiring into whether the treaty provision at stake had since its adoption *evolved* into a customary rule, not on whether that provision was codifying a pre-existing, or crystallizing an emerging, customary norm, something which the ICJ had already excluded.

This process for establishing custom through the prism of an originally purely conventional provision should have been considered by the *Cudak* jurisprudence in the light of the requirements set by the *North Sea Continental Shelf* decision itself. One of the chief reasons for doing so would have been that, insofar as material, the

be borne in mind that the Convention would have to be read in conjunction with the commentary prepared by the International Law Commission, *at least insofar as the text* [of the Draft Articles] *submitted by the Commission had remained unchanged*' (emphasis added).

[28] O'Keefe and Tams (n 26) xl. [29] *Cudak* (n 4) para 66.

[30] *North Sea Continental Shelf* [1969] ICJ Rep 3. [31] ibid paras 48–55. [32] ibid para 62.

legal situations before the ICJ in 1969 and the ECtHR in 2010 were comparable. Both courts were dealing with recent treaties, namely with a situation where the alleged customary rules would have emerged from conventional norms after a relatively short period of time since the conclusion of the treaties. The ICJ identified two conditions for a finding that a recent treaty rule has passed into customary law.[33] It stated, first, that 'a very widespread and representative participation in the convention might suffice of itself'.[34] This was not the case with the Geneva Convention which, although in force at the time of the judgment, had been ratified by 39 States only, a number, 'though respectable, hardly sufficient'.[35] As we know, and considering the substantial increase in the number of States since 1969, at the time of the *Cudak* judgment the UNCSI was not in force and had been ratified by a bare eight States. The second condition was that, within the period of time running from the date of adoption (or entry into force) of the treaty until the date of the judgment, 'short though [that period] might be, State practice ... should have been both *extensive and virtually uniform* in the sense of the provision invoked;— and should moreover have occurred in such a way as to show a general recognition that a rule of law or legal obligation is involved'.[36] As pointed out in the following section, such extensiveness and virtual uniformity of State practice in accordance with the employment exception in the UNCSI was in 2010, and remains to date, a chimera.

As to the attitude of the respondent State in *Cudak* towards the ILC Draft Articles and the UNCSI, the ECtHR resorted to a nutshell version of the doctrine of the persistent objector to customary rules.[37] It recalled that Lithuania had not made any particular objection to the wording of the employment exception in the ILC Draft,[38] which should be taken to refer to the debates in the ILC and the General Assembly Sixth Committee in the 1990s up to 2004, since the State in question gained independence in 1990. Nor, the Court continued, had Lithuania voted against the conclusion of the UNCSI in 2004,[39] a consideration which could conveniently be replaced throughout the case law in question with the simple reminder that the UNCSI was adopted by consensus. Of course, the foregoing remarks by the ECtHR implied that any other kind of objections put forward in fora other than the ILC and Sixth Committee, including in a string of uniform national jurisprudence deliberately deviating from the UNCSI, could be dismissed for want of uniformity across the board.

But what about the States claiming (and granted) immunity in the underlying domestic proceedings, such as Poland in *Cudak*? Consistency in the application of the persistent objector doctrine would also require an investigation into the attitude of those States towards the alleged custom. If such States were found to be persistent objectors, the customary rule could not be opposed to them, and the

[33] See recently, Tomka (n 20) 205–7. [34] *North Sea Continental Shelf* (n 30) para 73.

[35] ibid para 73. [36] ibid para 74 (emphasis added).

[37] See R van Alebeek, '*Oleynikov* Judgment on State Immunity' <http://echrblog.blogspot.it/2013/03/oleynikov-judgment-on-state-immunity.html> accessed 27 July 2018.

[38] *Cudak* (n 4) para 66. [39] ibid.

forum States conferring immunity could not be held responsible for a violation of the ECHR. Curiously, the only relevant decisions which appear to be mindful of this problem are those involving the United States as respondent in the domestic suit. In *Wallishauser*[40] and *Radunović*,[41] the Court pointed out that the United States had not objected to the ILC Draft and the UNCSI with regard to their rules on service of process and on the employment exception, respectively. By contrast, the attitudes of Poland,[42] France,[43] Kuwait,[44] and Sweden[45] towards the employment exception were ignored, as was—much more worryingly—that of North Korea[46] with regard to the commercial exception.

The impression is that the lip service paid by the ECtHR to the controversial notion of the persistent objector is somehow meant to make its groundbreaking holding, ie, that the ILC Draft Articles and the UNCSI as a whole reflect customary law, more digestible. It is indeed the correctness of this holding which remains the real bone of contention.

3. Dismissing the Customary Status of the Employment Exception under the UNCSI

It is now appropriate to clarify why, substantively, the view that Article 11 UNCSI[47] embeds a customary rule of international law is untenable. Even a

[40] *Wallishauser* (n 1) paras 31, 39, 69; see also *Wallishauser (No 2)* (n 1) paras 40, 71.

[41] *Radunović* (n 1) para 43. [42] *Cudak* (n 4).

[43] *Guadagnino* (n 4). To be sure, this is the only pertinent decision where the ECtHR did not take into account even the attitude of Italy in its capacity as respondent State, cf *Guadagnino* (n 4) para 70.

[44] *Sabeh El Leil* (n 1).

[45] *Naku* (n 4). The problem was, however, moot in this 2016 judgment, as Sweden had ratified the UNCSI in 2009.

[46] *Oleynikov* (n 6).

[47] The employment exception in Article 11 UNCSI reads as follows:

1. Unless otherwise agreed between the States concerned, a State cannot invoke immunity from jurisdiction before a court of another State which is otherwise competent in a proceeding which relates to a contract of employment between the State and an individual for work performed or to be performed, in whole or in part, in the territory of that other State.
2. Paragraph 1 does not apply if:
   (a) the employee has been recruited to perform particular functions in the exercise of governmental authority;
   (b) the employee is:
      (i) a diplomatic agent, as defined in the Vienna Convention on Diplomatic Relations of 1961;
      (ii) a consular officer, as defined in the Vienna Convention on Consular Relations of 1963;
      (iii) a member of the diplomatic staff of a permanent mission to an international organization or of a special mission, or is recruited to represent a State at an international conference; or
      (iv) any other person enjoying diplomatic immunity;
   (c) the subject-matter of the proceeding is the recruitment, renewal of employment or reinstatement of an individual;
   (d) the subject-matter of the proceeding is the dismissal or termination of employment of an individual and, as determined by the head of State, the head of Government or the Minister

cursory, non-expert look at the provision engenders much perplexity about that view. Its largely unnecessary prolixity, its frequently confusing wording, its 'labyrinthine technical complexity [and] structural convolution'[48] are clearly in tension with the prototype of custom as a norm made up of a few relatively broad and simple legal propositions offering reliable guidance for the evolution of practice. Certainly, this is not the end of the matter. International practice is replete of examples of lengthy and complicated treaty provisions that have nonetheless been acknowledged as reflecting customary rules, such as Article 31 of the Vienna Convention on the Law of Treaties (VCLT) about treaty interpretation. But those provisions must somehow prove to be reasonably amenable to a widely shared, acceptable construction which, *without rewriting them*, crystallizes consensus over their contents and meaning. By contrast, certain interpretative issues emerging from the text of Article 11 UNCSI can be regarded as virtually intractable.

After setting out an exception to the immunity rule for proceedings relating to contracts of employment between a foreign State and an individual for work performed in the territory of the forum State, Article 11(2) envisages six counter exceptions, that is, six situations where immunity however subsists. In two cases,[49] these counter exceptions are in turn qualified by circumstances which imply a loss of immunity. Crucially, the counter exceptions apply cumulatively, ie, none of them must be applicable in order to deny immunity to the employer State. This complex scheme raises fundamental problems about the appropriate standard of interpretation and the sharing of the burden of proof in concrete cases. The ECtHR has been very generous to individual applicants in these respects, by stating that the counter exceptions 'must be strictly interpreted'[50] and making it clear that the burden to prove their applicability essentially rests on the State claiming immunity or the respondent State in Strasbourg.[51] Yet it cannot be taken for granted that a standard of restrictive interpretation is correct with regard to counter exceptions to an exception from a general rule of State immunity.[52] Similarly, the structure of the UNCSI implies that a State enjoys prima facie immunity from the jurisdiction of other States, thereby making it substantially incumbent on the individual claimant to prove that one of the exceptions, as laid down in Part III UNCSI, applies.[53]

for Foreign Affairs of the employer State, such a proceeding would interfere with the security interests of that State;

(e) the employee is a national of the employer State at the time when the proceeding is instituted, unless this person has the permanent residence in the State of the forum; or

(f) the employer State and the employee have otherwise agreed in writing, subject to any considerations of public policy conferring on the courts of the State of the forum exclusive jurisdiction by reason of the subject-matter of the proceeding.

[48] Foakes and O'Keefe, 'Article 11' in O'Keefe and Tams (eds) (n 26) 183, 208. Such complexity is compounded by an enigmatic understanding with respect to Article 11 included in the annex to the UNCSI. The annexed understandings are an integral part of the Convention (Article 25 UNCSI).

[49] Article 11(2)(e) and (f), respectively.

[50] *Sabeh El Leil* (n 1) para 66; *Radunović* (n 1) para 80.

[51] *Cudak* (n 4) para 70; *Guadagnino* (n 4) para 72; *Sabeh El Leil* (n 1) paras 62–64; *Radunović* (n 1) paras 77, 80–81; *Naku* (n 4) paras 93–95.

[52] DJ Bederman, '*Sabeh el Leil v France*' (2012) 106 AJIL 125, 129.

[53] R van Alebeek, 'Introduction to Part III' in O'Keefe and Tams (eds) (n 26) 153, 160.

In essence, according to Article 11(2) UNCSI, State immunity survives in the following six situations: (a) the employee performs *jure imperii* functions; (b) she/he is a diplomatic agent, a consular officer, or 'any other person enjoying diplomatic immunity'; (c) the subject matter of the proceedings is the recruitment or reinstatement of an individual; (d) the subject matter of the proceedings is the dismissal of an individual, provided the employer State has determined that such proceedings would interfere with its security interests; (e) the employee is a national of the employer State not permanently resident in the forum State; or (f) the employee and employer State have concluded an agreement derogating from the jurisdiction of the forum State, unless this agreement is inconsistent with the public policy of the latter State.

In many of the cases discussed in this chapter, the ECtHR had to assess whether any of the foregoing counter exceptions applied to what is probably the thorniest situation potentially caught by the employment exception, ie, that of claims of compensation for wrongful dismissal filed by members of the administrative and technical staff of foreign embassies. Even in countries with 'progressive' jurisprudence in this area, there has always been widespread resistance to the notion that immunity does not, as a rule, cover labour disputes brought by such employees, on the assumption that they are inherently involved in activities of a public-law nature carried out at places, such as an embassy or a consular post, which are indeed a quintessential manifestation of sovereign authority. In *Cudak*, the ECtHR implicitly reversed its previous jurisprudence[54] and held that the UNCSI had removed from the scope of immunity 'a State's employment contracts with the staff of its diplomatic missions abroad',[55] except in the situations exhaustively enumerated in paragraph 2 of Article 11. None of such situations was triggered by the case at hand[56] and, therefore, Lithuania had breached the applicant's right of access to a court.[57]

The accuracy and reliability of the interpretation given to Article 11 by the ECtHR is questionable. At least two aspects seem problematic. The first concerns a mysterious limb of the counter exception in Article 11(2)(b). Not only does this provision restore immunity when the claimant employee is a diplomatic agent or consular officer, but also when she/he is 'any other person enjoying diplomatic immunity'.[58]

[54] Namely, the following holding in *Fogarty* (n 8) para 37: '[W]here the proceedings relate to employment in a foreign mission or embassy, international practice is divided on the question whether State immunity continues to apply and, if it does so apply, whether it covers disputes relating to the contracts of all staff or only more senior members of the mission. Certainly, it cannot be said that the United Kingdom is alone in holding that immunity attaches to suits by employees at diplomatic missions or that, in affording such immunity, the United Kingdom falls outside any currently accepted international standards'. See R Garnett, 'State and Diplomatic Immunity and Employment Rights: European Law to the Rescue?' (2015) 64 ICLQ 783, 792. Despite the misleading references to the 1991 ILC commentary, the reversal of the foregoing 2001 holding by the 2010 *Cudak* judgment shows that, in the eyes of the ECtHR, the real turning point in the evolution of customary law applicable in this field was the adoption of the UNCSI in 2004.

[55] *Cudak* (n 4) para 65. See also *Sabeh El Leil* (n 1) para 53; *Naku* (n 4) para 95. This *dictum* must *a fortiori* be taken to catch the service staff of diplomatic missions, as well as the administrative, technical, and service staff of consular posts.

[56] *Cudak* (n 4) paras 69–72.

[57] ibid paras 74–75.

[58] Article 11(2)(b)(iv) UNCSI.

According to the Vienna Convention on Diplomatic Relations (VCDR), members of the administrative and technical staff of a mission, provided they are not nationals of or permanently resident in the receiving State, do enjoy full immunity from the latter's criminal jurisdiction, as well as functional immunity from its civil and administrative jurisdiction.[59] Also members of the service staff of a mission—not nationals of or permanently resident in the receiving State—are entitled to functional immunity at large.[60] The possibility that the applicants in *Cudak, Sabeh El Leil, Radunović*, and *Naku* might indeed have been persons enjoying diplomatic immunity, by virtue of their position in the embassies concerned, should have been taken into account by the ECtHR, which limited itself to declaring that they were not diplomatic agents or consular officers.[61] That they were nationals of the receiving/forum States, as they were, would not be the end of the matter, given that the VCDR foresees that such members of the non-diplomatic staff of a mission may freely be granted immunities by those States.[62]

The problem was instead squarely triggered by the *Benkharbouche* case[63] before the English courts, which concerned various claims, including for unfair dismissal, brought by members of Moroccan nationality of the service staff of the Sudanese and Libyan embassies in London. The Court of Appeal got rid of the problem with the consideration that subsuming all members of the non-diplomatic staff of a mission, such as the claimants at hand, in the category of persons envisaged by Article 11(2)(b)(iv) UNCSI would be inconsistent with the scheme, purpose, and *travaux préparatoires* of that provision taken as a whole.[64] The Court relied entirely on the commentary to Article 11 by Foakes and O'Keefe.[65] In this magisterial commentary, the authors submit that the expression 'any other person enjoying diplomatic immunity' must be understood to refer to miscellaneous—albeit unspecified—persons or employees of diplomatic status not already listed in Article 11(2)(b).[66] They argue that any other expansive reading, covering employees who are part of the administrative, technical, and service staff of diplomatic missions, 'would fly in the face of the *travaux préparatoires*'.[67]

That remark is, however, questionable. The expression 'any other person enjoying diplomatic immunity' was contained in both alternative texts proposed in 2002 by

[59] Article 37(2) VCDR. [60] Article 37(3) VCDR.

[61] *Cudak* (n 4) para 69; *Sabeh El Leil* (n 1) para 60; *Radunović* (n 1) para 75; *Naku* (n 4) para 90. The failure to address this point in *Naku* is particularly unfortunate because the accreditation certificate issued to the applicant by the Lithuanian authorities had explicitly excluded that she was entitled to any diplomatic immunities or privileges, see *Naku* (n 4) para 12.

[62] Article 38(2) VCDR. For a telling example, see Court of Justice of the European Union, Case C-154/11 *Mahamdia v Algeria* (19 July 2012) para 15. The applicant was a driver at the Algerian embassy in Berlin. He possessed dual nationality, Algerian and German, so that in principle he would not enjoy diplomatic immunity as per the VCDR. However, German legislation confers immunity on all members of foreign diplomatic missions, regardless of their nationality, as well as on the members of the latter's families and their private servants.

[63] Court of Appeal, *Benkharbouche v Embassy of the Republic of Sudan* [2015] EWCA Civ 33.

[64] ibid para 38.

[65] Foakes and O'Keefe, 'Article 11' (n 48). Analogous, unconditional reliance on this commentary is placed by Garnett (n 54) 788 (n 8).

[66] Foakes and O'Keefe (n 48) 202. [67] ibid 201.

the General Assembly's Ad Hoc Committee on Jurisdictional Immunities.[68] For our purposes, it therefore seems rather inconsequential that most State delegates to the Sixth Committee favoured the less restrictive text, which was ultimately retained in Article 11. Moreover, there was no consensus in the Sixth Committee on removing immunity for employment claims by the non-diplomatic staff of embassies (and consulates). For instance, the United States delegate observed that jurisdiction over contracts of employment should not 'permit local authorities to intrude into the internal working of consulates and embassies, or to compromise diplomatic and consular immunities'.[69] As a matter of fact, the *travaux* prove to be inconclusive and they are by no means incompatible with the hypothesis that the phrase in question was meant to cover the non-diplomatic staff of embassies, thus acting upon, and taking further, a point which had been made in 1991 by the ILC in its commentary on the Draft Articles.[70]

On a general level, there surely is a limit to using the *travaux* (or the intention of the parties, for that matter)—however enlightening or significant they may be[71]—as a hermeneutic device supplanting the golden rule of textual treaty interpretation.[72] Foakes and O'Keefe seem to accept that it is appropriate to invoke the *travaux* in order to determine the meaning of Article 11(2)(b)(iv) because otherwise that provision would appear obscure, ambiguous, or manifestly absurd.[73] Actually, in and of itself, the wording of the provision is as clear as it can be. It stipulates that State immunity attaches to employment claims advanced by *any* person enjoying diplomatic immunity. Textual interpretation does not yield a result which is objectively unreasonable or such as to deprive the UNCSI's exception for employment claims by embassy and consular employees of all meaning. In principle, that exception is still available (at least) for consular employees enjoying consular—not diplomatic—immunity, as well as for embassy employees possessing the nationality of the receiving/forum State (or permanently resident therein) and not benefiting of a discretional grant of immunity by that State. It is, therefore, perfectly possible that the provision at stake reflects the best compromise that could be achieved in the early 2000s in order to placate State resistance to inroads into diplomatic and consular affairs, thereby overcoming the *impasse* on a key issue standing in the way of a successful conclusion of the UNCSI process.

Foakes and O'Keefe further observe that the controversial phrase in question arose from an Ad Hoc Committee's organizational change (vis-à-vis earlier proposals

[68] GAOR, 'Report of the Ad Hoc Committee on Jurisdictional Immunities of States and Their Property, 57th Session' (4–15 February 2002) Suppl no 22, UN doc A/57/22, 7.

[69] GAOR, '57th Session, Sixth Committee, 19th meeting' (24 October 2002) UN Doc A/C.6/57/SR.19, para 2.

[70] When discussing the counter exception relating to employees performing *jure imperii* activities, the text of which was more favourable to State immunity than current Article 11(2)(a), the ILC gave the following examples of 'covered' employees: 'private secretaries, code clerks, interpreters, translators and other persons entrusted with functions related to State security or basic interests of the State', ILC Commentary, Draft Article 11, para 9.

[71] JD Mortenson, 'The *Travaux* of *Travaux*: Is the Vienna Convention Hostile to Drafting History?' (2013) 107 AJIL 780.

[72] Article 31(1) VCLT.

[73] cf Article 32 VCLT.

by the ILC) which may have 'unintended consequences'.[74] Perhaps. At any rate, this observation suggests that the retention of the expression 'diplomatic immunity' may be regarded as nothing else than a glitch: in reality, the drafters wished to refer to any other person enjoying diplomatic *status* or *rank*. But if this is true, it is then strongly recommended that, as soon as the UNCSI comes into force, the States Parties adopt an amendment, or at least an interpretative declaration, dispelling any doubt into how Article 11(2)(b) should be read.[75]

The second problematic aspect associated with Article 11 UNCSI and its reading by the ECtHR involves the counter exception relating to claims for wrongful dismissal, which is triggered when such claims, *as determined* by the head of State or government or Ministry for Foreign Affairs of the employer State, 'would interfere with the security interests of that State'.[76] Also this provision was not included in the 1991 ILC Draft Articles and should be considered as retrogressive as compared to that Draft, which did not contain a national security clause and simply allowed claims for compensation (albeit not for reinstatement) arising from acts of wrongful dismissal by the employer State.[77] This is a stringent counter exception capable of nullifying what is probably the most recurrent remedy sought by ex-employees of foreign States. As worded, it leaves the viability of such a remedy entirely in the hands of the authorities of foreign States, whose unilateral determinations of national security risks arising from the proceedings in question appear to trigger near-automatic grants of immunity. Such determinations are seemingly not subject to second-guessing or review on the merits by the courts hearing the employment suit. Yet this is precisely what the ECtHR was prepared to do in *Cudak* when it stated that Poland's security interests were not sufficiently brought into play by 'the mere allegation that the applicant could have had access to certain documents or could have been privy to confidential telephone conversations in the course of her duties'.[78] In reality, the ECtHR could have relied on a different argument much more in line with the text of the UNCSI, namely, that the foreign State employer had not notified the domestic courts of any positive determination

[74] Foakes and O'Keefe (n 48) 191.

[75] A series of consistent reservations or interpretative declarations made by States on becoming parties to the UNCSI might also be a useful mechanism for that purpose. However, no such reservations or declarations have been formulated by the current 22 States Parties to the UNCSI.

[76] Article 11(2)(d) UNCSI. As spelled out in the first paragraph of the understanding with respect to Article 11, the reference to the security interests of the employer State 'is intended *primarily* to address matters of national security and the security of diplomatic missions and consular posts' (emphasis added).

[77] Draft Article 11(2)(b), read together with ILC commentary, Draft Article 11, para 10.

[78] *Cudak* (n 4) para 72. The Court further specified that the acts of sexual harassment experienced at the embassy by the applicant, which were at the basis of the dispute, 'can hardly be regarded as undermining Poland's security interests', *Cudak* (n 4) para 72; cf *Cudak* (n 4) paras 40, 51. A variation of the same approach may be found in *Guadagnino* (n 4) para 73. A misinterpretation of the same provision was also evident in *Radunović* (n 1) para 77, where the Court stated that the national security clause was not applicable, because *neither the domestic courts nor the respondent government* had shown how the applicants' duties were linked to the security interests of the US. As recalled in the text, the clause in question is triggered by a unilateral determination of the highest authorities of the *State claiming immunity* in the underlying domestic dispute.

of risks to its national security, an approach canvassed indeed in the subsequent *Sabeh El Leil* judgment.[79]

As spelled out in the next section, these remarks are not intended to ignore the progressive stance endorsed by the ECtHR on the merits of the cases in question. This stance is functional to the *ultimate end* pursued by the ECtHR, namely, an enhanced level of protection for the rights of employees of foreign States. It also prevents the employment exception to State immunity from virtually becoming a dead letter. Instead, the foregoing considerations raise doubts about the propriety of the legal *means* espoused by the Court to that end, ie, the wholesale recognition of the customary status of Article 11 UNCSI. At this juncture, one need only observe that the liberal interpretations given by the Court end up shaping an exception which, in several key respects, looks rather different from that provision. This is something which speaks *against* the professed customary character of Article 11.

In any event, incontrovertible evidence against that character is provided by the fact that Article 11 does not reflect generalized and consistent State practice, let alone *opinio juris*. Practice in the field of State immunity from employment claims shows that a variety of national approaches has invariably been pursued,[80] especially with regard to the key indicator(s) according to which a decision whether to uphold immunity must be made. Such indicators, which may apply cumulatively or alternatively, include the nature of the employee's duties, the place of work, the nature of the claim, and the nationality of the employee. The impression is that Article 11(2) UNCSI adopted compromise formulations of these indicators and elevated them to the status of distinct counter exceptions to the employment exception, whereas, in effect, their ultimate purpose has always been to inform an overall determination as to whether a given employment dispute against a foreign State interferes with the latter's sovereign interests.

The foregoing elements of State practice were readily available to the ECtHR when it was elaborating its *Cudak* jurisprudence. Most strikingly, the Court ignored altogether first-hand evidence coming from the Council of Europe (CoE), which in 2001—upon initiative from its Committee of Legal Advisers on Public International Law—embarked on a pilot project on State practice concerning State immunity with a view to collecting pertinent materials and drawing conclusions on the extent of convergence in the legal systems of CoE members. Twenty-eight CoE members (plus one observer State, ie, Japan) participated in the project and their contributions were posted online,[81] and later systematized and analysed in an academic publication.[82] As regards employment claims, that publication reported that the materials revealed

[79] *Sabeh El Leil* (n 1) para 61. See also *Naku* (n 4) para 91.

[80] See, eg, Opinion of the Advocate General in *Mahamdia* (n 62) paras 23–26 (24 May 2012); H Fox and P Webb, *The Law of State Immunity* (3rd edn OUP 2013), 439; Foakes and O'Keefe (n 48) 186–89; van Alebeek (n 37).

[81] The database in question is available at <http://www.coe.int/en/web/cahdi/database-immunities> accessed 27 July 2018. In addition to the original contributions, it contains updated materials which cover the law of international immunities at large, including for instance the immunity of international organizations.

[82] G Hafner, MG Kohen, and S Breau (eds), *State Practice Regarding State Immunities* (Martinus Nijhoff 2006).

'a rich and diverse judicial practice'[83] and 'disagreements'[84] in Europe about the scope of immunity in this area.

Given these widespread inconsistencies in the CoE legal space, it is unclear why the ECtHR looked further and felt the necessity of outsourcing the identification of (alleged) customary rules to the ILC and related UNCSI process. More fundamentally though, by disregarding the divergence of practice in Europe, the Court was able to bypass the problem of the lack of a European consensus in this field. It is well known that the absence of a European consensus usually militates against findings of violation of the ECHR.[85] Inter alia, that absence normally implies a wide margin of appreciation enjoyed by the States Parties in the discharge of their obligations.

4. Does the End Justify the Means? Insights from the English and Italian Jurisprudence

Now that certain flaws of the ECtHR's UNCSI jurisprudence have been highlighted, can its substance nevertheless be saved? Indeed, we should not lose sight of the *ultimate end* which, almost invariably,[86] has been canvassed by this jurisprudence, ie, a higher level of protection for the right of access to justice of individuals who are unable to pursue their claims by reason of State immunity. This is particularly significant for employees working at foreign embassies, consulates, or comparable State instrumentalities. Moreover, and regardless of confusing references to Article 11 UNCSI, the ECtHR's disavowal of the exclusion of forum States' jurisdiction over all employment disputes brought by such employees may eventually prove to be consonant with general international law or a decisive contribution to the crystallization of emerging customary norms.[87]

Richard Garnett, for example, asserts that the ECtHR is right in considering the test based on the nature and level of the employee's duties under Article 11(2)(a) UNCSI as a customary rule. The ensuing finding that suits filed by low-level employees engaged in generic, non-governmental duties are not in principle barred by immunity *wherever* they may be working, as well as the Court's restrictive approach to the national security clause in Article 11(2)(d), should therefore be applauded.[88] Irrespective of their appropriateness,[89] the problem with these views is that they

[83] U Köhler, 'State Immunity Regarding Employment Contracts', in Hafner, Kohen, and Breau (eds) (n 82) 69, 96.

[84] S Breau, 'Summary of State Practice Regarding State Immunities in the Council of Europe', in Hafner, Kohen, and Breau (eds) (n 82) 168, 177.

[85] For a recent, prominent example, see *Parrillo v Italy* App no 46470/11 (ECtHR, 27 August 2015) paras 169, 175–80 (no violation of Article 8 by a ban on donation of human embryos to scientific research, given especially the lack of a European consensus in this area).

[86] The exception being *Wallishauser (No 2)* (n 1).

[87] Garnett (n 54) 796, 805.

[88] ibid 806–7, 810 (n 117), 812.

[89] Garnett's views are not shared by many scholars who believe that the distinction between *jure imperii* and *jure gestionis* functions of employees as reflected in Article 11(2)(a) UNCSI is at best unhelpful (see, eg, Foakes and O'Keefe (n 48) 208), at worse an open-ended test lending itself to arbitrary solutions (see, eg, B Conforti, *Diritto internazionale* (10th edn, Editoriale Scientifica 2015) 273–75).

dilute and oversimplify the *Cudak* jurisprudence. The actual *Cudak* test is that *each and any* of the six counter exceptions in Article 11(2) must not apply in order to establish a violation of the right of access to a court, not only that concerning the nature of the duties performed by the employee. Garnett's position seems rather to be driven by the aforementioned perception of the ultimate correctness of the ECtHR's findings vis-à-vis general law and by requirements of substantive justice towards the aggrieved employees.

Largely similar considerations apply to the recent *Benkharbouche* decision,[90] where the English Court of Appeal had to assess the lawfulness (inter alia) under international law, particularly the ECHR, of the provisions of the UK State Immunity Act[91] (SIA) ruling out employment suits against foreign States by any member of diplomatic missions (and consular posts) and by any employee who was neither a national of the UK nor habitually resident there when the contract of employment was made. The Court of Appeal was quite critical of the ECtHR's holding that Article 11 UNCSI is reflective of customary norms,[92] and vindicated a substantial power to determine customary rules—especially in uncertain areas of international law—unimpeded by prior rulings of the ECtHR itself.[93] Yet it upheld the essence of the principle arising from the ECtHR's State immunity jurisprudence, pursuant to which grants of immunity constitute a proportionate restriction on the right of access to justice only when they are required by international law.[94] Accordingly, it carried out an accurate review of State practice and pertinent international instruments, within which the UNCSI was just one—albeit a very important one—of the various elements to be taken into account.[95]

On that basis, the Court of Appeal came to the conclusion that both provisions of the SIA at stake were inconsistent with international law,[96] and proceeded to make a declaration of incompatibility with the ECHR under Section 4(2) of the UK Human Rights Act.[97] Most significantly, it held that no rule of international law required immunity 'in respect of employment claims by members of the service staff of a mission in the absence of some special feature such as where the claim is for the recruitment, renewal of employment or reinstatement of an individual or where the proceedings would interfere with the security interests of the state'.[98] Although narrowly confined to members of the service staff of embassies, such as the claimants, the impact on this ruling of the bold stance taken in *Cudak* by the ECtHR seems undeniable. In addition, despite its scepticism over the customary nature of the UNCSI and similarly to the ECtHR, the Court of Appeal carefully considered whether any of the counter exceptions to the employment exception as envisaged by that Convention was triggered on the facts of the case. But of course this approach constitutes a reflection of the obligation to abide by the ECHR: given that the ECtHR has conditioned compliance with Article 6 ECHR on the observance of

[90] *Benkharbouche* (n 63). [91] Sections 16(1)(a) and 4(2)(b) SIA, respectively.
[92] *Benkharbouche* (n 63) paras 29–30, 36. [93] ibid para 21. [94] ibid para 30.
[95] ibid paras 33–45, 48–52, 55–65. [96] ibid paras 53, 65. [97] ibid para 68.
[98] ibid para 46.

each and any of the (allegedly customary) provisions in Article 11 UNCSI, domestic courts of CoE members should follow suit.

Consequently, two perverse effects arising from the ECtHR's UNCSI jurisprudence may be singled out. They raise doubts about the propriety of the *legal means* endorsed by the Strasbourg Court to achieve an enhanced level of protection for the rights of persons affected by grants of State immunity.

First, that jurisprudence ends up imposing the UNCSI *qua* purported customary law on ECHR Parties through the back door of ECHR obligations. This operation may involve even countries, such as the UK, which in all probability will withhold their ratification of the UNCSI for an indefinite period of time, and which moreover do not generally accept the primacy of customary rules over parliamentary legislation. Crucially, the problem is not only that the customary status of Article 11 UNCSI is highly questionable, but also that—substantively—indiscriminate reliance on some of the provisions of that norm may give rise to a *regression* in the protection of employees' rights. Take the example of claims for wrongful dismissal. The national security clause as worded in the UNCSI may turn out to be a stumbling block for those claims, one which was previously unknown to the practice of national courts which allowed dismissal proceedings against foreign States.

Accordingly, the second perverse effect is that, in the wake of the ECtHR's *Cudak* jurisprudence, the domestic courts of ECHR Parties may see fit to modify the criteria used hitherto for *denying* State immunity in employment disputes and respect instead the dictates of Article 11 UNCSI *in a scrupulous manner*. Again, some of these dictates can prove detrimental to the protection of labour rights as compared to the national practice followed in the pre-*Cudak* era. But denials of State immunity, whether in line *vel non* with customary law, are not the ECtHR's business. The Court is fundamentally concerned with grants of immunity which exceed the requirements of international law, thereby violating the right of access to justice. The situation in *Benkharbouche*, which involved statutory grants of immunity, may be kept distinct from the traditional case in this area where a domestic court has to review individual applications claiming that immunity should be denied in accordance with national precedents and constitutional rules, and/or the evolution of international law. The *Cudak* jurisprudence might bring about a major change in the methodology followed to address the latter situation and effectively freeze the law as enshrined in the 2004 UNCSI.

The Italian example is emblematic in this respect. In 2014, the Italian Supreme Court of Cassation finally acknowledged the existence of the *Cudak* jurisprudence, and consequently held that Article 11 UNCSI applies to employment disputes with foreign States as a matter of customary law, thus as the critical 'yardstick for assessing the compatibility of defendant States' jurisdictional immunity with the guarantees of fair trial'.[99] In the first of a trio of

[99] *Embassy of Spain to the Holy See v de la Grana Gonzales* No 9034/2014, ILDC 2436 (18 April 2014), author's translation. As pointed out by the Court, despite Italy's accession to the UNCSI (on 6 May 2013), the latter could not apply *qua* treaty law, pending its entry into force and given its non-retroactivity. Yet, an argument for relying on the UNCSI *qua* treaty law would have been that, as per Article 18(b) VCLT, Italy is bound not to defeat the object and purpose of the Convention, as long as

cases,[100] the Supreme Court granted immunity because the remedy sought by the dismissed employee was reinstatement, and as such it was unquestionably barred by the UNCSI *and* the earlier Italian case law. A distinctly beneficial effect on labour rights produced by the *Cudak* jurisprudence resulted instead from a major reversal of Italian precedents in the later decision in *Académie de France à Rome v Galamini di Recanati*.[101] Relying on the UNCSI as interpreted in that jurisprudence, the Supreme Court asserted jurisdiction over all of the pecuniary claims advanced by a senior administrative secretary of an instrumentality of France. Crucially, such claims included compensation for unlawful dismissal, a remedy hitherto regarded as covered by State immunity in a host of consistent judicial decisions.

Yet the dark side of the *Cudak* coin entered the stage in the third employment dispute with foreign States adjudicated by the Italian Supreme Court in 2014. In *Lasaracina*,[102] the United Arab Emirates pleaded immunity in a case concerning a claim for the retrospective adjustment of job status with ensuing monetary awards brought by a senior member of the administrative staff of its embassy in Rome. The lower courts afforded immunity because the employee's duties were found to be closely related to *jure imperii* activities *and* the claim at stake could not be regarded as one of a purely pecuniary nature. The Supreme Court upheld the lower courts' conclusion, but it gave substantially different reasons. On the one hand, the *Cudak* jurisprudence and the UNCSI—the Court reasoned—did not accept immunity for the claim at stake and for a suit filed by an employee engaged in duties such as those of the plaintiff. However, the Court went on with a meticulous review of the counter exceptions in Article 11(2) UNCSI and unexpectedly found that the *forum prorogatum* clause in Article 11(2)(f) was triggered in the circumstances as, in his contracts of employment with the foreign State, the employee had agreed in writing that the same State would have exclusive jurisdiction over all disputes arising from the contracts.

This is an amazing conclusion which is at variance, not only with recent decisions by the same Supreme Court,[103] but also—most importantly—with European Union law. After *Mahamdia*,[104] there is no doubt that the pertinent EU legislation[105] covers employment disputes with embassies of foreign States[106] and that an

its entry into force is not unduly delayed. Injudiciously, in its instrument of accession, Italy did not formulate any reservation with respect to the employment exception. However, the existence of this option raises the tricky question of whether the *Cudak* jurisprudence might even operate so as to trump reservations to the UNCSI by ECHR Parties. For further insights into the Italian jurisprudence at issue, see the commentary by P Rossi, (2014) 24 Italian Yearbook of International Law 468.

[100] *Embassy of Spain to the Holy See* (n 99).

[101] *Académie de France à Rome v Galamini di Recanati* No 19674/2014, ILDC 2437 (18 September 2014).

[102] *Lasaracina v Embassy of the United Arab Emirates* No 22744/2014, ILDC 2438 (27 October 2014).

[103] *Embassy of the Kingdom of Saudi Arabia v Omran* No 14703/2010 (18 June 2010); *Embassy of the Republic of Korea v Malysheva* No 1774/2011 (26 January 2011).

[104] *Mahamdia* (n 62).

[105] Regulation no 44/2001 on jurisdiction and the recognition and enforcement of judgments in civil and commercial matters, Articles 18–21 (OJ 2001 L 12), recast as Regulation no 1215/2012, Articles 20–23 (OJ 2012 L 351).

[106] At least when such a dispute, as that underlying the *Lasaracina* case, does not involve 'functions carried out by the employee ... [in] the exercise of public powers', *Mahamdia* (n 62) para 57.

agreement conferring jurisdiction on such a State is only applicable when it is subsequent to the emergence of a dispute or not exclusive of the ordinary jurisdiction of the courts envisaged by that legislation[107] (in *Lasaracina*, the Italian courts as those of the State where the foreign State employer was domiciled through its embassy). *Both* the latter requirements were plainly missing on the facts of the *Lasaracina* case.

The lesson coming from this decision is that, given the uncertainties associated with the interpretation of Article 11 UNCSI, a domestic court inclined to grant immunity in a given case will look to all commas, colons, and semicolons in that provision and most likely discover a legal avenue to deny jurisdiction. Probably though, the best is yet to come for the Italian jurisprudence post-*Cudak*. The truly hard cases will be those where the defendant State, on the strength of the relevant clauses in Article 11, will oppose claims of a pecuniary nature by reason of the nationality of the employee and/or the latter's senior position and public law duties. In and of themselves, these criteria have long been abandoned in the Italian jurisprudence relating to State immunity in labour disputes, whereas since the 1990s the pecuniary character of the claim has certainly represented the key test.

Finally, the preceding remarks point to a broader, systemic problem emerging from the ECtHR's UNCSI jurisprudence. The latter's expansion into areas other than employment cases has been accompanied by the indiscriminate recognition of the customary status of the pertinent UNCSI's norms. Again, this lack of discernment may indirectly result in regressive State immunity decisions by domestic courts.

A telling example is provided by the *Oleynikov* judgment,[108] which involved a claim for the recovery of a sum of money lent to a North Korean official. The ECtHR stated that the *provisions* of the UNCSI applied to Russia *qua* customary law.[109] Perhaps, the Court intended to refer only to Article 10 UNCSI on the commercial transaction exception.[110] At any rate, the correspondence of Article 10, taken as a whole (ie, including its enigmatic norm on State enterprises), with customary law should seriously be questioned, even more so when Article 10 is read together, as it must be, with Article 2(1)(c) on the definition of commercial transaction and Article 2(2)[111] on the criteria for determining whether a transaction is indeed commercial.[112] Article 2(2) definitely constitutes one of the most controversial provisions of the UNCSI, insofar as it provides that whether a given transaction is commercial should *only* primarily be established in the light of its

[107] *Mahamdia* (n 62) para 66.

[108] *Oleynikov* (n 6). See van Alebeek (n 37).

[109] *Oleynikov* (n 6) para 68. Improvidently, the Court added that also the pertinent provisions of the European Convention on State Immunity (ECSI) reflected customary law, *Oleynikov* (n 6) para 68. This must be ruled out altogether given the considerable difference among the norms on the commercial exception in the ECSI and UNCSI, the former being decidedly more favourable to the subsistence of immunity in this area, cf Articles 4 and 7 ECSI.

[110] cf *Oleynikov* (n 6) para 61.

[111] In the judgment under discussion, these provisions are indeed duly mentioned among the materials relevant to the case, see *Oleynikov* (n 6) para 42.

[112] See the compelling observations by S Wittich, 'Article 10' in O'Keefe and Tams (eds) (n 26) 167, 182: '[T]his trio of provisions raises almost as many questions as it answers . . . [O]ne can confidently say that *some form* of the commercial transaction exception reflects customary international law' (emphasis added). The author makes clear that such a form is not provided by the norms in question.

nature, as its purpose should also be taken into account if the parties thereto have so agreed or if this is in line with the practice of the forum State (Russia, in our case). In *Oleynikov*, Russia's position was indefensible as the domestic courts had denied jurisdiction simply by applying the defunct rule of absolute State immunity. However, the ECtHR—perhaps inadvertently—saw it fit to point out that '[t]he domestic courts did not undertake any analysis of the *nature* of the transaction underlying the claim'.[113]

Now, there is little doubt that Russia has to be included among the countries whose practice attaches importance to the *purpose* of a transaction in order to distinguish between acts *jure imperii* and acts *jure gestionis*. Until the very last minute of the negotiating process, it was a strenuous supporter of the provision in Article 2(2) UNCSI.[114] Does the latter really reflect a customary rule? If so, as the *Oleynikov* judgment might be taken to assume, ECHR Parties giving relevance to the purpose criterion should then be exempted from findings of violation of the right of access to a court. The most upsetting scenario, though, would be a reversal of the practice of ECHR Parties firmly anchored to the nature test. This reversal might possibly arise from reciprocity considerations benefiting those countries which accord broader immunity by application of the purpose test, as well as from an uncritical reading of the ECtHR's UNCSI jurisprudence with its emphasis on the customary nature of each and any of the Convention's provisions.

5. Conclusion

The concern for a potential regression in the immunity-related practice of States brought about by the UNCSI extends to many areas other than those addressed in this chapter, including the definition of State with its apparent preclusion of compensation proceedings against State officials responsible for grave violations of human rights,[115] the territorial tort exception with its alleged savings clause for military activities,[116] and the essentially absolute prohibition of prejudgment measures of constraint against State property.[117] In the wake of the *Cudak* jurisprudence, such a risk of regression may be averted only by ruling out the customary nature of the pertinent UNCSI provisions read in light of their wording, context, and *travaux préparatoires*.

With regard to the exceptions to the immunity rule set out in Part III UNCSI, probably no one better than Rosanne van Alebeek has encapsulated the key point. In her view, it is undeniable that 'the *broad contours* of Part III of the Convention reflect customary international law',[118] ie, that such exceptions do apply under

[113] *Oleynikov* (n 6) para 70, emphasis added.

[114] cf GAOR, '57th Session, Sixth Committee, 19th meeting' (24 October 2002) UN Doc A/C.6/57/SR.19, para 12. It is important to note that certain States had insisted on a more restrictive formulation of the provision which would accord relevance to the practice of the State party to the transaction (such as North Korea in the *Oleynikov* case!), see GAOR, '59th Session, Sixth Committee, 13th meeting' (25 October 2004) UN Doc A/C.6/59/SR.13, para 48 (statement of China).

[115] Article 1(b)(iv) UNCSI.

[116] Article 12 UNCSI.

[117] Article 18 UNCSI.

[118] van Alebeek (n 53) 163, emphasis added.

customary law 'in some form or other'.[119] Yet the key question, she continues, 'is whether the *precise formulation* of each provision is also consonant with custom',[120] a question which currently—save the evolution of practice—should be answered in the negative.[121]

Thus, basically and at least for the time being, the customary status of the UNCSI remains a myth. The ECtHR would consequently be well advised to be cautious in its future UNCSI jurisprudence and introduce qualifications and nuances thereto. A powerful example showing that this is the right path to follow comes from the CoE members themselves. In 2013, given various uncertainties arising from practice, a Declaration on Jurisdictional Immunities of State Owned Cultural Property[122] was elaborated under the aegis of the CoE's Committee of Legal Advisers on Public International Law and opened for signature. The Declaration is intended as a written document recording the *opinio juris* of States on the correspondence between the norms of the UNCSI[123] on immunity from execution for State cultural property and customary international law. This is the orthodox process according to which customary rules may come to light and subsequently be invoked, as opposed to one blindly relying on a multilateral convention finalized after decades-long, intricate, and extremely difficult drafting sessions and negotiations.

It can be expected that the real nature, purpose, and relation to customary law of the UNCSI will continue to generate debates for a long time to come. Beside the traditional options of codification versus progressive development of international law, the present chapter has intended to introduce an element of broader reflection by pointing to the possibility that the UNCSI may bring about an undue regression or ossification of the law. After all, the Convention, rather than a faithful reflection of the preponderant practice, should in the first place be regarded as a robust compromise between vastly divergent positions of States. This compromise was seen as a compelling necessity in order to pursue the harmonization and associated predictability of practice in this area. Yet it is open to question whether it was worth undermining the dynamism and progress of the law guaranteed hitherto by the absence of binding treaty rules.

To sum up, the legal means canvassed to pursue a given end do matter considerably. An inaccurate choice of means may even compromise the end sought to be achieved. This should be taken into account by the Strasbourg Court if it wants to make the best of its *Cudak* jurisprudence, thus preventing the latter's shadows from outnumbering its undeniable lights.

119 ibid. 120 ibid, emphasis added. 121 ibid.

122 The text of the Declaration is available at <https://rm.coe.int/declaration-on-immunities-en/168071bb2d> accessed 1 September 2017. As of 1 September 2017, 20 States, including the Holy See, have signed the Declaration.

123 Article 21(1)(d) and (e) UNCSI. On these themes, see R Pavoni, 'Sovereign Immunity and the Enforcement of International Cultural Property Law' in F Francioni and J Gordley (eds), *Enforcing International Cultural Heritage Law* (OUP 2013) 79.

Conclusion

Reflections on the 2015 Strasbourg Conference

Antônio Augusto Cançado Trindade

1. Introduction

I have been entrusted with presenting the concluding reflections in relation to the theme examined in this thoughtful Conference proceedings book, the result of a memorable Conference of 5 June 2015 at the *Palais des Droits de l'Homme* in Strasbourg. May I express my satisfaction for having, at the table, the company of Professor Luzius Wildhaber, with whom I share the memories of the times of solidarity when we presided at, respectively, the European Court of Human Rights (ECtHR) and the Inter-American Court of Human Rights (IACtHR).

May I begin by saying that, in the domain of the protection of human rights, one is guided by the principle *pro persona humana*, whereby, in face of two norms—an international and a national one—to be applied, it is the one which affords better protection to the human person that in effect applies. The so-called 'subsidiarity', if aimed at the (international) mechanism of protection, cannot at all be invoked so as to encompass material law.[1] International jurisdiction for the protection of human rights is not 'subsidiary' to national jurisdiction, nor are the concepts independent of each other; they are complementary to each other, standing in constant interaction in the protection of human rights.

I would like to refer to three points identified by President Dean Spielmann, at the opening of the Conference, which have been of much relevance to discussions and papers, namely: (i) the 'special character' of the ECHR, and other human rights treaties; (ii) the importance of general principles of international law; and (iii) the dialogues between courts, international and constitutional courts, ie, the dialogue between judges. I would add two other points, which have also permeated the debates, namely: (i) the aforementioned interactions between the international and the domestic legal orders in the present domain of the protection

[1] cf AA Cançado Trindade, *The Access of Individuals to International Justice* (OUP 2011) 211.

Conclusion: Reflections on the 2015 Strasbourg Conference. Antônio Augusto Cançado Trindade.

of the rights of the human person; and (ii) the common ground of treaty hermeneutics in Public International Law and in the International Law of Human Rights.

In these concluding reflections, I do not intend to repeat what the contributors have discussed in the preceding chapters. I shall, instead, single out the main points made on each topic and present some personal concluding reflections on them, also referring at times to the case law of the IACtHR. Keeping to the structure of the book, the distinct topics addressed (section 2) will be: (i) jurisdiction; (ii) responsibility and reparations; (iii) immunities; (iv) treaties; and (v) other sources of international law. In section 3, I dwell upon the common ground in treaty hermeneutics in Public International Law and in the International Law of Human Rights. Section 4 of this chapter deals with distinct conceptions of the exercise of the international judicial function. If one follows the conception of objective obligations, this leads to a reassuring view of the unity of human rights law: domestic and international, universal and regional (section 5). Regional systems are then appreciated within the framework of the universality of human rights (section 6). This paves the way to my final observations (section 7).

2. Observations on the Topics Addressed

2.1 Jurisdiction

The contributions on jurisdiction have examined the issue in its multiple aspects. As to jurisdiction of States in general international law, State jurisdiction is regarded as a factual issue: the State regulates its own *ordre public*, and exercises jurisdiction over its own territory and in relation to persons subjected to it. Moreover, a State occupying a territory which is not its own seeks to exercise its jurisdiction extraterritorially; human rights treaties thus apply also extraterritorially, to the extent that the occupying State seeks to do so.

We then come to the key issue of State obligations under human rights treaties. The State's jurisdiction, and its exercise of it, is in effect tied up to its conventional obligations under human rights treaties. States are bound to respect, and to ensure respect for, the protected rights. The obligations of States to ensure respect for the protected rights within their respective jurisdictions amount to *positive* obligations, which require due diligence on the part of States to prevent violations of human rights.

Such obligations have been asserted in the *jurisprudence constante* of international human rights tribunals (the IACtHR, from its very start, and the ECtHR, over the last three decades). Even if a State exercises jurisdiction over an occupied territory which is not its own, it is under the conventional *positive* obligation to secure respect for the protected rights of all persons under its exercised jurisdiction.

Human rights conventions being 'living instruments', calling for a 'dynamic interpretation' (as both the ECtHR and the IACtHR have acknowledged), it comes as no surprise that conventional rules on human rights protection may thus pave the way for the formation and development also of general international law.[2] Treaties and custom go together, in providing responses to the new and changing needs of protection of the human person.

2.2 Responsibility and reparations

Once jurisdiction is established (not without difficulties), the way is paved for the determination of State responsibility. The contributions in this volume to Part IV Responsibility have shown that case law of the ECtHR has elaborated on State responsibility in the most diverse circumstances of the cases lodged with it, including aggravating circumstances. An example is afforded by the handling by the ECtHR, in recent years, of cases concerning enforced disappearance of persons, among others.

In its judgment on the *Varnava and Others v Turkey* case (2009), for example, the ECtHR—in line with the ground-breaking decisions of the IACtHR in the *Blake v Guatemala* case (1996–98)—found that enforced disappearances of persons comprised violations of various human rights, some of which forming a *continuing* situation, a *continuing* violation of the close relatives' right of access to justice (or denial of justice), engaging State responsibility.

The lack of an effective investigation overcomes any temporal jurisdictional restriction, and amounts to a breach of a procedural obligation, prolonging in time, as long as the fate of the disappeared persons remains unaccounted for. The State concerned bears international responsibility for the entire period during which that *continuing* situation lasts and remains in non-conformity with the international obligations.

In its judgment on the case *Aslakhanova and Others v Russia* (2012–13), the ECtHR, likewise, referring to the *jurisprudence constante* of the IACtHR in the matter,[3] considered enforced disappearances of persons as 'a combination of several violations of protected rights', often entailing a violation of 'both the substantive and procedural aspects', eg, of the right to life, and of the close relatives' right to be free from degrading treatment (on account of the prolonged suffering caused by the absence of news about the fate of their beloved ones), as well as of the abducted person's right to freedom and security (para 64).

Such cases surrounded by aggravating circumstances have drawn the ECtHR's attention more closely to general principles. For example, in the aforementioned *Varnava* case, among others, the ECtHR has acknowledged the key role of general principles, in face of the lack of an effective investigation on the part of the respondent State, and its *continuing* obligation to account for the fate or whereabouts of the missing persons, and the needed adoption of consequent measures for redress.

[2] cf, recently, D Spielmann at al (eds), *La Convention Européenne des Droits de l'Homme, un Instrument Vivant—Mélanges en l'Honneur de Chr.L. Rozakis* (Bruylant 2011) 27–179, 207–18, 531–53, and 705–40; *The Judge and International Custom/Le juge et la coutume internationale* (Seminar Proceedings), Paris/Strasbourg, MRE/France—Council of Europe, 2012, 38–39 and 80.

[3] For a study, cf AA Cançado Trindade, 'Enforced Disappearances of Persons as a Violation of *Jus Cogens*: The Contribution of the Jurisprudence of the Inter-American Court of Human Rights' (2012) 81 Nordic Journal of International Law 507–36.

We can here see, in my view, an approximation between the European Convention on Human Rights (ECHR) and general international law.

In effect, once responsibility is established, breach and reparations (in all its forms) go together (cf section 3 in this chapter). In its judgment of 12 May 2014 in the case *Cyprus v Turkey*, the ECtHR clarified that, even in interstate cases, the reparations are due to the individuals concerned, the victims, who are their true *titulaires*. The individuals victimized suffered the breaches of their rights, and the corresponding reparations are owed to them. The ECtHR referred to the case law of the International Court of Justice (ICJ) (paras 41 and 46), in particular to the case *AS Diallo* (*Guinea v DR Congo*, 2012).

Let me turn to the issue of State responsibility and exemplary reparations (punitive damages) in cases of aggravating circumstances (grave breaches). State responsibility *aggravated* by the circumstances of cases of serious breaches of human rights brings about consequences for the reparations due to the victims or their relatives. In my understanding, in those cases, there is room for '*exemplary*' reparations, among others. At times, this type of reparation is also referred to as 'punitive damages' (but with a meaning distinct from that attributed to the expression in given domestic legal orders), being endowed with special importance, as judicial recognition of the suffering of the victims and in honour of their memory, as satisfaction to their relatives, and as a measure which seeks to guarantee the non-repetition of the harmful acts.

These are all distinct forms of reparation (of a non-pecuniary nature). It should not pass unnoticed that violations of human rights have diversified. In cases involving victimized members of entire communities, pecuniary reparation may not always be the most important reparation. Other forms of reparation that benefit the community as a whole may be just as important, if not more so. For example, in the case of the *Massacre of Plan de Sánchez v Guatemala* (judgment of 29 April 2004), the reconstruction of the destructed houses and roads and, in the case of the *Massacre de Mapiripán v Colombia* (judgment of 15 September 2005), in addition to the case of the massacre of the *Moiwana Community v Suriname* (judgment of 15 June 2005), the obligation of the State to guarantee the safety for voluntary return, to their ancestral lands, of the surviving inhabitants or their relatives.[4]

Distinct from the practice of some national tribunals, exemplary reparations (or 'punitive damages') in the framework of the International Law of Human Rights, do not necessarily have to be in the form of pecuniary reparations. The IACtHR has so understood, since the early days of its jurisprudential construction, in which I participated actively. One may recall, for example, that, in the case (of summary and extralegal executions) of *Aloeboetoe and Others v Suriname* (reparations, judgment of 10 September 1993), the Court ordered, as non-pecuniary reparations, inter alia: (i) the establishment of two trust funds and the creation of a foundation

[4] It is not my intention here to dwell upon this particular topic, which has formed the object of my reflections in individual opinions I presented to the IACtHR, eg, in the cases of *Myrna Mack Chang v Guatemala* of 25 November 2003; of *Blanco Romero and Others v Venezuela* of 28 November 2005; and of *Goiburú and Others v Paraguay* of 22 September 2006.

(for the benefit of the children of the murdered victims); (ii) the reopening of a public school in the locality of Gujaba, and (iii) the putting into operation of the small, local hospital.[5]

The *Aloeboetoe* case became the leading case for such reparations in subsequent cases of massacres adjudicated by the IACtHR. In the aforementioned case of the massacre of the *Moiwana Community*, for example, the IACtHR also ordered the establishment of a development fund for health, housing, and educational programmes, besides a public apology. In the case of the massacre of *Caracazo v Venezuela* (judgment of 29 August 2002), the IACtHR ordered, as a measure of reparation, the educational training of all members of the armed forces and of the security agencies on the fundamentals of human rights protection, so as to prevent or avoid the repetition of similar violations of human rights in the future.

Subsequently, in another leading case, that of the '*Street Children*' (*Villagrán Morales and Others v Guatemala*, reparations, judgment of 26 May 2001), the IACtHR ordered the respondent State, inter alia, to designate a public school with a name allusive to the five murdered adolescents, and to put in that school a plaque with their names.[6] Once again, in the case of the *Massacre of Plan de Sánchez*, also concerning Guatemala (reparations, judgment of 19 November 2004), the Court ordered the respondent State exemplary reparations, such as, inter alia, those of: (i) organizing, in the same town of Plan de Sánchez, a 'public act of recognition of responsibility' on the part of the State, and in honour of the victims of the harms in the present case, with the presence and participation of the leaders of the communities affected—a ceremony which took place eight months after that Judgment;[7] (ii) 'honouring publicly the memory of the persons executed' in the massacre of Plan de Sánchez (perpetrated by agents of the State on 18 July 1982);[8] (iii) rendering services of health treatment (including psychological and psychiatric) to the victims; (iv) 'providing adequate housing' to the surviving victims residing in the town of Plan de Sánchez 'who so require'; and (v) developing the study and dissemination of the culture *maya-achí* in the affected communities.[9]

This case of the *Massacre of Plan de Sánchez*—among others of the recent *cycle of massacre cases* adjudicated by the IACtHR—seems to indicate that such forms of exemplary reparations have contributed much to the present-day reality of advances

[5] *Case of Aloeboetoe et al v Suriname* (Judgment of 10 September 1993). Resolutory points 2–5 of the aforementioned judgment.

[6] Resolutory point 7 of the aforementioned judgment.

[7] In effect, on 18 July 2005, the respondent State organized the public act of recognition of responsibility, in honour of the victims, as determined by the IACtHR, in the same town of Plan de Sánchez; during the ceremony, the State of Guatemala, by means of the then-Vice-President of the Republic (E Stein), asked pardon from the victims of the massacre of Plan de Sánchez. During such an 'act of reparation', a reconstitution (in the form of a psychodrama) was performed, of what would have been the massacre of Plan de Sánchez of 1982. For a historical account, cf AA Cançado Trindade, *El Ejercicio de la Función Judicial Internacional—Memorias de la Corte Interamericana de Derechos Humanos* (3rd edn, Del Rey, 2013) 70–72.

[8] The massacre of Plan de Sánchez, of 18 July 1982, was perpetrated during the repressive regime of E Ríos Montt; the mass killing of 268 indigenous members of the ethnic group *maya-achí*—who had refused to integrate the patrols of paramilitaries (of 'civil self-defense', utilized by the army for repression of rural inhabitants (*campesinos*))—was denounced by survivors one decade later, in 1992.

[9] Resolutory points 2–3 and 7–9 of the aforementioned judgment.

in the international protection of human rights. Such advances form an irreversible process, now deeply rooted in the bases of national society in several countries, to the ultimate benefit of their inhabitants.

2.3 Immunities

The next section of the chapter focuses on *immunities*. In my understanding, State immunities cannot be approached in the void; they are related to the right of access to justice. In its judgment in the case *Stichting Mothers of Srebrenica and Others v The Netherlands* (2013), the ECtHR (Third Section) addressed the key issue of jurisdictional immunities (of States and international organizations). Relying upon the judgment of the ICJ of 3 February 2012 in the case of the *Jurisdictional Immunities of the State (Germany v Italy, Greece intervening)*, the ECtHR (Third Section) rejected the application as manifestly ill-founded, thus declaring it inadmissible.

Paradoxically, the ECtHR (Third Section) placed the alleged immunities of the State and of the United Nations above human rights, which it is supposed to protect as an international human rights tribunal. There are cogent reasons in support of the primacy of the right of access to justice over alleged State immunities in cases of international crimes, or of grave violations of human rights and of International Humanitarian Law.[10] In this case of *Stichting Mothers of Srebrenica*, the ECtHR (Third Section), in referring to the ICJ's majority decision in the case of the *Jurisdictional Immunities of the State*, applied dogmatically the law (as it understood it), rather than imparted justice. Its decision clearly portrays a divorce between law and justice.

The finding of particularly grave violations of human rights and of International Humanitarian Law provides a valuable test for the removal of any bar to jurisdiction, in pursuance of the necessary realization of justice. State immunity does not stand in the domain of redress for grave violations of the fundamental rights of the human person. There is nowadays acknowledgement as to the removal of immunity in cases of international crimes, for which reparation is sought by the victims.

In effect, to admit the removal of State immunity in the realm of trade relations, or in respect of local personal tort (eg, in traffic accidents), and at the same time to insist on shielding States with immunity in cases of international crimes—marked by grave violations of human rights and of international humanitarian law—in pursuance of State (criminal) policies, amounts, in my view, to a juridical absurdity. In cases of grave violations of human rights, the right of access to justice *lato sensu* is to be approached with attention focused on its essence as a *fundamental* right, rather than on permissible or implicit 'limitations' to it. Grave breaches of human rights and of international humanitarian law amount to breaches of *jus cogens*, entailing State responsibility and the duty to provide reparation to the victims. There can be no (State) immunity for international crimes.

[10] For a recent case-study, cf AA Cançado Trindade, *La Protección de la Persona Humana frente a los Crímenes Internacionales y la Invocación Indebida de Inmunidades Estatales* (IBDH/IIDH/SLADI 2013) 5–305.

This whole matter requires a people-centred approach, keeping in mind the humane ends of the State. The principle of humanity, as an expression of the *raison d'humanité*, imposes limits on the *raison d'État*. In cases of international crimes, attention is to be shifted from the vicissitudes of strictly interstate relations to the needs of protection and reparation to the persons concerned, in the light of the principle of humanity. This is in line with the idea of *rectitude* (in conformity with the *recta ratio*—human conscience) underlying the conception of law (in distinct legal systems—*Droit/Right/Recht/Direito/Derecho/Diritto*) as a whole.

The individual victims' right to reparation is the indispensable complement of the grave breaches of international law which harmed them. With the realization of justice—as a form of reparation—victims have their right to the law (*droit au Droit*) duly vindicated. In my own conception, through *reparatio* (from the Latin term *reparare*, 'to dispose again'), the law intervenes to cease the effects of its violations, and to guarantee the non-repetition of the harmful acts.

This indissoluble whole of breach and reparations is recognized in the *jurisprudence constante* of The Hague Court (PCIJ and ICJ): the wrongly assumed incidence of State immunity herein cannot dismantle that indissoluble whole. And the *realization of justice* is in itself a form of reparation (satisfaction) to the victims. It is the reaction of the law to those grave violations that brings one into the realm of *jus cogens*. The State's duty to provide reparation to individual victims of grave violations of human rights and International Humanitarian Law is a duty under customary international law and pursuant to a fundamental general principle of law.

Even in our days, juspositivists do not seem to realize the dangers of the *décalage* between *law* and *justice*, as they can only behold the former. State immunities—overworked in the past in legal doctrine—in face of international crimes, yield to the right of access to justice of the victims, so that *law and justice* do not move apart or clash. It is in the jusnaturalist thinking that the notion of *justice* has always occupied a central position, guiding *law* as a whole. *Justice* is found, in sum, at the beginning of all *law*, being moreover its ultimate end. *Jus cogens* stands above the prerogative or privilege of State immunity, with all the consequences that ensue therefrom, thus avoiding denial of justice and impunity.[11]

2.4 Treaties

Moving on to the section on *treaties*, it may be recalled that, over a decade ago, it was aptly pointed out that the special nature of human rights treaties calls for their teleological and evolutive interpretation, in harmony with Article 31(1) of the two Vienna Conventions on the Law of Treaties (of 1969 and 1986) (cf section 4 of this chapter). The terms enshrined into regional conventions on human rights have

[11] AA Cançado Trindade, 'The Primacy of the Right of Access to Justice over the Undue Invocation of State Immunities in Face of International Crimes' in *Mélanges Liber Amicorum en l'Honneur de D. Spielmann* (Wolf Publisher 2015) 65–72.

a meaning of their own, and the interpretation and application of their norms have led international human rights tribunals (such as the ECtHR and the IACtHR) to have recourse to general international law.[12]

In doing so, the ECtHR and the IACtHR have drawn attention to the importance of general principles of law (discussed later in this chapter), thus bringing together the international protection of human rights under the respective conventions and general international law. Reference can be made here to the principles of good faith (*bona fides*) in the due compliance with judgments and decisions, of *pacta sunt servanda*, of the equality of arms (*égalité des armes*), of equality and non-discrimination, of *jura novit curia*, of *estoppel*, and of the *effect utile* of the conventions.[13]

International human rights tribunals have, in recent years, developed, in a reassuring way, their work of jurisprudential cross-fertilization. In this connection, the ECtHR has issued, in August 2012 (and updated ever since), a useful research tool, the first of its kind, its *Report on References to the Inter-American Court of Human Rights in the Case-Law of the European Court of Human Rights*. This is a most commendable initiative, showing its open-mindedness to the labour of its sister institution in the American continent—which refers constantly to its case law—in the framework of the universality of human rights.

The jurisprudential cross-fertilization of our times encompasses other international tribunals as well (such as the ICJ, the International Tribunal for the Law of the Sea (ITLOS), and the international criminal tribunals (ICC, ICTY, ICTR), among others), thus aptly endeavouring to secure a harmonious development of their respective case law in distinct domains of contemporary international law. Another illustration of the open-mindedness of the ECtHR lies in its series *Dialogue between Judges* (from 2005 onwards). As far as the ECtHR is concerned, the dialogue between judges does not exhaust itself at international level; there is likewise the dialogue between international and constitutional judges.[14]

2.5 Other sources of international law

The remainder of this section focuses on *other sources of international law*. In effect, in the realm of the international protection of human rights, it is important

[12] L Caflisch and AA Cançado Trindade, 'Les Conventions Américaine et Européenne des Droits de l'Homme et le droit international général' (2004) 108 Revue Générale de Droit International Public 11–13, 19, and 47–48; AA Cançado Trindade, 'La Convention Américaine relative aux Droits de l'Homme et le Droit International Général' in Jonathan G Cohen and JF Flauss (eds), *Droit international, Droits de l'Homme et Juridictions Internationales* (Bruylant 2004) 59–63 and 67–69.

[13] Caflisch and Cançado Trindade, 'Les Conventions ...' (n 12) 6–7, 53, 55–58 and 60–61; Cançado Trindade, 'La Convention...', (n 12) 59–63 and 67–69.

[14] This is now attracting growing attention in expert writing; cf, eg, G de Vergottini and JJ Pardini, *Au-delà du Dialogue entre les Cours* (Dalloz 2013) 39–138; T Koopmans, 'Judicialization' in N Colneric et al (eds), *Une Communauté de Droit—Festschrift für G.C. Rodríguez Iglesias* (Berliner Wissenschafts-Verlag 2003) 51–57; A Nollkaemper, *National Courts and the International Rule of Law* (OUP 2011) 1–304; G Ulfstein, 'The International Judiciary' in J Klabbers, A Peters, and G Ulfstein (eds), *The Constitutionalization of International Law* (OUP 2011) 126–52.

to remain always attentive to principles and values.[15] The ECtHR has consistently done so in its *jurisprudence constante*. As to the mechanism of protection, the invocation of State responsibility under the ECHR, also in interstate cases in the exercise of a *collective guarantee* of the protected rights, for example, bears witness to the superior common values, to be preserved, lying in the foundations of the system of protection.[16]

General principles of law, enlisted among the formal sources of international law (Article 38 of the ICJ Statute), encompass those found in all national legal systems (thus ineluctably linked with the very foundations of law), and likewise the general principles of international law.[17] Such principles, in my own conception, inform and conform the norms and rules of international law, being a manifestation of the universal juridical conscience (the ultimate material source of the law of nations); in the *jus gentium* in evolution, basic considerations of humanity play a role of the utmost importance.

International human rights tribunals (like the ECtHR) and international criminal tribunals have ascribed great importance to such general principles of law.[18] Those principles have been reaffirmed time and time again, and retain full validity today. Legal positivism has always attempted, in vain, to minimize their role, but the truth is that, without those principles, there is no legal system at all, be it national or international. They give expression to the idea of an *objective justice*, paving the way to the application of the *universal* international law, the new *jus gentium* of our times.[19]

Like the ECtHR, other contemporary international tribunals (such as the ICJ and the IACtHR) have also resorted to general principles of law (recognized in domestic legal systems and in international law) in their *jurisprudence constante*. For their part, international human rights tribunals have always kept in mind the principle of the dignity of the human person,[20] as well as the principle (*pro persona humana*) of the application of the norm most favourable to the victim. After all, the *corpus juris* of the International Law of Human Rights is oriented towards the victims.

From this outlook, the basic posture of an international tribunal can only be *principiste*, without making undue concessions to State voluntarism. I had the occasion of pointing this out, as guest speaker, in the opening of the judicial year of the

[15] cf C Husson-Rochcongar, *Droit international des Droits de l'Homme et Valeurs—Le recours aux Valeurs dans la Jurisprudence des Organes Spécialisés* (Bruylant 2012) 1–941.

[16] LA Sicilianos, 'L'influence des Droits de l'Homme sur la Structure du Droit international—La Hiérarchisation de l'Ordre Juridique International' (2012) 116 Revue Générale de Droit International Public 13.

[17] It is not surprising that the heralds of absolute sovereignty of the past have resisted the applicability to the general principles of law at international level.

[18] To this effect, cf, eg, K Grabarczyk, *Les Principes Généraux dans la Jurisprudence de la Cour Européenne des Droits de l'Homme* (Presses Universitaires d'Aix-Marseille 2008) 375–473; FO Raimondo, *General Principles of Law in the Decisions of International Criminal Courts and Tribunals* (Nijhoff 2008) 73–163.

[19] AA Cançado Trindade, *International Law for Humankind—Towards a New Jus Gentium* (2nd rev edn, Nijhoff 2013) 1–726.

[20] cf, eg, B Maurer, *Le Principe de Respect de la Dignité Humaine et la Convention Européenne des Droits de l'Homme* (Documentation Française/Université d'Aix-Marseille1999) 7–491.

ECtHR, on 22 January 2004, at the *Palais des Droits de l'Homme* in Strasbourg, in the following terms:

La Cour européenne et la Cour interaméricaine ont toutes deux, à juste titre, imposé des limites au volontarisme étatique, protégé l'intégrité de leurs Conventions respectives des droits de l'homme, ainsi que la prépondérance des considérations d'*ordre public* face à la volonté de tel ou tel État, élevé les exigences relatives au comportement de l'État, instauré un certain contrôle sur l'imposition de restrictions excessives par les États, et, de façon rassurante, mis en valeur le statut des individus en tant que sujets du Droit International des Droits de l'Homme en les dotant de la pleine capacité sur le plan procédural.[21]

International human rights tribunals, such as the ECtHR and the IACtHR, have aptly resolved basic jurisdictional issues raised, eg, in the *Loizidou v Turkey* case (Preliminary Objections, 1995),[22] and in the *Constitutional Tribunal* and *Ivtcher Bronstein* cases (Jurisdiction, 1999),[23] making use of the techniques of Public International Law in order to preserve the integrity of their respective jurisdictions of protection of the human person, and thus to strengthen them.

Their position, leaning towards the protection of the weaker and most vulnerable, rather than threatening the cohesion of international law, enriches and strengthens it, in asserting its aptitude to resolve disputes also at intrastate level. Contemporary international law has thereby become more responsive to the fulfilment of the basic needs of the international community, of human beings, and of humankind as a whole, amongst which that of the realization of justice. The outlook of international tribunals such as the ECtHR and the IACtHR reflects the way contemporary international law is evolving, no longer indifferent to human suffering, in the construction of a *corpus juris* for the international community guided by the *rule of law* in democratic societies and committed to the realization of justice.

3. Treaty Hermeneutics in Public International Law and in the International Law of Human Rights: The Common Ground

The hermeneutics of human rights treaties contains elements, developed in international case law, deserving of attention, namely: the *effet utile* of their provisions; the objective character of obligations enshrined therein; the autonomous sense of

[21] 'Discours de AA Cançado Trindade, Président de la Cour Interaméricaine des Droits de l'Homme' in *Cour Européenne des Droits de l'Homme, Rapport Annuel 2003*, Strasbourg, CourEDH, 2004, 41–50.

[22] 15318/89 [1995] ECHR 10 (23 March 1995). Followed by the case of *Ilaşcu and Others v Moldova and Russian Federation* (2001) Application no. 48787/99.

[23] Followed by the case of *Hilaire, Benjamin and Constantine v Trinidad and Tobago* (Preliminary Objections, 2001). In the cases of the *Constitutional Tribunal* and of *Ivcher Bronstein* (competence, 1999), the IACtHR preserved the integrity of its own jurisdiction (not allowing the 'withdrawal' of the acceptance of its jurisdiction). In the case of the *Constitutional Tribunal* (Merits, 2001), the IACtHR furthermore intervened to safeguard the national jurisdiction, for the restoration of the *rule of law (État de droit)*. In the cases of *Barrios Altos v Peru* (2001), *La Cantuta et al v Peru* (2006), and *Massacre of Plan de Sánchez v Guatemala*, the IACtHR preceded national jurisdiction (in the first two cases, it also preceded even the Truth Commission), upholding State responsibility even before domestic courts held the former head of State responsible.

their terms (in relation to the domestic law of States); their uniform interpretation of the *corpus juris* of protection; the collective guarantee underlying them; their dynamic or evolutive interpretation; and the restrictive interpretation of permissible restrictions.

These elements of hermeneutics converge in sustaining the integrity of human rights treaties, in seeking the realization of their object and purpose, and, accordingly, in establishing limits to State voluntarism. This new outlook bears witness to the recognition that, ultimately, the State exists for the human being, and not vice-versa. In the face of the multiplicity of international instruments and mechanisms of human rights protection, it has been due to the prominent function exercised by their hermeneutics that there has been a significant *jurisprudential convergence* as to the pursuance of their proper interpretation, which has guided the path of their evolution.

3.1 The proper interpretation of human rights treaties and the autonomous sense of their terms

Human rights treaties have their interpretation oriented by the rules of international law, as enshrined in Articles 31 to 33 of the two Vienna Conventions on the Law of Treaties (of 1969 and 1986). The general rule, formulated in Article 31(1), is to the effect that provisions of treaties are to be interpreted in good faith, in conformity with the ordinary meaning of their terms and their context, and bearing in mind their object and purpose.[24] Such elements are found together, jointly, in one sole formulation, singling out the unity of the process of interpretation.

Underlying that general rule of interpretation (Article 31(1)) is the principle *ut res magis valeat quam pereat* (corresponding to the *effet utile*), whereby one is to secure to conventional provisions their proper effects. This principle has been widely endorsed in international case law. As a given treaty is governed by international law, the evolution of the latter is to be taken into account at the moment of its interpretation. The principle *ut res magis valeat quam pereat* has assumed, in the domain of human rights protection, particular importance in the determination of the wide scope of the conventional obligations of protection.

Besides such general rules of treaty interpretation set forth in the two Vienna Conventions on the Law of Treaties (1969 and 1986), there are specific directives in the ambit of the International Law of Human Rights.[25] It so happens that human rights treaties prescribe obligations of an essentially *objective character* (rather than reflecting reciprocal concessions or advantages, as in classic treaties), to be *collectively* guaranteed, with the prevalence of considerations of general interest and *ordre public*

[24] Article 32 foresees recourse (when needed) to supplementary means of interpretation (eg, their *travaux préparatoires*).

[25] cf, eg, American Convention on Human Rights, Article 29; African Charter on Human and Peoples' Rights, Article 60. It ensues from Article 29 of the American Convention, eg, the clear purpose of giving to the provisions of the convention the interpretation which secures the maximum degree of protection to the rights enshrined therein.

(transcending individual interests of States Parties). The special nature of human rights treaties has an incidence—and it could not be otherwise—in their process of interpretation: they all seek the realization of the ultimate goal of the protection of the rights inherent to the human person. There is nowadays a *jurisprudence constante* to that effect.

Given the special character of human rights treaties and the essentially objective nature of the obligations enshrined thereunder, they have been having a proper interpretation, which does not depart from the generally recognized rules of international law on the matter; on the contrary, it is international law itself that permits an interpretation which keeps in mind the special character of human rights treaties, giving due weight to the relevance of their object and purpose.

After all, distinct from classic treaties concluded in the stricter framework of *interstate* relations, the International Law of Human Rights has been formed and crystallized in a framework of *intrastate* relations, ie, relations among States and human beings under their respective jurisdictions, recognized as subjects of rights emanating directly from international law. An apparent tension arose: legal concepts and categories of Public International Law, conceived in the framework of a legal order of coordination in conformity with the principle of the juridical equality of States, were to no longer appear always adequate when transposed into the domain of the International Law of Human Rights, marked by the relations between factually unequal subjects, and oriented towards the safeguard of the factually weaker ones, of those who stand in greater need of protection (the victims of human rights violations).

In this domain of protection, one seeks—rather than to obtain an abstract equilibrium between the parties—to remedy the effects of disequilibrium and disparities to the extent that they affect human rights. Inspired by considerations of *ordre public* and common superior values, we are before a true *law of protection*, oriented towards that safeguard of the rights of human beings and not of States. The norms of the International Law of Human Rights are interpreted and applied always bearing in mind the pressing needs of protection of the victims, and in this way—as I have been pointing out for years—calling for the *humanization* of the postulates of classic Public International Law.

There is thus no reason to keep nourishing the aforementioned tension: on the contrary, the challenge today is precisely in the sense of overcoming that tension. The fact that the International Law of Human Rights has gone beyond classic Public International Law in the matter of protection of the human person calls for an interpretation of its norms in conformity with the innovative character of its *corpus juris*.

The very canons of interpretation of treaties permit giving greater weight to one or another of its component elements, better adapted to a given type of treaty; this finds ground in the relevant provisions on treaty interpretation of the two Vienna Conventions on the Law of Treaties. The *teleological interpretation*, stressing the fulfilment of the object and purpose of human rights treaties, has prevailed as the best method to secure an effective protection of human rights. It is, in effect, the one which most faithfully reflects the special nature of human rights treaties, and the one which has propitiated the configuration of the 'autonomy' of its own conceptualization.[26]

The recognition of the autonomous sense of the terms of human rights treaties (vis-à-vis the domestic law of States) has contributed to secure the unity of their interpretation. The fundamental unity of their object and purpose has led to the resulting convergence of the relevant jurisprudential construction of international tribunals of human rights, singling out the autonomous sense of the terms of human rights treaties.

The consolidation and constant evolution of the International Law of Human Rights in the hermeneutics of human rights treaties is a widely acknowledged phenomenon nowadays. There is a convergence in the hermeneutics of multiple human rights treaties and instruments of protection, whereby they have been reinforcing each other, to the ultimate benefit of the protected human beings. Such interpretative interaction has contributed to the universality of the *corpus juris* of the International Law of Human Rights.

It has, moreover, given precision to the extent of conventional obligations of protection, ascribing *primacy to the norm most favourable* to the alleged victims.[27] The proper interpretation of human rights treaties encompasses provisions of substantive, as well as procedural law. This has paved the way, in the concomitant interpretation of corresponding or equivalent provisions of distinct human rights treaties, for the application of the criterion of the *primacy of the norm most favourable* to the alleged victims.[28]

I have already referred to the commendable posture of international human rights tribunals in support of the integrity of the respective jurisdictions, opposing the voluntarist conception: to them, considerations of *ordre public* prevail over the individual 'will' of States (paving the way to higher standards for the behaviour of States and to the strengthening of the position of individuals as subjects of international law, endowed with international juridical capacity in the International Law of Human Rights.

[26] It is not to pass unnoticed that the preambles of the two Vienna Conventions on the Law of Treaties (1969 and 1986), in referring to the principles embodied in the UN Charter, expressly assert the principle of 'universal respect for, and observance of, human rights and fundamental freedoms for all' (sixth preambular paragraph, *in fine*).

[27] cf, eg, AA Cançado Trindade, *Tratado de Direito Internacional dos Direitos Humanos* (vol I, SA Fabris edn 1997) 434–36, and sources cited therein.

[28] A criterion which has found express support in human rights treaties, eg, at global level, Article 5(2) of the UN Covenant on Civil and Political Rights; Article 23 of the UN Convention on the Elimination of All Forms of Discrimination against Women; Article 41 of the Convention on the Rights of the Child; and, at regional level, Article 29(b) of the American Convention on Human Rights, and Article 4 of its Additional Protocol in the Matter of Economic, Social and Cultural Rights (Protocol of San Salvador); Article 53 of the ECHR, and Article 32 of the European Social Charter; Article 17(1) of the European Convention for the Prevention of Torture and Inhuman or Degrading Treatment or Punishment.

3.2 Dynamic or evolutive interpretation of human rights treaties

Human rights treaties are living instruments which accompany the evolution of times and of the social *milieu* wherein the protected rights are exercised. This has been stressed in the *jurisprudence constante* of international human rights tribunals.[29] The dynamic, or evolutive, interpretation of human rights treaties, which finds expression in international case law, takes into account the transformations that have occurred in the *corpus* of human society, and provides new responses to new needs of protection of the human person.

The case law of international human rights tribunals bears eloquent witness to a process of evolutive interpretation of human rights treaties. Such evolution, in turn, reflects a deeper phenomenon: the *corpus juris* of international protection itself is conceived, develops, and is applied, taking into account, and being moved by, new and constant value judgments which emerge and flourish within human society, and which are naturally reflected in the process of dynamic or evolutive interpretation of human rights treaties.

3.3 The uniform interpretation of the *corpus juris* of the International Law of Human Rights

The acknowledgment, in such evolutive interpretation of human rights treaties, of the special character of the latter, does not lead to a departure from the relevant rules of the law of treaties, in particular those set forth in Articles 31–33 of the two Vienna Conventions on the Law of Treaties (1969 and 1986). There is, in effect, no incompatibility or antagonism between the general rule of interpretation contained in Article 31(1) of those two Vienna Conventions and the methods of interpretation of human rights treaties which take into account their specificity. International human rights tribunals (and for a long time the ECtHR and the IACtHR), in developing their interpretation of the respective regional conventions, have kept in mind both their special character as human rights treaties and the elements of interpretation enshrined in the two aforementioned Vienna Conventions.

Endowed with their own specificity, human rights treaties have had their interpretation and application guided by superior common values which they embody and in which they inspire themselves; in this way, they differ from classic treaties which limit themselves to regulate the reciprocal interests between the parties. The special character of human rights treaties entails legal consequences with an incidence on the methods themselves of their interpretation, which render it possible, as already seen, to emphasize one or another of their component elements, with more aptitude to the correct application of the treaty at issue.

[29] For a review, cf, eg, AA Cançado Trindade, *Tratado de Direito Internacional dos Direitos Humanos* (vol II, SA Fabris edn 1999) 23–200; *La Convention Européenne des Droits de l'Homme* (n 2) 27–179, 207–18, 531–53 and 705–40; P van Dijk, F van Hoof, A van Rijn, and L Zwaak (eds), *Theory and Practice of the European Convention of Human Rights* (4th edn, Intersentia 2006) 340–41 and 538–39.

Human rights treaties establish objective regimes of protection, and there is no impediment for international human rights tribunals to pursue methods of interpretation of their own, without thereby departing from the canons of treaty interpretation in international law. The elements of treaty interpretation cover their whole work, from judgments in contentious cases to provisional measures of protection, from advisory opinions to resolutions and other decisions. By means of jurisprudential cross-fertilization, those international tribunals have, in their interpretative interaction, reinforced the respective instruments of protection, to the ultimate benefit of human beings.

The *uniform* interpretation of the *corpus juris* of the International Law of Human Rights, keeping in mind the rules of treaty interpretation, has been characterized, as we have seen, less by the objective of securing the uniformity of international law in general, in any contexts and circumstances, than by the concern and purpose to respond effectively to the needs and the imperatives of the international protection of human rights. Such concern and purpose, preponderant in the interpretation and application of treaties of protection, reflect the specificity of the International Law of Human Rights.

The reassuring results of the joint operation of the organs of international protection (such as international human rights tribunals) are reflected precisely in the *uniform* interpretation of the *corpus juris* of the International Law of Human Rights, which in no way challenges the unity of international law: on the contrary, it has contributed significantly to the development of the aptitude of the latter to secure, as from the necessary acknowledgment of the specificity of human-right treaties, compliance with the conventional obligations of protection of States vis-à-vis all human beings under their jurisdictions.

And with the evolution of the International Law of Human Rights, it is international law that legitimates—besides enriching—itself, in asserting principles, concepts, and juridical categories proper to the present domain of protection, on the basis of premises fundamentally distinct from those which have oriented the application of its postulates at the level of strictly interstate relations. One could not foster the development of the International Law of Human Rights to the detriment of the law of treaties; nor could one pretend to hinder the evolution of the International Law of Human Rights by attaching, to the classic postulates of the law, treaties making abstraction of the context wherein they apply.

One is thus to proceed rightly to the *humanization of the law of treaties*, in the understanding that it is thereby that their norms can be considerably enriched by the impact of the International Law of Human Rights, and can develop their aptitude to govern adequately the legal relations at both interstate and intrastate levels, under the respective treaties of protection. In sum and conclusion, the interpretation and application of human rights treaties confirm—as expected—the special character of such treaties, and, in this way, the International Law of Human Rights itself contributes to develop the aptitude of Public International Law to secure, in the present context, the faithful compliance with the international obligations of protection undertaken by the States to the benefit of all human beings under their respective jurisdictions.

4. Distinct Conceptions of the Exercise of the International Judicial Function

May I now recall that at the *Palais des Droits de l'Homme* in Strasbourg, seven years ago, in 2008, the first meeting (of dialogue) ever of the three regional human rights courts operating within the conceptual framework of the universality of human rights (the European, the Inter-American, and the African courts) was held. The meeting was coordinated by the then-President of the ECtHR, Judge Jean-Paul Costa, present also at the 2015 Strasbourg Conference—the basis of this book, this time as President of the International Institute of Human Rights (René Cassin Institute).

The aforementioned meeting of 2008 of the three international human rights tribunals—of which I keep a good memory—was a proper occasion for a fruitful dialogue, which covered relevant points of their common concern and work, such as, eg, their determination to safeguard the integrity of their respective jurisdictions, not yielding to State voluntarism, and the special attention they devote nowadays to such issues as reparations, provisional measures, and compliance with their judgments and decisions.[30]

With the operation of international tribunals, such as the ECtHR and the IACtHR (and, from 2006, the African Court on Human and Peoples' Rights—ACtHPR) there have, in effect, in the present era of contemporary international tribunals, gradually emerged two basic distinct conceptions of the exercise of the international judicial function. One—a stricter one—maintains that the tribunal has to limit itself to settle the dispute at issue and to handle its resolution of it to the contending parties (a form of transactional justice), addressing only what the parties have put before it.

The other, a larger one—the one I sustain—holds that the tribunal has to go beyond that and say what the law is (*juris dictio*), thus contributing to the settlement of other like situations and to the progressive development of international law.[31] In the interpretation itself—or even in the search—of the applicable law, there is space for judicial creativity; each international tribunal is free to find the applicable law, independently of the arguments of the contending parties, in pursuance of the principle *juria novit curia*.

[30] For accounts of that memorable meeting, cf AA Cançado Trindade, 'Quelques Réflexions à l'Occasion de la Première Réunion des Trois Cours régionales des Droits de l'Homme' (2009) 9 Revista do Instituto Brasileiro de Direitos Humanos 229–39; PH Weckel, 'La Justice Internationale et le Soixantième Anniversaire de la Déclaration Universelle des Droits de l'Homme' (2009) 113 Revue Générale de Droit International Public 5–17.

[31] AA Cançado Trindade, *Los Tribunales Internacionales Contemporáneos y la Humanización del Derecho Internacional* (Ad Hoc 2013) 148–62; AA Cançado Trindade, 'A Century of International Justice and Prospects for the Future' in AA Cançado Trindade and D Spielmann (eds), *A Century of International Justice and Prospects for the Future/Rétrospective d'un Siècle de Justice Internationale et Perspectives d'Avenir* (Wolf Publisher 2013) 16–17.

Furthermore, there are circumstances wherein the judgments of international tribunals may have repercussions beyond the contending States in a case.[32] Such repercussions tend to occur when the judgments succeed in giving expression to the idea of an *objective* justice. In this way, they contribute to the evolution of international law itself, and to the *rule of law* at national and international levels in democratic societies. The more international tribunals devote themselves to explaining clearly the foundations of their decisions, the greater their contribution to justice and peace is bound to be. Reason and persuasion permeate the operation of justice, and this goes back to the historical origins of its conception.

5. The Unity of the Law

The work of international human rights tribunals, as well as of contemporary international criminal tribunals, bears witness to the interactions between international and domestic law in the tribunals' respective domains of operation. The realization of justice becomes a common goal, and a converging one, at the domestic and international legal orders. They both testify to the *unity of the law* in the realization of justice, a sign of our times. The operation of the ECtHR, and other international human rights tribunals, has shown that, in the great majority of cases lodged with them, international jurisdiction is resorted to when there is no longer a possibility to find justice at domestic-law level.

And there have been occasions wherein the international jurisdiction has come to support national jurisdiction, so as to secure also within this latter the primacy of law (*préeminence du droit, rule of law*). In effect, the expansion of international jurisdiction has counted on the co-participation of national jurisdictions. After all, international law also attributes international functions to national tribunals.[33] The latter also have a role to play in the search of the primacy of the international *rule of law*.

Contrary to what keeps on being assumed in various legal circles, national and international jurisdictions, in our times, are not concurring or conflictive, but rather complementary, in constant interaction in the protection of the rights of the human person and in the struggle against the impunity of the violators of those rights. It is not certain either—also contrary to what is usually assumed—that the international jurisdiction for the protection of the rights of the human person is always and only 'subsidiary' to national jurisdiction, or 'autonomous' in relation to it. The two jurisdictions interact in the present domain of protection.

In the operation of international human rights tribunals, there have been occasions when international jurisdiction has supported, or even rescued, the national one, so as to secure, in the ambit of the latter, the *rule of law* (*prééminence du droit*). Furthermore, the rule of law (*préeminence du droit*) in a democratic society ultimately stresses the utmost importance of the right of access to justice *lato sensu* (comprising

[32] For an account, cf Cançado Trindade (n 21) 267–68.

[33] cf *Cançado Trindade* (n 1) 76–112 (on the interaction between international law and domestic law in human rights protection).

the formal access to justice, the guarantees of due process, and the faithful execution of the judgment)[34]—a true right to the Law (*droit au Droit*) in a democratic society.

In this respect, there are in effect significant illustrations, in certain situations of extreme adversity to human beings, of the international jurisdiction having even *preceded* national jurisdiction in the determination of State responsibility for the protection of the rights of the victimized and in the reparations due to them.[35] In the history of the relations—and interactions—between national and international jurisdictions, this particular point will surely keep on being studied by the present and future generations of internationalists and constitutionalists devoted to the protection of human rights.

It is also to be kept in mind that domestic remedies integrate the mechanism of international protection, with attention shifted from the formal process of their exhaustion (as a condition of admissibility of complaints) to the element of redress. International and national jurisdictions are here in interaction, to the benefit of the protected human beings. They thereby give testimony to the *unity of law* in our times. The incidence of the local-remedies rule in human rights protection is certainly distinct from its application in the practice of diplomatic protection of nationals abroad (in general or customary international law), and the rule at issue is far from having the dimensions of an immutable or sacrosanct principle of international law.

The criterion of the *effectiveness* of local remedies, and certain procedural techniques (such as the shifting of the burden of proof as to exhaustion) and presumptions will continue to be applied in favour of the alleged victims (the ostensibly weaker party) in order to secure the faithful realization of the object and purpose of human rights treaties and instruments. Local remedies form an integral part of the very system of international human rights protection, the emphasis falling on the element of redress rather than on the process of exhaustion.[36] The local-remedies rule bears witness to the interaction between international law and domestic law in the present context of protection, disclosing the *unity of the law*.

We are here before a *droit de protection*, with a specificity of its own, fundamentally *victim-oriented*, concerned with the rights of individual human beings rather than of States. Generally recognized rules of international law (which the formulation of the local-remedies rule in human rights treaties refers to), besides following an evolution of their own in the distinct contexts in which they apply, necessarily undergo, when inserted in human rights treaties, a certain degree of adjustment or adaptation.

Such adjustment is dictated by the special character of the object and purpose of those treaties and by the widely recognized specificity of the international protection of human rights. In sum and conclusion, international jurisdiction, rather

[34] On the matter, cf, AA Cançado Trindade, *El Derecho de Acceso a la Justicia en Su Amplia Dimensión* (2nd edn, CECOH/Librotecnia 2012) 79–574; AA Cançado Trindade, *Le Droit International pour la Personne Humaine* (Pédone 2012) 282–97.

[35] For a historical account of a trilogy of cases, cf, Cançado Trindade (n 21) 42–45; AA Cançado Trindade, *Os Tribunais Internacionais Contemporâneos e a Realização da Justiça* (Renovar 2015) 349–54.

[36] AA Cançado Trindade, *The Application of the Rule of Exhaustion of Local Remedies in International Law* (CUP 1983) 1–445.

than 'subsidiary' to, or independent from, domestic jurisdiction, is complementary to it, the two standing in constant interaction in the protection of the rights of the human person.

6. A Regional System within the Framework of the Universality of Human Rights

A further topic within the general theme of the book and the unity of law (section 5 in this chapter) is the place of regionalism within the framework of the universality of human rights. The ECHR was promptly drafted, and originally adopted in 1950, so as to avoid delays, such as those in the adoption, only one and a half decades later, of the two UN covenants on human rights. The ECHR was intended to secure the international protection of human rights in the jurisdictions of States Parties to it, which is not the same as creating a 'regional system'.

The ECHR, like other human rights conventions, is *not* a 'self-contained' regime. International supervisory organs under all human rights instruments, in their operation, make recourse to general principles of law (including of international law) and to rules of general international law. Conventional and general international law are here brought together. Human rights conventions are not 'self-contained' or 'self-sufficient' regimes, as they form an integral part of Public International Law.

After all, the ECtHR has always operated, as it does today, in the conceptual framework of the universality of human rights. The same can be said of the IACtHR and the ACtHPR. Thus, even regional systems, such as those set forth by the European and American conventions on human rights and the African Charter on Human and Peoples Rights, operate—may I reiterate—within the conceptual framework of the universality of human rights. They are not 'self-contained' regimes, and have never been conceived as such. They are attentive, and rightly so, to the jurisprudential construction of each other's international tribunals, operating at regional level. Contemporary jurisprudential cross-fertilization is most reassuring. International human rights protection is endowed with universality.

7. Final Observations

Last but not least, may I turn briefly to my final observations, which draw on the contributions of this book but also refer to the contributions from the floor at the Conference. It was remarkable to me that the stress on the importance of general principles of law came not only from some of the panellists, but also and firmly from the floor. Moreover, the Conference was open to other human rights systems (such as the inter-American one), with participants with knowledge and experience thereon,[37] as shown in their interventions in its debates.

[37] And coming from distinct sectors, eg, from the Legal Office of the Council of Europe (such as Andrew Drzemczewski) and from entities of the civil society (such as Mónica Feria Tinta).

From the work of this Conference as a whole, several lessons have been extracted. The international protection of human rights is oriented to those who stand in need of it, in the light of the principle *pro persona humana*. The ECHR, like other human rights treaties, sets forth (positive) obligations of an objective character, collectively guaranteed. In their implementation, considerations of *ordre public* prevail over the 'will' of individual States. International human rights tribunals (like the ECtHR and the IACtHR) have thus safeguarded the integrity of their respective mechanisms of protection. A true *law of protection* has been formed, on the basis of general principles of law and common superior values.

Contemporary international human rights tribunals (ECtHR, IACtHR, ACtHPR), keeping in mind the object and purpose of the respective conventions, have pursued a teleological interpretation. Furthermore, by means of their dynamic and evolutive interpretation, international human rights tribunals have for years been contributing to the progressive development of conventional, as well as general, international law,[38] oriented towards the protection of the human person.

Last but not least, such progressive development of the *corpus juris* of the International Law of Human Rights has helped to clarify many points which international legal doctrine used to regard as problematic; the age of dualism and monism, eg, is long past and overcome. In the present domain of protection, there are interactions between the international and national legal orders, and the norm most favourable to the victims is the one that applies. There have occurred instances when international jurisdiction has preceded, or even rescued, the national one, in times of extreme violence and social disruption.

The jurisprudential cross-fertilization of international human rights tribunals (ECtHR and IACtHR) has harmoniously reinforced their respective instruments, the *corpus juris* of protection as a whole. Human rights treaties (at regional and global levels) and general international law have set up the common ground for the undertaking of a noble mission. *Ex pluribus unum*. The international law of human rights has thus enriched and legitimized Public International Law in developing its aptitude to govern relations not only at inter-State but also at intrastate levels. And we are all fortunate to witness and to contribute to the ongoing historical process of *humanization* of international law, the new *jus gentium* of our times.

[38] A point which now seems to be grasping growing attention of expert writing, cf, eg, F Vanneste, *General International Law before Human Rights Courts—Assessing the Specialty Claims of International Human Rights Law* (Intersentia, 2010) 3–595.

Index